TRINITY OF PASSION

Trinity of Passion

The Literary Left and

the Antifascist Crusade

ALAN M. WALD

The University of North Carolina Press

Chapel Hill

Set in Quadraat types by Tseng Information Systems, Inc.
Manufactured in the United States of America

This book was published with the assistance of the
William R. Kenan Jr. Fund of the University of North Carolina Press.

The paper in this book meets the guidelines for permanence
and durability of the Committee on Production Guidelines for
Book Longevity of the Council on Library Resources.

Library of Congress Cataloging-in-Publication Data
Wald, Alan M., 1946–
Trinity of passion : the literary left and the antifascist crusade /
by Alan M. Wald.
    p. cm.
Includes bibliographical references and index.
ISBN-13: 978-0-8078-3075-8 (cloth : alk. paper)
1. Communism and literature—United States—History—20th
century. 2. American literature—20th century—History and
criticism. 3. Authors, American—20th century—Political and
social views. 4. Antifascist movements—United States—History.
5. Radicalism—United States—History—20th century. 6. Right and
left (Political science) in literature. 7. American literature—Jewish
authors—History and criticism. 8. American literature—African
American authors—History and criticism. I. Title.
PS228.C6W37   2007
810.9'358—dc22   2006019974

A section of Chapter 6 appeared in a somewhat different version
as "Between Insularity and Internationalism: The Lost World of
Jewish Communist 'Cultural Workers' in America," in Studies in
Contemporary Jewry: An Annual, vol. 20, ed. Jonathan Frankel (New York:
Oxford University Press, 2004), 133–47. It is reprinted here with
permission.

cloth   11 10 09 08 07   5 4 3 2 1

To my sister and brother,

                    Sharon and Michael

I speak to you, Madrid, as lover, husband, son.

Accept this human trinity of passion.

I love you, therefore I am faithful to you

And because to forget you would be to forget

Everything I love and value in the world.

Who is not true to you is false to every man

And he to whom your name means nothing never loved.

—Edwin Rolfe, "Elegia," 1948

I had started out as a true believer, not a zealot. . . . But when I saw what

was happening to the Jews in Europe, God's Chosen People dragged off to

concentration camps and slaughtered by the millions, I rebelled. I slammed

the door of the tabernacle in His face and went in search of another God.

Someone to help me in my fight with Adolf Hitler—someone like Karl Marx.

—Ossie Davis, *With Ossie and Ruby*, 1998

CONTENTS

ILLUSTRATIONS

PREFACE

Trinity of Passion is the second of three volumes that track the fortunes of several generations of left-wing writers, carrying forward the chronicle launched in *Exiles from a Future Time: The Forging of the Mid-Twentieth-Century Literary Left* (2002). It delves into literary, personal, and political trajectories of cultural workers in the era of "the antifascist crusade." This social and cultural campaign enthralled the hearts and minds of the mainstream of the literary Left at the time that the International Brigades fought in the Spanish Civil War (1936–39) and the United States battled in World War II (1941–45). The adjective "crusade," habitually used then and later, aptly captures the zealotry with which ideals were pursued at the price of blindness to complicating contingencies.

In *Exiles from a Future Time*, the writers discussed were principally shaped by the interplay of modernist impulses homologous to the 1920s and the feeling of civic emergency induced by the domestic crisis of the early 1930s. In *Trinity of Passion*, most of the authors initiate careers in the middle and late 1930s; they are drawn to what is by this time a dynamic and bustling movement whose predominant theme was opposition to fascism at home and abroad. The series of three volumes, spanning the years from the early 1930s to the early 1960s, will conclude with *The American Night: The Literary Left in the Era of the Cold War*.

Each volume of this cultural history stands alone as a self-contained book that investigates and appraises an interrelated assembly of writers, themes, publications, and organizations. The inquiry is designed neither as an encyclopedia of literary activists nor as a survey of "greatest hits," but as an interpretation of issues that engrossed the rank and file of the literary Left. Writers in the antifascist era, pro-Communist by ideological inclination and sometimes by Party affiliation, faced newly configured questions and challenges. Jewish Americans and African Americans were markedly conspicuous in the cultural field, which decisively affects the eight governing propositions and motifs in *Trinity of Passion*.

- More than ever, starting with the Spanish Civil War, Jews had to define manhood in terms of learning how to fight.
- African Americans in the same era increasingly had to negotiate their duty to contest racism at home with their obligations to halt fascism internationally.

- Women and homosexuals had to contend with a Left culture increasingly infused with putatively masculine standards of behavior—realpolitik, emotional toughness, direct action, and freewheeling personal mobility.
- The organizations and publications that sought to lead as well as to express the tradition of the Left experienced public defections, mysterious losses, and the arrival of ambitious younger voices.
- The cultural climate of the United States shifted rapidly from a relative apathy about fascism in the 1930s to an irresistible yet somewhat forced and illusory national unity during World War II.
- The immediate post–World War II moment brought a mix of disillusion, uncertainty, anger, and cynicism resonating in the new mass-market venues for radical writers.
- Some erstwhile pro-Communist writers subsequently devoted their fiction to working their way out of what they interpreted as misguided loyalty to Communism, yet most never relinquished pride in their antifascist idealism.
- Above all, writers had to come to terms with the formidable task of realizing their artistic potential amidst the contending claims of economic survival, the needs and responsibilities of personal life, changing audiences, the ideological loyalties that masked political contradictions, and psychological and physiological well-being.

Following the arrangement of *Exiles from a Future Time*, I treat discrete authors as components of a "humanscape" in relation to the peculiarities of their biographies.[1] In order to better re-create attendant conditions and patterns, and to convey the sweep of a literary and personal life, the straitjacket of strict chronology, before, during, and after the critical decade of the "crusade," is violated at times. This occurs especially in biographical narrative but also in the use of novels published decades later that reflect back on earlier events in which the author participated. Moreover, a range of strategies is deployed to convey personal and political commitments and their complex cultural expressions. Three such strategies are comparative biography in the instance of Spanish Civil War novels by Milton Wolff, Alvah Bessie, and William Herrick; the reconstruction of the African American Left community of the 1940s in the case of Ann Petry's Harlem writings; and the narrative of the career of activist Communist editor Morris U. Schappes in the investigation of Jewish Americans trapped between internationalism and insularity. Since the portraits of these and other writers overlap the eras and decades surveyed in the three-volume study, readers may feel a degree of arbitrariness in regard to the placement or omission of a particular writer or literary text in this volume. As before, my eventual aim is to present the literary and biographical material in a manner that affords fresh angles and issues in respect to particular figures and writings, while remaining faithful to an overall chronological sequence of events.

Furthermore, *Exiles from a Future Time* focused principally on the writing and lives of poets. *Trinity of Passion: The Literary Left and the Antifascist Crusade* is more concerned with prose writers. The title as well as principal leitmotif is drawn from the 1948 poem "Elegia," by Communist and Spanish Civil War veteran Edwin Rolfe (1909–54). In the poem, the antifascist cause of the 1930s and the 1940s is exemplified by the city of Madrid, capital of the Spanish Republic. Rolfe and other volunteers in the International Brigades had tried to defend Madrid from being overrun by fascists in the three-year armed conflict now considered to be the first major battle of World War II. The seven lines that are quoted as the first of the two epigraphs for this volume stress the complexly blended forms of passion (designated as a "trinity of passion") that bound Rolfe to the antifascist crusade. The cryptic nature of Rolfe's choice of "trinity" as a modifier is reflected in its reverberation of John Donne's sonnet "Batter My Heart, Three-Person'd God," as well as its selection as the code name of J. Robert Oppenheimer for the first atomic bomb test three years earlier.[2] In his reference to a human trinity, blending diverse loves that may lead to intensification as well as disharmony, Rolfe echoes passages from Ernest Hemingway's earlier *For Whom the Bell Tolls* (1940), a novel pitting love against delusion and betrayal.[3] Although Rolfe completed the poem nine years after Franco's triumph over the Spanish Republicans and three years after Allies' victory over the Axis powers, such passions blazed in his memory more fiercely than ever.

"Elegia" is also an appropriate epigraph because "passion" epitomizes one of the most captivating yet precarious aspects of the heritage of the literary Left, an especially seductive sentiment during the antifascist era of the Spanish Civil War and World War II. Passion rouses individuals to action and can spawn fervent idealism and predisposition to sacrifice. It is unimaginable to be able to effectively combat fascism, racism, and class oppression without passion. But passion can also generate oversimplified perceptions, blindness, misdirected rage, and wishful thinking. Passion often leads to the type of zealotry noted by the African American actor Ossie Davis in *Trinity of Passion*'s second epigraph. Not at all confined to those on the Left, zealotry may influence one's idealism in unsettling ways, without necessarily annulling either the intentions of the passionately motivated or the righteousness of their cause.

The consequences of political passion for literary creativity can be discomfiting. Passion may fuel the striving to create works of the literary imagination relating to social liberation, but passion by itself offers no guaranty of artistic success or guidance as to appropriate form and content. No matter how ardently and purely passion is felt, the creative act is perforce refracted through the peculiar psychology of the artist. It is only then transformed into literature through the writer's skills and interactions with editors, publishers, and audiences. Art aroused by passion on occasion burns most brightly in close proximity to political events; other times it flares in the afterglow of the events.

In re-creating and probing the intellectual and emotional panorama associated with the Spanish Civil War and World War II, this study focuses on a select group of writers and their careers. The merits of their various writings are appraised for the skill with which they convey the emotional landscape of antifascist struggles and its legacy, rather than for the particular political convictions held by the authors. *Trinity of Passion*'s introduction, "The Strange Career of Len Zinberg," features a forgotten writer of popular fiction; its final, climactic chapter, "Arthur Miller's Missing Chapter," concerns a major dramatist; and its conclusion, "The Fates of Antifascism," discusses diverse authors who fall in between. This is a book about a cross section of literary talent and achievement, as much as it dwells on the legacies of diversely unfulfilled political dreams.

One cannot concentrate exclusively on the presentation of the new without reference to the old. The narrative strategy of *Trinity of Passion* encompasses pivotal political events and landmark literary achievements while not rehearsing material that is familiar to the general reader or readily available elsewhere. Substantial attention is devoted to well-known authors such as Henry Roth or Arthur Miller when new information on their work and their relation to the Left warrants. Since biographical data and literary analysis are extensive for other prominent writers of the era—such as Ernest Hemingway, Lillian Hellman, Theodore Dreiser, and Richard Wright—they are considered sparingly.

Many of the conceptual approaches utilized in *Exiles from a Future Time* apply as well to *Trinity of Passion*. "Elective affinity" continues as the chief determinate for locating writers in an ongoing, evolving, and ardent pro-Communist cultural tradition. The utopian theme in *Exiles from a Future Time*—romantic idealizations of the USSR and dreams of an interracial partnership among proletarians—is still visible but is now part of a broader mix. The burden of "living in a state of emergency" and the weight of "force fields" of literary networks and institutions are more present than in *Exiles*.

No political concept is more central to *Trinity of Passion* than the definition and changing fortunes of the Communist-initiated policy of the Popular Front. The Popular Front became the official Communist orientation in August 1935, at the

Seventh World Congress of the Communist International. The Popular Front was theorized by German Communist Georgi Dmitrov as a "broad" version of the United Front (usually an alliance of working-class organizations around a common objective), and his speech was published in the United States as *The United Front* (1938). The novel revised policy was, however, anticipated in the United States by several efforts at creating united fronts in 1934, and the matter is complicated by the occasional use of the old term "united front" after 1935, with "People's Front" and "Democratic Front" employed as well.

The gist of the Popular Front policy was the subordination of the Communist Party's revolutionary anticapitalist program, which appears in Communist leader William Z. Foster's *Toward Soviet America* (1932), to the pursuit of unity with supporters of Franklin D. Roosevelt's New Deal. The political practice of the People's Front was less a call to build a coalition for unified action on a specific issue than it was a multiple strategy of preserving the existing socioeconomic-political system against the looming threat of fascism. Following the Hitler-Stalin Pact of 1939, however, the Communist Party jettisoned the Popular Front policy overnight. This hiatus lasted for eighteen months; the policy was essentially reinstated after the Nazis' attack on the USSR in 1941. Under the exigencies of wartime, the potential of the Communist Party for using the Popular Front in order to police the domestic U.S. Left was more in evidence than in the 1930s. Declaring World War II a "People's War," the Party sought to promote its version of national unity by enforcing the no-strike pledge, assailing African American labor leader A. Philip Randolph and his March on Washington Movement against discrimination in the military (first as pro-war, then as disruptive of wartime unity), collaborating in the prosecution under the Smith Act of the Trotskyists of the Socialist Workers Party, and endorsing the internment of Japanese Americans.

In Europe the Communists' wartime policy was called the National Front or National Freedom Front and was theorized as an extension of the Popular Front under new conditions. In the United States, the term "National Front" was mainly used in the Party's theoretical journal, *The Communist*.[4] Most importantly, Communist Party general secretary Earl Browder enforced his own interpretation, relentlessly mechanical in its retrogression to political positions to the right of those of many liberals, even those with pro-Soviet sympathies at the newspaper *PM* and the journal *New Republic*.[5] After the Teheran conference of Roosevelt, Churchill, and Stalin in 1943, Browder went even further, conceptualizing the need for unity between workers and their bosses as a permanent condition. The implications of this evolving concept for writers and literary culture are too multifaceted to be condensed summarily. Fine points about the theory and practice of the Popular Front will be taken up as pertinent in the ensuing chapters.

The writers of the antifascist crusade were associated with the Communist movement in particularized modes. Many passed through membership in the Communist Party. The originality of *Trinity of Passion* lies more in its research into writers' lives, writings, and institutional networks than in promoting any novel political theories of my own. The use of the term "Stalinism" to describe the Soviet Union and the ideology of the U.S. Communist Party in this era follows the prevailing Marxist scholarship of the late twentieth century, emphasizing Stalinism's historical character.[6]

No matter how commendable they were in other respects, pro-Communists lauded the USSR as a model of socialism and a force for world peace, supported journals and newspapers that hailed Stalin as a genius, and endorsed a succession of policy revisions championed by Moscow. Of course, in contrast to Stalinists in the USSR, they did not personally impose a state dictatorship. The essence of the political lives of most pro-Communist writers in the United States was an honorable one of fighting against the injustices of U.S. society and fascist dictatorships internationally. This perspective frequently outlasted their Communist Party affiliations and in succeeding years was occasionally coupled with protests against injustices in the Soviet Union. Nevertheless, there was a specificity to the version of communism they promoted, one that is blurred by euphemisms for tacitly Stalinist political allegiance such as "Progressive," "Left," and "radical" or even the unqualified use of the term "Communist."

Paradoxically, however, one aim of this book is precisely to bring the writers, as individuals and artists, out from under the shadow of the term "Stalinism," in accordance with an observation of the socialist writer Michael Harrington. Throughout his youth, Harrington had known Communists exclusively as political opponents in the radical movements in which he was an activist. Only after the 1956 revelations of Nikita Khrushchev about Stalin's brutal regime and the Hungarian revolt against Soviet domination "created turmoil in the Communist world" did Harrington experience his "first truly personal contacts with the Communists." He was then "surprised to discover . . . complex and often decent people who had served the wrong cause for right reasons while fighting courageously for social change in American society."[7] This sentiment provides an accurate profile of many of the writers portrayed in this study.

{ TRINITY OF PASSION

INTRODUCTION

The Strange Career of Len Zinberg

In 1967, the multimillion-copy selling, tough-guy mystery writer Ed Lacy published yet another of his highly successful mass-market detective stories featuring an African American protagonist, In Black and Whitey. The new novel was unlike Lacy's previous, award-winning series of mysteries about a Black private eye named Toussaint Marcus Moore. Moore confronted the subtleties of racism while solving crimes in unusual settings, such as small-town Ohio and Mexico City. Lacy's In Black and Whitey featured an African American police officer, Lee Hayes. Hayes is assigned, with a white partner, to cool off an explosively hot political situation in the Harlem ghetto.

In Black and Whitey is told entirely through the eyes of the young, very race-conscious Hayes, who sympathizes with many of the aims of the new Black Power movement even as he is skeptical of the motives and strategies of some of the self-proclaimed Harlem leaders. Moreover, Hayes is alternately intrigued and mystified by the personality of his white partner, Albert Kahn, who has a sort of dual ethnic identity. At times, Kahn is identified as "Whitey" by Hayes and also by some of the Harlem Black Power militants; he is undifferentiated from the Euro-American majority with its caste privilege. In other moments, the African American Hayes is acutely conscious of Kahn as a Jew, in ways that differentiate Kahn from other "whites." Hayes takes note of Kahn's supposed Jewish physical features (such as a "thick nose") as well as his putatively Jewish "braininess" and bookishness.[1] Kahn is also an obsessive weight lifter and consumer of natural foods. Moreover, some of the more fervent nationalists in the Black community, where Hayes and Kahn go under cover disguised as social workers carrying out an "Ethnic Survey," immediately direct anti-Semitic remarks at Kahn, calling him "Jewboy" and denouncing "Jew control."[2]

Kahn appears to have a classic left-wing attitude toward Jewish identity, abhorring anti-Semitism but making no concessions to Jewish particularism. Kahn is quick to mention that his parents "died in a Nazi oven."[3] However, he is equally quick to denounce Jewish nationalism and chauvinism. He admits that Jews can hold ignorant racist sentiments, even as he corrects one Black militant who thinks that the Yiddish word *schwartzer* (sometimes spelled *schwartze*) is necessarily tantamount to the epithet "nigger."[4] Expressing with a disconcerting articulateness his views about culture and history, Kahn goes so far as to repudiate all notions of ethnic heritage as the determinant of one's worth, Jewish, Black, or otherwise. Paraphrasing Henry Ford's famous comment on history, Kahn declares that "heritage is bunk" and argues in favor of "environment" as the explanation of differences in group behavior.[5]

Gradually the African American Hayes is attracted to Kahn, and indeed, so may be the reader who brings to the book a curiosity about or sympathy for radical politics. After all, despite Kahn's occasional odd proclamations, one begins to sense that he may be a secret Red. Early in the novel Kahn corrects one of his police superiors who is worried about "riots in the Negro community": "'Well, sir . . .' [Kahn] said, in that considered way he talked, 'I look upon them as rebellions, not riots. I think many Negroes have reached the breaking point in ghetto fatigue; they've had it. Marches no longer mean much, and at best they provided only a minor frustration release. . . . If I was in a Negro ghetto, I think I'd be leading a pretty fair revolt myself.'"[6] When one of the Harlem Black Nationalists offers a popular version of Frantz Fanon's theories urging "colonials to fight and destroy Western civilization, as a form of revolutionary therapy," Kahn steps in with a factual correction: "'Fanon was born in Martinique, where Negroes are the majority. And with the Algerian rebels, the FLN, Fanon was working in a country where he was again on the side of the majority. Hence his theories only apply to an area where the . . . colonials constitute the majority of the population and not to a country where the colonials are but a small minority. I've read his *Wretched of the Earth*, and he does not advocate his theory for the U.S.'"[7] At one point in the novel, another white cop, an overt racist, sneaks up on Kahn and knocks him out for being a "'nigger lover.'"[8]

The suggestion that Kahn, the Jewish cop, is a Leftist, as is Hayes, the Black cop, is reinforced if the reader recognizes that the names of the two officers who are trying to "do the right thing" in Harlem are the same as those of two famous pro-Communists: Lee Hayes (1914–81) was a singer and songwriter for Pete Seeger's Almanac Singers and the Weavers as well as a minor mystery writer who appeared in the same publications as Lacy; Hayes was white but known for his use of Black musical traditions.[9] Albert Kahn (discussed in Chapter 4) was the author of popular radical books on foreign policy, a contributing editor of the *New Masses*, a founder of the World Peace Council (generally regarded as a "Communist Front"), and co-owner in the 1950s of the left-wing publishing house Cameron and Kahn Associates. The use of Leftists' names in Lacy's novels is not merely coincidental. One of the villains in *In Black and Whitey* is named

Eugene Lyon; Eugene Lyons (1898–1985) was a famous apostate from Communism who wrote the classic 1941 anti-Communist work *The Red Decade: The Stalinist
Penetration of America.* Lacy's earlier Black private eye, Toussaint Marcus Moore,
was named after three political activists: Toussaint L'Ouverture, the leader of the
Haitian Revolution; Marcus Garvey, the founder of the largest Black Nationalist movement in U.S. history; and Richard B. Moore, the famed Caribbean-born
Communist who ran the Frederick Douglass Bookstore in Harlem. However, in
the astounding and unexpected denouement of *In Black and Whitey*, it turns out
that Kahn is not left wing but the villain of the novel. He has taken the Harlem undercover assignment precisely to ignite a race riot that will create a white
backlash, and in the end, Albert Kahn engages in a bloody hand-to-hand battle
to the death with Lee Hayes.

Can Ed Lacy's portrait of a Jewish betrayer who takes advantage of the kindness, trust, and generosity of his Black partner actually be a vile contribution
to anti-Semitic ideology? If so, of what race, ethnicity, and political orientation
might the author of *In Black and Whitey* actually be?

To the contrary, the novel is hardly anti-Semitic, because it turns out that
Officer Kahn is not really Jewish but the "100% Aryan" son of Nazi Party members who fell out of favor with Hitler over tactical differences and were sent to a
death camp.[10] Kahn is identified as not being Jewish near the end of the novel by
Mr. Herman, an "authentic" Jew—a shopkeeper who lives in Harlem and whose
daughter Ann is active in the civil rights struggle. Herman notes, "In Europe
a name like Kahn can be Jewish or gentile. One of Hitler's worst beasts was
a Rosenberg."[11] Moreover, the author of *In Black and Whitey*, Ed Lacy, although
thought by some readers to be an African American and, indeed, credited as the
creator of the first Black detective and included in at least one collection of Black
authors, was *himself* Jewish, born Leonard S. Zinberg.[12]

Despite the plot twist, the politics of the book are abundantly of the Left. Social reform, especially liberalism, is depicted as an insufficient solution to racist
capitalism. Hayes rejects the ultraleft nihilism of the extreme nationalists as
well, but he has something of a Leninist view of "the National Question"; that is,
Hayes does not equate the extremist nationalism of the oppressors (e.g., white
supremacism) and the Black nationalism of the oppressed. Such an equation is
the way that the other, more careerist Black officers choose to see things. Moreover, although the novel includes no didactic lectures on "the Jewish Question,"
its symbolic action seems to suggest that Jews can only oppose racism and fascist
movements by becoming "race traitors" to whiteness. The action of *In Black and
Whitey* argues that race hatred, in the form of white supremacism, is an American form of fascism, and the color line ("the visibility factor") is fundamental.

That is, race hatred takes root when any minority that can "pass" for white, such as Jews, allows itself to be absorbed even temporarily into the culture based on white identity and therefore privilege; the result will be that "the only minority in the U.S. will be colored." [13] Unlike the Jews of Europe, Jewish Americans have a choice about color, but to identify primarily as "white" could lead Jews to tacitly aid fascism. Most telling for Lacy's political education in the Old Left is his plot of American Nazis fomenting anti-Semitic ideology to ignite a race riot in Harlem in the late 1960s; this conspiracy theme is lifted directly from the controversial analysis by the Communist Party of the Harlem Riot of 1943, an episode that will be discussed at length in Chapter 4.

At the novel's end, the police, both white and Black, cover up the truth about Kahn. They place the blame for the Harlem troubles on the Black Power movement instead of on the white supremacists and facilitate Kahn being trumpeted in the newspapers as a heroic son of concentration camp victims who gave his life to stop racial violence. When Hayes reads in the papers a proclamation by the mayor of New York that the situation in Harlem was defused by "Negro-Jewish-Italian-Irish teamwork on the part of New York's finest, truly an all-American team," he renounces the police force for its "fink stink" and decides to accept his girlfriend's offer to move to the Caribbean.[14] The political implications of the overall narrative design express a Marxist sensibility: The state power constructs a false history in an almost "naturalized" way, the police infiltrate the Black ghetto in the guise of social workers conducting an ethnic survey, and the liberal rhetoric of "multiculturalism" is glibly invoked by the city administration to celebrate a spurious victory that changes nothing.

To what extent can In Black and Whitey be written off as an anomalous product of the late 1960s, a bizarre work by an unregenerate Leftist who happened to be on the scene and sought to capture the zeitgeist? Ed Lacy was, in fact, a mass-market phenomenon throughout the entire Cold War era; at his death in 1968, the year after In Black and Whitey came out, the New York Times reported that 28 million copies of his novels had been sold in twelve countries.[15] Moreover, Ed Lacy was far from atypical. His biography, political evolution, absorption with the ideology of racism, and dual literary career (before the Cold War as Zinberg, then under the name Lacy and other pseudonyms) are very much rooted in the generation that came of intellectual age during the antifascist crusade. Trinity of Passion will demonstrate that what, at first, might seem to be the strange career of Leonard S. Zinberg ends up being perhaps not so strange after all.

The career of Leonard Zinberg is offered here at the outset not merely to unveil the hidden identity of Ed Lacy—as a secular Jew, a former Communist, and a proletarian writer turned pulp writer extraordinaire. The career of Zinberg is also

LEONARD S. ZINBERG was a pro-Communist novelist in the
1930s and 1940s who reinvented himself during the Cold War as
a leading pulp fiction and mystery writer often featuring African
American characters. Under the name Ed Lacy he sold millions
of copies of his books and won a prestigious award. (From the
Zinberg Collection in the Howard Gotlieb Archival Research
Center at Boston University)

exemplary for its birthright in the antifascist crusade, its transit from the small magazines of the Left to the mainstream publications of mass culture, its manifold engagements with the ideology of racism and the travails of working-class life, and its dogged loyalty to fundamental class-based ideas of social transformation, albeit in a changing world.

Leonard S. Zinberg, known as Len, was born in 1911 in upstate New York to Max and Elizabeth Zinberg. The couple was divorced a few years later, and Elizabeth married Maxwell Wyckoff, a Manhattan banking lawyer. After age ten, Len resided with his mother and stepfather on West 153rd Street, at the edge of Harlem.[16] For a while, in the late 1920s, he attended City College of New York, and in the early 1930s he traveled across the country, working at odd jobs. Then his stories started to appear under his own name in pro-Communist publications such as the *New Masses*, *Blast*, and *New Anvil* and in commercial publications such as *Esquire*, *Coronet*, and *Story*. In 1940 he published *Walk Hard, Talk Loud*, about an African American boxer in love with a Black Communist activist. This was produced as a play in 1944 by the American Negro Theater Company in Harlem, with a script by an African American veteran of the Federal Theater Project, Abram Hill (1910–86). The responses to Zinberg's first novel by African American writers from a range on the political spectrum were sympathetic to his cross-cultural efforts. Ralph Ellison's comments in the *New Masses* merit quoting at length, inasmuch as they might seem surprising in light of Ellison's later reputation:

> For several years Len Zinberg, a young white writer, has been producing short stories that reveal an acute and sympathetic interest in the Negro's problems. . . .
>
> [In] *Walk Hard, Talk Loud* [he] indicates how far a writer, whose approach to Negro life is uncolored by condescension, stereotyped ideas, and other faults growing out of race prejudice, is able to go with a Marxist understanding of the economic basis of Negro personality. That, plus a Marxist sense of humanity, carries the writer a long way in a task considered extremely difficult: for a white writer to successfully depict Negro character. Another element in the author's success is a technique which he has modified to his own use, that of the "hard-boiled" school. This technique, despite its negative philosophical basis, is highly successful in conveying the violent quality of American experience—a quality as common to Negro life as to the lives of Hemingway characters.[17]

In one of two columns devoted to Zinberg in the African American newspaper *Pittsburgh Courier*, the editor George Schuyler wrote,

Len Zinberg, a young white author, has written a novel . . . which . . . is superior on several accounts to Richard Wright's *Native Son*. . . . Zinberg's Negroes are not caricatures as were Wright's. The red blood of authenticity pulsates through all of them. The Harlem jive is as realistic as it could possibly be. The picture of Harlem and the plight of its denizens, of all Negroes, is impressively authentic. . . .

[The protagonist's] sweetheart . . . is one of the finest female Negro characters yet created as characteristic of the modern age . . . far above the . . . liquor-sated Bessie of *Native Son*.[18]

In the era of the antifascist crusade, efforts by Euro-Americans to delineate Black life from an antiracist standpoint were often applauded by African American intellectuals. The situation would shift dramatically after the 1967–68 controversy about William Styron's *Confessions of Nat Turner*.[19]

During World War II, Zinberg served in the Army Air Corps from 1943 to 1945, rising to the rank of sergeant and spending most of his time in southern Italy. He was a correspondent for *Yank* magazine and won a Twentieth Century Fox Film Literary Fellowship award that brought him to Los Angeles for 1945–46. At the same time, Zinberg began contributing to the *New Yorker*, publishing a dozen and a half stories between 1945 and 1947. A number of these addressed the problem of the adjustment of ex-servicemen to the postwar climate and satirized both ultramasculine behavior and racism. Before the war, Zinberg held membership in the Communist-led League of American Writers; afterward he was active in the Communist-influenced National Council of the Arts, Sciences and Professions.

In the late 1940s, he published two more novels under his own name, including a radical one about the Depression-era Left, *Hold with the Hares* (1948). In this novel, the central character, Steve Anderson (the name anticipates one of Zinberg's later pseudonyms, Steve April), is a working-class WASP aspiring to a career in journalism. Steve's heart is with the Left, but he continually rationalizes the opportunistic choices he makes in the years between the Depression and World War II, under the delusion that, once he becomes successful, he will have the power to say what he "truly" thinks and will have some influence. Along the way, Steve meets several Jews who have responded to their Jewish identity in different ways, although anti-Black racism is a touchstone in each instance. One Jewish friend has assimilated simply to remove an obstacle blocking his career, and he frequently uses racist epithets; another, from the South, affirms his Jewishness, but he does so by refusing to fight the Jim Crow system because he does not want to reinforce the southern stereotypes of Jews, including the one of the Jew as a radical troublemaker.

7

Both of the Jews are doppelgängers, reflections of Steve's own political opportunism, and Steve likes them because their behavior confirms rather than challenges his own, although clearly the author Zinberg does not like them. What turns Steve around at the climax of Hold with the Hares is the influence of Pete Wormser, a revolutionary white sailor of unstated ethnicity who first fights with the International Brigades in Spain and then with antifascist partisans in World War II; finally, Pete travels to the Carolinas with Operation Dixie, an effort of the Congress of Industrial Organizations (CIO) to organize Black mill workers.

This section features a shootout with a racist, antiunion lynch mob in which Pete's Black comrade Oliver—whose name suggests Oliver Law, the African American martyr of the Abraham Lincoln Brigade in Spain—is killed. Pete then flees to New York and goes underground. Although the Communist Party wants Pete to return to stand trial, Pete feels he would have no chance in a southern court. Thus, in events somewhat based on those of Communist union leader Fred Beale and the 1929 Gastonia, North Carolina, textile strike, Pete decides to escape to Europe. At this point Steve quits his big-time journalism job and, breaking with his past, sneaks Pete out of the country. In the final pages of the book, Steve launches a new life as a radical writer by taking over a small-town newspaper that was being run by an aged member of the Industrial Workers of the World, in order to fight a kind of guerrilla war against the capitalist system.

The novel can perhaps be read as a psychohistory of Zinberg. Using the extent of opposition to anti-Black racism as a constant litmus test for one's morality, Zinberg rejects the possibility of presenting a protagonist who finds self-realization as a Jew, because he feels, and the novel suggests, that there were no individuals who joined the vanguard of the antiracist struggle on the basis of their Jewish identity. Zinberg thus, through his surrogate Anderson, opts for a proletarian internationalist identity, although apparently, in his support of Pete's flight, he indicates a preference to act as a radical free agent rather than a disciplined Party cadre.

With publication of the paperback crime novel The Woman Aroused in 1951, the same year the Communist Party leadership was jailed under the Smith Act, Zinberg became reborn under the name Ed Lacy to protect himself from blacklisting and harassment. As early as 1946, he had been named in a New York Times article reporting on allegations of Communist influence in a New York post of the American Legion.[20] Never again, during the next two decades, did he refer to his earlier career or earlier novels in autobiographical statements or in biographical information provided for book jackets. His multiple identities were not even known to most of his left-wing friends from the literary workshops and discussion groups hosted by editors of the Communist journal Masses & Mainstream that

he attended at the home of Dr. Annette T. Rubinstein, a blacklisted school principal, throughout the 1950s. Len Zinberg was married to an African American
writer, Esther Zinberg (1910–83), who contributed stories as Esther Lacy to the
New Yorker, the *Negro Digest*, the *Baltimore Afro-American*, and the *Contemporary Reader*
(published under the auspices of the Writing and Publishing Division of the New
York Council of the Arts, Sciences and Professions in the early 1950s). Esther
Zinberg was also an office worker and was employed for some years as a secretary at the Yiddish Communist newspaper *Freiheit*. The decision of the interracial
couple to adopt a child was another reason for Len to guard his new professional
name from any linkage to his political past in the era of red-baiting.

In the 1950s and 1960s Zinberg as Lacy became distinguished among mystery writers for his use of African American characters as protagonists, including two series characters, Toussaint Marcus Moore and Lee Hayes. A third series,
which features the character Dave Wintino, includes *Lead with Your Left* (1957) and
Double Trouble (1965). Wintino is part Italian American and part Jewish American
and has a Black police partner. Radical politics are pervasive in the Lacy novels;
Zinberg was the main opponent among hard-boiled mystery writers to the ultra-
reactionary author Mickey Spillane and Spillane's red-baiting private eye, Mike
Hammer. *Sin in Their Blood* (1952), his second novel as Lacy, depicts a right-wing
organization that is blackmailing African Americans who are trying to "pass."
Go for the Body (1954) tells of the interracial marriage of a Black boxer who lives in
exile due to racism in the United States and of a scheme to strike a blow against
elements of Italian and German fascism that are organizing for a postwar come-
back. *A Deadly Affair* (1960) and *Sleep in Thunder* (1964) treat racism against Puerto
Ricans. *The Napalm Bugle* (1968) attacks the U.S. government's role in Vietnam,
and *Breathe No More, My Lady* (1958) favorably depicts a blacklisted radical professor, formerly a professional boxer. Zinberg also published hundreds of short
stories in various mystery, pulp, and popular magazines.

The shift from novels in the proletarian tradition to pulp fiction by Lacy was
more a matter of entering the mass market than a change in his form or ideology.
In all phases of his career Zinberg's disconcerting irony and multilayered perspectives challenged prevailing constructions of racial and ethnic identity, and
especially white male pretensions to ultramasculinity. The post–World War II
effort to mask his earlier Communist persona actually functioned to heighten
and complicate his approach to such constructions. Starting with his pieces in
the *New Yorker*, Zinberg turned his skills to capturing the nervousness of the post–
World War II and Cold War cultural climate. For example, in his second work of
pulp fiction, *Sin in Their Blood*, Lacy rewrites Hemingway's modernist classic, *The
Sun Also Rises* (1926), for a new age.

Lacy's hero, Matt Ranzino, like Hemingway's Jake Barnes, emerges from a war—in this case the Korean War—with a mysterious wound. The doctors in the hospital insist that Ranzino, a former private eye, is cured, yet he continues to believe that he has symptoms. His friends are distressed about his condition, and his former girlfriend, now the mistress of his ex-partner, asks, in a reference to Jake Barnes's emasculation, "God, Matt, you weren't wounded there?"[21]

Matt was not; but his attitude toward women has changed, and he sees the world of the 1950s through new eyes. He is disgusted that his former partner has taken on a "new executive look" and has turned the detective agency into a red-baiting/blacklisting enterprise along the lines of *Red Channels*. The unnamed modern city he surveys, like T. S. Eliot's London, has became a commercialized wasteland: "I took in the skyscrapers, the movie houses, the gin mills, the bookie joints that passed as cigar stores, the radio station tower that disappeared into the blue sky, a modern monument to nothing. I watched the people hurrying by, the crowded restaurants and orangeade stands, the heavy traffic—and I knew the street didn't mean a thing to me any more."[22]

Events in the novel, though, force Matt out of his lassitude as he decides to combat the very detective agency for which he had once worked. Haunted by the mass murder he has witnessed in Korea, he refuses to cash in on his veteran status by playing the patriot. He finds himself no longer comfortable with the ideology of toughness to which he once adhered. Even more astounding, for a novel published in 1952, he is drawn to a woman who talks of the need for equal rights, dresses only to please herself, and makes him share the housework. Yet Matt must fight back in an effort to resist the triumph of this new and corrupted wasteland. In contrast to his onetime mentor Hemingway, who draws on the metaphor of the bullfight to promote the need for grace in the face of eternal meaninglessness, Lacy uses a boxing match—the exercising of skill in combat with human opponents. The need to survive and win rekindles Matt's memory of his old boxing coach, Pops—a moral and socially conscious alternative to the champion of the bullfight ethic, Papa Hemingway.

Twelve years after *Sin in Their Blood* challenged the Hemingway ethic, Lacy published a full-blown attack on the bullfighting paradigm as an elaborate fraud. *Moment of Untruth*, set in Mexico rather than Hemingway's Spain, depicts a Black private eye who exposes a charlatan matador, Cuzo, an Indian, notorious for his womanizing and macho antics. Once exposed, the bullfighter commits suicide— an apparent commentary on Hemingway's death the year before Lacy's book was published. Like Lacy's other books, *Moment of Untruth* is a troubled study of the difficulty of a modern sensibility coping with the myths of bourgeois society. His Black private eye (this time it is Toussaint Marcus Moore), a target of racism in the United States, is told that he will encounter "no color problems" in Mexico.[23] Instead, he finds that he is frequently perceived as if he were a white man and he needs to be repeatedly educated regarding his American chauvinism.

Even more disconcerting, Toussaint's task is to discredit a pure Indian, the bullfighter Cuzo, who is known as "El Indio," a member of the bottom rung of the racial hierarchy in Mexico, even as he, Toussaint, walks a sexual tightrope between two white women. One is a masculinized scientist specializing in poisonous snakes; the other, a blond bombshell with big breasts who seems to stalk Lacy characters throughout all his books.

In the last pages of the novel Toussaint painfully reflects: "For all my hatred of Cuzo, I knew he was born a slave and only generations removed from slavery. As an Indian in Mexico he faced the same general problems I had in the States. I could understand only too well what made him tick. . . . I [had] this terrible feeling I was being an Uncle Tom, doing the white folks a favor, somehow, by knocking off El Indio. It was driving me crazy . . . the idea that I was betraying my color." Toussaint's final thoughts, then, are far from triumphal at his successful resolution of the case. They show him reflecting an unhappy consciousness resonating with the author's awareness not only about contradictions of racism in a capitalist society; the passage also suggests that Lacy is disturbed by his participation in the mass culture industry, which by its nature dilutes and compromises the radical sensibility he aspires to impart to his writing. This melancholy mood, a sense of historic entrapment joined with a desperate need to fight on nonetheless, is characteristic of the legacy of the antifascist crusade in U.S. literature.

Many obscure careers in literary radicalism such as Zinberg's are evoked in *Trinity of Passion*, with the aim of deepening and complicating rather than creating a counterparadigm to the past five decades of scholarship about the U.S. literary Left. The marvelous founding studies tended to treat World War II as a sad coda: "The Long Retreat," in Walter B. Rideout's *The Radical Novel in the United States: Some Interrelations of Literature and Society, 1900–1954* (1956); "Disenchantment and Withdrawal," in Daniel Aaron's *Writers on the Left: Episodes in American Literary Communism* (1961); and "The Politics of Collision," in James Burkhart Gilbert's *Writers and Partisans: A History of Literary Radicalism in America* (1968). A few older books examine the literature of the Spanish Civil War in isolation from other U.S. writings of the Depression era to achieve a sustained analysis of the genre, sometimes in an international context.[24] Most books about radical fiction published since the 1970s are informed by theoretical perspectives and focus on the 1930s; none substantially takes up the broader Left in World War II.

In 1996, Michael Denning's *The Cultural Front: The Laboring of American Culture* in the Twentieth Century contributed a dramatic shift in perspective engaging a spectacular sweep of cultural references. Although Denning did not treat World War II as a discrete moment, he included a positive view of cultural workers of the 1940s in this treatise on the long-term liberating effects of Popular Front culture. Subsequent to Denning, and with comparable sympathies, several persuasive books examining the African American cultural Left have incorporated components of the 1940s into their narratives: Bill Mullen's Popular Fronts: Chicago and African-American Cultural Politics, 1935–46 (1999); James Smethurst's The New Red Negro: The Literary Left and African American Poetry (1999); and Stacy I. Morgan's Rethinking Social Realism: African American Art and Literature, 1930–1953 (2004). Earlier, Susan Schweik's A Gulf So Deeply Cut: American Women Poets and the Second World War (1991) had brilliantly explored the experience of war as an ideological construct in relation to gender.

There are additional studies to which I am particularly obliged that speak to aspects of culture and politics in World War II. I read Chester E. Eisinger's Fiction of the Forties (1963) as an undergraduate and was enraptured by his narrative sweep of politics and literature. I was also taken with the photographs on the cover of the paperback edition of the faces of Irwin Shaw, Budd Schulberg, Nelson Algren, James T. Farrell, and others who imparted an aura of realist and naturalist writers earnestly engaged with ideas. To George Lipsitz's Rainbow at Midnight: Labor and Culture in the 1940s (rev. ed., 1995) I owe many methodological debts, including Lipsitz's expansive notion of the category of class.[25] I much admire Andrew Hemingway's Artists on the Left: American Artists and the Communist Movement, 1926–1956 (2002) for its holistic approach and the author's effort to restore to the Communist movement the credit it merits without blurring its political flaws to the reader. Both Andrew Hemingway and I see the Popular Front as the continuation of a troubled tradition in new forms rather than a genuine solution to earlier predicaments.

There also exist numerous scholarly works that do not engage literature but nevertheless reflect on writers in relation to the major political controversies of the Spanish Civil War and World War II. The dispute over the 1939 Hitler-Stalin Pact and the political cost of later delusions about the USSR have been traced in works such as William L. O'Neill's The Great Schism: Stalinism and the American Intellectuals (1982). The political somersaults of the Communist movement before, during, and after the 1941 German invasion of the USSR were derided in Irving Howe and Lewis Coser's The American Communist Party: A Critical History (1957). Even the 1946 literary controversy surrounding screenwriter Albert Maltz, a critical episode in Trinity of Passion, has been a principal focus of scholarship since it was reported forty-five years ago in Aaron's Writers on the Left; most recently it was a centerpiece of Ronald Radosh and Allis Radosh's history, *Red Star over Hollywood: The Film Colony's Long Romance with the Left* (2005). Several of these books attack Communist foibles with such prosecutorial zeal that it is hard to see the reasoning by which intelligent, humane, and talented writers would choose to devote themselves to what is painted as predominantly a foolish and corrupt cause. But I do not dispute the rudimentary facts they present.

An exceptional work of political history that has not received attention commensurate with its originality is Frank A. Warren's *Noble Abstractions: American Liberal Intellectuals in World War II* (1999). Warren draws a distinction between the Popular Front of the late 1930s and the post-1941 confluence of liberals and Communists around the antifascist crusade in World War II. Neither, of course, was a genuine Popular Front in the sense of constructing a form of organization-to-organization unity achieving governmental rule. But Warren observes that the World War II coalition gave a lesser role to the political influence of the Communist Party. This is partly because the Communists, contrary to their image as extremists in the popular mind, repeatedly went farther to the right than many liberals in their idealization of the Democratic Party, their hostility to the militant wing of the African American civil rights movement, and their inclusion of rivals (Norman Thomas Socialists and Trotskyists) into their amalgam of a "fifth column" that needed to be governmentally suppressed. *Noble Abstractions* is not, however, just one more book about Communist blunders; Warren's principal attention is devoted to the liberals' own illusions that World War II was somehow "a democratic revolution" and an international civil war between democracy and fascism.

Trinity of Passion, in contrast, is about writers and literary trends, where there was a stronger continuity over the decades for those who perceived Spain and World War II as stages in an elongated contest to transform capitalism by defending it against the internal and external forces of the Far Right. Still, the antifascist crusade in culture was far from seamless, even for those pro-Communists who are the subject of this study. The belief systems of the writers were perpetually challenged by calls to alternately embrace and then flay liberal allies; to instigate and then oppose strikes; to urge, then resist, and then again urge U.S. governmental action against fascism; and to identify racism in the United States with fascism abroad, then to subordinate struggles against the former for the sake of national unity against the latter. With the exception of the unmitigated threat posed by the Nazis, the social and political terrain was fraught with contradictions. None of these obviated the need to destroy fascism by military force, but they did pose questions about the ideological and strategic aims of the Allies.

The capitalist democracies were compromised by their colonial empires, class oppression, and virulent racism, and their Soviet partners masked a brutal dictatorship behind the guise of "socialism." Moreover, the war in the Pacific had a disturbing racial character. By and large the Communist-led wing of the antifascist crusade, particularly strong in literary circles, demanded an exacting loyalty to shifts in Soviet policy that would permanently taint Communist Party claims to be consistently prolabor and antiracist. In 1946, in the course of a bitter postwar debate in the pages of the *New Masses* about the slogan "Art as a Weapon," the Communist Party's political and cultural leadership stuck fast to its tradition of judging literature by current Party policy; thus the fault lines first exposed by intra-Left debates in the 1930s were visibly deepened.[26]

Most novelists in the pro-Communist tradition sought to accomplish meaningful ideological work in their creative efforts. Many drew considerably on models of the realist and naturalist schools and sporadically on modernist strategies, to restore historical consciousness to the reader by reproducing the forces shaping character, society, and belief. Their aim of dereifying the reader's mental world is an honorable artistic objective, but creative work is always revelatory in aspects unexpected and even unintended by its authors. That is why a cardinal concern of *Trinity of Passion* resides beyond formal ideology. Although a comprehensive reconstruction of all of the elements shaping a writer's consciousness is unattainable, the discernment of the intricacies of his or her political passions can modify, enrich, and challenge earlier interpretations of novels, poems, and plays. Traces of the piercing convictions of the day can also be detected in works published decades later, frequently in forms that are masked and modified.

More than fifty years later, signs of the literary origins of Len Zinberg and many others who launched careers in the antifascist era are far less decipherable than those of writers who came into their maturity during the 1930s. Writers of the Depression forthrightly declared their aims of producing "revolutionary poetry," "workers theater," and the "proletarian novel." Writers of the 1940s were more integrated into mainstream and popular literature.

The argument of *Trinity of Passion*, as is that of *Exiles from a Future Time*, is not that Communism has been the secret glue of U.S. literature in the 1930s, 1940s, and 1950s. To the contrary, Communism, or even political commitment in general, is by itself a deficient and distorting prism through which to view the narrative imagination. Too often a preoccupation with Communist affiliations leads to the deductive fallacy of making presumptions about the artistic process according to supposed political loyalties of authors. *Trinity of Passion* intends to offer a judicious assessment of the intricacy of the lives of those writers in which a shared yet individualized political commitment played an indispensable part.

14

It also aims to consider the implications of the transit through the antifascist crusade that are dispersed across the horizon of mid-twentieth-century literary history. To that end, the account begins with literature that responded to the founding moment of the antifascist crusade, the civil war in Spain, and proceeds to several fronts of World War II.

{ 1

Tough Jews in the Spanish Civil War

UNMANLY DOUBLES

Near the climax of *Another Hill* (1994), an autobiographical novel of the Spanish Civil War (1936–39), there is a dramatization of the cardinal debate about art and political responsibility that consumed the mid-twentieth-century literary Left before, during, and after the antifascist crusade. The novel's author is Milton Wolff (b. 1915), the Jewish American commander of the Abraham Lincoln Battalion, the largest constituent of volunteers from the United States serving in the Fifteenth International Brigade.[1]

Wolff's fictional surrogate, Mitch Castle, initiates a sharp exchange between two "real-life" characters among a group of antifascist intellectuals clustered around a table at the Hotel Majestic in Barcelona, shortly before the 29 October 1938 farewell parade for the foreign volunteers. One is Joseph North (1904–76; born Joseph Soifer), an editor of the Communist *New Masses*. The other is Ernest Hemingway (1899–1961), the epitome of the virile artist in modern literature. Although Wolff depicts the two men at variance in relation to literary matters, Hemingway and North later collaborated on the pamphlet *Men in the Ranks: The Story of 12 Americans in Spain* (1939).

The issue that prompted the intellectual sparring match between the Communist Party cadre, North, and the fellow traveler, Hemingway, was the question of how a militant antifascist author should treat the Spanish Civil War in fiction. North's remarks are based on his sense that Mitch Castle's style of narrating the exploits of the Lincoln Battalion in his native "Brooklynese" tends to accentuate the sensationally dangerous and downplay the heroism of the ordinary. Anticipating Hemingway's predictable rejoinder, that the writer's only obligation is to be "true to his art, to be a craftsman, and to tell it truly,"[2] North warns, "If for the sake of drama . . . or self-pity and a mistaken sense of humor and humility, we emphasize the negative aspects . . . if we allow these occasional weaknesses to upstage the main drama, then, and I must say I am putting it as strongly as possible because we are dealing with not a few lives here, but millions, then we are aiding and abetting the murderers of mankind."[3] North's remarks offer a "soft," Popular Front variant of the Communist movement's "Art Is a Class Weapon" orientation, with which Mitch Castle is conspicuously in accord.[4] Yet the reverberations of this warning on the mind and art of the pro-Communist Milton Wolff thirty years later, when he began writing *Another Hill* in the late 1960s, appear ambiguous.

Another Hill forcefully recounts the adventures of a range of representative Lincolns, none of whose exploits and sexual encounters, however, approaches the romanticized ones of Hemingway's celebrated Spanish Civil War volunteer Robert Jordan in *For Whom the Bell Tolls* (1940). As the consummate exemplar of Hemingway's code—a strong, silent type who greets his destiny with little complaint—the college instructor Jordan diverges from most of Wolff's Lincolns as neither ethnically distinguished nor a Communist.[5] As the sole U.S. volunteer in the hills behind enemy lines, Robert Jordan is also something of a cross between the Lone Ranger and an acrobat of the sleeping bag, who makes love as well as adroitly shoots a fascist from under his blankets.

Yet, *For Whom the Bell Tolls* ascends to a poignant but politically noncontroversial execution, when Jordan shoots the fascist Lieutenant Paco Berrendo.[6] In contrast, Wolff's *Another Hill* drives relentlessly toward the moment when Mitch Castle executes not a fascist but a fellow Jewish American member of the Lincoln Battalion, Leo Rogin. Moreover, although accused of being a malingerer, Rogin is not the political opposite of Castle, as Berrendo is of Jordan.

The similarities between Wolff's two characters are so compelling that Rogin can be justly considered as a doppelgänger to Castle, a haunting double who is a projection of the kind of overtly pusillanimous attributes that Castle discerns in himself as dormant but nonetheless must act decisively to quell. Castle and Rogin are both New York Jews of a comparable age, handsome, and with backgrounds in the Young Communist movement. They are differentiated chiefly by their public "masculinity." Castle is strikingly fearless in battle, like Hemingway's Robert Jordan, as opposed to Rogin's uncontrollable fearfulness in the front lines. Augmenting the similarities of the two men, Milton Wolff inserts doubts into the narrative as to the military indispensability of Castle's act of violence against Rogin, insinuating that there are personal and political rather than strictly martial reasons for the summary execution.

Moreover, given the inordinate strain under which the outgunned and outnumbered Lincoln volunteers served, and the propensity of the Communist movement to persecute suspected heretics, one may be dubious about the genuine cowardice of Rogin. Although Rogin is executed at a moment parallel in *Another Hill* to the shooting of Berrendo in *For Whom the Bell Tolls*, Rogin's weakness

17

and fate evidently mimic the role in Hemingway's novel of the insecure Russian guerrilla, Kashkin. In events that antedate those recounted in *For Whom the Bell Tolls*, Kashkin is wounded by fascists; he was then shot by Robert Jordan to prevent his capture and torture, because Kashkin lacked the nerve to take his own life. Later, Jordan is disconcerted by what he regards as Kashkin's unmanly behavior, just as Castle is haunted by Rogin's numerous desertions, his own unmanly mirror.

Thus it appears that Wolff's novelistic response to North's admonition to Hemingway to use art as a weapon on behalf of the antifascist cause is half-hearted. Wolff faithfully depicts more ordinary events of the war than does Hemingway, but he is not inclined to sugarcoat the sordid aspects. Wolff's obstinate reluctance to accentuate the positive is corroborated rather perversely by the concluding action of *Another Hill*, as the Lincolns make ready to quit Spain and Mitch Castle confronts another "real-life" character. Castle is depicted as providing a sharp retort to pro-Loyalist *New York Herald Tribune* reporter Vincent Sheean's eulogy for James Lardner, son of the writer Ring Lardner. James Lardner is alluded to as being "The Last Volunteer," which was in fact the title of the sixth chapter in Sheean's 1939 book *Not Peace but a Sword*. When Castle hears the questionable claim that a person from such a celebrated family was literally the last Lincoln killed, he scoffs derisively. To Mitch, such a romantic but highly dubious story is opportunistic mythmaking, which leads to writing that will falsify life to uplift morale.

Mitch proceeds, in an act dripping with cynicism, to contrive his own myth. During the farewell parade of International Brigades volunteers, he encounters Leo Rogin's abandoned Spanish lover in the streets of Barcelona. In a brief conversation with her he reports that "the last volunteer" killed in battle was probably Leo—leaving out the details that Leo was a deserter and had been shot by Mitch himself months earlier. Almost assuredly the invention of this myth as a finale would have caused Joseph North, had he lived to see the publication of Wolff's novel, to declare *Another Hill* a "negative" account potentially upstaging "the main drama." The circulation of one bogus story in place of another also provides a disturbing gloss for the famous tribute that La Pasionaria (Dolores Ibarruri, the Spanish Communist Party's "spiritual" leader) would deliver in her speech to the departing Lincolns: "You are legend."[7]

Seventeen years after *For Whom the Bell Tolls* appeared, Alvah Bessie (1904–85), a Jewish American Lincoln Battalion warrior like Milton Wolff, published a political and psychological rejoinder to Hemingway's fictionalized portrait of an ultramasculine, non-Jewish volunteer. In *The Un-Americans* (1957), Bessie employs

ALVAH BESSIE, shown in Spain in April 1938 during the
Spanish Civil War, joined the Communist Party before
volunteering with the International Brigades to fight fascism.
The author of novels, memoirs, and screenplays, Bessie served
a prison sentence as one of the Hollywood Ten. (Courtesy of
Abraham Lincoln Brigade Archives, New York University)

flashbacks and flash-forwards between the Spanish Civil War and the House Committee on Un-American Activities (HUAC) hearings in the early 1950s to relate the adventures of Ben Blau, his own fearless, semiautobiographical version of Robert Jordan and Mitch Castle. Blau, a journalist turned Communist and a combat veteran of the Lincolns, is the author of an acclaimed nonfiction chronicle of the war experience in Spain called *Volunteer for Liberty*, which echoes Bessie's own *Men in Battle* (1939).

Residing in New York City after the publication of *Volunteer for Liberty*, Blau attends the opening-night performance of *Better to Die*, a play by the eminent radical journalist and radio broadcaster Francis Xavier Lang. Lang had befriended Blau in Spain and later commended *Volunteer for Liberty* just as Hemingway and the journalist Vincent Sheean had praised *Men in Battle*.[8] Lang, a character recalling Hemingway and especially Sheean, had reported on the war as a correspondent but was motivated principally by his love for a beautiful Spanish Communist who was later killed in an air raid.[9] When Blau sees Lang's *Better to Die*, he is appalled at the production, noting, "It was romantic, it was nostalgic, it revived the painful memories of Spain without demanding anything of its audience but laughter and tears."[10] In an episode based on the public protest initiated by Bessie and Wolff in 1940 of *For Whom the Bell Tolls*,[11] Blau and other veterans of the Abraham Lincoln Brigade issue an "Open Letter to Francis X. Lang," stating in part, "From its defeatist title—a perversion of La Pasionaria's stirring call to battle—to its hopeless final curtain . . . *Better to Die* is a violent distortion of the recent struggle in Spain. . . . We cannot recognize in Charles Wilton, the hero, the archetype of the American volunteer in Spain."[12]

The Un-Americans, while entertaining, is Bessie's anti-McCarthyite witch-hunt morality play, with uncomplicated polarities of good and evil. Hence the increasingly depraved Lang morally decays as relentlessly as Dorian Gray's portrait in Oscar Wilde's *The Picture of Dorian Gray* (1891). Ultimately, Lang, who was a casual member of the Communist Party until 1939, gives testimony before HUAC that plays a role in consigning Blau to prison. Once incarcerated, Blau is brutally beaten in an attempted murder by Levine, a Jewish semi-gangster. Levine at first befriends Blau, then assaults him in the name of anti-Communism, hoping that the near-fatal attack might shorten his own sentence.

The Levine episode combines features of two infamously savage events that occurred during the McCarthy era. One was the assault in prison by a Yugoslav fascist on the Communist and Smith Act victim Robert Thompson, who was also a Lincoln veteran and a World War II hero. A metal plate had to be inserted in Thompson's skull, which may have contributed to his sudden death at age fifty. The other bloody event was the knifing and murder of Jewish Bohemian poet and former Communist Party member Maxwell Bodenheim (1892–1954; born Maxwell Bodenheimer) and his wife by a Jewish American, Harold Weinberg, who had posed as a friend. Afterward, Weinberg defended himself at his trial by affirming that "I ought to get a medal. I killed two Communists."[13] In the novel Levine clobbers Blau with two baseball bats (the Yugoslav used an iron pipe) with the result that Blau, like Thompson, will require a steel plate in his head. After this attempted murder of Blau, Levine, echoing Weinberg, cries, "I killed the dirty Red son of a bitch!" and "I'll be sprung for this!"[14] As Levine is placed in handcuffs and Blau is taken to the prison hospital, one of the guards comments, "Two less Jew-boys."[15]

Inasmuch as the two "Jew-boys" present ideological contrasts, the confrontation between Blau and Levine can be seen as a rather disconcerting reference to the violent encounter between Hemingway's Robert Jordan and Paco Berrendo. Blau is a former Lincoln, while the would-be assassin Levine is an anti-Communist exemplar of the gangster elements attracted by fascism. Levine, of course, lacks Lieutenant Berrendo's cultivation and better resembles the kind of thugs (some Jewish) used by bosses and mobsters to smash Left-leaning trade union organizing efforts. Levine also reflects what Bessie views as a post–World War II fascism in the United States, nourished by the growing right wing in the Cold War era, akin to the mobs that had disrupted Paul Robeson's Peekskill, New York, concert in 1949. However, the burgeoning expression of fascism in the United States is further linked to a section of the intelligentsia in the sense that Levine was abetted by the cowardly and opportunistic Lang, who provided the intellectual rationale for Blau's imprisonment. Further, as in Wolff's violent encounter between Castle and Rogin in the months prior to the victory of the fascists in *Another Hill*, two Jewish Americans, Blau and Levine, battle it out, with the latter attempting to kill the former in the historical and literary context of the ascendancy of a right-wing surge that also has an anti-Semitic component.

In each of the three novels, the theme of masculinity—dramatized in the relationship of Jordan to Kashkin, Castle to Rogin, and Blau to Lang—is pivotal. Collectively, the three fragile "doubles" of the steadfast protagonists are associated with what the respective authors seem to consider as a weakness that is decidedly "feminine" in the face of bellicose adversity. Hemingway's efforts to craft a virile persona long preceded *For Whom the Bell Tolls*, and Wolff's Mitch Castle is constructed as manly in that precise tradition. Bessie, too, was categorically emphatic about his masculinist ideal in his aptly titled *Men in Battle*, in which a less virile volunteer is judged "more of a woman than a man" and the war experience was considered to be "necessary for me, at that stage of my development as a man."[16] Moreover, in *The Un-Americans* the dilemma of rescuing masculinity from the threat posed by the unmanly doppelgänger, Lang, is more centrally displaced and reworked through an expressedly sexual contrast.

All three protagonists (Jordan, Castle, and Blau) redeem their masculinity in confrontations with effeminized doubles (Kashkin, Rogin, and Lang). However, in the first two instances, physical annihilation of the doubles is required, whereas Bessie establishes his mastery over Blau's double through his description of sexual relations with females. Lang, a moral and physical coward, degenerates from an inveterate womanizer who nonetheless maintains an attractive wife and a mistress to a pathetic drunk repudiated and even exploited by the women whom he once dominated. Blau, in contrast to Lang's growing impotence, upholds his virility not by shooting his double but through his willingness to martyr himself for his principles. Prior to being confined in jail, he referred to himself as "Ben the Blue" because of his inability to cement a durable romantic relationship. Yet he emerges from his prison tribulation with his Communist political convictions reinvigorated and seemingly his testosterone level increased. At the conclusion of Bessie's novel is the text of Blau's frank marriage proposal to Sue, his long-suffering girlfriend, in which he signs himself as "Ben the Red." [17]

A third response to Hemingway's portrait of a volunteer from the United States in Spain is by the disillusioned Lincoln combat veteran William Herrick (1915–2004), author of some ten novels, several of which are about Spain and the Lincolns. Herrick is usually compared to George Orwell (1903–50), chiefly because of Orwell's socialist critique of Stalinism in *Homage to Catalonia* (1938). [18] Herrick was, like Wolff and Bessie, a Jewish American; his birth name was Horvitz, and he joined the Lincolns under the name Bill Harvey. Yet Herrick affords a sensational contrast with Hemingway, Wolff, and Bessie in his political rendition of the Spanish events. Such political complications are manifest in literary design as well, even as Herrick joins the latter two in the tradition of retorting to Hemingway's alleged inauthenticity and shares their fixations on dramatizing the intersection of radical secular Jewish identity and masculinity during the era of the Popular Front in arms. [19]

JEWS WITH GUNS

The life stories of Milton Wolff, Alvah Bessie, and William Herrick are notably disparate, except in two instances: All were raised in secular New York Jewish families with religious traditions at some distance from their lives, although a Yiddish culture was present. All suffered the loss of or alienation from their fathers at a young age. Two were won to radicalism in the early Depression; the first was initiated by teenage acquaintances, and the second by the arguments of his fellow intellectuals. The third was born into a revolutionary family during

World War I. Their routes to Communism, Spain, and writing novels collectively comprise a vital subset of the literary Left, as well as a hitherto neglected segment in Jewish American cultural history.

Wolff was the youngest son of unhappily married Jewish immigrants in Brooklyn.[20] He grew up assuming that his birth was undesired. His father was a self-employed man hired for odd jobs, and money was always in short supply. Nearly overwhelmed by the constant fighting of his parents and the resultant schisms among his siblings, the young Milton Wolff also battled neighborhood bullies and Italian American anti-Semites. He retreated into adventure novels, movies, and the studying of painting. Then he withdrew from high school and joined the Civilian Conservation Corps (CCC), leaving his family, which enabled them to go on relief. Although apolitical, he was drawn into a victorious demonstration in the CCC camp against mismanagement of the camp's food money. He was eventually forced to leave the CCC when he supported the grievances of the family of a friend in the camp who had died of blood poisoning.

When Wolff returned to Brooklyn to take a job in the garment industry and to study drawing at night, he discovered that his old buddies had joined the Young Communist League (YCL). Soon he became an activist YCL member himself, revealing an aptitude for speaking on street corners; as a result, he was transformed from a pacifist into an antifascist partisan. Most vitally, for the first time, as a member of YCL he enjoyed a resplendent family life through a community of friends and a common political association.

Wolff's socialist education was widened by internal YCL classes and reading the Communist Party press. But in an unpublished autobiographical manuscript made available in the 1990s, he suggests that his decision to go to Spain was partly due to complications in his personal life, even as his political convictions grew. In "A Member of the Working Class," the fictionalized Wolff persona, again called Mitch Castle, is drawn into love affairs with two women, including the girlfriend of a brother. He is also implicated in a stock-skimming operation at the hat factory where he is employed. Thus he readily offers himself for military service in Spain when a YCL organizer asks for volunteers at a meeting.

Wolff arrived in Spain in early 1937, training first as a medic and then as a machine gunner. After fighting in the battles of Brunette, Quinto, and Belchite, he was promoted to commander of a machine gun company for the battle of Fuentes de Ebro. By the battle of Teruel, he was a captain and an adjutant. At age twenty-two he was elevated to commander of the Lincoln Battalion after the death of his predecessor, Dave Reiss. In this post, Wolff led the Lincolns in a notable attack over the Ebro River and into the Sierra Pandois.

Wolff returned to the United States a hero to the Left. For the remainder of

CAPTAIN MILTON WOLFF, shown in 1938, served as the last commander of the Abraham Lincoln Battalion in Spain. Decades later he published a revealing novel reflecting his experiences in war. (Courtesy of Abraham Lincoln Brigade Archives, New York University)

his life he was known as a spokesperson for the veterans of the Abraham Lincoln Brigade, where pro-Communists comprised a substantial albeit declining constituency. Although Wolff maintained that he was not technically a Party member, the ideals of Communism continued to guide him. In the early days of World War II Wolff wrote to a friend about the course of his personal journey: "I looked for an argument in favor of purity, faithfulness and love. And I found them— in the theory of the party and in the broad, active material sweep of party practice—even though I did not find it in the individuals thereof." As for his decision to enlist in the U.S. Army a year after the Soviet Union was attacked, he added, "Only in war have I found peace. . . . Here I know my way." [21]

Wolff was singularly tall and sinewy, with a full head of dark hair that evolved into a gray mane as he grew older. In contrast, Bessie was of average height, fairhaired and blue-eyed. He balded early, and, according to his elder son, by the 1950s "Pop's face, that of an aging basset, frequently got him mistaken for the British actor Sir Cedric Hardwicke." [22] Bessie claimed that he never finished his autobiography because he had become "bored with the central character," but to the contrary he was a theatrical personality who incorporated much of his life into his short stories, novels, and three memoirs. [23]

Nurtured in prosperity, Bessie was the son of American-born parents. [24] His father was an inventor and an occasional stockbroker and was also quite conservative. Bessie attended good schools and summer camps and became enchanted with natural history. He was, however, stifled by his father's constant pressure on him to conform, to the point where he turned his back on the law career that he was ordained to follow, electing instead to study English and French at Columbia University. Although his father died in 1922, two years before his graduation, Bessie spent the rest of his life trying to exorcise the demons of what he perceived to be the elder Bessie's middle-class values.

Upon graduation from Columbia, he began a short career as an actor and a stage manager. By 1928 he had written two unpublished novels. After failing a physical exam for the U.S. Army Air Corps (he had hoped to become a pilot), he spent a few months in Paris and then returned to New York and a series of jobs on the fringes of publishing. In 1930 he married Mary Burnett, who was six years older and an aspiring writer, painter, and puppet maker. They moved to rural New England where they had two children and lived very frugally. Bessie was now publishing short fiction regularly, and in 1936, with the help of a Guggenheim Fellowship, he completed the novel *Dwell in the Wilderness*, the subject of which was the ill fortune of a midwestern family as it evolved from the later nineteenth to the early twentieth century. The characters are modeled on Mary Burnett's relatives, and the novel chiefly chronicles the impact of the parents' puritanism on the lives of three children.

To the extent that Bessie's political awareness was developing, a growing social consciousness was reflected in a stream of book reviews he produced at the time. Most influential among his friends was Kyle Crichton (1896–1960), an editor for *Scribner's* and later *Collier's* magazines who was living a semi-clandestine double life as a contributor to the *New Masses* under the name Robert Forsythe. Toward the mid-1930s he bought Bessie a *New Masses* subscription and bombarded him with Communist pamphlets. Bessie's correspondence with Columbia classmate Guy Endore (1900–1970) between January and March 1934 documents the steps by which he drew closer to the Party.

At the beginning, Bessie felt that he was unable to emotionally identify with Communism, and he was rather frightened by the suddenness and urgency with which so many of his intellectual friends had embraced the cause.[25] Within two weeks, however, Bessie seemed to have switched to a new view: "As a political faith, C'ism [Communism] is the faith I embrace. Only I cannot permit, feel no compulsion to allow, a political faith to supercede my other faith or faiths, overshadow every department of my life."[26] He argued that an artist must transcend any particular political ideology, inasmuch as politics are irrelevant to the process required to produce an outstanding novel. Toward late March, Bessie was mainly being put off by the mutual sniping among intellectuals on the Left, as well as by the categorical statements to which Communists seemed heavily attracted. As an example, he quoted to Endore from a recent Marxist literary essay: "'The greatest writers have been those who have assimilated the best ideas of their time. The best ideas of our time emanate from communism, the methodology of the revolutionary working class.'" In his characteristically blunt manner, Bessie responded, "I say shit to that."[27]

Returning to New York in 1935, Bessie became an assistant editor and critic for the *Brooklyn Eagle*. Soon after, his involvement in the 1936 East Coast strike of seamen in the National Maritime Union led him to a twenty-year membership in the Communist Party. His decision to join the Party came at about the same time that he separated from his wife, the marriage having been weakened by infidelity by both parties. He then began writing for the Left press. In 1937 he was enthralled when he had the chance to interview the French novelist André Malraux (1901–76), who was then touring the United States to gain support for the Spanish Republic. However, a disagreement with the publishers of the *Brooklyn Eagle* over the content of his Malraux piece led to his resignation. Soon he found himself working in the Public Relations Office of the Spanish Information Bureau in New York. In January 1938, at age thirty-three, his marriage terminated, Bessie volunteered to fight in Spain in order to fuse his writing with his politics and turn his focus away from himself toward the plight of others.

Weeks later, as he walked over the Pyrenees from France to Spain, Bessie began keeping a pocket diary. After training, he was moved to the front in the Aragón hills. Subsequently he was involved in a number of harrowing adventures, including one where Bessie with his machine gun stumbled into a fascist camp. After several months of moving from one position to another while a major Loyalist offensive was being prepared, he was ordered in July to cross the Ebro River, where he endured another month of harsh combat. Finally, in late August, he switched from combat to writing for the brigade paper, *Volunteer for Liberty*, spending his remaining months in Spain in Barcelona.

Like Milton Wolff, Bessie repatriated to great celebrity in radical circles as a Spanish Civil War veteran, although he was saluted more as a writer who had taken up arms than as a seasoned warrior. The popular press was not interested in publishing articles by him, but Scribner's Publishing House, prodded by Hemingway, accepted *Men in Battle*, which accrued much literary praise but sold poorly. Residing in New York, Bessie was delivering public lectures on Spain when an event in his personal life turned his literary life in a unforeseen direction.

His former wife, Mary, with whom he had maintained a friendship, had moved with the Bessie children to rural Pennsylvania. There she met and married a local handyman, Harold Frisbie. Meanwhile, Bessie pursued and eventually married an editor from McGraw-Hill whom he had met at a party for Lincoln Brigade veterans. Although Frisbie seemed to have a gentle nature and was good with the Bessie children, there were cryptic aspects of his personality that were bothersome. He was incapable of finding and holding employment, and at intervals he vanished for days at a time. Then he asked to borrow a gun from Bessie to kill porcupines and skunks around the property. Hesitantly, Bessie gave him a 7.65 Estrella automatic pistol he had acquired from Spain. Ernest Hemingway had taken a set of two such pistols from the body of a fascist officer and passed them on to poet Edwin Rolfe, who in turn gave one to Bessie. In a bungled effort to rob a store several hundred miles distant, Frisbie killed the driver of a car that he tried to commandeer in an escape attempt. Shortly, he was apprehended.

Bessie found himself deeply moved by the tragedy of Frisbie's life and the situation that led to his misfortune. Wanting to do something to prevent Frisbie's execution after he pleaded guilty, Bessie wrote *Bread and a Stone* (1941). The novel was a graphic and sensitive fictionalized narrative of Frisbie's life, illuminating the factors leading to his destruction in a manner recalling Dreiser's *An American Tragedy* (1925) and Wright's *Native Son* (1940). As with his prior two books, reviews were laudatory but sales were meager.

Bessie then supported himself in the early 1940s by working as the drama critic for the *New Masses*, to which he also contributed dozens of book and film reviews as well as a few feature articles. Naive about the Soviet Union, he accepted the Communist Party's view of the Hitler-Stalin nonaggression pact, then became an ardent pro-intervention propagandist when the Nazis invaded the USSR in 1941. Unexpectedly, in June 1941 he was offered a position as a contract screenwriter for Warner Bros., and he moved to Hollywood, where he enjoyed a modestly successful career until he was subpoenaed to appear before HUAC on 23 October 1947.

In *Inquisition in Eden* (1965) Bessie recounted the full story of his conviction for contempt of Congress, his imprisonment, and his being blacklisted. He survived the 1950s by working as an assistant editor and a public relations assistant for the *Dispatcher*, the paper of the left-wing International Longshoremen's and Warehousemen's Union, and as an announcer, stage manager, and light man for the "Hungry i" nightclub in San Francisco. He also wrote numerous reviews under four pseudonyms—David Ordway, Jonathan Forrest, N. A. Daniels, and William Root—for the West Coast newspaper of the Communist Party, *People's World*. Under his own name he published articles discussing Spain and the blacklist. Following the issuance of *The Un-Americans* by a left-wing publishing house, he attained some commercial success with *The Symbol* (1967), a fictionalized account of the psychological repercussions of Hollywood culture on an actress suggestive of Marilyn Monroe.

Bessie's only significant return to film after his blacklisting was for the prize-winning *España otra vez* (*Spain Again*) (1968), about the return of a doctor to Spain thirty years after the civil war. This book was succeeded by Bessie's reminiscences of his own return to Spain, which was also titled *Spain Again* (1975). To little notice he published a novel based on his former life in a nightclub, *One for My Baby* (1980), and a largely retrospective collection of his short stories, *Alvah Bessie's Short Fictions* (1982). Married now for the third time, Bessie lived his remaining years in the San Francisco Bay Area, defending the honor of the Lincoln Battalion, excoriating the Hollywood blacklist, and cooperating with one of his sons, Dan Bessie, on a film interpretation of *A Bread and a Stone*.

William Herrick was the only one of the three New York Jews born into a Communist let alone a radical family.[28] His mother was a founding member of the Communist Party. Atop Herrick's crib hung "a piece of tin embossed with the stern physiognomies of Vladimir Ilich Lenin and Leon Trotsky."[29] His father, a wallpaper hanger, died when Herrick was four. In Byelorussia the family name had been Gurevich, which U.S. immigration transformed into Horvitz. Herrick's brother changed the name to Herrick in 1939, to deflect anti-Semitic prejudice in his effort to get a job at the Metropolitan Life Insurance Company. He included William in the application to the courts for a name change. Herrick's mother was a seamstress whose beauty facilitated her dabbling in the Yiddish art world. After his father's death, Herrick was tormented by her love affairs and on one occasion he jealously took a knife to a suitor. Subsequently, when other admirers appeared, he simply left home without telling her and wandered about.

During the time that his family resided in the Bronx in cooperative housing where mostly pro-Communists lived, Herrick attended meetings of the Young Pioneers of America, the children's organization of the Communist Party, and went to Young Pioneer camps. As soon as he was old enough, he joined the YCL. He also spent some time with an aunt and uncle on the Sunrise Cooperative Farm outside Saginaw, Michigan, which was run by anarchists. After high school Herrick tramped about the country, sporadically pausing to work as a busboy in cities such as New York and Miami Beach and in a summer camp in the Catskills. Although he was not a formal YCL member while traveling, when crossing through the South Herrick spent some time assisting a Communist Party organizer who was working with sharecroppers.

Returning to New York in the mid-1930s, Herrick took a job in the fur market, rejoined the YCL, and began organizing in his workplace. Although he felt uneasy with the proclamation of the Popular Front policies in 1935, he volunteered to fight in Spain at an early opportunity. He was quickly wounded and, during his convalescence, began to feel his allegiance slipping from Communist policy toward that of the POUM (Workers Party of Marxist Unification) and the anarchists, who had sought to combine a social revolution with the antifascist war. When he came back to the United States, he was given a job as a combination guard and receptionist for Communist Party leader Irving Potash (1902–76), who was also a leader of the International Fur and Leather Workers Union. However, Herrick was seen by a Communist Party member at meetings of the Socialist Party and the Independent Labor League, a former faction of the Communist Party that had been expelled in 1929.[30] Herrick believed that he was fired by the union for this reason at the time of the Hitler-Stalin Pact. After that, he regularly attended meetings of Max Shachtman's Workers Party, although he remained an independent socialist.

Herrick felt no call to become a creative writer in his youth. Ultimately he found employment as a court reporter from 1943 to 1969. However, he read insatiably and, during the 1940s, began to consume works by Victor Serge, Arthur

WILLIAM HERRICK, a former Communist and a veteran
of the Spanish Civil War, wrote several novels dramatizing the
emotional and political loyalties of the Left. (Photograph by
Dick Duhan; courtesy of William Herrick)

Koestler, and Albert Camus. He also read publications by the Workers Party, the Socialist Workers Party, and the Independent Labor League as well as the social democratic *New Leader* and the liberal *Reporter*. In New York City in the 1950s, he met Bernard Wolfe (1915–85), a novelist who had been a Trotskyist in the 1930s; it was Wolfe who, after hearing stories of Herrick's adventures in Spain, encouraged him to write.[31] In 1967 Herrick published *The Itinerant*, a gritty, autobiographically based novel about the American Left, with a sequence that occurs in Spain that he partly modeled after the work of Henry Miller. Over the next quarter of a century he published ten more books, most dramatizing revolutionary illusions frequently held by beguiled Communists and "terrorists" of the 1960s generation.

WHOSE REVOLUTION?

In his virulently anti-Stalinist *Hermanos!* (1969), Herrick depicts Richard Jordan Prettyman, a ruthless, college-educated Lincoln Battalion officer denounced as "Murderman" by other Lincolns behind his back. The middle name, "Jordan," is an obvious reference to Robert Jordan, and the surname, "Prettyman," suggests Hemingway's primary model for Jordan, the Lincoln commander Robert Merriman, who was killed in action. But Herrick's Prettyman is just one of a cast of incompetent and sometimes cowardly officers of the Lincolns whose fanaticism leads them to deploy their troops as cannon fodder.

Although masculinity, on the battlefield and in bed, is as much an abiding concern in Herrick's work as in Hemingway's, Wolff's, and Bessie's, *Hermanos!* is a far more ambitious effort than *For Whom the Bell Tolls* or the other novels to present a history of the Spanish Civil War in fiction. The character based on Hemingway's Robert Jordan turns out to be a minor figure, although Prettyman is a good indication that Herrick is like the other veterans in striving to deromanticize the hero of *For Whom the Bell Tolls*. The effort of Herrick to reveal a more authentic Lincoln Battalion soldier in fiction is split between two friends—an idealist, young Communist functionary, Jake Starr, and a realist, rank and filer, Joe Garms.

Herrick, also like the others, includes a climactic execution-type episode involving an unsettling double, but in *Hermanos!* the incident is elaborately transformed into a form of suicide. The symbolic action of the novel, embodied by the trajectory of the idealist Starr, the naive Communist functionary, reveals how a romantic illusion in the grip of Stalinism must necessarily kill its revolutionary other. In this instance, the other is a militant of the POUM, which is depicted in *Hermanos!* as expressing indigenous Spanish proletarian aspirations. Herrick brilliantly presses the narrative forward using allegory; once the romantic idealist under the spell of Stalinism crosses the line onto the terrain of the unredeemable, his own destruction, and hence the destruction of the remnant of idealism in the Communist International, becomes inevitable.

The character of Jake Starr is used to dramatize representative Lincoln Brigade members. The fictional Starr has some similarities to Herrick but is primarily modeled on the Jewish American Communist Arnold Reid. Reid was born Arnold Reisky in New York City in 1911 to Communist parents who moved to the Soviet Union in the early 1930s. In 1925 he joined the YCL, and in 1931 he became a member of the YCL's New York State Committee and was to work on a secret radio communications operation, to which he periodically returned. He also traveled to Latin America to establish contact with underground Communist parties there for the Caribbean Secretariat of the Communist International, under the direction of the veteran Communist Alexander Bittleman (1890–1982). During that time he received training from a Comintern instructor on the key national and colonial issues and gained experience in illegal work.

By 1935 Reid had learned to write and speak Spanish fluently and was sent to Mexico. On his return to the United States he became a member of the National Committee of the YCL, serving as chief of agitation and propaganda at cadre schools. In 1936 he was assigned to the editorial board of the *New Masses*, where he wrote editorials and political articles. In February 1937 he was sent by the Communist Party to France to organize the passage of International Brigades volunteers to Spain and to maintain liaison with the Comintern organizations involved in recruiting volunteers. In October 1937, with permission of Robert Minor (1884–1952), a former political cartoonist who was the representative of the Communist Party of the United States in Spain, Reid moved to Valencia, Spain, to work with the Spanish Communist Party in handling matters relating to the American volunteers. He was soon assigned to combat and graduated from the Fifteenth Brigade officers training school in January 1938. Seven months later he died in battle.

Reid was ubiquitously praised for his idealism. Indicative of his temperament, Arnold Reid in Spain used the Party name Jack Reed, after the romantic author of *Ten Days That Shook the World* (1919). While at the University of Wisconsin, the young Reisky had befriended the poet Edwin Rolfe. He was eulogized by Rolfe in an article in the 4 October 1938 issue of the *New Masses*, in the poem "For Arnold Reid" (published in July 1939, after which the title was changed to "Epitaph"), and in Rolfe's *The Lincoln Battalion* (1939).[32] Al Richmond, editor of the *People's World*, remembered Reid as "a brilliant young intellectual . . . sailing out of Brooklyn as a cadet on the old Red D Line and guided by revolutionary exiles

ARNOLD REID, a young Communist activist who inspired
poetry and fiction, died on the battlefield in Spain under
controversial circumstances. (Courtesy of Abraham Lincoln
Brigade Archives, Tamiment Library, New York University,
Postcard Collection)

from Latin America" who was "instrumental in reestablishing the Venezuelan Communist Party which had been shattered by the dictatorship of Juan Vicente Gómez." [33] As a member of the editorial board of the *New Masses*, Joseph Freeman regarded Reid as "the political rabbi" of the younger writers.[34] Although the character Jake Starr in *Hermanos!* imaginatively projects Reid's psychology, the basic biographical facts are the same as Reid's. The resulting portrait of a young man driven by a blind love for the Communist Party and a need to personally incarnate romantic heroism defies conventional literary realism by the near-superhuman exploits attributed to him. Yet the portrait cogently expresses one aspect of the profile of revolutionary commitment that Herrick held to be emblematic of his generation.[35]

Complementing Starr, to dramatize another aspect of authentic members of the Lincolns, is the character Joe Garms, who declares that he loves Jake "like a *hermano* [brother]." [36] Garms is a Catholic workingman but is clearly modeled on Herrick's Jewish friend Joe Gordon, a tough-talking proletarian who survived Spain but was later killed in World War II.[37] Garms, a macho reminiscent of the initial delineation of the tough proletarian character Yank in Eugene O'Neill's *The Hairy Ape* (1922), is ignorant of the totality of factors at work in the Spanish conflict, unlike Starr, who is a sort of Stalinist Sir Galahad. Garms is interested only in killing fascists and showing his loyalty to his working-class battalion brothers, no matter who gets in his way—including incompetent brigade officers. In contrast, Starr seeks the Holy Grail of revolutionary self-sacrifice and progressively internalizes and rationalizes the brutal suppression of "internal enemies" such as members of the POUM, anarchists, and suspected Trotskyists.

In the turning point of *Hermanos!* Herrick enlists the most complicated version of the execution incident first depicted by Hemingway as between Jordan and Berrendos, then reworked in various ways in the novels of Wolff and Bessie. In Herrick's novel, Starr executes the POUM supporter Daniel. The shooting of Daniel is a horrific scene. This symbol of selfless revolutionary internationalism is embodied in a consumptive Spaniard prefiguring the asthmatic Che Guevara but also carrying the name of the sixth-century-B.C. Jewish prophet Daniel. He is put to death by the Jewish American übermensch Jake Starr, who gains his almost superhuman power from his belief that he has found his place in the historical process.

As cartoonish allegories of various human types, found among the Communist movement as well as elsewhere, Herrick's characters embody a disturbing truth; they hold the power of other extravagant literary creations in famous works, such as Dr. Bledsoe in Ralph Ellison's *Invisible Man* (1952) or Blanche DuBois in Tennessee Williams's *A Streetcar Named Desire* (1947). However, the effort to transform such caricatures into "fact" renders a significant distortion of political reality. In the pages of *Hermanos!* anarchists are unconditionally idealistic carriers of true morality and the Popular Front orientation is a total falsehood.[38] Most important, the power structure of the International Brigades is depicted as corrupt from top to bottom, even practicing a perverse kind of affirmative action. This policy provides one of the most scandalous episodes in the novel, involving an unqualified Black officer named Cromwell Webster, whose name alludes (via the association with Oliver Cromwell) to real battalion commander Oliver Law, the first African American officer to command white troops in U.S. history.[39] The cowardly Webster is placed in charge of a battalion unit and leads his men to disaster. Consequently he is assassinated by other Black as well as white Lincolns, who subsequently urinate on his body. The novel also presents an imaginary love affair between Arnold Reid and Charlotte Haldane, wife of the famous scientist J. B. S. Haldane (1892–1964), who is shamefully vilified in the text.

In sum, *Hermanos!* manages to dredge up virtually every horror story about the International Brigades that exists. Nonetheless, it is the only artistic effort by a Spanish Civil War veteran from the United States to forthrightly address the political complexities avoided by Hemingway, Wolff, and Bessie.[40]

Unhappily, the discussion about Spanish Civil War literature is so politically charged that Herrick's novel, fascinating as a quasi-history registering the psychology of romantic commitment, is too often treated as thinly veiled fact.[41] The degree of Herrick's embellishment and transformation of historical events can be measured to some extent by his depiction of the storming of the Nazi ship *Bremen* in New York harbor in 1936, a famous incident in which a group of U.S. Communists, including Bill Bailey, raided the ship and tore off its Nazi insignia and tossed it into the sea. A number of aspects of the plan went wrong, so that Bailey and others were nabbed and beaten by the German sailors and then by the police before being arrested.[42] Here is how Herrick transforms the event: "One thunderous night raining shotguns a few weeks after his [Jake Starr's] return [from Cuba], a group of men raided a German Nazi warship visiting New York harbor and painted hammers and sickles in blood red over the decks and raised the red flag to the top of the radio mast, coincidentally bludgeoning a few sopping supermen. Those in the party now knew Jake Starr was in town."[43] The more prosaic "facts" of the incident are reworked to recast Starr as a Red Superman: the night is raining shotguns, the passenger ship becomes a warship, the tearing down of the swastika becomes the raising of the red flag and the painting of hammers and sickles in blood red over the decks, the beating of the Communists becomes the bludgeoning of the Germans, and so on. In personal correspondence, Herrick stated that his source for the re-creation of the *Bremen* episode was neither an eyewitness nor a newspaper account, but his memory of an oral report he heard immediately after the event from some Party members who were involved.[44]

In 1983 Herrick published the novel *Kill Memory*, which Paul Berman in the *Village Voice* asserted to be a faithful recounting of events involving a nurse at the Republican hospital where Herrick was recuperating.[45] In both fiction and life, the nurse and Herrick were having an affair, calling to mind the situation in Hemingway's *A Farewell to Arms* (1929), but she nevertheless reported him to the International Brigades police for making anti-Soviet remarks. However, Berman fails to acknowledge a crucial difference between the novel's version and actual events: the Herrick surrogate in the novel is shot through the heart by a brigade officer, while the real Herrick was only asked to prove his loyalty by reading some letters sent by U.S. and English truck drivers. Once again, Herrick's writing is misleading if considered factual, although compelling as allegory. From an artistic point of view, the bullet through the heart is a potent symbol. It makes for a dramatic contrast with the fascist bullet that the fictionalized Herrick surrogate had earlier received in the spine. The fascist bullet had threatened his masculinity by disabling him, but his sexual well-being is regained through the affair with the Stalinist nurse. However, her betrayal of his trust—for the purpose of maintaining her standing in the Communist movement—results in the deadly bullet through his heart.

In Herrick's novels, as in those of Hemingway and the other writers, the war against fascism is depicted on at least one level substantially as a test of iron-fisted masculinity as sharply differentiated from allegedly feminine traits. Herrick goes further: The Communist delusion held by idealists, if undone, threatens the core of one's entire reason for being. The suggestive philosophical implications of such symbolic dramatizations extend far beyond the specificities of Spain. However, the treatment of the details of such episodes in *Hermanos!* as literal by neoconservatives and antiradicals for the purpose of scoring political points against the Left imputes to Herrick an intention that he did not have when writing his novels.[46]

As political fable, *Hermanos!* works powerfully on a metaphorical and psychological plane. Herrick captures select elements of the psychology of battalion members ensnared in a tragic situation. This is possible because Herrick risks confronting the alarming political values that Wolff and Bessie, consciously or unconsciously, suppress in their narratives. The extraordinary devotion and self-sacrifice of most Lincoln Battalion members seems in Herrick's novel to be explained by their adherence to a kind of pure and naive faith in the notion that the highest morality is subordination of one's individuality to the collective needs of the Communist Party. Unfortunately, the demands of the Party were often expressed by some Party disciplinarian who gained authority mainly by his fealty to pro-Soviet policy. Thus, the person to whom one was handing over one's super-ego, in the belief that one would gain personal and political redemption, was unworthy of one's trust. The phenomenon of misplaced idealism extends far beyond the experience of Communism, although the intensity of the Communist experience and the egalitarian ideals it so betrayed impart to that experience a unique poignancy.

Alternatively, to treat the content of *Hermanos!* as one treats Orwell's nonfiction is to transform a work of art into a political hatchet job. To be sure, literary license and the use of exaggeration may allow Herrick to dramatize certain unverifiable speculations as incidents that might have happened in Spain. In the case of the episode involving the African American Cromwell Webster, it is assuredly conceivable that an officer in the battalion might turn out to be cowardly and incompetent and that a fervent desire to demonstrate their antiracism might have encouraged battalion leaders to move too quickly in promoting a Black member.[47] In contrast, the assassination of incompetent officers, something known to have happened in conscript armies, seems less likely in a volunteer army such as the Lincolns, where a "community of belief" is shared, and especially when the officer is an African American.[48] Urinating on the body of the dead African American seems even more implausible in light of the hostile sentiments most Lincolns would have held toward the desecration of Black bodies during southern lynching rituals. Yet, in a 1986 *Village Voice* article, this literary episode is treated as a factual claim that Oliver Law was executed by his own men, despite a good deal of evidence to the contrary.[49] A careful reading of the evidence on which Herrick based this episode reveals that the allegation is based solely on a conversation over drinks that Herrick had with two men, one of whom died in 1938 and the other in World War II.[50] To date, the more credible account is that several brigade members doubted Law's courage, which gave rise to rumors and anecdotes that were exaggerated over time.

In contrast, Herrick's fictional treatment of Arnold Reid as Jacob Starr appears to be closer to the truth of Reid's death—truth so far as it can be established. As late as 1997, Herrick, working with information originating with former Party general secretary Earl Browder and seconded by former *Daily Worker* editor John Gates, knew only that Reid had been demoted from his leadership position and sent to the front.[51] He was also aware of Charlotte Haldane's memoir, *Truth Will Out* (1950), and her suspicions that Reid had been somehow betrayed by his own side. But with the opening of Communist International archives in the former Soviet Union, specific correspondence by two U.S. Communist officials concerning the fate of Reid in Spain has become available.

Most important is a letter dated 8 February 1938 from Earl Browder, on the eve of his departure for the United States, stating that Reid must be defended against any slurs originating in a subcommission of the Spanish Communist Party regarding his past political record. Browder also notes the high esteem in which Reid is held by the Communist Party in the United States. Yet three weeks later Robert Minor sent a personal letter to André Marty, the commander of the International Brigades, telling him that "I was mistaken about Jack (Arnold Reid)," who was now on a course of trying "to make himself appear as an innocent victim of 'mistakes' of the Party or of myself." While Minor would not confirm Marty's suspicions that Reid had secretly made a trip to Europe before his International Brigades assignment or that Reid may have come to Spain with "contacts" apart from those that were "the natural result of duties given him by myself or by the Spanish C.P.," Minor did assent to "the essential thing—the judgment of the man—you were correct." As for the fate of Reid, Minor presented Marty with a dilemma: Characters such as Reid "have no place in Spain today." However, if Reid were to be sent back, it would require "the necessity of first informing Paris that it is necessary to restrict his contacts while passing through Paris, and that also the American Party be given information." [52] In view of Marty's reputation for zealously searching out and dealing violently with alleged traitors, Minor's letter must be interpreted as giving a "go ahead" signal to consider the most extreme measures against Reid. The precise details of his death in battle are not known, but there is no doubt that, following Minor's statement that Marty's "judgment of the man" was "correct," Reid's value to the International Brigades leadership had been reduced to little more than that of Milton Wolff's character Leo Rogin.

Despite Herrick's fictionalizing historical fact in his novels, *Hermanos!* should not be dismissed as knee-jerk anti-Communism. [53] Although *Hermanos!* is scarcely equal to *Homage to Catalonia* as a document, the novel's politics are actually to the Left of Orwell's in the 1930s. At the opening of the novel, in events that precede Starr's assignment in Spain, the site of moral conscience in *Hermanos!* resides within the Communist movement. This is dramatized in the episode involving the character Morales, whose name suggests "morals." Morales is a Cuban Communist who does not share the doublethink of Starr and his evil mentor, the older Communist Carl Vlanoc, who have been sent to Cuba to impose the Stalinist line. This moral center, represented at first by Morales, is then progressively driven outside the Communist movement. Eventually it comes to reside in dissident communists, represented by Daniel Nunez, the member of the Spanish POUM. Daniel began as a Party member and embodies the spirit of Morales in his confrontation with Starr.

Jake Starr progresses from being a passive witness of Vlanoc's execution of Morales to becoming himself a junior Vlanoc by executing Daniel; that is, Starr falls from being a purist revolutionary to becoming an agent of the counterrevolution. Yet in another dazzling move, Herrick makes the vehicle of Starr's self-recognition and doomed effort at redemption his love affair with Sarah, the character modeled on Charlotte Haldane. Starr realizes that Sarah is deluded about him in the same way that he has been deluded by the Communist International. That is, in Sarah's need to idealize the love that she manifestly feels, she simply cannot discern the actuality of the situation—that Starr is barely different from the Stalinist thugs like Vlanoc whom she despises, with the exception that Starr is handsome and not so crude. Even more intriguing is the next stage. Once Herrick has Starr recognize his own delusion about Stalinism by apprehending Sarah's idealization of himself, it might seem that such a recognition will lead to redemption. But Herrick's view is that the tragedy of Stalinism for revolutionary idealists is so profound that the recognition of truth only seals Starr's doom. There is no redemption.

Herrick is closer to the "truth" of the Spanish Civil War than Milton Wolff or Alvah Bessie in his general portrayal of the POUM as an authentic expression of the revolutionary desire of the Spanish Left, with the Soviet Union and the Spanish Communist Party cast in the role of the "policemen" of the Left. Yet the use of allegory—or, in instances such as the character Prettyman, satire—overrides all else in his effort at fusing literature and politics. Wolff's *Another Hill* has little to offer in political analysis, although Wolff presents no exaggerations comparable to Herrick's. Paradoxically, *Another Hill* may be closer to Orwell's *Homage to Catalonia* in its effort to depict the truth as the author saw it at the time as well as later on. That said, one must immediately dismiss any hope that Wolff's novel "plays fair" by dramatizing or otherwise offering a plausible case for the anarchist or POUM perspectives before discrediting them by associating them with his unmanly antihero, Leo Rogin. Wolff and Herrick are similar in giving no quarter to their political enemies on the Left, although Herrick insisted that he was not a polemicist but merely following the "energy" of his characters.[54]

Wolff's doubling of Castle and Rogin focuses the novel on what appears to be the real terrain of consciousness on which the Lincolns fought their primary struggle—that of masculinity. Wolff is admirably frank in his autobiographical portrait of Castle as the relatively ill-informed youth that Wolff himself was. Castle reads only the *Daily Worker*, and his choice to go to Spain is largely due to escaping romantic entanglements. Once in the midst of battle, he discovers his main virtue—that he does not crack under fire. From then on, Castle's leadership skills emerge, as well as his ability to avoid ending up as a casualty, expertise that becomes almost mythical. Moreover, the affirmation of masculinity on the battlefield is augmented by his sexual exploits as he steals a gorgeous woman from the Ernest Hemingway character and later has an affair with another beautiful blond.

Mitch's family background is marked by a tyrannical father and a devoted mother, and his behavior in Spain exhibits possible manifestations of an Oedipal rebellion. His doppelgänger, Leo Rogin, in contrast, is out to please his father and joins the Lincolns mainly because his surrogate family—his two singing partners from a Communist folk music group—bring him along. Prior to battle Leo sleeps childlike between his buddies. When they are killed, Leo finds himself incapable of facing fire at the front. Retreating repeatedly to the rear—sometimes by desertion, occasionally by subterfuge—he starts a new family of his own, taking on an abandoned and very ordinary Spanish woman and her child. This behavior contrasts to Mitch's virile, freewheeling womanizing.

Perpetually ambivalent, Leo can neither desert nor fully participate in the battalion. He also feels warmth toward his new Spanish family but ultimately intends to abandon it. When Mitch summarily executes Leo as a deserter, Wolff displays unexpected candor in bringing to light a fairly damning revelation of one aspect of Lincoln Battalion life. Leo, after all, had returned voluntarily to the front. He swears that he will make a good-faith effort to fight, although the reader has to be skeptical, based on what has been revealed about him. Mitch knows far less than the reader about Leo's actions and motives; he simply identifies Leo as a risk and interprets the statement of political commissar John Gates (born Solomon Regenstreif, yet another historical figure in the novel) to "take care" of Leo as if it were a Communist Party order to execute him. No trial is held. Mitch and Abrams (a fictional Lincoln Battalion member who is later killed in battle) pretend to take Leo out to guard duty in an area where they had previously dug a trench. Mitch shoots Leo point-blank, and the trench becomes his unmarked grave. Back in camp, Mitch and Abrams lie to the other men about Leo's fate.

In his introduction to Wolff's novel, Cary Nelson stresses that the incident may never have really happened. The implication is that Wolff, as a commander who took responsibility for the battalion in Spain, is now taking responsibility for the execution, which may have occurred but with other protagonists. Nonetheless, most of *Another Hill* is factually grounded, and the events chronicled therein accord almost exactly with what is known about the execution of Bernard Abramofsky.[55]

Abramofsky, a young fellow traveler associated with the Group Theater in New

York, arrived in Spain in early 1937, along with his first cousin, a gifted musician and Communist Party member, Harry Melofsky. They had become part of a left-wing vaudeville troupe, The Convulsionaries, but were sent to the front. When Melofsky and another soldier were killed, Abramofsky was traumatized. Wolff told historian Peter Carroll that he was convinced that Abramofsky was faking it when he collapsed at Brunette and had to be carried behind lines in a stretcher.[56]

During the course of several desertions and subsequent returns, Abramofsky complained with some justification to the American Consulate that he was being kept in Spain longer than the time to which he had consented. Although John Gates agreed to take Abramofsky back into the battalion once more, he was heard muttering that Abramofsky ought to be shot. The night before May Day, Abramofsky was taken for a walk, and a single bullet was put in his head. When rumors of Abramofsky's death began to spread, Gates angrily confronted Wolff, but the latter told him not to worry and claimed total ignorance of Abramofsky's fate.[57]

In *Another Hill*, Wolff displays exquisite artistry in his layering of the ugly incident with ambiguities. The circumstances of war demand a fighting unit in which all men can have full confidence in one another, and Leo Rogin can hardly be judged trustworthy. Still, how can fear at the front be judged a sufficient reason for execution? At one point Mitch Castle is prophetically criticized for his pragmatism by a friend who insists, "You have to live the principles for which you're fighting while you're doing the fighting" or else "the war will change its character, and when you've won you'll find that you've won nothing, or only half the battle."[58] The manner in which Leo Rogin is killed is more likely a violation than a realization of the Communist principles held by Mitch. That Mitch must lie to his men shows the incompatibility of his action with the ideals of the battalion; it also links Mitch to an earlier warning by Hemingway regarding the dirty, secret deeds being done in back of the front lines about which Mitch is lucky enough to be ignorant.[59]

Perhaps the most significant self-revelation is that Mitch Castle insists that the execution of Leo Rogin was so automatic that he never once thought of Rogin in the next six months. When the name comes up, mentioned by a friend who also tells him that "a life's a life," Mitch retorts, "I don't know what you mean by that," in a manner that is at once defensive and shamefaced.[60] Yet the novel is testimony to the opposite. The memory of Leo, mostly based on Abramofsky but also a composite of all those who did not pass the masculinity test, haunted Wolff for the rest of his life and forced its way into the center of his fictionalized memoir.

GOLEMS AND GIMPELS ON THE BARRICADES

There are many quirky aspects to the record of left-wing novelists writing about the Spanish Civil War. One is that the lasting artistic contributions of Spanish Civil War fiction written by veterans may be far less in the realm of politics than of psychology—especially regarding such matters as gender and ethnicity. What is consistent in Hemingway, Wolff, Bessie, and even Herrick is the primacy of their inner wars—against the cowardly father in Hemingway, against the weak Jew alter ego in Wolff, against the opportunism of intellectuals in Bessie, and against the romantic will to power masked as self-sacrificing self-abnegation in Herrick. Politics may be present as raw background material, but in the dramatizations of the narratives the authors resist ideological coherence beyond generalities. Thus the denunciations of Hemingway's novel that came from all sectors of the Left in 1940 for the author's political failings simply confirm that For Whom the Bell Tolls, however atypical its protagonist Robert Jordan in comparison with the more representative volunteers, actually is a novel that fits comfortably, perhaps archetypically, within the Left fiction of the period.

Critics of Hemingway within the pro-Communist Left believed that the "reality" of the war was subordinated to a personal view with a highly anomalous volunteer as the protagonist in a romanticized and outlandish love affair.[61] Moreover, he was accused of defaming La Pasionaria and André Marty. Alvah Bessie wrote in the New Masses that "this constriction . . . to the purely personal, has resulted in a book about Spain that is not about Spain at all! [The result is] a personal attack upon André Marty . . . as could be . . . delivered upon him by the French fascists themselves!"[62] How impromptu this reaction to Hemingway was on the part of all the Lincolns is not entirely clear. Steve Nelson, a political commissar of the Lincoln Battalion, in his 1986 interview published in Salmagundi, asserts that he was given Communist Party orders to condemn Hemingway's novel: "I thought it was a fine book. My comments were printed in the People's World. . . . After this some Party people from New York paid me a visit. They told me to withdraw my comments. . . . I had to say I was hasty in judging the book. I was a Party member and I had to accept Party discipline."[63]

What is intriguing is that criticisms of Hemingway's novel from intellectuals associated with Trotskyism and left-wing anti-Stalinism were quite similar to those of the Lincolns and the New Masses in their avowal that Hemingway exchanged the personal for the political. The paramount disagreement was that the anti-Stalinist Marxists focused their appraisal on the fact that Hemingway had smeared the anarchists and revolutionary international Left rather than Marty. In his column for the January–February 1941 issue of Partisan Review, Dwight Macdonald observed that "Hemingway lacks the equipment to handle [a political] theme. Instinctively, he tries to cut the subject down to something he *can* handle by restricting his view of the war to the activities of a small band of peasant guerrillas behind Franco's lines. . . . The most politically revealing thing in the book is Hemingway's vindictive picture of the Anarchists."[64] In the same issue, Lionel Trilling's book review concluded that "it is the isolation of the individual ego in its search for experience that Hemingway celebrates in this novel."[65]

For Whom the Bell Tolls is one of those recurrent instances where it is nearly impossible to disentangle judgments of literary quality from the political questions. It is rare for a knowledgeable reader to feel delight in reading what he or she judges to be historical falsification. Yet with the fervor generated by the world conditions at the time, both the *New Masses* and *Partisan Review* were variously engaging in correlations between literary quality and factual accuracy or political "line." In fact, for those holding the Popular Front view that the Republican government was simply leading an antifascist war for bourgeois political democracy, and that the issue of economic justice could only be addressed once the fascist threat had been beaten back, *For Whom the Bell Tolls* is faithful to the character of the war and the role of the anarchists (whose economic program may have been unrealistic and whose tactics were dubious), if not entirely fair to individuals such as Marty and La Pasionaria. But the perception of the novel is quite different for those who came to believe—as did Macdonald, Trilling, and William Herrick—that the rank and file of the International Brigades were unwittingly part of a Soviet-led counterrevolution in the wake of an authentic revolutionary uprising of the working class that had beat back the fascist coup attempt. From this perspective, Hemingway serves tacitly as a Stalinist apologist.[66]

More than six decades later, however, Hemingway's book has acquired more authority because of his refusal to enlist the novel as a partisan text of either version of the Spanish Civil War. Indeed, an increasing number of scholars, as well as surviving veterans, have come to recognize that arguments supporting both perspectives existed in Spain, and it remains an open question as to whether the failure of the Popular Front verifies the validity of the perspectives of the Front's left-wing critics. Historian Paul Preston, although sympathetic to the Popular Front view, notes in the introduction to his 1984 collection *Revolution and War in Spain, 1931–1939* that Spain "was many wars" fought simultaneously.[67] Moreover, in his aforementioned *Salmagundi* interview, Steve Nelson, who never repudiated the basic Popular Front strategy, concedes that Orwell's anti–Popular Front *Homage to Catalonia* is "a good book," and that Orwell was "right to condemn these acts of the Communists" against anarchists and Trotskyists. "I see this now," Nelson concludes, "although I didn't see it when I was in Spain, under the spell of the Party."[68] Similar sentiments were held by the late Saul Wellman, a political commissar of the Canadian Mckenzie-Papineau Battalion, and expressed by Abe Osheroff, a prominent figure among the veterans of the Abraham Lincoln Brigade.[69]

More specifically, the above survey of three novels by Jewish American Spanish Civil War veterans of the first phase of the Popular Front's antifascist campaign fits into yet also complicates several of the debates of the past decade about Jewish masculinity and heterosexuality. In particular, the protagonists in these novels challenge the popular idea that twentieth-century Jewish American culture primarily carries forward the "ethic of mentshlekhkayt." This is a term for the "compassionate, socially responsible, intellectually dedicated" Ashkenazic notion of the "mensch," which was projected as an alternative to the violent Jewish thugs of the Old Testament as well as an Eastern European Jewish alternative to the "muscled, aggressive manliness" that predominated in Christian Western Europe.[70] The three Spanish Civil War novels even call into question the most sophisticated challenges to the mensch hypothesis, by Paul Breines in *Tough Jews* (1990) and Warren Rosenberg in *Legacy of Rage* (2001). These two scholars hold that the gentle mensch, in its weakest form, Gimpel the Fool, Isaac Bashevis Singer's character, and the out-of-control Golem, a mythological figure supposedly created by a gentle rabbi to forcefully defend the Jewish people, exist as interdependent, symbiotic counterparts.[71]

In contrast, in the novels of Wolff, Bessie, and Herrick, there are some Golems, backed by the authority of the Popular Front, who bludgeon and in some cases kill the Gimpels. Such a dynamic differs significantly from the literature of another minority group, that produced by the African American Left during and in response to World War II at home and abroad. As will be demonstrated in the next chapter, literature of the latter centrally foregrounds the pivotal ideological questions of minority group politics, masculinity as a political or even human rights issue, and of course, a critical view of the politics of the Popular Front.

In fact, of the Spanish Civil War fiction by Jewish American veterans, only the work of Herrick candidly considers the Popular Front. Herrick strongly criticizes the Popular Front as suppressing the democratic dynamic essential for oppressed groups to emerge victorious against capitalism and fascism; yet his anti-Stalinism is so "over-the-top" that *Hermanos!* also seems to be anti–Popular Front simply because the Popular Front was promoted by the Communist International.

African Americans, however, were in a different position in World War II. They were segregated in the military as they were in society at large and were not so blinded by anti-Communism; they knew that Communists had fought for Black rights when liberals stood by on the sidelines. Thus the narrative strategies employed in their fiction of World War II carry ideological meanings that point more clearly and fairly to the bitter contradictions of the Popular Front, especially to the one between the rhetoric of the "People's War" and the reality of racial capitalism in the United States. For them, the affirmation of African American "manhood" could imply an implicit struggle against certain aspects of the Popular Front. Ironically, the wartime position of African Americans was not unlike that of the anarchists and the POUM in Spain. Both aspired to combine a social movement against immediate oppression—of urban capitalism in the United States and semifeudal landholdings in Spain—with the military fight against fascism. For the Far Left in Spain, the Popular Front subordination of the former to the latter was regarded as an unacceptable concession. Likewise, in the United States, a number of African American writers came to believe that, if a minority group was going to wholeheartedly take up arms against an external enemy, considerations of that group's dignity and interests must be included among the goals of the struggle.

The Agony of the African American Left

"THE WAR IS EVERYWHERE WE FIND IT"

In the inaugural chapters of *And Then We Heard the Thunder* (1963), the World War II novel by former Communist John Oliver Killens (1916–87), Killens's autobiographical character, the Black soldier Solomon "Solly" Saunders, finds himself trapped between two exceedingly attractive African American women. What is absorbing about this romantic triangle is that each of Solly's lovers is emblematic of the major radical political trends within the African American community at the time that the United States entered World War II.

One of the women is his new wife, Millie Belford Saunders, from a well-to-do, upwardly mobile Brooklyn family and, like Solly, a Left-liberal on the fringes of the Communist Party. Millie espouses the view promoted by the Communist-led Popular Front, looking upon World War II as a democratic war against an external threat far greater than the domestic racism that this charming and accomplished middle-class woman has endured herself. In her view, loyal participation and advancement in the segregated military provides an opportunity to aid not only the cause of "Negro Rights" but also the career of her handsome, well-spoken, and talented husband. Dividends will certainly come in the postwar era. Millie advises Solly, "Forget about the race problem at least for the duration. Be an American instead of a Negro, and concentrate on winning the war, and while you're in the Army work for those promotions just like in civilian life."[1]

While enduring basic training in Ebbensville, Georgia, Solly is drawn to Fannie Mae Branton, an activist in the National Association for the Advancement of Colored People (NAACP) and daughter of a militantly antiracist school principal. Living in the Deep South, where conditions for African Americans more closely approximated the oppression of Nazi Germany than in the urban North, Fannie Mae is less concerned with personal advancement than the preservation of dignity, and she frequently admonishes Solly, "Never sacrifice your manhood."[2] Fannie Mae is ardently anti–Popular Front and firmly supportive of the policy of the Double V (Double Victory) campaign, which she explains to Solly as "Victory against the fascists overseas and against the crackers here at home."[3] The official definition of the Double V campaign, launched by the African American newspaper the *Pittsburgh Courier*, was "Victory over discrimination at home / Victory over the Axis Abroad."[4]

Solly's encounters with white supremacism in the army have already begun to sap his optimistic political ideology, and he would rather shift the conversation topic to something less contentious. Nonetheless he finds himself retorting, "How can we win a war against the enemy if we fight amongst each other?" Fannie Mae responds, "Where is the enemy? Who is the enemy? Why should we discriminate? A fascist is a fascist and a cracker is a cracker. The War is everywhere we find it."[5]

At this point Solly's emotions are rent by a conundrum: Should he seduce Fannie Mae by agreeing with her or by angrily attacking all her arguments so that she comes to blindly worship him? He instinctively opts for the latter approach: "Look at it realistically. This is a house, and you and I are a family. We're having a family spat between us. A character very dangerous to both of us tries to break into the house and take it over. What do we do? Continue fighting each other and let him take over? Or do we stop and band together to fight him off and settle our family differences later?" "Let him have the house," Fannie Mae angrily replies. "What good is it? If you never let me breathe easy in it? . . . Let the house go down and we can build another one." Appalled, Solly asks, "What if the working men of this country had the same attitude? There wouldn't be any no-strike pledges and there'd be strikes all over the place and we wouldn't be able to produce enough to win the war. The whole nation would be completely demoralized." Fannie Mae shakes her head. "A nation that can be so easily demoralized is pretty sick to begin with. Double V could help to heal it and make it stronger for the battle."[6] Solly batters away at Fannie Mae until she succumbs; it is she who pleads to shift the subject. Soon he triumphantly seduces her without divulging that he is married.

Solly is nonetheless unnerved by the discussion as his outfit prepares to be sent to the Pacific as an all-Black unit commanded by white officers. Unrelenting racist harassment of Black soldiers corroborates Fannie Mae's conviction that the antifascist struggle during World War II is hamstrung by the segregationist culture and practices of the army. Solly begins, at least subconsciously, to consider the possibility that the white supremacist American nation really does need to be torn down and rebuilt on new egalitarian foundations if the postwar era is to be liberatory rather than repressive.

Accordingly, the violent climax of *And Then We Heard the Thunder* turns out not to be the anticipated democratic, antifascist battle against the Japanese in the

47

Pacific theater; rather, it is a full-scale race battle between Black and white American troops stationed in Bainbridge (Brisbane), Australia.[7] This is a battle between fellow countrymen, one that calls to mind the origin of the title of Killens's pathbreaking novel and the titles of its sections; all of these derive from an observation by African American abolitionist Harriet Tubman at the time of the U.S. Civil War.[8]

The violent race confrontation in Australia is precipitated by the harassment visited by white military police upon the Black soldiers. The Blacks attempt to enter a social club from which they had been banned due to fears on the part of white soldiers that the African Americans might interact with white Australian women.[9] As the battle unfolds, the African American soldiers commandeer a tank with the name Fannie Mae written on it above a Double V insignia, and even the most cynical and supposedly shiftless Black soldiers rise to heights of heroism, courage, and selflessness.[10] Such transformations occur because the Black soldiers take up Solly's view about the rebellion: "This is my war, not that Murder Incorporated up on the islands. This is my beachhead."[11]

Further, as the lines are drawn for the savage showdown, every professed ally of the Black soldiers is put to the test, especially those white soldiers who always "meant well" in verbally supporting ideals of racial democracy but "did so poorly" when it came to taking personal risks.[12] The Jewish lieutenant Robert Samuels, a supporter of the Popular Front's subordination of all other struggles to the antifascist crusade, had failed the test the first time in the South. In Australia, however, Samuels clearly breaks with white privilege when forced to choose sides. "You're a colored man tonight, old buddy," Solly tells Samuels as the "Battle of Bainbridge" finally winds down.[13]

John Oliver Killens's 500-page fictional critique of the limitations of the Communist-liberal Popular Front in World War II concedes that the policy did have a kind of commonsense allure. After all, who would disagree that the Nazi German state was considerably worse in its barbaric implementation of a "final solution" for non-Aryans than was the racist U.S. state? Moreover, how can one have sufficient national unity to fight an external threat without a willingness to sacrifice other issues? In the instance of the Popular Front, the mandate was to sacrifice demands for desegregating the military, for the right to strike, and in the case of the colonies, such as India, for national independence—which, if pursued during wartime, could disrupt the colonies and make them vulnerable to attack.[14] Writing in the Communist Party's theoretical journal, *The Communist*, in 1944, General Secretary Earl Browder bragged, "My party, the Communist Party, is the only national political organization which has renounced all thoughts of partisan advantage and completely subordinated all other considerations to the needs of the quickest and most complete victory in the war." [15] The statement is logical and not without appeal, especially as a temporary measure. Of course, exactly what the ruling elites were sacrificing in this Popular Front bargain was never clear. However, a paramount factor for many liberals and radicals after 1941 was that the ruling elites were for the first time allying with the Soviet Union against fascism, and thus objectively aiding defense of what Communists and their supporters believed to be the socialist motherland.

Yet for Killens, from his post-Communist perspective in his novel finished in 1962, the ultimate superiority of Double V stemmed from its demand that subordinate groups not make sacrifices that undermine their capacity to participate in the war effort with dignity. Moreover, the Popular Front strategy would leave unaffected the homegrown racists, fascists, and other reactionary forces, who would make no comparable sacrifice of their own. They might even grow stronger and carry out postwar state-sponsored repression, as noted by radical journalist Randolph Bourne at the time of World War I: "War is the health of the state." [16]

In *And Then We Heard the Thunder*, the minor and major rebellions against subordination presented by Killens are impelled by political imperatives. Killens repeatedly points out that a divided fighting force is a crippled fighting force and therefore morally compromises the antifascist cause. The bloody Battle of Bainbridge and all the internecine racial frictions that antedate it are not produced by reckless Double V advocates seeking to weaken resistance to fascism. They are a product of the inescapable repercussions of policies and practices that manifest an authoritarian white supremacist culture parallel with that of the enemy, insofar as it affects African Americans in the United States.

Solly explains this view to the third woman in his life, the white Australian nurse Celia Blake, as he engages in the race conflict that he now calls "the profoundest battle for democracy that any Yankee Army fought on all the far-flung battlefronts of World War II." He declares, "All my life, everything that has ever happened to me has brought me to this very moment, every place I ever was, everything and everybody, every street I ever walked." [17]

Killens's novel did not cohere as a narrative during World War II, although it was clearly derived from many of his experiences and it is likely that some chapters were drafted while he was in the army. His alter ego, Solly, is himself at work on a war novel, although he is terribly blocked writing it. *And Then We Heard the Thunder*, according to Killens, was written in its final form in the late 1950s and early 1960s, after the publication of his notable first book, *Youngblood* (1954), and following his departure from the Communist Party around 1956. [18] By the 1960s Killens had embraced a revolutionary form of Black nationalism, yet one informed by his long-held vision of socialism.[19] *And Then We Heard the Thunder* is not only a major contender for the finest U.S. novel of World War II; it is also a text that is critical for understanding the elements of continuity between the old and new African American Left. Critical to a comprehension of the book's historical significance is Killens's life preceding, during, and following his army service in the Pacific.

BLACK BOLSHEVIK FROM GEORGIA

Killens benefited from growing up in a sturdy, proud, and literate family and having a childhood marked by several meaningful interracial relationships that helped take the edge off the brutality of white supremacy in Georgia, of which he was a native. The middle sibling of three brothers, Killens was born in 1916 in Macon. From an early age he was entranced by the storytelling of his great-grandmother, Georgia Killens, a former slave whom he called Granny. Shattered by her death when he was five or six, he began nourishing his now-famished imagination by devouring library copies of the adventure series featuring the Rover Boys and Tom Swift. His mother, president of the Laurence Dunbar Literary Club, inspired him to read more widely, and Killens recalled that his father introduced him to Langston Hughes's writings.[20]

Killens's parents were eventually divorced, and his father remarried, a development distressing to Killens, who partially portrayed them as a devoted married couple in *Youngblood*. The radical and working-class sentiments Killens acquired from his family while growing up were fulfilled years later, when the Killens home was an organizing center for Operation Dixie, the CIO's attempt to create interracial unions in the South after World War II. Moreover, there were two momentous events from his Georgia days that had an intense impact on his understanding of southern racism and the response of the Black community. In the first, a number of African American boys were arrested for fighting with white boys; although not picked up by police, Killens observed Black parents beating their sons afterward at the behest of the white police. In the second, he was greatly affected at age sixteen by an incident in which his father, Charles Myles Killens Sr., with a pistol drove a drunken and abusive white man from a restaurant that he managed.

As an elementary school student, Killens had access to many books in his house, and by the eighth grade he was attempting to write novels. Killens also had a happy and auspicious four-year high school career at the Ballard Normal School in Macon, a private institution with an interracial faculty founded by the Congregational Church and the American Missionary Association. One of the white teachers imbued in Killens the notion of becoming a professional who

JOHN OLIVER KILLENS served in the army during World War II and wrote a major novel dramatizing the experiences of African Americans with racism. (Photograph by Carl Van Vechten; courtesy of the Van Vechten Trust, Lancaster, Pa., and the Carl Van Vechten Collection, Yale University)

could also "be in the service of your people."[21] After he graduated in 1933, Killens took a year off and then went to Jacksonville, Florida, where he attended Waters College for 1934–35. Then he spent one semester in the fall of 1935 at Morris Brown College in Atlanta.[22]

For the subsequent several years, Killens's biography parallels Solly Saunders's in And Then We Heard the Thunder. Both emerged from their teens with the fantasy of becoming highly regarded professionals who also aided the cause of African American freedom. However, after an incident in which he reacted badly to the sight of blood gushing from a cut toe, Killens decided that medicine was not for him and turned toward law. In the spring of 1936, he moved to Washington, D.C., to accept a position on the staff of the National Labor Relations Board (NLRB) until 1942. An attraction to radical movements as well as the New Deal grew logically out of Killens's background. As he finished high school, the Georgia newspapers were brimming with attacks on the 1932 Communist Party election campaign with its Black candidate for vice president, as well as the Communist-led defense of the Scottsboro Boys. Franklin Roosevelt assumed office in January 1933.[23]

Starting in 1937, Killens took night classes at Howard University, where he was captivated by the sociologist E. Franklin Frazier and his harsh censure of the Black middle class. Killens also took a course with the poet Sterling Brown, with whom he remained friends over the years.[24] Then he enrolled for evening classes at the Robert H. Terrell Law School from 1939 to 1942, during which he became enthralled by the political example of singer, actor, and activist Paul Robeson (1898–1976). Thereafter he began to associate with members of the Communist Party while continuing to be under the influence of radical Howard professors such as Eugene Clay Holmes.[25] In the pre–World War II years, Washington, D.C., was an intellectual as well as activist center for Black Marxists, and many friendships acquired at this time would continue for decades.[26]

Killens's FBI file reveals that he initially attracted government surveillance in the fall of 1941. He drew the attention of the bureau when he represented the Terrell Law Students Association as a delegate to the American Youth Congress, which at one time had been a broad Popular Front coalition but after the Hitler-Stalin Pact of 1939 was primarily comprised of pro-Communist activists.[27] FBI agents further reported that Killens, then holding a job as assistant mail and files clerk at the NLRB, shared his Thirteenth Street lodgings with two suspected subversives. One was a member of the Communist Party, and the other was an officer of the National Negro Congress—another once-robust Popular Front organization that had been mainly reduced to pro-Communist members by this time.[28] Subsequent reports, while not attributing Communist Party membership to Killens, relayed information from informants (whose names are blacked out on documents released to the public) to the effect that Killens invariably followed the Party line and collaborated with Party members in various organizations. However, in an FBI transcript of an interview that agents conducted with Killens, he denied knowledge of a Communist presence in any organizations with which he was affiliated. As a result, no action was taken against his employment.

On 3 July 1942, Killens was inducted into the U.S. Army, where he spent the next forty-one months, "twenty-seven of them island-hopping, ducking bullets in the South Pacific." He served primarily as a company clerk in the 813th Amphibian Truck Company, and he eventually became a staff sergeant. Killens never wrote more than a few nonfiction sentences about his years in the army, stating that he spent them "soaking up material for my second novel, *And Then We Heard the Thunder.*" [29] There is little doubt that many of Solly Saunders's adventures, and to some degree Saunders's fellow-traveling perspective, coincide with Killens's while he served in the army. The Battle of Brisbane, Australia, on which the fictional Battle of Bainbridge is based, occurred in March 1942, four months before Killens joined the army, suggesting that he re-created the battle from accounts he had acquired from other Black soldiers. [30]

In June 1943, Killens married Grace Jones, a radical activist from Brooklyn. Jones's family had come from Barbados, and her father was a podiatrist. After she graduated from Brooklyn College, she worked briefly in Washington, D.C., where she encountered Killens, then with the NLRB. They first met at a dance. Soon after, during a visit to New York City, Killens called her on the phone, and the courtship commenced. [31] By the time he was discharged from the army in December 1945, his dream of law school had been extinguished by his bitter experiences during the war. He had migrated so far to the Left that he considered the legal profession to be inappropriate for a revolutionary. He also had commenced to gather material for writing fiction while in the army. [32]

Initially the Killenses returned to Washington, D.C., where he briefly returned to the NLRB and then began to engage in trade union organizing for the United Public Workers of America (CIO). He served as business agent of Local 10, a union that was at that time regarded by the FBI as Communist-led. [33] Grace Killens also held jobs with left-wing affiliations; one was with the Bulgarian Embassy in Washington, D.C., and another was with the Armtorg Trading Corporation, a buying and selling agency for trade organizations of the USSR. While the couple was campaigning for Henry Wallace and the Progressive Party in 1948, Killens arranged to take a 1948 summer session creative writing course at Columbia University. There he worked with Dorothy Brewster (1883–1979), a Communist fellow traveler for several decades, who gave him strong encouragement. Soon after, he and his family moved to New York with a new dream—that of becoming a revolutionary novelist. He took another year at the School of General Studies at Columbia University, 1948 to 1949, and his writing skills were further honed in a workshop with Saul Bellow at New York University. Even more significant was a writers' group that he attended in Greenwich Village led by a blacklisted Communist screenwriter, Viola Brothers Shore (1891–1970).

In New York, Killens was soon traveling in African American Left cultural circles, meeting Paul Robeson, W. E. B. Du Bois, and Langston Hughes. He also worked with Dr. Alpheus Hunton, an African American Communist, at the Council on African Affairs, an organization promoting a militant anticolonialist policy.[34] Grace Killens became a secretary on the staff of a public workers' union in New York.

Although the FBI attempted to document all of Killens's political statements, the bureau missed a lucid exposition of his revolutionary political outlook that appeared in the summer 1949 issue of *New Foundations: A Student Quarterly*. The publication, designed to be "militantly progressive, with the aim of stimulating Marxist thought and practice," was politically connected with the Labor Youth League, founded in 1949 as the replacement for the YCL.[35] Killens's essay, "For National Freedom," is a protracted and unreservedly laudatory article about the importance of Harry Haywood's 1948 book *Negro Liberation*.

Despite a rocky career in the Communist Party, Haywood (1898–1985) was the principal Party advocate of the policy of self-determination for African Americans, a program that included the right to form a separate territory if the African American population so desired. Born Haywood Hall in Nebraska, son of one-time slaves, Haywood served in the army in France in World War I. In the postwar period he joined the African Blood Brotherhood, a revolutionary organization that believed in armed self-defense and was increasingly attracted to the international Communist movement. Recruited to the Communist Party in 1925, Haywood was the first Black student at the Lenin School in the USSR. He returned to the United States as a principal theoretician on the national question, but he became increasingly peripheral in the Party after the turn to the Popular Front in 1935 and also after his relatively undistinguished service record in the winter of 1937 as an adjunct political commissar in the International Brigades in Spain.

Following the February 1946 expulsion of Communist Party general secretary Earl Browder for "social imperialism"—as a result of the excesses to which Browder had steered the Popular Front policy during the war—Haywood's conceptions of the national question became more acceptable. A subsidy from Paul Robeson permitted Haywood to finance his book-length treatise on the question. However, within a few years after the publication of *Negro Liberation*, Haywood

54

declared himself in opposition to the Party leadership, and he was expelled in 1959. Following a sojourn in Mexico, Haywood returned to the United States to find a new political atmosphere where his ideas found great favor among Maoist revolutionary groups, who regarded the traditional Communist Party as "revisionist." In 1978 Haywood published an absorbing autobiography, *Black Bolshevik*.[36] Killens's 1949 essay on Haywood's view of national oppression is critical for grasping Killens's succeeding political growth and change as he evolved from Communism to embrace a variation of Third World Marxism.

In 1963, following the publication of *And Then We Heard the Thunder*, Killens explained, "When I wrote *Youngblood* . . . I was not as nationalistic in my beliefs as I am now."[37] Yet the essay on Haywood shows that Killens was by no means a recent convert to Black nationalism in the 1960s; what had changed between his Communist and post-Communist periods was less his understanding of Black culture and identity than his discovery of the source of potential new allies in the movement for Black liberation—former colonial subjects in lieu of the now-bankrupt Euro-American working class. Killens's 1949 identification with Haywood's militant view of Black nationalism as being compatible with Communism was unqualified; moreover, Killens personally incorporated the argument into his own outlook as an incipient novelist. He began his review essay by extolling the book not only as a political beacon but also as "one of the most important contributions to American literature."[38]

What attracted Killens to Haywood's viewpoint was not a "racial" argument, which does not exist in *Negro Liberation*. Rather, it was the view that African Americans in the South must endure a form of "super-exploitation" based on the northern-controlled economic life of the South. Despite the abolition of slavery, the advent of some degree of industrialization, and substantial migration to the North, in the 1940s the plantations were still the "dominant form of large scale ownership" that "in many respects . . . takes on aspects of a colony."[39] The three final sections of the essay are titled "A Nation within a Nation," "Right of Self-Determination," and "Status of National Consciousness," all formulas that Killens could embrace fifteen years later with the rise of Black Power and the dissemination of the writings of anticolonial theorists such as Frantz Fanon and Amical Cabral. There was a strong line of continuity between the "internal colonialism" hypotheses of the 1960s and Haywood's earlier view paraphrased by Killens that "the special character of the exploitation of the Negro people in the Black Belt has led to their development into an oppressed nation" with the result that "the so-called racial persecution of the Negro people in the United States is a particular form and device of *national* oppression."[40] Thus from Killens's perspective it was completely logical that African Americans, even while striving for equal rights, should vigorously build mostly Black organizations, especially the NAACP, that tended to have a "militant rank and file" even though "much of its national leadership is conservative."[41]

The primary concern of Killens, like Haywood, was the evolution of national consciousness on the part of the African American population in the South as the means of access to a socialist future. Little time is wasted assailing Euro-American workers for their white chauvinism. When white workers allow themselves to be separated from their natural allies and diverted from confronting the true source of their own oppression, they only debilitate their latent power. Racial solidarity given by whites is appreciated, but it must emerge from self-interest, not "humanitarianism or paternalism."[42] Over the next two decades nearly all of this theorization remained consistent in Killens; what changed was his confidence in the capacity of the Euro-American working class to discern its own self-interest, although he admired a few heroic white martyrs in the civil rights movement. Instead, an alternative and much more formidable ally was found in the emergence of Third World revolutionary movements in the former colonies of the Western nations.

In the late 1940s and early 1950s, Killens was transforming himself from a professional revolutionary into a novelist. Harlem Communist Party leader Howard "Stretch" Johnson recalls urging Killens to become a full-time Party functionary, but Killens felt such a job would detract from his literary projects.[43] Although he seems to have dropped beneath the FBI radar at that time, subsequent reports refer to his having been allegedly active in the Bedford-Stuyvesant section of the Kings County, New York, Communist Party leadership. The federal government's surveillance of Killens resumed more ardently when his public activities were largely connected with lectures, some of which were under the auspices of Communist-led organizations such as the Council of the Arts, Sciences, and Professions (which replaced the Party-led League of American Writers after World War II), and when Killens became active in a local chapter of the NAACP. What caught the bureau's attention once more was primarily the prominence he achieved with the publication of *Youngblood*.

YOUNGBLOOD VERSUS TRUEBLOOD

In 1952 and 1954, amidst the onerous Cold War years of the McCarthyite anti-radical witch hunt, two mammoth first novels by African Americans, each nearly 600 pages, were published to acclaim in the popular press. The authors were about thirty-eight years old when their books were issued;[44] they were veterans of at least a decade of intimacy with the Communist movement in the United States and had been acutely shaped by the early writings of Richard Wright, who was six to eight years their senior and ten years before had been the most famous public Black Communist writer in the United States.[45] Accordingly, both authors wrote novels copiously focused on African American radicalism in the 1930s, with episodes in the Deep South as well as the urban North and a range of African American and Euro-American characters of different classes and political persuasions.

Ralph Ellison's *Invisible Man* is decisively in the modern mode, mostly eschewing realism or naturalism in favor of a gripping strategy of symbolic action. Through the odyssey of his nameless narrator, Ellison furnishes the reader with a sequence of brilliantly realized and eminently memorable lampoons and satires redolent with historical analogies and philosophical ambiguities. These include portraits of the Black college president, Dr. Bledsoe, corrupt to the bone; the sex-starved white female Negrophile, Sybil, desperate to be raped by Black men; the Machiavellian Communist leader, Brother Jack, one-eyed and Cyclops-like; the nihilistic Black nationalist, Ras the Exhorter, carrying a spear on horseback in Harlem; and the neurotic white liberal, young Mr. Emerson, opposing racism because of homosexual desire for Black males.

In contrast, John O. Killens's *Youngblood* marshals the techniques of social realism, presenting a continuum of ostensibly accurate Black responses to racial oppression in the North and South. At each point on the continuum, seemingly authentic and credible characters engage in the tense encounters that arise from an intersection of class and family backgrounds and the ambient factors of specific environments. Ideology and psychological drives are present in Killens's novel but are not conferred Ellison-style as idées fixes conveying the essence of character. In *Youngblood*, Black nationalism is clearly an operative philosophy, but the nationalist response is dramatized via the limited options of Black workers in the South, who are excluded from white unions and then denounced as "scabs" by their working-class white brothers. Killens also reveals how Communist dreams animate the fervent youthful idealism of Black revolutionary students at Howard University during the Great Depression.

As might be expected, two novels rendering such contrasting postwar interpretations of the radical legacy of the 1930s became polarized as literary artifacts in their subsequent interpretations and destinies. Ellison's *Invisible Man*, generally regarded as the superior artistic achievement, won the National Book Award and other prizes in 1953 and is today widely read as an avowal of free will and individual choice against racists, Communists, nationalists, assimilationist sellouts, and all "scientists" (Ellison's term) who aspire to project an identity for the "invisible" Black Man, who is essentially an "Everyman."[46] To escape power-hungry individuals and their attempts at psychological castration, the nameless narrator must survive "underground" through personal cunning. This is the individualist philosophy ultimately affirmed by the narrator, who declares, "After first being 'for' society and then 'against' it, I assign myself no rank or any limit. . . . My world has become one of infinite possibilities. What a phrase—still, it's a good phrase and a good view of life, and a man shouldn't accept any other."[47] Such an outlook in the published version of Ellison's novel (earlier versions and the unedited manuscript suggest other potentialities)[48] is consistent with the cataclysmic shift in political perspective of a generation of onetime Marxists during and after World War II. A thematic hallmark of the fiction of this generation— typified by Lionel Trilling, Edmund Wilson, Mary McCarthy, and Saul Bellow, among others—is a naive counterposition of rigid ideology to varieties of purported ideology-free experience.[49]

Killens's novel is magisterial in its own right, as an example of the precision with which the author crafts his social and political vision and his intricate interweaving of national oppression and patriarchy in the lives and psychology of his characters. This artistic accomplishment is unlikely to be attributed to his reading of Marx, which was presumably restricted to the classics available in translation and filtered through the prism of the Communist Party. In contrast to his literary practice, Killens's formal ideology of the time seems to express some of the worst excesses of the "art as a weapon" tradition, as indicated by his egregious review of Ellison's novel in Paul Robeson's newspaper, *Freedom*:

> The thousands of exploited farmers in the South are represented by a sharecropper [Ellison's infamous Trueblood] who has made both his wife and daughter pregnant.
>
> This book would give the impression that the Negro people as a whole are a hopeless bunch of dehumanized beings. This is precisely the Big Lie that the enemies of Negro Freedom have been telling the world since slavery time.[50]

It is probable that the "freakishness" of Ellison's characters, including Trueblood, was principally a commentary on contradictions of the human condition and especially the distortions wrought by racism. A more generous reading of *Invisible Man* might acknowledge the power of the novel in Ellison's capacity to mobilize Black cultural traditions, especially the forms and themes of urban blues, in ways entirely worthy of the African American heritage. Instead, Killens's review represents a knee-jerk hostility to disquieting allegory and a tendency toward a shallow political coding characteristic of a political polemicist.

There can be little doubt that Killens's Youngblood family is a potent and commanding rejoinder to what he judges to be the slander perpetrated by Ellison's depiction of Trueblood; the Youngbloods of Crossroads, Georgia, are credible as they exemplify an exceedingly unpathological, un-"damaged" Black family with both parents intact and a Protestant work ethic that would be highly desired by any fair-minded employer. What is most consequential is that both Ellison and Killens, for all their conspicuous contrariety in style, literary strategy, and political development, are both very deferential to Black culture as a unique and resplendent phenomenon. Yet neither is limited to a "narrow nationalist" or "essentialist" representation of that culture in their novels. In this sense the two writers are bound together in representing two profoundly divergent manifestations of the Black Marxist cultural tradition in the post–World War II United States.

Their dissimilar paths are particularly significant in light of the impact of Richard Wright's *Native Son* (1940) a dozen years earlier. Both writers were jarred by the novel but were affected differently. Ellison saw *Native Son* as an expansion of the possibilities of African American literature, while Killens felt it a betrayal of the course charted by Wright's *Uncle Tom's Children* (1938) and still evident in *Twelve Million Black Voices* (1941). Both writers were engaged in their own apprenticeships during their wartime service in the mid-1940s, so the delay in publishing their responses to Wright in their novels is not as significant as it might seem. Each drew different conclusions from the bombshell that Wright had thrown into the traditional Black Marxist schema, which had balanced a complex relation between national oppression and class unity.[51]

For Killens, the task was to repair the damage—to supplant Wright's protagonist Bigger Thomas, bereft of a Black cultural identity as well as a relationship to productive labor—with characters capable of developing a grasp of racism and its foundations. Such a race and class consciousness could inspire Blacks, both in the North and in the South, to continue to fight for their rights, in contrast to the external and internal versions of exile from the U.S. Left respectively promoted by Wright and Ellison.

For Ellison, the project was to deepen the fissure in the traditional Marxist schema brilliantly exposed by *Native Son* with its debunking of the roots of racial solidarity that was sometimes facilely promoted by the Communist Party. In the process of writing *Invisible Man*, he shifted from what may have been an effort to correct Marxism to one of obliterating the altruistic claims of the Black Marxist tradition that had attracted and frustrated both himself and Wright since the 1930s.

No doubt there were abundant reasons in the 1950s to pursue such an objective, including disillusionment and a cynical view of human motives. Most important, there was, despite some heroic attempts, a failure of the class unity aspect of the Communist project to materialize significantly in the nearly fifteen years since Ellison's first encounter with Communism. There was, too, the on-

59

going degeneration of the impact of the Russian revolution under Stalin, who turned the USSR into a police state, although Ellison's criticisms of Communism in the 1940s were mainly focused on the blunders of the Communist Party in the United States. Finally, there was a postwar renewal of the tendency in Communist cultural circles to judge art by knee-jerk political criteria. Even as the Communist movement continued to give voice to nascent writers from subordinate groups who had been largely excluded by the mainstream cultural apparatus, the narrow applications of "socialist realism" in the United States, combined with the knowledge that a literary deviation might be conflated with a political deviation, could certainly constrain the full flowering of the literary imagination. To be sure, the final, published version of *Invisible Man* was ideologically complicit with the Cold War, and its unprecedented coronation by the literary establishment was not entirely disconnected from Ellison's playing, in his own brilliant way, the "anti-Communist card."

Killens, despite his misreading of Ellison's novel as a vulgar smear of Black culture rather than an attempt at more substantive questioning of American society as a whole, drew on his literary instincts with a passionate response to the writings of his longtime intellectual mentor, W. E. B. Du Bois (1868–1963). Through characters, consciousness, and a wide range of dramatic episodes, he presented in *Youngblood* a critique of the ideology of racism, class oppression, and patriarchy more challenging than Ellison's and considerably closer to that of William Attaway's in *Blood on the Forge* (1941).[52] *Youngblood* is steeped in a composite dialectical vision that recalls Hegel's famous master/slave dialectic in *The Phenomenology of Mind* (1807).[53] In Killens's paradigm, there are two subordinate groups in the South: Black and white workers, both of whom have nothing to lose but psychological and social chains. Yet they live according to two social constructs—"Niggers" and "crackers"[54]—that falsify their interdependency and mask their subordination to their true economic master. The former construct is an outright fraud—a subhuman category derived primarily from the white patriarchy's projection of its own desires and, not infrequently, its own practice onto an economically weaker sector of the population. Yet in its demonization of African Americans, the "Nigger" construct provides the convenient scapegoat whom poor white men and women can blame for their problems. Thus working whites are flattered by the illusion of a dignified position of superiority and can also imagine themselves to be higher on the economic ladder.

Of course, Killens recognizes that those who affirm the privilege of white skin do have some economic advantages to buttress their illusion of racial superiority; however, he believes that such advantages are not so great as to be worth the overall cost. As a poor African American youth says to a poor white boy, "Just 'cause your skin is white and you live in a three-room shack and I live in one room, that don't make you no better than me. You ain't got as much sense as I got and you damn sure can't beat me. You poor white trash and I'm a Negro—So what goddammit have you got to be so glad about?"[55]

Accordingly, Killens capitalized on *Youngblood* to affirm an updated if nonetheless classical Marxist route to social liberation that would serve as a personal guide throughout the 1950s and 1960s. In disparity, Ralph Ellison seems to have lived out the political philosophy of *Invisible Man*, including the contradictions and illusions of his "underground" character. Although a brilliant analyst of African American music and culture, Ellison remained aloof from the new Black Arts movements of the 1960s and distanced himself from the civil rights movement. Yet he was hardly apolitical, distinguishing himself as among the very few outspoken African American intellectual defenders of the U.S. war in Vietnam, directly in opposition to Martin Luther King Jr. Indeed, Ellison became an active supporter of the hawkish wing of the Democratic Party as well as a tacit member of neoconservative intellectual circles in New York.[56]

Killens embarked toward a rather different destination. In the late 1940s he emerged as a guiding figure in Communist-influenced cultural organizations such as the Committee for the Negro in the Arts (founded in 1947) and the Harlem Writers Guild (1950), the latter of which began to distance itself from the Communist movement after the first several years.[57] In these years, many Black writers in the guild or the Party worked their way out of the painful illusions of the Stalinist version of Communism. None became informers, and all distanced themselves from the public anti–Communist Party polemics of their onetime colleague and contemporary Harold Cruse, whose *The Crisis of the Negro Intellectual: From the Origins to the Present* (1967) was mainly aimed at Killens.[58] They also refrained from public criticism of onetime mentors such as Paul Robeson and W. E. B. Du Bois (who joined the Communist Party in 1961), both of whom never publicly expressed any misgivings for their pro-Stalin loyalties. Killens, while welcoming constituents of the new Black Arts and Black Power movements of the 1960s, never completely discarded the ideals of class-based internationalism that drew him to the Communist Party in the first place.

For a decade, from the time he finished *Youngblood* until the mid-1960s, Killens was extremely active in the civil rights movement and its spin-offs. At first he was associated with Martin Luther King and was an activist in the Montgomery bus boycott. Then he was drawn to Malcolm X and embraced the left-wing Black nationalism of Malcolm's final phase, helping Malcolm to put together the Organization of African American Unity, his political group after he broke with the Muslims.[59] Years later Killens wrote, "Philosophically speaking, Du Bois was my grandfather, Robeson my father, Malcolm was my brother."[60] Both a 1965 collection of essays, Black Man's Burden, and another long novel, 'Sippi, published two years later, embody Killens's Third World Marxism. His last two novels were The Cotillion (1971), an elaborate satire of the Black elite, and Great Black Russian (posthumously published in 1989), a fictionlized life of Alexander Pushkin. For young people, Killens wrote books about Denmark Vesey and John Henry; he also composed plays and screenplays.[61] He was associated with Harry Belafonte's production of Odds against Tomorrow (1959), a classic of film noir and the first to feature a Black protagonist.[62]

Killens's persona in his fiction and his essays throughout the Black Arts and Black Power periods, and long after, was prevalently "tough-guy shrill" and rhetorical. His literary criticism continued to be polemical rather than subtle, although he came to disavow his early remarks about Ellison.[63] A representative statement of his philosophical and political position was "There is no such thing as art for art's sake. All art is propaganda, although there is much propaganda that is not art. We must join a crusade to decolonize the minds of Black people. No one else will do this work, so we must."[64] Nonetheless, despite his hard-line public persona, Killens was a low-key, soft-spoken, and gentle man, devoted to nurturing young Black artists.[65] During the mid-1960s Killens organized numerous conferences for African American authors and served three years (1965–68) as a nationally prominent writer in residence at Fisk University. After several other teaching positions at Columbia University, Howard University, and Bronx Community College, he obtained a faculty post at Medgar Evers College of the City University of New York in 1981, which he held at the time of his death from cancer in 1987.

A DOUBLE PERSPECTIVE ON DOUBLE V

John Oliver Killens's literary treatment of Double V in And Then We Heard the Thunder is enhanced by a double perspective, one indicative of his post-Communist maturation when he retrospectively probed the circumstances that led initially to his Communist commitment during and after World War II. As such his novel is a profound testament to the agonizing ordeal of the post-1930s African American cultural Left as it ultimately came to terms with the contradictions of the Communist experience as a whole. The ideological climate of the late 1950s and early 1960s in which Killens's novel was written is the critical ingredient. During the years in which he formulated and wrote Youngblood, approximately 1947 to 1953, Killens was most likely an active and devoted member of the Communist Party. The coincidence of his literary success with Youngblood and the 1956 revelations of Nikita Khrushchev seems to have brought that membership to a close.

Consequently, the anti–Popular Front political perspective of *And Then We Heard the Thunder*, although it certainly existed in the 1940s, was not one to which Killens adhered as he went through the military experiences depicted in the novel or, for that matter, in the immediate aftermath of the war. He would not conceivably have joined, or rejoined, the Communist Party, which he most likely did in 1946, if he had then believed that the Party held a position conciliatory to white supremacism—a view that he articulated in 1963. More probably, the political clarity and consistency of *And Then We Heard the Thunder* is retrospectively projected back on the period. Thus, despite the setting of the narrative amidst the left-wing debates during World War II, the politics of Killens's novel actually reflect the race as well as labor and gender relationships of the civil rights movement of the late 1950s and the rise of Third World radicalism in the 1960s.

Even with this anomaly, Killens can be seen as a representative figure for understanding how left-wing African American writers negotiated the so-called People's War in relation to race, masculinity, and the often misunderstood politics of the Popular Front.[66] What is portrayed in Killens's projection of his emerging politics of the 1960s back into his World War II experiences in the mid-1940s is also quite implicit in most Black Marxist novels treating the domestic and international fronts of World War II; as a group they create a counterpoint to the political ethos of World War II antifascist unity, which much of the Euro-American left wing supported. The probability is that nearly all radical Black writers of the World War II era were, like Killens, affected politically by the Communist movement in diverse ways; yet, notwithstanding that the Popular Front was categorically counterpoised by the Communist Party to Double V, the logic of life experiences in which writers were immersed tended to push them toward a practical or at least implied Double V perspective in fiction writing at the time and later. Moreover, Fannie Mae's declaration that "the War is everywhere we find it" is an apt touchstone for any investigation of how one locates and theorizes the Black Marxist literary response to the antifascist crusade.

Novels with combat episodes such as those Killens presents in *And Then We Heard the Thunder* are rare because although the nearly 1 million African American troops in World War II were occasionally in combat, they were largely relegated to work gangs in both the Pacific and European theaters.[67] Considering World War II as "everywhere we find it" is a vital strategy for resuscitating the radical countercultural dimensions of a sweep of World War II era books by African Americans. The novels by Black writers significantly connected with the Marxist cultural Left in the 1940s include William Attaway's *Blood on the Forge*, Chester Himes's *If He Hollers Let Him Go* (1945) and *The Lonely Crusade* (1947), Ann Petry's *The Street* (1946), William Gardner Smith's *Last of the Conquerors* (1948), and Willard Motley's *We Fished All Night* (1951). (The last two authors will be discussed in the next volume in this series.)

The Popular Front, especially after 1941, created a dilemma for movements of the racially oppressed, because these rebellions often had their own dynamic and the most militant of the oppressed participants refused to wait for Euro-Americans to change their consciousness. In this sense, the advocacy of a "nascent" Double V strategy for African American liberation is plainly inscribed in Attaway's 1941 historical narrative of the 1919 steel strike near Pittsburgh, Pennsylvania, *Blood on the Forge*. As with Killens's *And Then We Heard the Thunder*, the date of its writing is decisive for an understanding of its ideological assumptions. Attaway's novel was written between 1939 and 1941, that is, during the eighteen-month interlude when the Communist Party abandoned the Popular Front strategy, due to the Hitler-Stalin nonaggression pact.[68] Consequently, the anti–Popular Front facets of Attaway's *Blood on the Forge* were not strictly at odds with Communist policy when the novel was written. For Attaway, Black oppression is so acute that, even though Black workers assuredly have many of the same anticapitalist objectives as Euro-American workers, unity cannot come through Black integration into a rotten "house of labor." Rather, the house must be reconstructed on new foundations to allow Blacks to fight for their own interests alongside Euro-Americans struggling against a mutual adversary. Indeed, in a long document describing the "plan of work" for his projected novel, Attaway rebutted the conventional criticism of the conservative role that African Americans had played in the steel union: "Nobody took into consideration the fact that the strike issues in the mills were to the Negroes trivial by contrast to the terrible labor conditions under which they had so lately suffered."[69]

Unluckily, *Blood on the Forge* was released after Hitler had invaded the Soviet Union and the Communist Party had changed its orientation back to supporting the Popular Front. Thus the novel was criticized by Ralph Ellison and others then in the Communist Party cultural apparatus for its nationalist positions and its failure to dramatize positive routes to class unity.[70] The failure of *Blood on the Forge* to link up with the prevalent Popular Front mood of the liberals and the Left during the mid-1940s is surely central among the reasons for the "disappearance" of this arresting novel until it was reprinted in the 1960s and 1970s. Moreover, although he served in World War II in North Africa, William Attaway never wrote about his own war experiences; indeed, he never published fiction again, except for one 1947 allegorical short story that implies the abandonment of his art.[71]

Attaway, like Killens, surely revealed that the autonomous dynamic of Black resistance to racial oppression cannot be subordinated to class considerations, let alone to "national unity" that involves those who perpetuate or accommodate white supremacism, and that "the War is everywhere we find it." Yet Attaway, too, remained a Communist Party member through the Cold War. The two authors first met at a Party-led cultural meeting shortly after World War II, and it was Killens who would write the foreword to the 1987 Monthly Review reissue of Attaway's novel that was published one year after Attaway's death.[72] That both men, who supported Double V at heart, would nevertheless find the Communist Party an attractive political home long after the commonly believed peak of Communism in the 1930s illustrates the still-underestimated allure of the Communist movement for Black cultural workers through the mid-1950s. Notwithstanding the contradictions of its World War II policy, the Communist Party persisted in encouraging, or at least providing a milieu for, a counterculture to capitalism. This counterculture nurtured many talented and often influential African Americans who started writing after the war, such as Lorraine Hansberry (1930–65), Julian Mayfield (1928–85), Lance Jeffers (1919–85), Douglas Turner Ward (b. 1930), Alice Childress (1916–94), Audre Lorde (1934–92), Sarah Wright (b. 1928), Rosa Guy (b. 1925), and Lonne Elder III (1931–96).[73] Of course, whatever uneasiness Killens, Attaway, and the others may have felt about the Communist Party's World War II policy probably was partially assuaged when Earl Browder was expelled from the Party in 1946 and the Party's backpedaling on the race issue was repudiated—although Browder was perhaps unjustly scapegoated.[74]

William Attaway's *Blood on the Forge* foreshadowed the approach explicitly taken by Killens in 1962, and implicitly by other writers during the 1940s and 1950s, to U.S. white supremacism during the World War II phase of the antifascist crusade. But it does not follow that there was a clean sweep for Double V in Black literature at the time of the war. In particular, the publication *Negro Story*, based in Chicago and with a strong contingent of pro-Communist supporters, tended to tilt toward the Popular Front and therefore against Double V in its fiction and poetry about the war.[75] It featured the 1944 story "Private Jeff Johnson," by Margaret T. Goss, later known as Margaret Burroughs (b. 1917), the founder of Chicago's DuSable Museum of African American History. Goss tells of a northern Black soldier sent into the Deep South for basic training. Like Killens's Solly Saunders, Jeff Johnson soon has a serious run-in with the white military police.[76] Nevertheless, instead of retaliating when an MP uses the hate epithet "nigger," Johnson thinks along Popular Front lines of unity above all else: "To win this war, black and white ought to be fighting Hitler, not each other." So, to the jeers of the other Black soldiers, Johnson backs off. When it is later disclosed that the MP's provocation was a setup to instigate a riot in which many Blacks could have been killed, one of those who jeered Johnson apologizes and says, "You're just a clear-thinking man and a real soldier. A riot here today would have been just what Hitler wanted. The guy we want is Hitler."[77]

Nonetheless, subordination of the domestic antiracist struggle to the ideology of the Popular Front is not a theme that found its way into most memorable Black fiction of the era. In 1940 Chester Himes (1909–84), who had been friendly to the Communist Party following his release from prison in 1936, and especially during his 1939–40 association with the radical journal Crossroad in Cleveland, moved to California, where he charted an idiosyncratic course combining pro-Soviet and Double V politics. During the months following the Hitler-Stalin Pact, Himes's short fiction appeared to be absorbed in race and class dilemmas; the possibility of being involved in an international war was broached only as a distraction from the Depression.[78] Yet a few months after the USSR was invaded by Germany, Himes burst into print with "Now Is the Time! Here Is the Place" in Opportunity, monthly magazine of the Urban League.

Surely one of the most eloquent and passionate defenses of Double V in print, Himes's appeal embraces the "unity" aspect of the Popular Front. He explains the policy as an alliance of the oppressed with their former oppressors against a greater evil: "At this time, we 23,000,000 Negro Americans are united with all Americans of all races, colors, and creeds, with their allies, the Chinese Republic, the Soviet Union, the white ruler races of the British Empire . . . in a war to defeat and destroy nazism." However, the struggle against discrimination cannot slide into second place, for this war will not be won unless a second front is opened against "our native fascists"; this second front "must be a contemporaneous, a concurrent effort." Himes's formula could well be the epigraph for And Then We Heard the Thunder: "How can we participate in this greater war without giving the same effort to our home fight against our native enemies? What pride will there be to urge us on? What ideal for which to fight? What love of country to inspire us with patriotic ardor?" Diplomatically, Himes did not criticize the Communist Party by name, but he directed a deliberate polemic against its policy: "One of the unfortunate aspects of the Negro Americans' fight for freedom at home is the discovery that many organizations, humanitarian ideologists, and realistic political groups, Americans who have long been in the front ranks of the Negro Americans' slow march toward equality, are now deserting them, advocating that this fight be set aside until the greater fight for freedom is won. Only by doing so, they state, will it be possible to achieve the national unity necessary to win the war."

CHESTER HIMES, drawn to the Communist movement in the
late 1930s and early 1940s, published fiction and essays about
the domestic front in World War II. (Photograph by Carl Van
Vechten; courtesy of the Van Vechten Trust, Lancaster, Pa., and
the Carl Van Vechten Collection, Yale University)

Himes's views paralleled those of Wright and Ellison, who also did not believe that the Communist Party's formal statements about Black equality were being implemented.[79] Himes thought that it would be a "travesty" if, following a victory of the allies in "their fight for the freedom of all people in the world, we 23,000,000 Negroes remain in virtual bondage."[80] Less than a year later Himes reintroduced his scrupulous position with "Zoot Suit Riots Are Race Riots!" an essay in the *Crisis*, the monthly magazine of the NAACP. Here he gave no quarter to patriotic rhetoric or deference to men in uniform, referring to the sailors who attacked Mexican Americans in zoot suits as "vigilantes" and "Klansmen," concluding bitterly that "the South has won Los Angeles."[81] Such straightforward Double V polemics were then followed by his curious essay, "Negro Martyrs Are Needed."

This article, in the May 1944 issue of the *Crisis*, is where Himes for the first time presents his theory of social revolution. He states unabashedly that the only nation in the world to have approached the goal "wherein everyone is free" is "the communist dominated socialist state of the USSR." In contrast, in the United States only the "ruling class or race is free," and in the fascist states, "no one is free." Thus a revolution initiated by middle-class "Negro Martyrs" to bring about the "overthrow of our present form of government and the creation of a communistic state" is required—a revolution in which the Communist Party of America will play a leading role and will have "fair chances of success." The guarantor of this victory, however, is not the dictatorship of the proletariat but merely the "enforcement of the [U.S.] Constitution" by the majority of the population, with violence as a threat but perhaps avoidable. As a result, "a Negro American revolution will cease to be a revolution and become a movement of the people to stamp out injustices, inequalities, and violations of our laws."[82]

In a December 1945 interview by the *Chicago Defender*'s Earl Conrad (a Communist fellow traveler and former Party member under his birth name, Earl Cohen), Himes clarified why he politically supported Communism as it existed in the Soviet Union, without necessarily favoring an economic transformation of the United States. Concerning the "race problem," he told Conrad, "I have always thought it was a problem more psychological than economic." Moreover, he believed that "if we had a government of the people . . . who themselves believed in the principles of democracy as set forth in the constitution, that they could, through the structure of government we have now, [give] a dignity of citizenship to all minorities and oppressed groups that would psychologically prepare citizens to accept each other, and after that, the security that would be offered by jobs would make the solution complete." Thus, at the end of the year in which his novel *If He Hollers Let Him Go* was published, Himes still ardently believed that the Soviet Union was "a nation that represents a new ideology in which the masses of people have more freedom . . . that has passed from theory to practice." While the United States must also move forward to this "new way of life," the immediate task is to "put more responsible legislators into office, and it also lies with the liberal press and the school system to teach the truth about the Negro."[83] In a peculiar rendition of the Communists' Popular Front slogan "Communism Is Twentieth-Century Americanism," Himes saw the USSR as the embodiment of the U.S. Constitution's pledge of political equality (more important than economic justice), and, through elections, he hoped for a nonviolent eradication in the United States of racist practices and the psychology of racism.[84]

Himes's short fiction in the first half of the 1940s was uncommonly obsessed with the figure of the Black soldier and the dilemmas of wartime racism. As a prelude to his dramatizations of wartime bigotry, in late 1942 he published "Lunching at the Ritzmore," a satire of discrimination that reminded the reader that the Communist Party had been accurate in its claims about the persistence and ubiquity of race bias.[85] This was followed by a burst of fiction in 1943 that starts out by promoting an optimistic outcome of the Double V debate but becomes progressively skeptical about the antifascist crusade achieving its promise. Most graphically, in Himes's hopeful phase, "Two Soldiers" recounts a white racist soldier driven to love a Black man in uniform due to the latter's fatally heroic acts in confronting the Nazis.[86] "So Softly Smiling" is about the love affair of an African American U.S. Army lieutenant on leave from North Africa, in which the ideology of Double V is foregrounded. The officer, educated at "Chicago University," had begun the war disaffected, thinking, "Let the white people fight their own war—I've got nothing to win." But articles by Walter White of the NAACP and A. Philip Randolph of the Brotherhood of Sleeping Car Porters convinced him that "America belonged to the Negro as much as to any one." Thus he had gone off to fight with an outlook similar to that of Solly Saunders in the opening sections of *And Then We Heard the Thunder*.[87] In "Heaven Has Changed," Himes portrays a Black soldier, killed in battle, who ascends to heaven, where he leads a successful revolution by ballot that abolishes Jim Crow.[88]

In a more caustic vein, "All He Needs Is Feet" tells of a Black man in the South with two brothers in the army. After being horribly tortured by whites in Georgia for resisting their violence, he loses both feet. He then moves to Chicago, where his circumstances improve. Prior to watching the World War II movie *Bataan* (1943), with its heroic portrayal of an African American soldier, he is clobbered by a white southerner because he is incapable of standing for the national anthem. But the story nonetheless is perversely optimistic, perhaps an expression of Himes's last effort to redeem the promises of the Popular Front. It satirizes the notion that a display of patriotism should be expected from those brutalized by the system, but the source of the racism in the story is rooted mainly in southern prejudice rather than being endemic in the United States. Moreover, the racism is offset somewhat by the film, which was a work of liberal war propaganda.[89]

By 1944–45, Himes had shifted toward treating the war as being without redemptive potential. "Let Me at the Enemy—an' George Brown" is a satire in which a Black man proclaims himself pro-war after losing his girlfriend and being tricked out of money owed him for a supposedly well-paying job. The man's cynical attitude toward the war expressed here more closely parallels the one that Himes held in 1939.[90] "A Penny for Your Thoughts" tells of a racist Texas lawman who prevents the lynching of a Black soldier accused of rape only because of his respect for the soldier's uniform.[91] "He Seen It in the Stars" humorously depicts a worker named Accidental Brown who falls asleep during a movie called *Hitler's Children* and dreams of encounters with Hitler just before the Allies stage their final attack on Germany.[92] In "All God's Children Got Pride," Himes provides flashbacks of the 1930s experiences with racism of a soldier now in the guard-house; his fierce pride had always brought him to the brink of trouble, and this time he is definitely "guilty" of refusing to conciliate racism.[93]

In his last published story of the World War II era featuring a veteran, Himes's emphasis has switched: He is disconcerted by the threat to traditional gender relations created by the employment of women during the war. "Make with the Shape" describes how honorably discharged Sergeant Johnny Jones returns home to find his wife, Jessie May, working the night shift in a pipe factory. He also learns that she has become a judo expert. Disconcerted when she tells him that he might get a job as her helper, or perhaps that he need not have to work at all, Jones tries to make her jealous by hooking up with a chorus girl. In the brawl that ensues, the chorus girl humiliates Jessie May by beating her up; Jessie May then reverts to her pre-war role as the "sweet little wife."[94]

By the time Himes published *If He Hollers Let Him Go*, his central concern with the antifascist crusade was principally the failures of wartime equal employment policies to address racism and of the Communist Left to militantly fight against discrimination. Himes's dazzling narrative records five days in the life of African American shipyard worker Bob Jones in Los Angeles. Jones's commonplace name suggests that he is an ordinary man. Early in the novel, Himes registers a forceful objection to the internment of Japanese Americans, which was whole-heartedly defended by the Communist Party. This illustrates Jones's instinctive identification with all victims of racist epithets and persecution: "I was the same color as the Japanese and I couldn't tell the difference. 'A yeller-bellied Jap' coulda meant me, too."[95]

Himes's disappointment at the wartime policies of the Communist Party is also reflected in a scene where Bob Jones is warned by the manager of a segregated restaurant that he will not be served in the future. The waiter who delivers the manager's note is sympathetic to Jones and tells him, in the hope of making him feel better, that he is going to quit his job and publish an exposé of the restaurant in the West Coast Communist Party paper, *People's World*. Jones retorts, "If you're thinking about how I feel, when you should have quit was before you brought the note."[96] The episode implies that the Communist Party is reluctantly complicit in perpetuating racism but is interested in unmasking bigotry after the fact for its self-aggrandizing propaganda.

Later Jones engages in a debate about Richard Wright's *Native Son* with Tom Leighton, a Euro-American friend of Jones's girlfriend, Alice, who represents the liberal pro–Popular Front point of view. Jones's political notions are indistinguishable from those of Himes or those published in the *Chicago Defender*. Although college educated, Jones is employed as an industrial worker in the aircraft industry and objects to Leighton's belief that economic security will lessen racial tensions. "No," Jones interjects, "It's a state of mind. As long as the white folks hate me and I hate them we can earn the same amount of money, live side by side in the same house, and fight every day." In his description of the necessary revolution that is required to abolish racism, Jones concedes that white allies—ones who will act and not just talk—will be fundamental for victory. When Leighton proposes, instead, that African Americans put aside the notion of a revolution in the United States and "participate and co-operate in the general uprising of the masses all over the world," Jones bluntly asks, "Are you a Communist?"[97] In other words, Jones makes no distinction between the Communists and the Left-liberal view that the subordination of African American demands for justice to the war effort will guarantee international postwar democracy. In yet another reference to Communist Party policy, Jones, out of sorts and looking for some friends with whom to socialize, muses, "There was Vivian Williams; there used always to be something going on at her house back in the days before the Communist Party dealt the race issue out."[98]

Jones finally takes his grievance about the on-the-job racism perpetrated by a southern white woman, Madge, to the union representative Herbie Frieberger, a Popular Front supporter who is baited as a Communist by Jones. The argument that ensues substantially anticipates by two decades some of the debates over Double V in *And Then We Heard the Thunder* between John Oliver Killens's own Black and Jewish pair, Solly Saunders and Robert Samuels.

[FRIEBERGER:] "You forget we're in a war. This isn't any time for private gripes. We're fighting fascism—we're not fighting the companies and we're not fighting each other—we're all fighting fascism together and in order to beat fascism we got to have unity. We got to have unity in the union and unity on the job—"

[JONES:] "That's fine, Comrade Marx, that's wonderful. . . . Let's you and me unite and start right here fighting fascism. Let's go down and give this cracker dame some lessons in unity and if she doesn't want to unite let's tell her about the war—"

Frieberger then urges Jones to read the editorial by Mrs. Baker in a Los Angeles weekly newspaper, a likely reference to Charlotta Bass, editor of the pro–Popular Front *California Eagle*, a weekly Black publication. Jones irreverently retorts, "Mrs. Baker's not my mama. . . . Get these crackers to unite with me. . . . But I ain't gonna even try to do any uniting without anybody to unite with." He then adds, "What the hell do I care about unity, or the war either, for that matter, as long as I'm kicked around by every white person who comes along?"[99]

There is one probable Communist with whom Jones shares a sense of comradeship: Don, a white worker in the plant. But Don turns out to be insidious. After several times expressing his affection for and trust in Don, Jones is drawn to confide in him, even though he suspects Don of being a Party member. When Jones describes the racist behavior he has experienced from Madge, Don nonchalantly hints that a sexual encounter with a Black man might "cure" Madge. He then gives Jones Madge's address, and a sexually explosive confrontation with Madge at her apartment at night ensues. In a subsequent encounter with Madge, Don acts as if consummation (which was in fact thwarted by Madge's screaming that she wanted to be raped) had actually occurred, greatly heightening the tension.[100] This precipitates the novel's disastrous conclusion in which Jones is falsely accused of rape and is sentenced to join the army as an alternative to going to prison.

It is surprising, therefore, that Himes's novel was hailed by the major organs of the Communist press without a single word of criticism of his portraits of Communists and his critiques of the Party's wartime policy. The explanation for this uncharacteristic generosity may be provided by *Daily Worker* reviewer Eugene Gordon (1891–1974),[101] an experienced African American Communist cultural critic: "Communists should read the book, so that they might be reminded of much we forgot in the past period. It will shock many of them. It will suggest that there is a hell of a lot of work to be done." Although Himes certainly began writing the novel before the expulsion of Earl Browder, the date of Gordon's review (late December 1945) is six months after the famous Jacques Duclos letter against Browder's policies, which was first published in French in April 1945 and as a front-page story in the *Daily Worker* on 24 May 1945. The Communist Party was already in the throes of considerable self-flagellation for having held some of the very positions attacked by Himes. Moreover, Gordon was explicit about the novel's relevance in light of the Party's self-criticism that the Party had not backed up its claims to belief in racial equality with appropriate actions: "It is a warning to anybody who pretends any kind of interest in the Negro question to live up to his pretensions or be damned by on-rushing events."[102]

If Gordon's desire to use Himes's novel for political rectification blinded him to the deeper and more troubling subtext that suggested that the psychology of racism is omnipresent and a paramount issue, Herbert Aptheker, writing in the *New Masses*, was even more obtuse. Empathizing completely with Bob Jones's battle against "the walls of the obscene ghetto into which he and his people have been forced," Aptheker ironically mimicked Himes's character Herbie Frieberger by calling on African Americans to take up the movement toward unity as their burden: "We say to Bob, and we say to Himes: others suffer, too, and others aspire, too. Come, in the name of humanity, come join hands with us. Add your strength to ours, and so lose your weakness and your terror."[103]

However, three years had transpired since Himes wrote "Now Is the Time! Here Is the Place!" and the time and place had now passed. For him, the possibility of revolution through Double V was contingent on Euro-Americans joining with African Americans in support of their immediate struggles against white supremacism, struggles that would certainly not have Euro-American radicals play the leading roles. As was the case with Killens's Jewish lieutenant, Robert Samuels, it is the professed allies who have the burden of "taking off their whiteness," acting at the appropriate time, and making demands on the oppressors, not the oppressed.

African American literature, then, directly dramatizes the weakness of the Popular Front in ways only implicit in Spanish Civil War writing by William Herrick and possibly Ernest Hemingway. The pattern of evasion found in Wolff and Bessie is repeated to some extent by Jewish American writers fixated on German fascism during World War II. They embraced the Popular Front encumbered by analogous blinders regarding political alternatives on the Left, as had most of their predecessors in regard to the Spanish Civil War. Where the Jewish American World War II writers differed from one another was primarily in regard to the makeup of European fascism itself.

{3

The Peculiarities of the Germans

"A JEW MUST LEARN TO FIGHT"

In 1944 a gifted young Jewish American Marxist playwright, scenarist, and fiction writer, Albert Maltz (1908–85), published a novel that would become the most highly regarded work of his literary life. *The Cross and the Arrow*, commended in the *New York Times* for "the scope of its vision of humanity,"[1] adopted the form of a fast-paced political mystery to reveal the events underlying an act of sabotage in Nazi Germany in 1942. Through a succession of well-crafted flashbacks, Maltz reconstructs the circumstances motivating a German worker, Willi Wegler, a recent recipient of a Service Cross in recognition of his exemplary labor, to betray his country. During an August night, Wegler ignites an enormous arrow formed out of hay, fashioning a flaming signal to the British bombers searching for the location of a concealed tank factory. The novel opens with Wegler prostrate in a German hospital, mortally wounded in the abdomen by gunshots fired by the German guard who apprehended him. The drama unfolds from the endeavor of local officials to ascertain what motivated Wegler.

Maltz constructed this fictionalized anatomy of a feat of antifascist insurgency to contest a burgeoning assumption among the wartime Allies about the singular culpability of the German people for fascist atrocities. Many were asking, Was there something unique in German history and culture that led ordinary people to acts of aggression and barbarism that were outside the norms of what was considered to be Western Civilization? Maltz was distressed by his learning that there was, indeed, strong sentiment, even on the part of liberals and members of the Left, for the conception that the German people stood apart from people in the rest of Europe and the United States in their capacity to tolerate and collaborate in atrocities. There was even an attitude that ordinary Germans—not just the leaders of the Nazi party and regime—would eventually require punishment if they did not undergo a postwar program of reeducation. The foremost advocate of this position was the British diplomat Baron Robert Gilbert Vansittart (1881–1957); hence the stance was known as "Vansittartism."[2]

In the U.S. Communist movement, there was a recurrent slippage between caustic denunciations of Germans in general and Nazis in particular. One article in the Daily Worker of November 1944 was titled "The Degeneration of the German Woman." It began, "Let no one doubt that the Nazi women are moral cesspools," and the conclusion was that "Nazi women have become a nation of prostitutes."[3] The popular Daily Worker columnist Mike Gold (1894–1967) leaned more consciously toward conflating the German people with the Nazis, as well as advocating a severe form of collective punishment. In an October 1944 column devoted to the subject, Gold used language that suggested an almost genetic explanation for the appearance of Nazism: "For generations they [the Germans] have been bred to revere force; and only force can now change their national habits." Without distinguishing between conscious Nazi supporters and sectors of the population terrorized into complicity, Gold declared, "They must suffer so much that at last they repent. They must purge themselves of their Nazi disease. . . . Until that time they are the rattlesnake nation."[4] Most appalling, however, were the views of the journalist and novelist Ilya Ehrenburg (1891–1967), a leading cultural figure in the Soviet Union. Ehrenburg was capable of writing wartime newspaper columns that included such statements as "Now we understand the Germans are not human. . . . If you have killed one German, kill another. There is nothing jollier for us than German corpses."[5]

In the ensuing decades, disputes about the peculiar degeneracy of German culture into Nazism, the responsibility of ordinary Germans, and the appropriate measures that should have been taken by the victorious Allies emerged in new forms that sporadically spilled over into popular culture. While academic studies circulated among scholars, Stanley Kramer's 1961 film Judgment at Nuremberg and the appearance of Hannah Arendt's 1963 book Eichmann in Jerusalem brought the controversy into the public domain. Finally, scholarship and publicity in the media blended to create the most comprehensive and notorious treatment of the issue in 1996, following the publication of Daniel Jonah Goldhagen's Hitler's Willing Executioners: Ordinary Germans and the Holocaust. Although many scholars protested, Goldhagen tenaciously argued that the ingrained anti-Semitism that preceded the Nazi regime created a nation ready-made to commit genocide.[6]

A direct link between certain strands of Communist thinking in the 1940s, echoing that of Vansittart and Ehrenburg and foreshadowing Goldhagen's thesis, is rendered clear in a column by Mike Gold published just one month after The Cross and the Arrow was discussed in the Communist press. Gold anticipated the most sensational part of Goldhagen's title: "The crimes [of Nazi Germany] needed millions of criminals to be carried out, and Germans were willing to be instruments of the insane program" (emphasis added). Moreover, like Goldhagen,

Gold maintained that the root cause of this criminal behavior predated the Nazi seizure of power: "The Nazis did not invent their horrific program. They were merely the last heirs of the historic philosophy of German nationalism and imperialism."[7]

Albert Maltz joined the Communist Party in 1935 and would remain affiliated for more than two decades.[8] Despite a noted conflict with Party cultural policy in 1946, he was willing to suffer imprisonment for ten months in 1950–51 rather than betray his convictions, and he did not separate from the Party until sometime after the Khrushchev revelations of 1956. However, he judged the thinking of Vansittart and Ehrenburg to be forms of racism unacceptable to internationalists; their premises might generate simplistic and monolithic explanations for fascism that weakened a Marxist understanding of the phenomenon. *The Cross and the Arrow*, originally a novelette, was thus partially conceived of as an "intellectual platform" to dispute such presumptions. It was grounded in primary research in journalistic articles, including those by U.S. writers who were in Germany until 1941, and thereafter by Swedish and other reporters from neutral countries. An important source for Maltz was interdenominational religious magazines that attended to current events in Germany. Moreover, Maltz had visited Germany, and he was in immediate contact with German refugees, including a former Nazi party member who provided intimate details of the structure of the fascist organization.[9]

The Cross and the Arrow is infused with an ambition and intricacy that energized and vivified its thesis. The 450-page book was illustrative of the singular mettle and temper of its creator. Maltz ripened as a writer from a background that fashioned him into an utterly earnest, serious, and driven man whose most unforgettable attributes were rigidity and abundant compassion. Born in Brooklyn as the youngest of three brothers, Maltz was bedeviled by the misfortunes endured by his parents; they drove him to overachievement while concurrently instilling in him a grim sense of life's dangers.[10]

Maltz's father, Bernard Maltz, immigrated at age fourteen from Lithuania near the German border. He subsequently rose from an indigent peddler to an increasingly thriving housepainter and eventually to a prosperous building contractor, although he continued to act as if poverty were a threat and money was tight. Then, in his forties, he was stricken with an unexpected illness, diagnosed as Buerger's disease; he underwent the amputation of both legs as a result, and the illness exacerbated other medical infirmities that brought him to an early death in 1933. Albert Maltz's mother, Lena Sherashevsky (her last name was changed to Sherry at Ellis Island), was a Polish Jewish immigrant slightly older than her husband. She suffered from an eye disease, trachoma, that produced

ALBERT MALTZ was a leading writer in the Communist
movement who published influential novels in the 1940s and
later served a prison sentence as one of the Hollywood Ten.
(From the Maltz Collection in the Howard Gotlieb Archival
Research Center at Boston University)

near-blindness; this prompted her to ban library cards and most books from the house under the belief that her son must also have weak eyes, which should be saved for college. A few months after Maltz's father died at age fifty-six, she also passed away.

The two parents colluded in fashioning an ambience in which the young Maltz absorbed a great deal of what an analyst later described as "free-floating anxiety." They demanded perfection and gave approval only when Maltz excelled. Consequently he felt that he had to outdo his contemporaries in athletics as well as academics. Dread of failure drove him to run a great distance to elementary school each morning, as he was panicked about the repercussions of being late. His grades at Erasmus Hall High School in New York were so spectacular that he was awarded a scholarship to Columbia University upon graduation in 1926, in spite of his repeatedly failing the qualifying entrance exam. In sports he drilled himself to become superior at tennis and swimming, setting records in college, and also at wrestling. To his astonishment, at age fifty, while living in political exile in Mexico, Maltz was diagnosed by a doctor as having suffered from a "hidden polio" in childhood that rendered his left leg and foot substantially smaller than his right ones. Yet Maltz's physical exertions since his youth had caused his body to find ways of compensating. Hence the discrepancy was unnoticeable in his gait and carriage and only apparent in the fact that his right shoe size was noticeably larger than his left.

As the Maltz family moved into better neighborhoods during his boyhood and teen years, Albert encountered anti-Semitism, not infrequently accompanied by violence. Although the Maltz family was assimilationist, the Jewish identity of his parents was evident in their celebration of the high holidays with an extended family, their attendance at the Yiddish theater, their maintenance of a kosher household (mainly for in-laws who lived with them), and their speaking of some Yiddish at home. These early painful anti-Semitic incidents, which he saw as analogous to anti-Black race discrimination, left Maltz fiercely opposed to injustice in any form. He later recalled, "Wherever I met injustice . . . I revolted against it automatically, as though I were touching a red hot stove."[11] Moreover, he was acutely influenced by his father's advice that "a Jew must learn to fight."[12] The elder Maltz would relate exemplary stories of resistance. One entailed a powerful Jew who fought back against an anti-Semitic pogrom in Russia with a nail-studded club, and another recounted a small Jew on the East Side who was able to defend an elderly Jew from harassment because he had been a professional boxer.[13] Eventually Maltz began to take boxing lessons from a professional, even preparing to enter the Golden Gloves competition while at college. A preoccupation with self-defense continued into his middle age. In 1950, at age forty-two, Maltz studied judo on the eve of incarceration in a federal prison, in order to be confident that he could take care of himself if challenged by violence from right-wing prisoners.

During his high school years, his only social analysis related to his view of World War I. At the time, he engaged in expressions of support for the war, reinforced by his knowledge that several uncles were in the service. Afterward, he became upset by the amount of war profiteering that had taken place, and he read antiwar novels and memoirs in college. By the time he gained an intellectual focus at Columbia, he had become intensely interested in discerning why things were the way they were. In the succeeding years Maltz became captivated by the study of history, but in college he devoted himself to philosophy and graduated Phi Beta Kappa in 1930.

Through courses in philosophy with Professor Irwin Edman and in great books with Mortimer J. Adler and Mark Van Doren, Maltz pursued questions of epistemology—what are the grounds of our knowledge of reality? Later, he would find that the classics of Marxism, especially the writings of Engels, provided explanations with which he concurred. But at Columbia he was attracted to the philosophical masterpieces and became engrossed with logic and ethics. However, literary distractions were germinating in the background. In high school he had become attracted to the romantic poetry read by one of his teachers. While at summer camp, he mostly engaged in sports but concluded that he had acting ability. This inclined him toward the theater, and he promptly started going to performances at every opportunity, captivated by playwrights of many types—including Luigi Pirandello, Eugene O'Neill, and August Strindberg. He started taking courses in drama as well as in short story writing. In the latter he was drawn instantaneously to the short fiction of John Galsworthy, Maxim Gorky, Leonid Andreyev, and Liam O'Flaherty.

Although Maltz was still absorbed in philosophy, a desire to produce a creative work began to emerge, in a form that presaged his later writing. An uncle had been convicted of robbery and was sent to Sing Sing Prison. Probably the uncle had been guilty of a lesser offense, but he was already unpopular in the Maltz family and was now disowned by Maltz's father. Albert nonetheless chose to visit his uncle during the years of his imprisonment, and from their discussions he began to weave a concept for a play. He also drafted part of a novel that included a lynching, another sign of his enduring sensitivity to injustice. Concurrently he immersed himself in Aristotle, reasoning that the *Poetics* was the bedrock of robust dramaturgy. All these facets of his craft ultimately came together in a conviction that he could employ philosophical logic and the search for moral values in creative writing, especially in exploring the motivation of characters and the logic of events. He resolved that in his art he would always go to the facts and never make up episodes.

Maltz was drawn forthwith to the Yale School of Drama in 1930, where Professor George Pierce Baker ran a renowned workshop in playwriting that particularly appealed to Maltz's desire to pursue all sides of his art. Baker's workshop taught not only writing but also directing, lighting, scene design, and costumes, under the theory that a writer must comprehend all of these facets of theater. Among the revelations to Maltz in this new environment was that homosexuality was widely accepted in the theater as well as in the Yale department; in light of the esteem he had for the accomplishments of his new gay and lesbian colleagues, he could no longer share the derisive homophobic attitudes of many of his contemporaries. More significant was his recent acquaintance with George Sklar (1908–88), a radical from a working-class socialist family who had won a scholarship to study Latin at Yale. After graduating Phi Beta Kappa, Sklar had been unable to find a teaching position. Subsequent to taking a playwriting class at Columbia University, Sklar returned to Yale and entered the School of Drama.[14]

Maltz and Sklar started to write together in the fall of 1931, and their lives would be joined over the years in the New York theater, Hollywood screenwriting, and the era of the blacklist. By 1932 Maltz was reading the *New Masses* and talking with Sklar about Communism. Earlier Maltz, still troubled by the tribulations of his upbringing, had planned to write a personal family novel, but in 1931 Sklar urged him to read a journal article about the frame-up of a Cleveland bellboy for a gangland murder. This article became the basis of their 1932 collaboration, *Merry-Go-Round*, which opened at the Provincetown Playhouse. Centering on a portrait of the bellhop who was set up, Ed Martin, the plot was also an exposé of the corrupt politics of a large city. The subject garnered much attention, and the play subsequently made it to Broadway for six weeks, followed by a movie version, *Afraid to Talk* (1933). Sklar and Maltz then left Yale in a fruitless effort to find work in Hollywood. Returning to New York City, they found that their playwriting had drawn the attention of Charles Rumford Walker (1893–1974), the guiding spirit of the Theater Union.[15]

The Theater Union was formed in 1932 as a coalition to build a professional social theater at affordable prices, with a board comprised of members of the Socialist Party and the Communist Party as well as liberals and unaffiliated individuals. Maltz joined the executive board of the Theater Union, and another play by Maltz and Sklar was its first production. *Peace on Earth*, the depiction of a pacifist professor framed and martyred like the bellhop in *Merry-Go-Round*, ran for eighteen weeks in 1934. In 1935 came Maltz's first solo production, a full-length play called *Black Pit*. *Black Pit* continued Maltz's strategy of presenting well-researched portraits of men under political duress. A Polish mine worker, Joe Kovarsky, is taken on a long journey that begins with his imprisonment and blacklisting for union activity. By the close of the drama, poverty and exploitation have transformed him into an informer, shunned by fellow workers and forced to leave his family.

Maltz's determination to focus on a scab and informer precipitated a minor if tedious altercation in the Communist press. The realism of Maltz's setting, based on primary research that he undertook in the coalfields, was admired by all. Nonetheless, the review in the *Daily Worker* questioned Maltz's decision to give the despicable informer laudable credentials as a former union militant, since "only the rottenest and weakest elements in the working class become stool pigeons."[16] Joseph North, writing in the *New Masses*, questioned the centrality of the informer in the narrative on grounds of his atypicality, presaging the line of argument that he apparently used in his discussions with Hemingway in Spain: "It seems to me the selection of this emphasis—the stool-pigeon story—undoubtedly derives from Maltz's relatively recent initiation into proletarian environment. Else, the spectacular, this unhealthy and atypical aspect of the labor movement, would not have caught his dramatist's eye."[17] Surprisingly, Maltz was defended by a Party functionary, Jack Stachel, who argued that the problem of the stool pigeon was a vital question and that Maltz's approach was educational.[18]

WILLING EXECUTIONERS?

His experience with the Theater Union further expanded Maltz's political education. Moving beyond his earlier focus on war profiteering and race discrimination, he read Marx, Engels, and Lenin and traveled around the United States to gather material about coal miners, vigilante groups, strikes, flophouses, and tenements. Maltz had no hesitation about going directly into violent situations, such as the Flint, Michigan, sit-down strikes, or even into reactionary regions in the South. He regularly picked up hitchhikers to mine them for material, and at one point he engaged in factory work as part of his research. He soon branched out into one-act plays. "Private Hicks" (1935) was yet another portrait of martyrdom, in which a national guardsman is sent to prison for refusing to fire on striking workers. Other short plays include "Rehearsal" (1938) and a radio drama called "Red Head Baker" (1937). During the late 1930s he became recognized for distinguished short stories, starting with "Man on a Road" (1935) and "Hotel Raleigh, the Bowery" (1937; better known as "Season of Celebration") and culminating in the collection *The Way Things Are* (1938).

In the summer of 1935, Maltz inaugurated a serious relationship with Margaret Larkin (1899–1967), the executive secretary of the Theater Union and a woman whose background was markedly dissimilar from his and that of his acquaintances. With high cheekbones, smooth olive skin, and expressive dark eyes that shined with intelligence, Larkin hailed from an old English and Scottish family dating back to the seventeenth century in the United States on both sides; her great-grandfather and four of his brothers had fought under George Washington in the Revolutionary War. Born in Las Vegas, New Mexico, she was nine years older than Maltz. A committed veteran of the Communist movement, by the mid-1930s she had become a personality in radical cultural circles.

Larkin's mother wrote verse, her father sang, and Margaret learned the guitar at an early age. In the fall of 1919 she enrolled at the University of Kansas to study journalism but soon left to tour as a folksinger. By the time she arrived in New York City on the eve of the Depression to try her luck, she had authored a published prizewinning play, *El Cristo* (1926); a classic in folklore, *Singing Cowboy: A Book of Western Songs* (1931); and verse that had appeared in *Poetry* and the *Nation* magazines. Stunned and appalled by the violence she witnessed during a textile strike in New Jersey, she changed the course of her life to devote her talents to the Communist movement. In August 1929 she traveled to the site of a vicious textile strike in Gastonia, North Carolina, where she was introduced to Ella May Wiggins, famous for her singing at union meetings. Three weeks later, Wiggins was gunned down by an armed mob. Larkin took it upon herself to tell Wiggins's story in the publications to which she had access, and she published tributes and lyrics in both the *Nation* and the *New Masses*.[19] Moreover, in a style anticipating that of the young Joan Baez, she performed Wiggins's ballads at parties in the early 1930s.

Larkin had been previously married to Liston Oak, a Communist functionary who would become disillusioned with the Party's policy during the Spanish Civil War; he then passed briefly through the Trotskyist movement before becoming a fixture in the anti-Communist *New Leader* by the end of the decade. Maltz and Larkin began living together in 1936. Late in 1937 they decided to adopt a child and got married. They adopted a second child in 1942. However, early in their relationship Margaret began suffering from various illnesses, so that she was in bed and indisposed for almost half of each year from 1939 to 1950, generating burdensome medical and psychoanalytic bills. Only when Albert was imprisoned did she become roused from her afflictions, sending him a letter every day of his incarceration.

In 1951 they moved to Mexico, partly to live more cheaply but also so that Albert could extricate himself from his political responsibilities and focus on his writing. In these years Margaret became active as a research assistant to the anthropologist Oscar Lewis and worked in a family planning agency in Mexico. In 1961 she published a mystery novel, *Seven Shares in a Gold Mine*, based on her experience in a plane that was disabled by a bomb. In 1965, following research in Israel, she published *The Six Days of Yad Mordecai*, the story of a kibbutz that repulsed an attack by three Egyptian brigades in 1948. The marriage, however, dissolved in the early 1960s. Albert returned to Los Angeles, and Margaret stayed in Mexico. A divorce was finalized in 1964, and Margaret died three years later. Albert went on to marry Rosemary Wylde in 1964, and following Wylde's suicide in 1968, he married Esther Engleberg.

Maltz joined the Communist Party in the fall of 1935, shortly after his romance with Margaret Larkin began. He had been moving in that direction since 1931. In New York he associated with a branch of selected professionals, individuals whose positions meant that their Party membership could not be disclosed even to other Party members. This unique branch engaged in classes and study, but members were not assigned political work beyond attending meetings. After Christmas in 1936 Maltz went to Detroit to research material for his novel, *The Underground Stream* (1940), about a Communist auto union organizer murdered by the fascist Black Legion. There he was aided by Michigan Party leader William Weinstone. Learning that the head of the state police in Michigan delighted in reading Marxist pamphlets and then arguing with the Communists he arrested, Maltz decided to appropriate these characteristics for his chief villain, Jeffrey Grebb, who was also modeled on Harry Bennett, the head of the Ford Motor Company's security personnel.

The protagonist of the novel, the Communist auto union organizer Fred Prince (called Princey), embodies yet another example of sacrifice as a staple of Maltz's writing. Moreover, through a sequence of conflicts, Princey grapples with his sense of masculinity by striving to reconcile his total commitment to the cause with his wife's feelings of neglect. Finally, he proves his loyalty to his comrades by dying at the hands of Black Legion fascists rather than betraying their names. In the final moments of the narrative, Maltz's voice merges with Princey's thoughts to articulate a credo of left-wing manhood: *"A man must hold to his purpose. This—nothing less—is the underground stream of his life. Without it he is nothing. I cannot yield. A Man is nothing who yields his purpose"* (emphasis in original).[20] Problematically, in the context of the novel and Maltz's own future, "purpose" appears to be synonymous with blind loyalty to the Communist Party as the trustee of the interests of the working class. However, the main objection to the novel raised in the Communist press concerned its ending. Michael Gold, who in his introduction to *The Way Things Are* had praised Maltz for adding "a chord of tragedy and psychological brooding" to proletarian literature, objected that the climax focused on the martyrdom of Princey rather than on the victory of the autoworkers and the union.[21]

The late 1930s were for Maltz a time of endless political activities. He participated in a small seminar led by a Jewish Communist scholar on anti-Semitism, and he wrote the anonymous introduction to the League of American Writers pamphlet on the subject, We Hold These Truths (1939). He devoted much time to Equality, an antibigotry magazine that he had helped to found in 1939. In the League of American Writers, Maltz served as a member of the Executive Committee in 1935 and of the National Council in 1939 and 1940, and he was elected vice president in 1941. He authored numerous league statements and taught at the league's New York Writers School and elsewhere.

Early in 1941 the Maltzes moved to Los Angeles. Albert planned to find work in Hollywood with his friends from the New York theater days, George Sklar and Michael Blankfort (1907–82). Before long Maltz became attached to a Communist Party branch in the film section, remaining a member for seven months. Over the next six-and-a-half years he was in several other Party branches whose members tended to be writers, studio readers, and secretaries. He attended weekly meetings, held in different homes, where there were thoughtful discussions of the Party's programs and other issues. Although he was not involved in inner-Party work at any time, he carried out such activities as building the League of American Writers in Hollywood and reading the works-in-progress of other members. He never publicly acknowledged his Party membership, believing that, even before the notorious blacklist period, no studio would hire an open Communist. Prior to his blacklisting in 1947, he annually earned as much as $43,000; immediately after, in 1948, his income dropped to $15,500.

By the time of the 1944 publication of The Cross and the Arrow by Little, Brown and Company, Maltz was greatly esteemed in the Communist movement. With his sensitive face, wrestler's build, and an aura of decency and unshakable integrity, he was admired not only by fellow Communists but by actors, directors, and producers. His earlier fiction had been warmly praised by the rising radical literary critic Alfred Kazin and others in the popular media.[22] The first reviews of the new novel in the Communist press were positive, as were the preponderance of reviews in other publications. Then signs of an impending controversy appeared in the 3 October 1944 issue of the New Masses, where Samuel Sillen (1911–73) identified the essential question of The Cross and the Arrow: "Is there an inherent national viciousness that pre-ordains the Germans to be accomplices in the aggressive brutishness of their militaristic leaders? Or does the ghastly corruption of civilized values in Germany betray a rottenness at the core of mankind?" Sillen sees the genius of the novel in Maltz's dual focus. The novel effectively explained the precise circumstances under which Willi Wegler came to an understanding that Germans like himself, who did not regard themselves as Nazis, were nonetheless complicit in the horrors of the regime and thus had a responsibility to resist. At the same time, the novel was able to transcend "its particular subject matter, enabling us to understand human types everywhere. It does not comfort us with the illusion that only in one country could men descend to such evil depths, nor does it suggest that fascism is a mystic inflection of the German bloodstream." While Sillen felt that more might have been added about the particularity of German social conditions shaping the distinctive expression of "anti-human reaction," he saw the novel as optimistic in that it augured hope for the post-Nazi German future. The character expressing views close to Vansittartism, Dr. Zoder, is lost in passivity and cynicism as he awaits the complete destruction of his hopelessly corrupt fellow countrymen.[23]

A week later, the *Worker Magazine* section of the *Sunday Worker* featured a commentary by writer Howard Fast (1914–2003), who agreed that the novel "is not only a tale of Germany, but of all people." Fast noted that the portrait of Wegler is that of "a good man" by the norms of most societies that privilege the minding of one's own business, and that the novel is "as complete and merciless an indictment of our times as has appeared on paper." However, Fast seems to have suspected that Maltz's choice of subject, a good German, might cause a controversy, as had Maltz's previous portraits of an informer in *Black Pit* and a Communist martyr in *The Underground Stream*. Consequently Fast insisted that Maltz's novel should in no way "aid the 'soft peace' crowd," because its indictment of fascism was ferocious. Rather, the novel served as a warning to the United States and intended to aid citizens in comprehending humanity even at its worst.[24]

In view of the compulsion of Sillen and Fast to defend Maltz against potential critics, it was not a complete surprise when the *Worker* published a second, more fault-finding review six months later, called "The Problem of German Evil in *The Cross and the Arrow*." The author, Harry Martel, the educational director of a union, who had a particular interest in Marxist philosophy and ethics, faulted Maltz for suggesting that German "evil" was similar to other evils in the twentieth century and for ostensibly disapproving of the view that "the German people as a whole must pay the cost of their defeat." Martel's appraisal entailed a virtual identification of "Germans" with "Nazis." He insisted that, inasmuch as "evil has penetrated the pores and mental processes of Germans," it was contradictory for Maltz to use a German worker to demonstrate "the emergence of Good out of the Evil that is Germany." Martel postulated that the novel lent itself to a melange of antithetical interpretations. He closed by stressing that Maltz's principal error was in his failure to recognize "that quantity turns into quality, and that the qualitative uniqueness of German evil, so excoriatingly exposed by Ilya Ehrenburg, is the basic fact that must shape our judgments."[25]

Martel's critique turned out to be unpopular among readers of the Communist paper. The deluge of protest letters sympathetic to Maltz was so great that the issue of 1 April 1945 featured three rebuttals to Martel with no rejoinder. Robert Raven, a blinded veteran of Spain, argued that Maltz's approach "strengthens our hatred, and makes it more intelligent," and is superior to simply adopting "the Nazi concept in reverse, that Germans are by their nature 'sub-men.'" Raven insisted that, while acknowledging the unique features of "German evil" due to the Germans' embracing of fascism, Maltz was justified in using Wegler to illustrate that other potentials exist: "The crimes of German fascism are not qualitatively, but quantitatively, different from that of the crimes of fascists of other nations."[26] But another response, by National Maritime Union official Howard Silverberg, seemed to confirm Martel's point about the ambiguity of the narrative. Silverberg insisted that The Cross and the Arrow was precisely about the "qualitative uniqueness" of "German evil" and "the first successful literary analysis of the exact nature of the guilt of the German people to come from any pen other than Ehrenburg's." Silverberg saw Wegler's act of desperate resistance not as a token of "goodness" but more as a symbol of the kind of "payment" the German people as a whole will have to make as part of their "rehabilitation." Maltz's "contribution" was to show the German people to be "crocodiles with human heads, human speech, and a vast well of tears—but crocodiles none the less."[27]

That the novel partly served as a litmus test for its readers' diverse reactions to the enigma of calibrating the ordinary German's accountability for Nazi atrocities is further confirmed by Maltz's copy of one of the unpublished communications to the Worker. The author was Brooklyn College Communist philosophy professor Howard Selsam, who argued that the "qualitative" difference in Germany was not in the "Nazi hangmen, murderers, torturers," because "individuals just as evil and perverted" can be "found in other times and places." What has never been seen before, however, is "a whole people, a whole nation, act as one with such individuals. The qualitative change here is that never before has such degeneracy and wickedness become accepted, unified, recognized national policy." Thus the logic of Maltz's novel is that "punishment must be visited on the people as a whole," with retribution "exacted from the German nation, and not from just as many individuals."[28]

To be fair, a more detached reading of the novel might suggest that Maltz did, indeed, have doubts about the wisdom of "collective punishment," but Soviet policy was so adamant on the matter that it is improbable that he would have asserted them.[29] More intriguing is Selsam's conjecture that the particular crimes of German fascism were part and parcel of modern civilization. What was unique about Nazism—the "qualitative" difference—was the open and explicit national acceptance of such crimes. Selsam's thinking flowed logically from the dramatic and symbolic action of *The Cross and the Arrow* but went beyond explicit references in the text. His speculation invites attention to the perspicacity as well as the defects of the body of writing that would be bequeathed by most of the Jewish American novelists with Communist backgrounds and sympathies who came to dominate World War II fiction in the 1940s and early 1950s.

Maltz's calling attention to German opposition to fascism, which resonates with his portrayals of resistance and martyrdom in his earlier works, was disregarded by almost every other left-wing novelist who wrote about the anti-Nazi crusade in Europe during World War II. Like Mike Gold, other writers variously leaned toward the view that practically all "Germans were willing to be instruments of the insane program" of the Nazis. Maltz's novel is likewise in accord with his earlier writings in its failure to include a Jewish character (or at least a surrogate Jew) among the protagonists. Indeed, Maltz's fiction and drama of the Depression and World War II years was distinctive for its lack of autobiographical elements. He customarily depicted individuals whom he had met and situations that he had researched firsthand, but when a "Maltz-like" character appeared, he was in the background, such as the driver in "Man on a Road."

Maltz believed fervently in his obligation to personally defy and resist anti-Semitism. Yet he customarily deflected the issue in his drama and fiction of the 1930s and 1940s. Conceivably Maltz anticipated that his attempts to clarify the conduct of men brutally trapped by the systems under which they lived would implicitly create a broader human cognizance of social evil that would include a revulsion to anti-Semitism. He also declined to show acts of personal revenge and retaliation by his victims of oppression, preferring to highlight their exemplary acts of self-sacrifice. Although his main characters—Private Hicks, Princey, and Willi Wegler—may have resisted and even revolted, their deeds are never aimed at a particular people and they all paid the ultimate price. In this sense his writing, at some distance from his personality and political stances, was not truly expressive of the "tough Jew," who tended to imaginatively unleash vengeful Golems in his literary efforts.

"AN EYE FOR AN EYE"

Diametrically the opposite of Albert Maltz in this regard was Irwin Shaw (1913–84; born Irwin Shamforoff).[30] At the outset of his career, Shaw was the Jewish pro-Communist writer of his generation most devoted to sensational dramatizations of brutal retaliation against oppression, accentuating the need for Jewish avengers. Shaw's archetypal fantasy of violence, "Residents of Other Cities," appeared in *Esquire* in 1939. It was reprinted in his first collection, *Sailor off the Bremen and Other Stories*, that same year, but thereafter it was omitted from all subsequent anthologies of his work. Set in Kiev at the height of the post–Russian Revolution civil war in 1918, the story recounts the ordeal of the sixteen-year-old Jew Daniel, an aspiring painter.

Daniel repeatedly witnesses pro-czarist soldiers and anti-Semitic mobs physically and sexually humiliating members of his family. Subsequently non-Jewish neighbors, the Kirovs, volunteer to hide and protect Daniel and his relatives in their basement, but they end up gang-raping Daniel's aunt and bayonetting her protesting husband. Daniel fantasizes a brutal revenge, and when the Bolsheviks seize the town, he obtains a gun from the compassionate Red Army soldiers. Accompanied by one of these armed fighters, the boy coldly executes every male who participated in the crimes of the Kirov family. Daniel regrets only that "they had died too easily. They had not suffered enough pain. They had come off best in the bargain, finally."

A commanding feature of the story is the ongoing debate between the Jewish father and son about a suitable reprisal for the anti-Semitic outrages that they have endured together. Daniel's father offered no resistance and is persuaded of the immorality of killing for any purpose. The father's response would be more fathomable if it had been due to cowardice or a sober assessment of the relationship of forces, but it seems to have been determined by a conviction that Jews are meant to be nonviolent. Bloodshed is a barbarism perpetrated by non-Jews; even when wronged, "it is not our part to punish." At the climactic moment, the father urges his son not to shoot the Kirov men, and he even lies to the Bolshevik soldier in an attempt to halt the slaughter. But Daniel's mother and aunt take Daniel's side.[31]

The depiction of the father is uncharitable in that Shaw identifies his indefensible conduct with a weak religiosity. Shaw, however, is also mindful of establishing that the father stands for only one current within the Jewish community that is not to be identified with all Jews, or especially with all believing Jews. Daniel's brother, David, also dreams of violent revenge; his uncle, Samuel, is killed trying to prevent the rape of his wife; and, of course, his mother and victimized aunt endorse David's views. The Bolsheviks are depicted sympathetically. They defeat the anti-Semitic pro-czarists and they assist the Jews. However, Daniel's alliance with them is expedient, not ideological. They and the new Soviet regime that they represent enable Daniel to carry out the Old Testament injunction "an eye for an eye."

A no less shocking, but far better known, variant of the same situation can be seen in Shaw's "Sailor off the *Bremen*," also published in 1939. This hair-raising story gained extra notoriety because it fell outside the *New Yorker*'s traditional practice of avoiding violent tales and its customary word limit on short fiction. Prior to the beginning of Shaw's narrative, a group of Communists, including a gentle artist named Ernest, staged a protest at the New York docks onboard the German ship *Bremen*, in league with a secret Communist German deck officer, Preminger. In the melee that followed, a group of German ship stewards surrounded Ernest. Two held him while a particularly vicious steward, a Nazi Party member from Austria named Lueger, pounded Ernest's face, knocking out his teeth, blinding him in one eye, and permanently deforming his features.

In a meeting at the apartment of Ernest and his wife, Sally, a brutal retribution is plotted. Ernest's older brother, Charley, a non-Communist college football player, suggests that Sally lure Lueger, a notorious womanizer, off the ship and take him to Twelfth Street in Greenwich Village. There Charley, assisted by a mild-mannered dentist named Dr. Stryker, will jump Lueger and extract the appropriate revenge. Ernest urges his brother and Stryker not to do this, expressing his Communist view: "It is not a personal thing. . . . It is the movement against Fascism. You don't stop Fascism with a personal crusade against one German." The German Communist, Preminger, who has firsthand familiarity with the Nazis, dissents. "Speaking as a Party member," he agrees with Ernest; however, "speaking as a man," he is with Charley.[32] The scheme works, and Lueger is pulverized by Charley in an unforgettably grisly beating.

The brothers are never identified as Jewish. However, there is an autobiographical parallel in that Shaw, a Brooklyn College football star, had a younger brother, David, who was an artist and for whom he felt protective.[33] Moreover, the high proportion of Jews in the Manhattan branch of the Communist Party, especially those who would relish an anti-Nazi action, makes it likely that the brothers are Jewish. Jewishness itself, however, is not stated as Shaw's theme, and the anti-Semitism of the Nazis is never explicitly mentioned.

Shaw's message is aimed at all those menaced by a violent, fascist-like enemy. One must not be deterred by abstract considerations that allow no immediate response, such as Ernest's explanation of the Communist Party line, and one must take any assault personally. As Charley put it: "I am disregarding the class struggle, I am disregarding the education of the proletariat, I am disregarding the fact that you are a good Communist. I am acting strictly in the capacity of your brother." Ernest's assessment of Charley is that "he has a football player's philosophy. Somebody knocks you down, you knock him down, everything is fine."[34]

Shaw's agreement with his stance, analogous to Daniel's revenge against the

Kirovs, is indisputable. Yet Shaw knows that the "football philosophy" is at bottom an emotional response that contains latent dangers, one of which is succumbing to group prejudice, ironically, a leading characteristic of the fascists. Preminger narrates the events on the *Bremen* in a manner that incites Charley's bias; he refers to "my people, the Germans," by saying that "you must always expect the worst from them." Moreover, even though Lueger has been clearly identified to Charley as an Austrian, Stryker calls him a "lousy German bastard" in the moments prior to the assault.

Stryker's behavior during the assault further suggests an element of corruption. Although he fears to participate in the actual violence and turns his head from the carnage, he puffs up like a gangster when a passing car slows down: "'Keep moving,' he said, very toughly, 'if you know what's good for you.'" Also compromising the idealism of Charley's actions are implications that, for Charley, his motivation may be as much a desire for masculine domination as seeking revenge for his brother. He consistently compares the assault on Lueger with the action in a football game and insists on using his hands instead of a weapon. Moreover, he employs his brother's wife as sexual bait and then makes certain that the damage inflicted by the beating will make Lueger unattractive to women in the future. As he pounds Lueger, he makes no mention of politics or even his brother, only muttering, "Oh, you dumb, mean, skirtchasing, sonofabitch, bastard." [35]

Significantly, the weakness associated with the Jewish father in "Residents of Other Cities" is here transferred to Sally. At the last minute, she cannot stomach complicity in the beating and tries to warn Lueger. This is an act of betrayal, comparable to the lies of Daniel's father on behalf of the Kirovs; it reinforces the identification of courage and honor with masculinity. Charley sobs while clobbering Lueger, but this only underscores the intense relief he feels at finishing the job properly—after a prolonged and thorough beating systematically designed to break Lueger's nose, knock out his teeth, tear loose his jaw, and blind his eye. Unlike Daniel's wail of frustration and dissatisfaction at the ease of his revenge, Charley knows when he has been appeased and contentedly withdraws on his own terms.

There is no evidence that Shaw ever engaged in such violence; during World War II he carried a rifle but never shot at anyone. Yet the kinship of Charley through his brother Ernest to the Communist Party is useful for achieving a biographical vantage point from which to examine Shaw's personal political commitment in the late 1930s. Charley has his own agenda, yet Communism is near at hand in the person of his brother, to whom he is devoted. Charley's actions against the Nazi stem from his emotional response to an assault on a loved one by an evil fascist. His individual solution is heretical from the perspective of Communist political strategy; yet it is nevertheless attractive to the German Communist militant, Preminger, as well as two others who also love Ernest, Sally and Stryker, weak individuals who have to be pulled along by a Golem-like avenging force.

Shaw's dramatization of Charley's reluctance to completely embrace the Communist Party, however, is not principally political. After all, the Communists' politics inspired his fictional characters to take the initiative against the *Bremen*. Lueger, who shows Sally a picture of Hitler in his watchcase, is a malignant representative of the swastika-sporting ship vaunted by the Nazi regime. Rather, Shaw's criticism is that the total ideological immersion of most Communist Party members blots out their normal, human reactions, which may be emotional but are nonetheless necessary. Ernest is so devoted to the Party's belief in the effectiveness of mass action that he voluntarily placed himself in a perilous situation for which he was unsuited. Ernest's change in personality and loss of the capacity to paint after his beating suggest that his subordination of self to ideology prevented him from grasping the potential consequences of his actions against the fascists. Preminger is more explicit in affirming that his manhood demands Charley's revenge on Lueger, his Communist Party image of himself notwithstanding. Dr. Stryker, apparently a fellow traveler, insists that he is motivated by a belief that the vengeance will heal Ernest, but he steps outside his selfless persona by reveling in his own vicarious acquisition of a sense of masculine power.

The parallels between "Residents of Other Cities" and "Sailor off the *Bremen*" are conspicuous. The debate is between those who carry out the biblical injunction of "an eye for an eye" and those who are opposed to behaving as badly as one's enemies because of either ethical considerations or politics that deflect what Shaw sees as a human response. The enemies are anti-Semites, although this paramount aspect of the Nazis is not emphasized but subordinated to a broader perspective on the evil of fascism. In both instances, a son acts in the absence of a father. In both stories Communists facilitate revenge while not directly participating in it. Indeed, that one must not only participate in but have full control over revenge seems crucial; perhaps this is why Daniel's using a borrowed gun seems to be less satisfying than if he had used his own knife to kill the Kirov males.

Yet there are also curious contrasts. In "Residents of Other Cities," the avenger of the violated woman is a painter; in "Sailor off the *Bremen*," the violated person is a painter and the avenger is an athlete—a type of Jew not found often in the literature of the Eastern European Jewish ghettos. In the former story, the victimized woman supports revenge; in the latter, the male victim is opposed to revenge, and his wife commits a last-minute betrayal. Clearly Shaw's visions of violence were not produced according to a seamless, doctrinaire philosophy but were interconnected with issues in his background and psychology. The plot in "Residents of Other Cities" involved a Jew taking direct action. Yet the Jew, at least in his Eastern European setting, neither was trained nor had the necessary resources to carry out a fully satisfactory act of revenge; he required the indispensable aid of a Red Army soldier. In "Sailor off the *Bremen*," the Americanized Jew, a football player, remote from Jewish tradition but no less devoted to defense of his people, becomes a Golem—one fashioned out of the new soil of the United States but ultimately beholden to no one but himself. From what family, culture, and social circumstances did Irwin Shaw, the creator of such narratives, arise?

Shaw was five years younger than Albert Maltz, and the two men were barely acquainted. Although they shared many superficial features of background and early careers, a closer investigation lays bare a contrast at every point. Both were from immigrant Jewish families, although Shaw's parents were lower on the economic ladder. Both were obsessed with sports in their youth, although Shaw's prowess was more natural and less forced. Both began as politically radical playwrights, although Shaw toiled his way from the bottom, graduating to Broadway and the Left theater movement from radio hackwork rather than from the Yale School of Drama. Both were drawn to the Communist movement in the early 1930s, although Shaw stayed organizationally at an arm's length and began to differentiate himself from the Party as early as 1940–41.

Shaw's father, William, born in the Ukraine, dreamed of becoming Americanized and became a land speculator during the boom of the early 1920s. Yet by the end of the decade, he had brought the family literally to the brink of impoverishment. Shaw's mother, the American-born artistic daughter of a Lithuanian Jewish intellectual, instilled in their two sons, Irwin and David, a love of music and literature. Like Albert Maltz, the young Shaw felt the anguish of anti-Semitism. However, in Shaw's case the cause was primarily a reaction to the shame his parents had to endure when their fortune crumbled, as if their plunge into poverty was the result of William's status as a Jewish immigrant. Irwin chose to respond by affirming his Jewishness, even if only outwardly. Although his father changed the family name from Shamforoff to Shaw for business reasons shortly after settling in Brooklyn, Irwin continued to call himself Shamforoff until his enrollment in college. He also demanded a bar mitzvah, although his parents were so committed to assimilation that they were reluctant to speak Yiddish.

Shaw also had a craving to prove himself among his Christian friends. Before the family's financial disaster, he had daydreams of attending Princeton University, and his love of football flew in the face of his parents' view that the sport was "goyim nochas"—a game inappropriate for Jews.[36] According to Shaw's biographer, the precocious student who graduated high school at fifteen took "as much pride in his athletic prowess as in his writing."[37] In the end, his rugged, brawny build and thick Brooklyn accent, in tandem with commercial success in film and popular novels, would always present obstacles to his being taken seriously by the literary elite, which was his abiding goal.

THE NATURAL

Even as he struggled through Brooklyn College, at that time attended mainly by Jews, Irwin Shaw sustained a dream of becoming a writer as he secured his primary standing as a varsity quarterback. Shaw was a "natural" at both sports and writing. Unlike Maltz, who determinedly researched every subject for his books and agonized over plot, structure, character, and psychological motivation, Shaw's words flowed in stories and columns that showed a high degree of professionalism. Later he would brag that he never rewrote any of his original drafts and that many of his first stories came to him in a day at most.[38] He was taken under the wing of speech professor David Driscoll, who admired Shaw's efforts at playwriting and who produced a number of Shaw's short dramas on the campus. An English professor, David McKelvey White, was so taken with Shaw's talent that he told him that he worried that "you're going to be successful too early."[39]

Shaw found a cheap way to see classic dramas by Henrik Ibsen, Anton Chekhov, Leo Tolstoy, and Maxim Gorky at the Civic Repertory Theater. He read widely in Balzac, Chekhov, Tolstoy, the Romantic poets, the Old Testament, Homer, Thomas Wolfe, William Faulkner, and Aldous Huxley. Hemingway held a magnetic attraction for Shaw, not only because of his literary style but for his larger-than-life persona as a sportsman, drinker, and womanizer. To make money, Shaw churned out English papers for New York University students to whom he was introduced by an old friend. He evinced no evident political consciousness during his college years, although David McKelvey White was a Communist who later resigned his position to fight for the Spanish Republic. The tenor of Shaw's newspaper column at Brooklyn College emitted the aura of a young man cynical and embittered, although simultaneously self-confident. On two occasions his published campus writings got him into difficulty with the administration—not for radicalism but for insinuating obscenity and disrespect.

When Shaw graduated from Brooklyn College in 1934, he had no job prospects and continued living at home. Then David Driscoll put him in touch with a radio producer. Soon Shaw was writing scripts for a series based on the *Dick*

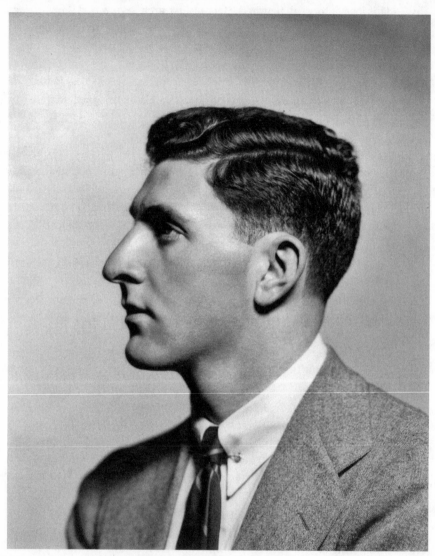

IRWIN SHAW, a left-wing playwright and fiction writer of the 1930s, dramatized antifascist themes. (From the Shaw Collection in the Howard Gotlieb Archival Research Center at Boston University)

Tracy and *Gumps* comic strips. For the next two years Shaw turned out five scripts in the first three days of the week, then devoted most of the rest of the week to his own short stories and plays. He found that he could make a living as a writer and even provide for his family. Never again would he take a job outside the writing profession.

Shaw found immense enjoyment in writing and began deluging the magazine market with short fiction in 1934. Following an initial lack of success, he changed to writing plays. A year later, his most notable play, *Bury the Dead* (1936), appeared on Broadway. It was a robust, one-act, agitprop play similar in form and strategy to Clifford Odets's *Waiting for Lefty* (1935), which it equaled in popularity. As his main characters, Shaw used dead soldiers who recount uncomplicated, poignant narratives of how they died and what they yearned for when they were alive. For decades after, the play was performed throughout the world to assail war as the instrument of corrupt rulers despoiling youth for their own greedy ends.

Bury the Dead, together with some notoriety Shaw had obtained from his radio writing, led to his first Hollywood film contract, *The Big Game* (1936). He was thereby launched on a fifteen-year trajectory of shuffling among theater, fiction, and film on two coasts, concluding only when he became an expatriate in Paris in 1951. Film was the primary source of his income during the Depression and World War II years, although not many of his films became classics.[40] Among his subsequent plays, only *The Gentle People: A Brooklyn Fable* (1939) was moderately successful. Others have vanished from memory, including *Siege* (1937), *Second Mortgage* (1938), *Quiet City* (1939), *Retreat to Pleasure* (1940), *The Shy and the Lonely* (1941), *Sons and Soldiers* (1944), *The Assassin* (1946), and *The Survivors* (1948; with Peter Viertel). Collections of his short fiction, however, mostly from the *New Yorker*, continued to augment his standing in the 1940s: *Sailor off the Bremen and Other Stories* (1939), *Welcome to the City and Other Stories* (1942), and *Act of Faith and Other Stories* (1946). Finally, with his World War II novel, *The Young Lions* (1948), Shaw established himself as a major-league player in the literary arena. Starting in the mid-1930s, Shaw's Hollywood connections also consolidated his ties with the Communist movement. These were always tenuous and mainly formed through personal and professional friendships and political affinities rather than adherence to the full Communist Party program. They were, nevertheless, consequential in understanding his fiction and drama.

Doubtless in response to the mood among young intellectuals in the early 1930s, Shaw, like Maltz, cut his literary teeth on his censure of war as a butchery of ordinary people on behalf of the affluent and powerful. The politics of *Bury the Dead* dovetailed with Communist antimilitarism while at the same time being attractive to non-Communist radicals, including pacifists.[41] As the antifascist mood grew after the beginning of the Spanish Civil War in 1936, Shaw turned increasingly to a theme that ordinary people must actively strike back against evil, most famously dramatized in *The Gentle People*. In this "Brooklyn fable," a middle-aged Jew, Goodman, unites with a Greek worker, Anagnos, to exultantly murder the gangster, Goff. Goff has been extorting money from both men by making them pay for "protection," as well as seducing and corrupting Goodman's daughter. The Left politics of the play reflect the Communist view (it debuted six months before the Hitler-Stalin Pact) yet go further. The Jew is an old socialist, and the gangster is several times associated with Hitler and Mussolini, in addition to having a past as a strikebreaker. As was the case with the response to Maltz's *Black Pit*, Communist publications acclaimed the play's political rectitude (especially its call to stop appeasement) yet also warned against its heretical dimension (the privileging of individualist rather than collective action).[42]

In later years Shaw would proudly embrace his antifascist past, giving special weight to his support of the Spanish Republic's resistance to Franco. In 1980, long after he had become resolutely anti-Communist, he told an interviewer that he had been on the Left "mostly because of the Spanish Civil War." But he qualified his statement by contending that giving money to the Abraham Lincoln Brigade was "about as far as my Leftism went."[43] He omitted entirely any references to his pro-Sovietism, a partisanship that was quite normal for many individuals with antifascist politics, liberals as well as radicals, in the Popular Front years, insofar as the Soviet Union was perceived as taking the most significant steps against Hitler. However, antifascism alone or even a vague appreciation of the Soviet Union as "progressive" cannot account for Shaw's signature, along with 122 others, on a very specific 1938 statement giving unequivocal support to the Moscow Trials verdict condemning to death alleged "Trotskyite-Bukharinite traitors."[44]

Shaw was ordinarily very careful, suspicious, and self-protective when making political commitments; if he were merely pro-Soviet on a broad antifascist basis, he need not have taken sides in the conflict between Stalin and Trotsky and others whom the brutal dictator sought to eliminate in his quest for personal power. Debate about the validity of the trials had been widespread among U.S. intellectuals since 1936, and Shaw could not have been unaware that other antifascists and radicals believed that the trials were a sham.[45]

Moreover, when the news of the 1939 Hitler-Stalin Pact broke, Shaw did not unite with those writers who protested by publicly leaving the Communist-led League of American Writers. Some, like Malcolm Cowley (1898–1989) and Granville Hicks (1901–82), had also signed the 1938 statement, but they wished to be able to continue to pursue militant antifascism after the Party abandoned the

Popular Front. Instead, Shaw became one of the teachers at the league's Hollywood School for Writers set up in 1940 in the wake of the Hitler-Stalin Pact, in part to provide a home for those who stuck with the Party during the pact.[46] Shaw was listed as a teacher at the school through 1942, although Albert Maltz recalled that Shaw had begun to move toward a pro-war position after the battle of Dunkirk in the spring of 1940.[47] This is confirmed by the recollections of his close friend Peter Viertel, who was also opposed to the pact and bonded with Shaw during this period.[48] Shaw's political evolution was perhaps announced in a 1942 entry in *Twentieth Century Authors: A Biographical Dictionary*, where he stated, "My political convictions are liberal."[49] Before then, the evidence confirms the recollection of writer Budd Schulberg that Shaw "seemed to maintain a quizzical attitude toward the party itself while being sympathetic toward the general movement."[50]

Shaw's bid to be taken seriously as an artist was above all else based on his commitment to the dramatization of the personal dimensions of political concerns—war, violence, and exploitation—in his plays and much of his fiction. Lionel Trilling argued in the early 1950s that Shaw "has undertaken the guidance of the moral and political emotions of a large and important class of people, those whom he once called 'the gentle people.'"[51] During and after World War II, Shaw's work began to receive increasingly harsh treatment in the Communist press, as his distance from the Party became more pronounced. Nevertheless, it is hard to detect any pointed criticism of the Soviet Union or the Stalinist character of the Communist Party in the United States in Shaw's creative work or public statements of the era. Such reproaches emerged only with the advent of the postwar Red Scare and were precipitated by the appearance of Shaw's name as an alleged Communist in *Red Channels*, a publication purporting to expose Communists in the entertainment industry.

In 1947 when Shaw was called a Communist by Jack Warner, vice president of Warner Bros., he wrote an opinion piece for the *New York Times* on 2 November distancing himself from the Party and the *New Masses*.[52] In 1950 he went further. In a letter to the *New York Times*, he explained his efforts to prevent Communist groups abroad from performing *Bury the Dead* and branded Communists as "double-tongued" and "killers."[53] In 1951 he published *The Troubled Air*, the story of Clement Archer, the director of a popular radio show called *University Town*. Archer is commanded by his show's sponsor and the station management to fire five suspected Communist employees who have been named in a red-baiting newsletter circulated in the industry called *Blueprint*. Out of respect for Archer's integrity, the sponsor allows Archer a grace period of two weeks to ascertain the truth of the accusations before determining what course he will take. Although

Archer ends up blacklisted himself and joins the opposition to the witch hunt, Shaw's novel was as anti-Communist as it was anti-McCarthy and included references to the possibility of U.S. Communists performing espionage for the Soviet Union.

Communists, although habitually treated as being imperfect, had never been truly demonized in any of Shaw's fiction or drama before *The Troubled Air*. The callow radicals Matthew and Ernest in *Sons and Soldiers*, the dogmatic Communist Lucien Gerard in *The Assassin*, and the tough-talking Abraham Lincoln Brigade recruiter Parrish in *The Young Lions* are neither evil nor sinister. For the most part, Communists represent the more committed sections of society and are depicted as individuals willing to take progressive actions at personal risk in spite of—or perhaps because of—a naive faith in humanity. As Victor Carnick says to Andrew in *Sons and Soldiers*, "I admire communists. They subsist on a noble delusion. They think that the human race is reasonable. I laugh at them, but I'm glad to know that such people exist."[54] In *The Young Lions*, the New York liberal intellectual Michael Whitacre compares himself unfavorably with the Communist Parrish at the outset of the novel: Parrish is willing to fight and die for his convictions, while Whitacre can barely salve his conscience by contributing money to the Abraham Lincoln Brigade. Only in the final pages of the novel, when Whitacre, now a soldier in World War II, personally hunts down and coldly executes the Nazi, Christian Diestl, does he redeem himself and achieve manly self-respect.

Indeed, whatever the idiosyncrasies of his political migration from 1930s radicalism to 1940s liberalism, Shaw was closely bonded to a number of individuals in and around the Communist Party during both decades. These personal connections to some extent explain Shaw's reluctance to engage in activities that might be construed as red-baiting, although some critics considered this a tactical opportunism that they linked to his supposed literary flaws, such as his tendencies to state the obvious, rely on simple characterizations of complex issues, and lapse into sentimentalism. In 1956 Leslie Fiedler described Shaw as "not a Communist a month past the time when being a Communist seems (to the most enlightened) a credible excess; not against war a month past the point when true liberalism demands it . . . able to read the right books in the morning but play a good game of tennis in the afternoon."[55]

Most vital among the various individuals binding Shaw to the broad Left was his first wife, the actress Marion Edwards, whom he met in 1936. At the time she was earnestly dating her high school sweetheart Richard Collins, who was already en route to becoming a notable Hollywood Communist.[56] Marion's closest friend was Virginia "Jigee" Ray, to whom Shaw was also attracted. By her own account, Jigee held membership in the Communist Party from 1936 to 1945. In 1936 Jigee married the screenwriter Budd Schulberg, who likewise became affiliated with the Communist movement that year.[57] In 1940 Jigee began an affair with the young novelist Peter Viertel, scion of a famous left-wing Hollywood family, who had been a Communist fellow traveler.[58]

Shaw, who was close to both men, knew about the adulterous liaison and protected Viertel. Viertel finally married Jigee after her divorce in 1944. By the start of the 1950s, the political and personal ties of Shaw's friends had become hazardous to everyone. Unexpectedly, Collins, Schulberg, and Jigee's sister appeared as friendly witnesses at the HUAC investigations in 1951. Jigee, soon caught up in a romance with Hollywood Ten victim Ring Lardner Jr., bitterly scorned the others. Yet in 1956 Jigee became an informer, naming her ex-husband Budd Schulberg, Ring Lardner Jr., Albert Maltz, and many others as Communists.[59] Shaw and his wife had good reason to fear that they might be implicated in some manner, which accounts in part for Shaw's 1950 *New York Times* letter, some aspects of his *The Troubled Air*, and their flight to Europe at the outset of the 1951 hearings.

The Communists in *The Troubled Air* are different from those in Shaw's earlier work. The memories and images of Communist idealism and self-sacrifice are still there as explanations for why individuals joined or at least collaborated with Communists. The actress Frances Motherwell, who proudly admitted to Clement Archer her Communist membership, provides the following description of the pilot, killed in World War II, who inspired her to join: "Back in college, he'd had a couple of friends in the Party and they'd been very good about Mexicans and Chinese and Jews and Negroes and a living wage for apricot-pickers and things like that. Then, to prove they weren't kidding, they went off and got themselves killed in Spain."[60] Motherwell, however, turns out to be mentally unbalanced. When called on to address a protest rally against *Blueprint* at the novel's climax, she announces that she has become an anti-Communist and proceeds to reveal the names of secret Party members to the audience.

More consequential for Shaw's new appraisal of Communism in the novel is Victor Herres, a former college football hero turned radio actor. Herres was the favorite student of Archer in the 1930s when Archer taught history at a midwestern college; subsequently, Herres persuaded Archer to come to New York to embark on a career in radio. During more than a decade of intimate friendship between the Archer family and the Herres family, Archer presumed that Herres's politics were confined to a sympathy for antifascist causes and unions.

Archer explains to Herres that he is going to put his reputation on the line by insisting to the show's sponsor that Herres has no Party affiliation; Herres confirms that he is not a Party member and encourages Archer to report this to the sponsor. Alas, Herres turns out to be one of the secret Party members exposed by Frances Motherwell. Worse, he is the head of the Party unit, and in an act of unspeakable treachery, he concocts a maneuver to provide information to the witch hunters, including a forged signature on a document, implicating Archer as pro-Communist.

Herres's wife, Nancy, loves him but recognizes that he is a fanatic. She makes it clear to a bewildered Archer that Victor would sacrifice anyone to the Communist cause, "because he thinks he's so reasonable and a reasonable man gives up little things like a friend or a wife for the future of the world." Moreover, Victor and other members of the Communist Party were certain that, whatever betrayal they committed, a man of Archer's character would "still fight their battle for them just the same." Her characterization of her husband as "so God-damn logical and disciplined and cold as ice," echoes a previous revelation experienced by Archer.[61] It came at the time he witnessed a Communist longshoreman exploit the funeral oration he was delivering for the composer, Manfred Pokorny, who committed suicide when faced with deportation: "God, Archer thought, the Communists don't understand anything because they are not human."[62] To be sure, murkier versions of such descriptions can be traced back to "Sailor off the *Bremen*," where Charley realized that a fervent submission to Party ideology blocked out normal, human responses. Is Shaw in 1951 revising his own politics to accommodate the realization that Charley's idealistic Communist brother, Ernest, was in 1939 en route to becoming a Victor Herres?

While an isolated reading of the text might suggest precisely that, imparting to the novel a theme similar to the chastened liberalism of Lionel Trilling's *The Middle of the Journey* (1947),[63] its curious autobiographical references prompt an alternate reading far more entangling and engaging. Archer appears to be Shaw's spokesman in the novel, like John Laskell in Trilling's *The Middle of the Journey*; yet it is Herres who has by far the closest resemblance to Shaw. Herres is a former star college football quarterback with a broken nose, and he brims with confidence. A natural at sports and in his profession as an actor, with a commercial radio background that parallels Shaw's trajectory, he is also a veteran of World War II. Dissimilar are Herres's blond hair, his wealthy background, and of course his choice to lead a secret life as the head of a Communist Party unit.

Archer is more likely a composite of Shaw's two influential college professors, David Driscoll and David McKelvey White. Following Shaw's graduation from college, Driscoll was offered a job writing radio scripts by a former student, Himan Brown (later a famous broadcaster who was attacked by *Red Channels*),[64] paralleling the manner in which Herres entices Archer into the field. Driscoll arranged for Shaw to join him in radio and also loaned Shaw money with the same generosity that Archer makes loans in *The Troubled Air*.

The character of Archer may be traced to White as well. Like Archer, White had become bald at an early age[65] and has an Ohio background (Archer taught college in Ohio, and White was the son of the former governor of Ohio). He achieved what Shaw considered to be martyrdom as the victim of a treacherous informer during the Rapp-Coudert anti-Communist hearings.[66] Moreover, Herres had first seen Marx's *Das Kapital* on Archer's bookshelf and borrowed it, which may well be a reference to the influence of White's Communist beliefs on Shaw. Finally, in a devastating moment of truth, Archer's long-suffering wife, Kitty, accuses him of romantic infatuation with his younger friends, Nancy and Victor Herres, which accounts for his blindness to their faults and extraordinary willingness to sacrifice himself for them. Pointing to the sad condition of their own sexual intimacy, Nancy declares that Archer is "in love" with both his young friends to the point where "it's sick. It's psychopathic." She describes Archer as "a middle-aged man tagging after another man like a puppy, calling him up all the time like a kid calling up his girl, running to him with your troubles, bringing gifts to his children, mooning over his wife."[67]

In reality, Shaw's mentor White was a proud bisexual, which was known to several of his students, one of whom he brought under his wing as a prelude to a sexual relationship.[68] White and Shaw were personally close, and it was White who took the good-looking young football star as his guest to the first classical music concert, Brahms at Carnegie Hall, that Shaw attended. If Shaw was not fully aware of White's sexual orientation, he may have detected some sign of it or had heard rumors. In the personal dynamics between Archer and Herres there is also likely an echo of Shaw's affectionate relation with his own best friend, the younger and more handsome Peter Viertel, who was married to the fascinating and alluring Jigee.

Herres cannot be considered the diabolical antithesis of Archer, Shaw's ideological spokesperson. He is a secret sharer, a doppelgänger, of both Shaw and Archer. In part, Herres is Shaw as he might have evolved had it not been for the accidents of life. Herres's psychosexual role in Archer's biography suggests a symbiotic relationship between those reluctant to act, "gentle people" like Archer, and persons of action. Moreover, the synergy between the two is manifest in a manner far more troubling than relationships depicted in Shaw's earlier writings, calling to mind the symbiotic connection of mensches, or even Gimpels, to Golems, described in Chapter 1. The persons of action—Daniel and Charley, who collaborate with Communists, and Party members such as Parrish and Herres— are exemplars for the gentle people, who must transform themselves to combat evil. Yet taking action means getting one's hands dirty and, under certain circumstances, even taking on the full characteristics of one's opponents, as suggested by the Communists' decision to frame Archer and finger him to the red-baiters.

Without a doubt, Archer is another version of Whitacre in *The Young Lions*, a man hesitant to act but basically decent, and one who rises to the occasion in the end. Herres, on the other hand, might be arguably linked to Christian Diestl, the idealistic young Nazi who originally had been a Communist but became corrupted by an ideology that he did not fully understand. However, Whitacre and Diestl meet as enemies on the battlefield. In contrast, Archer and Herres are enmeshed in a long-term love affair, characterized by the submission of the former to domination by the latter. Lloyd Hutt, the president of the advertising agency that sponsors *University Town*, imparts more than he intends in warning Archer: "Nobody can stand investigation. Nobody. If you think you can you must have led your life in deep freeze for the last twenty years."[69] Archer sets out to investigate others, which ultimately ends in a devastating self-investigation that leaves him with little more than the remnants of his marriage, a conviction that Victor Herres is his deadly enemy, and a suspicion of all those enamored of their own virtue.

THE BLOOD AND THE STAIN

The Troubled Air entails a reworking but by no means a disavowal of the cardinal themes that Shaw explored in addressing anti-Semitism in earlier writing. His fundamental principle of violent reprisal, "an eye for an eye," was conspicuous in his collection *Welcome to the City and Other Stories* nine years earlier. In one of these stories, "Select Clientele," two couples residing at an artists' colony in upstate New York are bicycling through the hills when they are set upon by four toughs. The thugs brand the male cyclists as "lousy Jew bastards" and hurl stones at them.[70] After the couples return to the colony, the two women retreat to their rooms, trying to forget the incident, while the men plot revenge. One, Sam, is a Jew; the other, Max, is a non-Jewish refugee from Germany. Both link the experience they have just undergone to larger forces at work in the world. Max says, "I left Berlin, I left Vienna. . . . I thought I wouldn't see any more things like that." Sam, whose wife is pregnant, thinks to himself, "Pogroms are being planned in odd corners of the United States for my kid who still has five months to go before he comes out of his mother."[71]

Max and Sam ask the assistance of Thomas, the handyman at the colony, whose job includes keeping the residents free of harassment from local gangs. The three men grab pitchforks and a baseball bat and walk back to the scene of the altercation. However, it turns out that the troublemakers are all friends and drinking buddies of Thomas, so they are allowed to slink away with an insincere apology. Sam and Max achieve no satisfaction from this hollow victory. Max ends up speechless in his suppressed rage, while Sam, emulating the Jews of Germany who got out in time, plans to move to the West Coast prior to the birth of his son. Unstated is the obvious truth that, had Max and Sam been successful in retaliating against the thugs, their devastating sense of impotency would have been transformed into confidence and optimism.

Like "Residents of Other Cities," this story was dropped from all post-1950 collections of Shaw's fiction. The only short story by Shaw surviving from the 1940s in later anthologies that directly addresses anti-Semitism in the United States is one that lends itself to possible misinterpretation if taken out of context. "Act of Faith," which appeared in a 1946 collection by that name, tells of a soldier, Norman Seeger, whose father sends a long letter to him in France at the end of the war. The elder Seeger reports that his other son, Jacob, discharged after being wounded in the leg, is obsessed with Nazi crimes and fears that Jews everywhere are still threatened. The father also describes anti-Semitic incidents reported in the press and his own experiences with anti-Semitism in his community. The letter ultimately discloses that Mr. Seeger has begun to suffer from self-hatred and is resentful of Jews who draw attention to themselves and make demands.

As a safeguard against untoward incidents upon his return, Norman Seeger resolves to bring back to the United States a luger he had taken from an ss major whom he had killed. Yet in an impulsive last-minute turnabout, Seeger decides to sell the gun to obtain money for himself and his two non-Jewish buddies to spend on an enjoyable leave in Paris. The story has been interpreted as signaling a new shift in Shaw's outlook, displaying confidence in the postwar United States and in the returning soldiers to guarantee a prejudice-free democracy; in this interpretation, Shaw is rejecting Seeger's father's unraveling as paranoid.[72] However, a reading that places the story in the context of *The Young Lions*, published shortly thereafter, suggests that Shaw is actually revealing Norman Seeger's naïveté. Through his powerful narrative in the novel of the ordeal of the persecuted and harassed Noah Ackerman, Shaw recounts a monumental anti-Semitism in the ranks of the army that can only be defeated by demonstrating that Jews such as the Seegers will resolutely fight back.

In *The Troubled Air* anti-Semitism appears as a theme but in a new form. Pokorny, the composer, insists to Archer that his Jewish identity is central to his being targeted by the *Blueprint* red-baiters as the first person to be fired, and as the one person for whom the sponsor will not entertain a compromise. Archer is skeptical of the claim of anti-Semitism but modifies his view when he finally holds a meeting with the show's sponsor, Sandler. Archer learns that Sandler is Jewish, too, yet expresses anti-Semitic views, especially in his contempt for left-wing Jews.

Similarly, the proposition of "an eye for eye" is present in the novel, albeit in more complex form. Such a strategy is expressly proposed at the protest meeting against the blacklist by Woodie Burke, a non-Communist who was among the first to lose his radio show. Burke suggests that the blacklistees carry out an investigation of those behind Blueprint, which he is convinced will reveal direct links to pro-Nazis and followers of the racist Father Coughlin: "We're in a fight and we're getting our eyes gouged out. Let's stop calling for the referee and do a little eye-gouging ourselves."[73]

Archer rejects this philosophy as oversimplified and based on a belief that all of one's opponents must embody absolute evil. But shortly afterward Archer has his final meeting with businessman Lloyd Hutt. He discovers not only that Hutt is the financial backer of Blueprint but that Hutt indeed shares the ideology of the fascists and racists. In a reference to Pokorny, Hutt rants against Archer's "filthy immigrant friends whose families haven't been here long enough to learn to speak the language without degrading it," and then he makes a threat: "We'll hound and defame you and we won't stop until you're all behind bars or swinging from trees." At this point, "Archer sprang across the room and hit him." Prevented by others from delivering any further blows to Hutt, Archer leaves feeling "dissatisfied that it had been so ineffectual."[74]

In response to the Cold War witch hunt, Shaw no longer feels he can offer violent retaliation as an adequate program for action. The enemy is not an alien force creeping over from Europe but is deeply rooted in the social structure of his own country; the persecutor of the Jew can just as easily be another Jew in league with anti-Semites out of blind greed. The exemplars for the gentle people, the people of action who went to Spain, are themselves corrupted. Archer's thoughts turn to the one man who had escaped and survived the witch hunt—the African American actor Stanley Atlas, who never counted on his radio career as a safety net and who went into exile in Paris without waging a fight: "Atlas had survived because he was suspicious and despairing from the beginning and had built a defense for himself out of a protective combination of shrewdness and loathing."[75]

Shaw's own move into exile in Paris in 1951 was parallel to Atlas's in both motivation (flight from political reaction) and destination, and it also echoes the move of Richard Wright to Paris four years earlier. But Shaw did not conclude that the United States had fallen into the grip of an equivalent of German fascism, which remained his prototype of evil. The Troubled Air deals with a rot that has emerged; but the corruption has not fully enveloped the land, and there

IRWIN SHAW in military uniform in Paris in the last days of
World War II. (From the Shaw Collection in the Howard Gotlieb
Archival Research Center at Boston University)

still are upright people who have retained their decency. Such positive qualities are conspicuously epitomized by Emmett O'Neill, an assistant to Hutt whose humanity impels him to regularly subvert his boss's orders.

This approach stands in dramatic contrast to Shaw's treatment of the German and Austrian societies in *The Young Lions*; these societies are subjected to a caustic investigation as to their comprehensive effects on the human character, as well as what the requisite political response should be. Christian Diestl's Communist past was not revealed by Shaw to suggest parallels between Communism and fascism but to provide a pointed contrast. Diestl is a symbol of the ordinary European who failed to find answers in Communism because of its emphasis on the rational: "Until last year I was a Communist. Workers of the world, peace for all, to each according to his need, the victory of reason. . . . Nonsense! I do not know about America, but I know about Europe. In Europe nothing will ever be accomplished by reason."[76] Shaw's residual sympathy for committed Communists is suggested by his choice of the name Parrish for the novel's open Communist; it is the name of his close friend of forty years, Robert Parrish, a filmcutter he had met in liberated Paris at the end of the war.

The positive view of Communism is further embodied in the trajectory of Michael Whitacre. He is a tepid fellow traveler of the Communist Party who, like Shaw, is dogged throughout his military career by an FBI report calling him a "Red."[77] Whitacre is powerfully affected by an incident early in the novel when he stands helplessly by while a fellow playwright attempts suicide and is saved by the timely intervention of Parrish. Whitacre's eventual redemption by coldbloodedly avenging Ackerman's death restores him to a moral stature comparable to that of his old Communist acquaintance. Whitacre is one of the gentle people, basically decent but hesitant to act; it is necessary for his intellect and emotions to come into balance before he can achieve maturity in the post-1930s world.

In contrast, Diestl, although he is an Austrian, fervently identifies with the German people as a repository of strength and dignity in a society that feels shamed and defeated. Shaw's subsequent narrative of Diestl's adventures in the German army as well as in Berlin illustrates that German culture stands not in contradiction to fascism but as its most fertile ground. Shaw's treatment of the Germans in his fiction incited the literary critic Chester Eisinger to rebuke him as an "implacable hater" who "writes about Germans as though he were cutting them to pieces, systematically and joyfully." To Shaw, "no reconciliation is possible . . . with the German mind." Like Vansittart, Shaw believes that "Germans are obsessed with war" and "the only good German is a dead German."[78]

This aphorism is surely insinuated by Shaw's penultimate scene in *The Young*

Lions. Diestl, after killing the Jewish American soldier Noah Ackerman, faces Whitacre unarmed and grins, "Welcome to Germany."[79] In violation of the Geneva convention, Whitacre coldly executes Diestl. Such an unforgiving attitude was already prefigured in Shaw's short fiction, such as "Retreat." In this 1946 story, a repentant German major encounters a Parisian Jew who has survived the occupation. The German asks, "What can I do . . . to wash my hands?" The Jew replies, "You can cut your throat . . . and see if the blood will take the stain out."[80]

Whitacre is surely on the side of rationality, but all-encompassing rationality cannot address the full threat of the peculiar evil of Nazism; heartfelt personal action, to the point of levelheaded execution, is the only way. Lieutenant Green, a character parallel to Whitacre who enters the story near the end, knows that, too. Even after the Nazis are defeated, Green sets up a phalanx of machine guns to protect from their non-Jewish fellows the liberated Jewish concentration camp inmates who want to conduct a service in Hebrew for the dead. Anticipating Goldhagen's *Hitler's Willing Executioners*, Green knows full well that the poison of anti-Semitism springs from the bottom of the population as much as it trickles down from the top of the regime. Moreover, like Michael Gold, Green believes that ruthless measures are required to stamp it out—in this instance, even against recently liberated non-Jewish inmates from the same camp as the Jews, who may seek revenge against those perceived as the cause of their misery.[81]

The enigmas and challenges of the World War II antifascist crusade were hardly limited to the fiction by Jewish radicals debating the peculiarities of the Germans. While Shaw and Maltz responded to fascism in the European theater of World War II, a young African American political activist, Anne Petry, was engaged in a communitywide battle against domestic racism on the home front that would eventuate in some of the most unforgettable fiction of the war years.

{4

A Rage in Harlem

In February 1942, the Reverend Adam Clayton Powell Jr. (1908–72), a flamboyant Harlem politician nicknamed "King of the Cats" by his biographer, launched an iconoclastic African American newsweekly that had Far Left politics.[1] The *People's Voice* was published in an office atop the Woolworth's Department Store at 210 West 125th Street, across the street from the Apollo Theater. The paper's editorial manifesto called World War II "one of the great crossroads of history" and invoked the obligation of all people to forge a unity against fascism. Indeed, the editors had earlier called their mission "The Crusade"—with the hope that it would advance in the tradition of the abolitionist Frederick Douglass, under the leadership of editor-in-chief Powell, who was elected to the New York City Council in 1941 and the U.S. Congress in 1945.[2]

In this spirit the *People's Voice* editors and staff crafted the following covenant: "We are men and women of the people. The people are ours and we are theirs. We respect no authority except their authority. We obey no mandate except their mandate. We look to no one to judge us except—they the people!" To underscore its pro-socialist perspective, the editorial went on to state, "THIS IS A WORKING CLASS PAPER. We are a working class race. We pledge to the trade union movement our fullest co-operation." The editors righteously boasted that they would eschew coverage of crime, the mainstay of most urban newspapers. Instead, "we . . . will fight to break down the walls of our ghetto by crusading for lower rent, better housing conditions, more and better health facilities, removal of restrictions against Negroes in the secondary school system . . . a just quota of jobs in all city, state and federal agencies."

The manifesto's political stance was slightly to the left of the Popular Front in its conspicuous stress on class and race. Thus it is surprising that the paper was silent regarding the pivotal war issues of Double V and the segregated military. On domestic issues the editorial was precise and programmatic, but of World War II the *People's Voice* waxed rhetorical, affirming a capacious but ultimately evasive vision: "We believe firmly that this is the people's hour to make democracy real and thereby make it world triumphant. If this is not done, we may lose this war. If this is not done, even though we win it, we lose the peace. . . . We are against Hitlerism abroad and just as strongly against Hitlerism at home."[3] Such a formulation camouflaged an ambiguity about what precisely constituted "Hitlerism" in Harlem and what might eventuate if antiracist activity should hamper war production for the anti-Nazi military effort in Europe. Nevertheless, it effectively created space in the pages of the *People's Voice* for a plurality of approaches focusing on, but also extending slightly beyond, the Popular Front.

Powell to a certain extent resembled other independent leaders of the African American Left in the early 1940s, such as Paul Robeson, Langston Hughes, and W. E. B. Du Bois.[4] The three were strongly attracted to the Soviet Union and variously sympathetic to the Communist Party, but they were uneasy with the Party's policy formulation that "the greatest service that can be contributed to Negro rights is unconditional support of the war, without which equality and freedom is impossible for any people."[5] Accordingly, versions of both Double V and the Communist Party's position appeared in the paper's pages.

Backing for the *People's Voice* came from several entrepreneurs associated with Harlem's famed Savoy ballroom. From the time it opened in 1926 on Lenox Avenue between 140th and 141st streets, the Savoy welcomed integrated dancing to swing and jazz orchestras. Moe Gale (born Moses Galewski), one of two Jewish brothers who founded the Savoy, gave financial support to the paper, while Charles Buchanan, a Black Harlem real estate broker who managed the ballroom and was an ally of Powell's, was the publisher.[6] The paper was printed on the presses of *PM*, a daily Left-liberal paper founded by the millionaire Marshall Field III in 1940.[7]

Equally vital to the paper's success was the technical support Powell received from his African American confidants in the Communist Party. Powell had been friendly to the Communists since the mid-1930s, welcoming them to the Abyssinian Baptist Church where he had succeeded his father as pastor. The church was the largest Protestant congregation in the United States, boasting more than 15,000 members.[8] Powell was a self-promoting left-wing maverick, but his pro-labor activities often coincided with the positions of the Communist Party. He had tended to be antiwar during the Hitler-Stalin Pact but became ardently pro-war after Germany's invasion of the USSR.[9]

The Communist intellectual most pivotal to Powell's *People's Voice* was the brilliant Harvard-educated Black lawyer and Party leader Benjamin Davis (1903–64). Davis had ample journalistic experience as editor of the Communist Party's *Harlem Liberator* and also as a member of the editorial board of the *Daily Worker*. He collaborated frequently with Powell in the 1930s, although they had sporadic disagreements. In 1943 Powell launched a campaign for Congress and urged that Davis be elected his successor on the New York City Council, which he was. Davis was reelected in 1945 in a landslide victory that united the Blacks of Harlem with Leftists in working-class neighborhoods across Manhattan. In 1949, two years after Powell broke with the Communists and the People's Voice collapsed, Davis was sentenced to five years in prison under Smith Act charges of conspiring to teach the overthrow of the government. During his confinement in the federal penitentiary in Terre Haute, Indiana, until 1955, Davis wrote his autobiography, Communist Councilman from Harlem, but federal authorities would not release the manuscript until after Davis's death in 1964, when it was published.[10]

Another member of the insurgent African American left-wing brain trust that Powell attracted to the People's Voice was Doxey Wilkerson (1905–93). Wilkerson was a onetime doctoral student at the University of Michigan who joined the faculty of the School of Education at Howard University in 1935. He then became a researcher and cowriter of Gunnar Myrdal's An American Dilemma (1944) and served as vice president of the American Federation of Teachers from 1937 to 1940. Wilkerson joined the Communist Party in 1943 at the time he became a journalist for the People's Voice. He rose immediately to the post of executive editor, which he held for the next four years. Subsequently he became a leading Communist Party educator until he resigned from the Party in 1957. Completing his doctorate at New York University in 1959, Wilkerson tried teaching at a college in Texas, but red-baiters forced his resignation within a year. He spent the last decade of his academic career, 1963 to 1973, as chairman of the Department of Curriculum and Instruction at Yeshiva University in New York.[11]

Another notable Communist writer for the People's Voice was Max Yergan (1892–1975), a former activist in the Young Men's Christian Association who had lived in India and Africa. Joining the Communist Party after visiting the Soviet Union in 1936, Yergan became a leader of the National Negro Congress and the Council on African Affairs, as well as a Harlem celebrity. In 1948 he suddenly lurched to the right; he first metamorphosed into a hired informant against Communists and then became a pro-apartheid lobbyist.[12]

The first phase of recruiting writers for the People's Voice entailed a raid on the Amsterdam News, the established Harlem weekly that had long been denounced by Powell and the Left for its use of sensational headlines and the negligible attention it paid to social issues. Most significant among the talented journalists who made the switch was the distinguished writer Marvel Cooke (1903–2000), who had been the first woman reporter on the Amsterdam News in its forty-year history. Hired in 1931, Cooke had been drawn to the Communist Party in 1935 through her collaboration with Black Communists such as Benjamin Davis in activities supporting the strikers of the American Newspaper Guild. She joined the Party the following year but kept her membership secret for fear of losing her job. After leaving the Amsterdam News in disgust over its sensationalist coverage of crime, Cooke became the de facto managing editor of the People's Voice throughout most of its existence, although sexism prevented her from holding the official title.

During the Cold War Cooke made front page news in the New York Times when she was subpoenaed by Joseph McCarthy in 1953 to testify about her People's Voice activities. McCarthy asked Cooke questions such as "Were you known by the other employees [at the People's Voice] as 'Mrs. Commissar'?" and "It has been testified by a number of witnesses that you held a position so high that you gave orders to the Communist National Committee. Would you tell us whether that testimony is true?"[13] Like most Leftists who did not want to be legally coerced into "naming names," Cooke pleaded the Fifth Amendment and declined to answer.

This public assault on Cooke transpired at the very time when alleged Communists were being fired, beaten up, driven into exile, and imprisoned and when the Rosenbergs were executed. Her subpoena, and the overwrought testimony of a few former People's Voice staff members who claimed that the paper was Communist-controlled, in all likelihood put a permanent damper on the willingness of people connected with the newspaper to discuss their activities and personal associations in subsequent years. Cooke, however, remained undaunted in her Communist commitment.

From 1950 to 1952 she was a reporter and feature writer for the Daily Compass, which was one of several unsuccessful efforts to continue the Left-liberal tradition of PM. Its most well-known reporter was the radical I. F. Stone (1907–89). In 1953 Cooke became the New York director of the Communist-led Council of the Arts, Sciences, and Professions. In 1970, at the request of the Communist Party, she became coordinator of New York activities for the National United Committee to Defend Angela Davis, the Communist philosophy professor who was falsely accused of involvement in a courthouse shooting in Marin County, California. Until 1989, Cooke was vice-chair of the National Council of Soviet-American Friendship.[14]

Conspicuous among the talented left-wing artists who congregated around the People's Voice was the noted cartoonist Oliver "Ollie" Harrington (1912–95), creator of the character "Bootsie." On any given Wednesday, when the People's Voice appeared, one might find an article by Paul Robeson, a poem by Langston Hughes, an excerpt from a work by Richard Wright, an essay by Alain Locke, or a theater review by Owen Dodson (1913–83), all of whom also appeared in the New

Masses and sometimes in the *Daily Worker*. With the onset of the Cold War, Wright moved to Paris, Robeson's passport was revoked, and Dodson pulled back from the Left. Harrington, at that time a political independent whose cartoons during World War II reflected a Double V outlook, moved to Paris in 1951. In 1961 he moved to East Germany, where he lived for the rest of his life, sending his cartoons to the U.S. Communist press for publication after 1968.

At the climax of its six-year run, the *People's Voice* was looking pretty Red. Powell would often be away on business, delegating day-to-day affairs to a Communist who was executive editor, Doxey Wilkerson. The duties of managing editor—including the supervision of all writing—were under the direction of another Communist, Marvel Cooke. And Communist Party official Ben Davis had his own column, in which he aggressively promoted Communist positions. FBI operatives frequently questioned staff members in the hope of uncovering Communist control of the publication, but the autocratic Powell was the paper's unifying personality.[15] While all writers adhered to the "crusade" championed in the *People's Voice*, not all staff members had political associations as conspicuous as those of Wilkerson, Cooke, and Davis.

Among the cadre of defectors from the *Amsterdam News* to work for the *People's Voice* was an aspiring young writer named Ann Petry (1908–97), who was born Ann Lane in Old Saybrook, Connecticut. Petry was proud that four generations of her family hailed from Connecticut, but she felt that her "outsider" status as an African American woman gave her a "tenuous, unsubstantial connection with New England." As a young girl she felt a strong identification with Jo March, "the tomboy, the misfit, the impatient quick-tempered would be writer" in Louisa May Alcott's *Little Women* (1868–69). Fairy tales and mystery stores enriched her imagination, as did family stories that bequeathed to her a "powerful oral-narrative tradition."[16] Some of these were about her maternal grandfather, who had escaped from slavery, and her father, Peter Clark Lane Jr., who had defied racist threats when he opened Old Saybrook's first black-owned drugstore in 1902. Many more stories came from uncles who had lived all over the world and worked at many jobs. One had served in the Spanish American War, and another had been sentenced to five years on a Georgia chain gang. Petry's mother, Bertha James Lane, was one of three sisters who had refused the role of housewife to become successful businesswomen who were financially independent; Petry's mother's company was called Beautiful Linens for Beautiful Homes.

At age four Petry accompanied her older sister to first grade; no one asked her to leave, so she commenced an early education. Although Petry was already writing stories and plays in high school, she chose to follow her father's occupation by attending the Connecticut College of Pharmacy, from which she graduated in

ANN PETRY was a radical journalist and activist in Harlem in
the 1940s who became an outstanding novelist and short story
writer. (Photograph by Carl Van Vechten; courtesy of the Van
Vechten Trust, Lancaster, Pa., and the Carl Van Vechten
Collection, Yale University)

1931. Thereafter she worked for nearly seven years in the two family drugstores. During this time she met George David Petry, originally from Louisiana, on a trip to Hartford. In 1938 they were married. They moved to New York City, where George lived, to test their literary inclinations.

Petry quickly found a job with the *Amsterdam News* selling space for the advertising department, while her husband worked in a Harlem restaurant and attempted to write mystery stories before he eventually turned to working as a writer on the Federal Writers Project and then in marketing. A year later Petry published her first piece of fiction, a pulpish story, "Marie of the Cabin Club," under the pseudonym Arnold Petri, in Baltimore's left-wing *Afro-American*. The story is noteworthy for its anticipation of Petry's evolution by the time of the publication of her most popular novel, *The Street* (1946). Like many episodes in *The Street*, the setting in "Marie" is an interracial nightclub recalling the Savoy ballroom and features a thriving African American trumpet player who takes the heroine for a ride in his fancy car. There are also stock characters from standard spy stories, including a sinister Englishman working for the Japanese government and a mysterious white woman who turns out to be a secret agent for the French. The former elements, closer to Petry's own experience, would intensify, while the latter would vanish in her later fiction.[17]

In 1940 Petry joined the American Negro Theater, of which she remained a part for more than two years. During the first year, she played Tillie Petunia three nights a week in Abram Hill's radical critique of the Black middle class, *On Striver's Row* (1940). Among the left-wing African American actors and actresses associated with the American Negro Theater in the 1940s were Ruby Dee, Ossie Davis, Alice Childress, Canada Lee, Sidney Poitier, Frank Silvera, and Harry Belafonte. Concurrently, Petry furthered her studies in painting and the piano. During 1941 she joined her onetime *Amsterdam News* colleague Marvel Cooke on the staff of the *People's Voice*.

While journalism at the new radical publication provided novel and edifying adventures, Petry still yearned for success as a fiction writer. She enrolled in a Columbia University writing class in 1942 and then a writers' workshop in 1943, both led by Mabel Louise Robinson. Her next short story, "On Saturday the Siren Sounds at Noon," was published in the *Crisis* in 1943. Although never reprinted, it constitutes another critical marker en route to *The Street*. Both the novel and the story focus on impoverished Harlem residents struggling against the economic odds and emphasize the special costs to children. In the short story, an exhausted Black worker returns home on a Monday to learn that his three children have been trapped in a fire in his apartment building; one is killed and two are injured. On the following Saturday morning he learns that the three youngsters had been locked in the apartment while his wife was with another man. In a daze he strangles her and then leaves for work in the late morning. When an air raid siren sounds at noon, the horror of the crime that he perpetrated is pulled to the surface of his consciousness, and he commits suicide by jumping in front of a subway train.[18]

The idea for "On Saturday the Siren Sounds at Noon" originated in a newspaper article that reported that two children had been burned to death while both parents were at work. Petry added the adultery and the revelation of the wife's betrayal as the turning point in the story, and she used a flashback technique in which the guilt-ridden husband is prompted by the noonday siren to recall the events precipitating the murder.[19] The story attracted the attention of an editor at Houghton Mifflin who encouraged Petry to plan a novel and apply for the company's literary fellowship.

Petry competed for the fellowship after leaving the *People's Voice* in 1944 and received $2,400 in 1945. When she reworked some of the material of her story into *The Street*, Petry retained mainly the discovery of sexual betrayal and a climactic Black-on-Black killing. She departed markedly, however, from the story by complicating gender roles in ways that contested the customary male and female stereotypes in "On Saturday the Siren Sounds at Noon." *The Street* presents a cheating Black woman, Jubilee, but the woman defends herself with a knife against her outraged lover, Boots Smith. Later Boots Smith becomes the betrayer of another self-reliant woman, Lutie, and he ends up the victim of her murderous rage.

"TALENT AS A WEAPON"

Petry was fully committed to the *People's Voice* throughout the 1940s, ideologically and as an activist. During her two-year tenure on the paper's staff, she was editor of the women's page, a reporter for stories dealing with the Harlem community as well as national protests, the author of a weekly column of announcements and gossip called "The Lighter Side," and the editor of the politically focused "National Roundup" of news.[20] In "The Lighter Side" column Petry's maturing familiarity with the Left was in evidence as she publicized and commented on cultural, social, and political events held under the auspices of the anticolonialist Council on African Affairs and at radical venues such as Café Society. Among the many left-wing writers, artists, and musicians whose activities were reported in "The Lighter Side" were Anton Refregier, Leonard Zinberg, Josh White, Earl Robinson, Paul Robeson, Aaron Douglas, Andy Razaf, Elizabeth Catlett-White, Augusta Savage, Jacob Lawrence, Langston Hughes, Sterling Brown, Angelo Herndon, and Theodore Ward.

Politically parallel to Petry's journalism was her role in organizing Negro Women, Inc., in May 1941. Sometimes shortened to Women, Inc., the group was described by Petry in the *People's Voice* as the women's auxiliary of the People's Committee, in which any woman is welcome if "you believe in a fighting program for the rights of Negro women."[21] The People's Committee had been set up by Adam Clayton Powell with his left-wing allies to quickly mobilize people in Harlem to protest and picket. The FBI carefully monitored the organization because of the central roles played by pro-Communists such as Ferdinand Smith, Max Yergan, Audley Moore, Benjamin Davis, and Theodore Bassett.[22] Petry remained an officer of Negro Women, Inc., until 1947. Starting in 1942 her community activism broadened to include collaborating with the Laundry Workers Joint Board to devise programs for the children of laundry workers. In 1943 she became assistant to the secretary of the Harlem-Riverside Defense Council.

However, in interviews with and autobiographical statements made by Petry after the onset of the Cold War, references to her engagement in the Harlem "crusade" are sparse and entirely depoliticized. She customarily gives the impression that her work at the *People's Voice* was merely a paying job on a traditional newspaper, or she confines her Harlem journalistic experience to the *Amsterdam News*.[23] There are no references to the People's Committee. Negro Women, Inc., is described by Petry as "a Harlem consumers' watch group" that provided "working-class women with 'how-to' information for purchasing food, clothing, and furniture."[24] In glaring contrast, at the time Petry first came to national attention with the publication of *The Street* in 1946, she was straightforward about her radical convictions and activities, including her friendly attitude toward the Communist Party. Similar documentation is evident in African American, mainstream, and Left publications prior to 1950.

In a *Chicago Defender* profile and interview with Earl Conrad in early 1946, Petry is described as belonging "to the great, hopeful phalanx of labor advocates." When asked what her solution to segregation was, she replied, "The group that would, more likely than any other, solve this question is labor. The labor unions primarily have fought for the Negro interest. If Christianity would be a living thing, it would be all right, but it does not live. The bulk of the population gives only lip service to the thoughts of Christianity. Labor and the Negro must mark off a path to each other." Petry also insisted that there was not "much difference between the Republican and Democratic parties"; she believed that "a third party" is "feasible" if "the people can find a leader around whom to rally."[25]

In an *Ebony* magazine interview and profile a few months later, Petry is described as "active in fighting for greater social rights and security for women.

ANN PETRY (third from left) at a meeting of the Laundry
Workers Joint Board in 1946. (From the Petry Collection in the
Howard Gotlieb Archival Research Center at Boston University)

She is executive secretary of Negro Women, Inc., a kind of pressure group of New York Negro women who are dedicated to advancing the status of Negro women and all women." Politically, Petry is said to "consider herself a 'definite progressive' on political and social matters. She finds the label 'liberal' a trifle vague and a little confusing."[26] Two years later, the Progressive Party electoral campaign supporting Henry Wallace for president would be launched, opposing President Truman's Cold War policies and his domestic anti-Communism.[27] However, before then, throughout the era of the Popular Front, the term "progressive" usually meant a radical who was willing to collaborate with Communists and who looked on the Soviet Union favorably as a force for peace and anticolonialism. Pro-Communists and nonpublic Party members sometimes called themselves progressives as well when they did not want to be labeled as Party supporters or members.

Petry first gained notice in the Daily Worker in March 1945, when she was awarded the Houghton Mifflin literary fellowship. She was identified as "executive secretary of Negro Women, Inc."[28] Added attention came after the publication of The Street, her novel about a single mother in Harlem, Lutie Johnson, driven to kill a Harlem nightclub band leader who tries to turn her into a prostitute. In the Daily Worker in March and April 1946, The Street was the subject of a review, a column, and a letter, and Petry was featured in a combination profile-interview. In May The Street was reviewed in the New Masses, and another review appeared in the first issue of the Communist-sponsored Mainstream in 1947.

The most positive commentary on the novel was by John Meldon, a writer who at one time covered waterfront issues, in the Daily Worker. Meldon characterized The Street as a "Harlem Tragedy" that unabashedly exhibits the good, the bad, and the ugly among Harlem residents but also "presents, with a cold and savage logic the underlying economic and social reasons" explaining the various types "who parade through The Street with an ominous tread." Meldon anticipated a possible criticism by readers of the absence in the novel of any mention of the "progressive movement" in Harlem led by Adam Clayton Powell and Benjamin Davis. He insisted that the book was nevertheless realistic because such forces in Harlem were still a minority and inadequate; therefore many women, like Lutie, would not know to whom to turn for help.[29] Shortly after, a letter to the editor praised the novel but contended that "somewhere along the line in 436 pages and in some corner of Ann Petry's mind there should be minimum knowledge about a developing unity between Negro and white."[30]

As it happened, the Meldon review and the letter to the editor appeared as the Party was in the midst of a debate over a New Masses essay by Albert Maltz published in February.[31] One of Maltz's chief antagonists in the debate, Communist literary critic Samuel Sillen, wrote a *Daily Worker* column linking Petry and Maltz. Sillen pointed out that Maltz had insisted that an artist could legitimately depict one "sector of experience," such as an impoverished man committing a theft and being sent to prison, without having to include "the whole truth" of the national political situation or introduce into the narrative a council for the unemployed that would save the day. While Sillen concluded that Maltz's claim had some veracity, he nonetheless felt that Petry confirmed the dangers of Maltz's view by her omission in *The Street* of any "genuinely affirmative pressures in the Negro community."

Sillen admired Petry's novel in general but believed that her strategy rendered the final conflict in the novel "self-enclosed, circular," resulting in "awkward and enforced melodrama." While Sillen did not object to Petry's writing tragedy, he felt that the climactic "Black-on-Black" violence was unilluminating. In a swipe at both Meldon and Maltz, he concluded that Petry's art would be superior if she had resisted "the conventionally bourgeois divorce between the sector of experience" and "our total comprehension of reality."[32]

Sillen was not linking Maltz and Petry hypothetically. Only a month before his column appeared, the *Daily Worker* had published writer Beth McHenry's interview with Petry, in which Petry mentioned that she had been carefully following the debate over Maltz's essay. The literary perspective embraced by Petry attests to her partisanship of Maltz's approach, and she appears to offer the opinion that an open debate would enable Maltz's perspective to triumph. Petry also generously praised Meldon's "Maltzian" review as "one of the best," because it went "to the heart of what I was trying to say." Affirming her solidarity with the Left cultural movement, Petry described her role as an artist as an "emotional arouser" and said that she aimed to write a series of books that would "move [the public] to action." Yet, aligning with Maltz's perspective, she indicated some discomfort with the slogan "Art as a Weapon," which Maltz felt could lead to formulaic writing. As an alternative, Petry stated that she looked on her own "talent as a weapon," by which she meant that she was equally committed to the use of genuinely artistic methods.

Not surprisingly, Petry told the *Daily Worker* that she profoundly disagreed with the critics who maintained that her novel would have been more effective if it presented a hopeful ending: "I feel that the portrayal of a problem in itself, in all its cruelty and horror, is actually the thing which sets people thinking, and not any solution that may be offered in a novel." Regarding *The Street*, Petry alluded to one of Maltz's most critical arguments—that the reader does not approach a novel with an empty head. She speculated that most people who would bother to read a novel such as *The Street* would already hold antiracist sentiments, "but they'll have to be made to feel—anger, horror, indignation—before they'll actually move on any program to solve the problem."

Petry concluded the interview by stating that she was "not affiliated with any party" but regarded this as a "mistake" because she "believes the only way a responsible human being can be an effective one is to join the party of his choice and become involved in its activities." As an example of her activity, Petry mentioned her job as executive secretary of Negro Women, Inc., "which functions as a progressive community organization in Harlem." Although Petry announced her intention to eventually move to a small town, she stressed that she was going to combat political isolation by dividing her time so that she "can come across with full-time community activity for at least three months of every year."[33]

The next month the *New Masses* carried a review far more disapproving than any of the commentary in the *Daily Worker*, a review that addressed problems that had been raised in the critical letter to the editor and the Sillen column. Writing under the pseudonym Alfred Goldsmith, the short-story writer Saul Levitt (see discussion in Chapter 6) linked Petry to Richard Wright, now regarded by the Party as a betrayer of the Left, because of her "opportunism" in the creation of character. Levitt saw the predicament of writing about African Americans as being that an author is faced with the unique complexities of African American life—characters caught between desires to "change" and to "escape," as well as seething "with the interaction of national and class drives." Unfortunately, Petry evaded this complex challenge by resorting to a juxtaposition of dark, stereotyped Black male villains and "the two-dimensional effect of an early movie starring Lillian Gish."

Assuring his readers that he was not demanding that Petry should show "a way out," Levitt insisted that the character of Lutie should have been more extensively realized. This would allow the nature of Lutie's individualist desire for escape and the one-sidedness of her "hatred of the tragically malformed personalities around her" to stand out more boldly.[34] Like Sillen, Levitt was selling short the capacity of the likely readers of Petry's fiction to contextualize the action of the text.

A year later, a final evaluation of *The Street* appeared in the Communist press. In the inaugural issue of *Mainstream*, a literary journal launched in 1947, African American playwright Theodore Ward (1902–83) included Petry's novel in a survey of five African American novelists. All five are variously indicted for failing to make the necessary link between the contemporary racist horrors of capitalism and "the new being born within the old."[35] The charge echoed the pivotal issue in the Party's debate with Maltz over the linking of sectors of experience. More specifically, Ward accused Petry of seeing African Americans "caged in by white prejudice, economic injustice and hate." Ward called this a vision of "despair" and an example of "burning support of the theory that in America life for the Negro inevitably ends in a cul-de-sac." Both Levitt and Ward linked Petry to Richard Wright and Chester Himes, but inasmuch as Petry did not explicitly attack the Communist Party, Ward noted that "it should be stressed that unlike Wright and Himes she employs it without political bias."[36]

Petry's final unabashed expression of her politics during the Harlem years appeared three years later. In a photographically illustrated essay about Harlem that Petry contributed to *Holiday* magazine at the end of the 1940s, she featured photographs of Powell's Abyssinian Baptist Church (with the caption "Progressive institutions and courageous individuals offer Harlem hope") as well as of Powell and W. E. B. Du Bois, accompanied by two poems by Langston Hughes. Without mentioning the now-defunct *People's Voice*, she repeated its traditional criticism of the *Amsterdam News* for its headlining of "the ripest scandals and the goriest murders" alongside editorials that are "as sedately written and as innocuous as those in the *New York Sun*."

Petry concluded her survey with the description of an invented Black worker named George Jackson as a symbol of the Harlem population. The fictional Jackson was politically educated by Adam Clayton Powell's 1941 election campaign for the City Council, after which he helped elect Powell to Congress for two terms: "This same George Jackson has twice helped to elect Benjamin J. Davis., Jr., a Communist, to the seat that Powell held in the City Council." This did not mean that Jackson had actually joined the Communist Party: "The chances are that he voted for Ben Davis because he felt Davis would never sell Harlem down the river."[37] Jackson's political evolution likely mirrors her own. Moreover, her statement was an implicit act of solidarity with Davis. Petry would surely have been aware that, nine months earlier, six FBI agents had burst into Councilman Davis's home and arrested him on the charge of teaching the violent overthrow of the U.S. government. Petry's choice to stress the controversial Ben Davis over Adam Clayton Powell may also reflect her disillusionment with Powell's shift toward anti-Communism.

It was the bravery and commitment of Ben Davis, not the Communist Party, that shaped her esteem. In all probability, the publication in the *Daily Worker* of the Sillen column and in the *New Masses* of the Levitt review alienated Petry from the Communist Party's cultural milieu. If the two sectarian appraisals of her novel did not do the job, then assuredly she was estranged by Maltz's humiliating self-criticism only a few weeks after the publication of her interview endorsing Meldon's "Maltzian" interpretation.[38] Her anger was still evident four years later, in "The Novel as Social Criticism," an essay she published in an anthology called

The Writer's Book (1950). The essay was among the last nonfiction expressions of Petry's fading commitment to the quasi-Marxist spirit of the World War II era progressive crusade in Harlem.

In her essay, Petry was still unrepentant, and even belligerent, in referring to *The Street* as a novel of social criticism. Noting that the latest fashion among critics was to condemn novels of social criticism as "deplorable," she claimed a long and noble genealogy for such literature, extending from the Bible to Willard Motley's recent *Knock on Any Door* (1947). Contrary to those who disparaged "propaganda novels," Petry argued that "all truly great art is propaganda," and she offered a common axiom of historical materialism: "The novel, like all other forms of art, will always reflect the political, economic, and social structure of the period in which it was created."

Yet Petry insisted that a social critic need not be a Marxist but merely "a man or woman of conscience." She quoted Richard Rumbold's 1685 oration on the scaffold about class oppression, 150 years before Marx, and suggested that the reading public has a psychological need for literature that reminds society of its failings. But she warned of the danger that a social perspective might transform a novelist into a "pamphleteer" and "romanticist." In a rejoinder to her Communist critics, as well as the critics of Maltz, she repudiated those who demanded the appearance in the text of "a solution to the social problem [the author] has posed. He may be in love with a new world order, and try to sell it to his readers; or, and this happens more frequently, he has trade unions, usually the CIO, come to the rescue in the final scene, horse-opera fashion, and the curtain rings down on a happy ending as rosy as that of a western movie done in technicolor." This criticism seems a bit unfair when applied to the Communist literary tradition of the United States, but it reveals the depth of her frustration with the critics of her bleak description of Harlem life.[39] She then provided a persuasive insight into one of the principal challenges facing all left-wing writers of committed literature, including herself. She pointed out that in indicting society, one must avoid the temptation to place blame totally on social, political, and economic circumstances, lest characters become cardboard due to the absence of "each individual carrying on his own personal battle against the evil within himself."[40] This statement helps explain why Petry resisted creating characters in *The Street* and her other writings whose views and behavior might be mechanically due to their status as social victims of racism and class oppression.

LUTIE JOHNSON'S WAR

Indications of Petry's increasingly intricate social vision and approach to literary characterization are discernible in the third and last short story she published before *The Street*. "Doby's Gone" appeared in 1944 in *Phylon*, the magazine founded by W. E. B. Du Bois at Atlanta University four years earlier. It concerns a six-year-old African American girl, Sue Johnson, and her imaginary male friend, Doby. Sue has moved from an isolated rural existence into a small town, and Doby accompanies her everywhere. As the only Black child in the town's school, Sue is subjected to expressly racial harassment and threats of violence by the other children, who force her to run home every day. Yet she explains to her mother that "Doby doesn't like the other children very much."

Finally Sue is trapped by a group of white children and decides to fight back, hitting them with her fists. In the midst of this struggle, she realizes that Doby has disappeared, but she continues fighting until the white children flee. At first she searches for Doby but realizes that "he had gone for good. . . . She decided it probably had something to do with growing up." A few minutes later several of the white children return and befriend her. When she arrives home late that afternoon, in their company, with scratched legs and a torn dress, she explains to her mother that "Doby's gone. I can't find him anywhere."[41]

In 1988 Petry published a memoir revealing the origins of "Doby's Gone." When Petry was four, she and her older sister were walking home from their first day at school when a gang of older white boys began stoning and insulting them. The sisters fled to their house in tears, but their parents told them that they must return to school the next day and that they would be safe. Although dubious, the girls set out for home the following afternoon. When the gang of boys appeared and started to throw stones, "two of our uncles appeared, quite suddenly, and started knocking the attackers down — some of them they held and knocked their heads together, as they threatened them with sudden and violent death."[42] After that the sisters strolled home from school without harassment.

The modifications Petry made between the factual occurrence and the fictionalized rendition are instructional. Petry was born in Old Saybrook, Connecticut, but the fictional Sue is a new resident from upstate New York. Petry was only four, but Sue is six, the same age as Ann's older sister. Ann accompanies her sister as Doby accompanies Sue. The sisters are attacked by older boys, but Sue is beaten by boys and girls who are the same age. The sisters are rescued by male uncles who meet violence with violence and terrorize the harassers, while Sue defends herself and ultimately earns the friendship of her antagonists. No doubt the most dramatic modification is the disappearance of the uncles from the fictionalized version. If the uncles had remained in the fictional version, there would have been no need for Sue's dramatic change. This change occurs because, in defending herself, Sue frees herself of her dependence on a fantasy friend and learns how to cope with painful reality. In the context of the racist assault against Sue, this is a crucial step to her reclaiming her human agency in an unjust world of which she had been previously ignorant.

The other changes are significant as well, in that the story was published exactly six years after Petry moved from Old Saybrook to Harlem. It insinuates an allegory of the dramatic adjustment Petry had to make in her own sensibilities as she moved from her relatively protected small-town life to the shocking world of urban racism. No longer could her imagination continue to be nurtured by the fantasy and mystery reading of her youth, which was still evident in "Marie of the Cabin Club." What was required was a new sense of reality as portrayed in "On Saturday the Siren Sounds at Noon." Equally important was Petry's growing consciousness through her activities in Negro Women, Inc., of the triple oppression of African American working women by race, gender, and class. Thus it was crucial, in her literary depiction of social forces as well as her characterization, to consciously turn her back on the customary portraits of African American women being trapped in religious ideology, passivity, or sexual promiscuity that had dominated American culture, including fiction by Black authors such as Richard Wright.[43]

The Street is set in 1944, a pivotal year in World War II. It was the year that the Allies liberated Italy and opened a second front with the invasion of Normandy. The Soviet Union drove the Germans out of Finland, Latvia, Estonia, and Lithuania, and the United States retook the Philippines. In the United States, Franklin Roosevelt won his fourth term, and the Communist Party dissolved into the Communist Political Association. In *The Street*, however, the only battles that occur are on the streets of Harlem, and the conflict is largely between African Americans and the environment in which they live, or between Black men and Black women. Prostitution and graft are rampant, and the only antiracist utopia extant is the white-owned Junto Bar and Grill, where African Americans with money are treated with respect.

When the World War II antifascist crusade is discussed in *The Street*, it is from a standpoint that challenges the Popular Front at its roots and even the more moderate versions of the Double V outlook. The most sustained reference to Nazism comes when Boots Smith, a former Pullman porter who leads the band at Junto's, receives a draft notice and tells his boss that he needs to have it "fixed." In answer to Junto's questions about why he won't fight the Nazis, Boots explains that "none of it means nothing. . . . They hate Germans, but they hate me worse. If that wasn't so they wouldn't have a separate army for black men."

When Junto persists in asking what would induce Boots to fight, Boots responds, "Them white guys in the army are fighting for something. I ain't got anything to fight for. . . . I got a hate for white folks here . . . so bad and so deep that

I wouldn't lift a finger to help 'em stop Germans or nobody else." When Junto protests that "I don't see—," Boots interrupts him: "You never will because you ain't never known what it's like to live somewhere where you ain't wanted and every white son-of-a-bitch that sees you goes out of his way to let you know you ain't wanted. . . . Don't talk to me about Germans. They're only doing the same thing in Europe that's been done in this country since the time it started." [44] The war in Europe, let alone the one in the Pacific, is seen through Boots's eyes as immaterial to the survival of the Blacks of Harlem.

For Petry, the antifascist crusade could only have meaning to Boots and other African Americans if it also proposed action that addressed issues that immediately affected the lives of Harlemites. To be sure, the Popular Front policy promoted by the Communists at least rhetorically proposed to combine domestic antiracist struggles with antifascism, but its action program was constrained by the axiom that the defeat of the European fascists and Japan was the precondition for enhancing democracy in the United States. Publications such as the *People's Voice* reflected a degree of overlap between radical expressions of the Popular Front and restrained expressions of Double V, although it seems that Petry's characters, like those of John Oliver Killens in *And Then We Heard the Thunder* and Chester Himes in *If He Hollers Let Him Go*, could only be inspired by the most combative aspects of Double V—ones that proposed immediate struggles to uproot racism at home by means of militant mass action, work stoppages, and civil disobedience, regardless of whether they obstructed the Roosevelt government's efforts in waging the war. To those beyond the constrictions of the Communist-led Popular Front, advocacy of rebellion in the streets was not excluded, or at the minimum, it was an understandable response to the insufferable state of affairs for most African Americans.

Boots, flush with the security of his new job at Junto's, appears to have withdrawn from the battle of the streets as he also avoids the draft. Lutie Johnson, however, is still waging a war for daily survival; she shows no interest in the antifascist crusade, which appears principally in background conversation as remote. But Lutie's war is waged under an obfuscating veil. Although she has partial insights into her situation, she cannot cut through the reified class and race oppression that dooms the efforts of herself and her son, Bub, to escape the fate of most African Americans. She knows that she is primarily in a war against the street, which symbolizes the poverty, the dirt, and the threat of violence surrounding the lives of the Harlem poor. She also wages a war against other African Americans—predominantly men who seek to exploit her for sexual gratification.

Perhaps more ominously, Petry sees an impending race war emerging from the tension in the Harlem community following incidents such as the stabbing of a poor Black man by a baker who claimed he was being robbed. The following day, as Lutie walks by the bakery, she sees "two cops right in front of the door, swinging nightsticks. She walked past, thinking that it was like a war that hadn't got off to a start yet, though both sides were piling up ammunition and reserves and were now waiting for anything, any little excuse, a gesture, a word, a sudden loud noise—and pouf! It would start."[45] Lutie never verbalizes an attitude toward World War II similar to that expressed by Boots Smith. Instead, she is trapped in a wartime totalitarian-run house of her own, one that recalls the ghettoization of European Jews: "Streets like the one she lived on were no accident. They were the North's lynch mobs, she thought bitterly; the method the big cities used to keep Negroes in their place. . . . From the time she was born, she had been hemmed into an ever-narrowing space, until now she was very nearly walled in and the wall had been built up brick by brick by eager white hands."[46] From the perspective of the Popular Front versus Double V debate, as presented in Killens's *And Then We Heard the Thunder*, this is a house of racism that clearly cries out to be immediately torn down and built on new foundations—not one to be defended in the hope of gaining postwar rewards.

Petry's literary strategy in *The Street* partially simulates the strategy of other radical urban novels—including James T. Farrell's *The Studs Lonigan Trilogy* (1936) and Richard Wright's *Native Son* (1940)—in its use of naturalist imagery, like the wind ripping down the street, to reify social oppression. While such motifs promoted critics to classify this type of literature as "naturalism," the outlook of such Left writers cannot be reasoned out in terms of the passivity in relation to the power of environment or the denial of human agency that the term "naturalism" connotes. Ironically, the aim of Farrell, Wright, and Petry was to spur the reader to surmount the apprehension of social forces as the fixed forces of nature, which was how their fictional protagonists misunderstood their situations. In that these novelists were variously drawn to Marxism, they wished to move their audience to a clear critical consciousness that apprehended the class basis of institutionalized poverty and racism. This "dereified" understanding in turn would point the way toward the collective efforts needed for social transformation. But how does an author use the techniques of art to accomplish this end?

Farrell chose to confront the reader with the banality of Studs Lonigan's musings and perceptions, while posing on the horizon an alternative perspective through the means of a minor character, Danny O'Neill, and intimations of a growing radical movement. Wright used a lengthy courtroom speech by his alter ego, Mr. Max, a humanitarian Jewish lawyer and Communist fellow traveler. Ann Petry, in her quest to develop characters shaped by yet beyond the determinations of social existence, fashioned a third, riskier way.

Lutie Johnson commences her war against the street—in effect, the domestic equivalent of fascism—with an inappropriately elitist philosophy. Her middle-class assessment of 116th Street in Harlem as a "jungle" filled with "the snakes, the wolves, the foxes, the bears that prowled and loped and crawled on their bellies" would ultimately segregate her from any possible community, setting the stage for her isolation and consequent downfall.[47] Additionally, Lutie finds nothing in her understanding of African American culture to assist her efforts to resist. Unlike Petry's own experience, the stories of Lutie's Granny are simply "nonsense" to her.[48] The Black church, a force for change in Harlem at the time, is perceived as meaningless by her. Adhering to an ideology of self-reliance inappropriate to her circumstances, Lutie thinks she understands the street; she believes that one can fight it by way of a personal resolution to earn money in a dignified manner and rise above others. Yet she ends up killing another victim of forces stronger than himself, Boots Smith, and as a result condemns her son to a destitute childhood without his mother.

The method that Petry used to avoid the pitfalls of reductive characterization and the interpolation of idealized solutions might be identified as one of subtraction. Subtraction occurs in the sense that a general view of potential social solutions—such as those found in the 1942 *People's Voice* editorial—was familiar to Petry. These in all probability shaped her approach to many aspects of the novel but were deliberately excluded from dramatic representation either in the form of events or by articulation of her fictional protagonists. *The Street*'s characters are destined to proceed in the absence of such solutions. Negative factors are very much present, and some characters become increasingly cognizant of them; but Petry excludes dialogue or symbolic actions that point the way to a positive resolution of her characters' situation.

Her strategic decision not to dramatize facile answers remains grounded in a social-realist strategy, quite unlike the modernist and postmodernist advocacy of an open-ended play of signifiers wherein the reader may construct his or her own contingent meanings. The distancing of social cause in Petry's novel is used for the artistic purpose of accentuating her characters' internal struggles. Thus the reader principally witnesses Lutie not as determined by particular societal agents but as psychologically ensnared by her unsuitable philosophy that was inspired by the writings of Benjamin Franklin. This leads to Lutie's uncharitable, occasionally racist perceptions of her fellow Harlemites, as well as her reified, naturalist view of the street.

Consequently she acts in ways that show little understanding that the class and race domination of her fellow Harlemites requires a collective response. As in James T. Farrell's work, one sees glimmers of ambient factors that could, under other circumstances, lead toward a dereified consciousness and eventual social amelioration. These include Lutie's startling recognition that the women in the waiting room at the Children's Shelter were bonded by poverty, not race, and her momentary sense of community and power as she emerges from the subway in Harlem after being in the white sections of New York.

The raw materials of The Street are substantially based on what Petry saw and learned during her activities as a People's Voice reporter. In 1943 Petry joined Harlem's Play School Association Project at Public School No. 10, working as a recreation specialist developing community programs "for parents and children in problem areas."[49] Petry could conceivably have been Lutie, if she had been suddenly deposited as an unemployed single mother in Harlem without the strong nurturing family and professional skills she had acquired in Connecticut and the political consciousness she had gained from her experiences at the People's Voice.

Although its name, Junto, is the same as that of a business club associated with Benjamin Franklin, the interracial lounge in the novel derives certain of its features from the Savoy ballroom. The Savoy's owner was white, but he remained in the background while a Black man managed the ballroom. Perhaps the character of Junto appropriates elements of Dutch Schultz (a pseudonym for Arthur Flegenheimer), who grew up in Jewish Harlem and later forced his way into a partnership with the Black gangsters who ran the numbers game.[50] The political implications of the novel suggest that Petry had formulated an outlook on antiracist politics during World War II influenced by yet broader than the Communist-led Popular Front.

"HITLER'S UPRISINGS IN AMERICA"

Her politics are abundantly evident if one scrutinizes a story that Petry published a year later, one that is less beholden to the strategy of subtraction and comes closer to addressing the politics of social change. "In Darkness and Confusion" appeared in the third of Edwin Seaver's annual literary anthologies, Cross-Section: A Collection of New American Writing (1944).[51] The twenty-page story is a forceful literary portrait of the Harlem rebellion (customarily called the Harlem Riot) of 1943; it also presents poor African Americans in a light acutely different from Lutie Johnson's conceptions of them. Most significant, perhaps, is that the political take on the rebellion in the story is categorically at odds with that of the Communist movement at the time of the rebellion, which occurred four years prior to the publication of the story.

The Detroit and Harlem riots and the so-called Zoot Suit Riot in Los Angeles about which Chester Himes wrote in 1943 were disconcerting jolts to the Popu-

lar Front strategy during World War II. The violence in Harlem, which had a dis-
tinctly anti-Semitic component—Jewish shopkeepers were central targets—was
a clear disruption of the war effort, since work was halted and resources had to
be diverted to quell the disorder and looting. Moreover, the episodes were major
embarrassments to the effort of the United States to present itself as the beacon
of freedom and democracy. In addition, it would be easy to conclude from these
and similar urban revolts that the Blacks and Chicanos involved in them did not
share the view that the only road to liberation was through the subordination of
all other struggles to achieving victory over the Axis.

The urban rebellions created a dilemma for the Communist Party, which was
fiercely committed to antiracism. It had a long and honorable history of defending oppressed people who had committed violent acts or committed crimes as
a consequence of the deprivations and pressures of class society and bigotry.
How could the Communists maintain their antiracist stance and simultaneously
oppose any activities that might jeopardize war production? The Party's solution was to take the position that all three "riots" were instigated by profascist
agents and their domestic allies (fifth columnists); such elements were accused
of manipulating the racially tense situations in all three cities to create "insurrections" against a pro-Allied government in a manner calculated to assist the fascist and Japanese war efforts. This enabled the Communists to denounce racism
and appropriately link it to fascism, but at the cost of minimizing the horrific
conditions of ghetto poverty and of depicting the African Americans and Mexican Americans who exploded in pent-up rage and frustration as the unwitting
agents of Germany and Japan.

No evidence at that time (or later) came to light giving credibility to the Party's
explanation of the riots. Of course, there were racist and fascist-like groups in
all urban centers. Detroit was home to Father Coughlin's Christian Front and
Gerald L. K. Smith's America First Party, and there was at least one clash there
in which Ku Klux Klansmen played the instigating role. Pro-Japanese propaganda circulated in a number of African American communities. Moreover, in
New York, anti-Semitism had been present in Harlem long before the war, inflamed by African American distrust of Jewish shopkeepers and resentment of
the "Bronx Slave Market" where Black women gathered each morning to make
themselves available as domestics to a clientele that was heavily Jewish.

These facts notwithstanding, all available evidence indicates that the three
riots were triggered by different instances of interracial conflict, although in
each case the incidents became extravagantly distorted as accounts of them were
spread by word of mouth. In Detroit and Harlem, the incidents ignited long-

simmering rage and distrust in the Black community, not only about the persistence of racism and economic oppression, but about the mistreatment of Black soldiers in the segregated military.[52]

In "Fifth Column Diversion in Detroit," a protracted report published in the Communist Party theoretical journal, *The Communist*, Max Weiss claimed that "the nation has been the shocked witness of . . . Axis-inspired riots in Mobile, Beaumont, Los Angeles, Chester, Newark—and their culmination in the insurrection in Detroit—which brought the full extent of these Hitler diversionary tactics to the attention of the nation." Moreover, the fascist conspiracy had been successful: "The direct results achieved by the fifth-column forces responsible for these outrages can actually be measured in terms of the man-hours of war production lost—more than a million in Detroit, and hundreds of thousands in Beaumont, Mobile, and other places." Further, Weiss claimed that this "Axis fifth-column plan to disrupt and divert the home front" was also evident in the strikes of the United Mine Workers.

Weiss held that anyone who insinuated that the Detroit and Los Angeles riots were "purely American" race riots similar to post–World War I riots in Chicago and East St. Louis was guilty of absolving "the Axis and its American fifth column from their direct and immediate responsibility." Moreover, any attempt to suggest that the violence was caused by growing "tension" between whites and people of color would be tantamount to saying that the Nazi persecution of Jews was the outcome of tension between the two groups. To the contrary, he maintained that Negro-white unity in the United States had been clearly on the upswing during the war.

What had occurred, according to Weiss, were "insurrections against the war effort, consciously and deliberately organized by Hitler's fifth column in America, with the weakest link in the chain of our national unity—the integration of the Negro people into the war effort—selected as the sector of the home front on which to make a break-through." Weiss conceded that in Detroit "90 per cent of the Negroes killed were killed by the police" and "85 per cent of those arrested by the police were Negroes." However, this toll only confirmed that the "fifth column has, through one or another of its many agencies, penetrated quite extensively into the police forces in a number of cities."[53]

Following the August riot in Harlem, the 14 September 1943 issue of the *New Masses* featured Earl Browder's article "Hitler's Uprisings in America." The episodes in Detroit, Los Angeles, and Harlem are described as "Hitler at work on our own soil, dealing us blows heavier than those he has inflicted against us on the battlefield." Detroit, according to Browder, was "the clearest and most outstanding example of Hitler's invasion of America to date." Browder was particularly rankled by the statements of those who "deny any Hitlerite origin or significance" to the events and who claim that "these disturbances are all of domestic manufacture, one hundred per cent American." The "cold truth" was that the Los Angeles, Detroit, and Harlem explosions had occurred precisely "in the middle of 1943, on orders from Berlin, at a moment chosen by Hitler, for objects that benefit Hitler."

Browder also took a strong rhetorical stand against the segregated military. He observed that the racist practice hindered the efficiency of the army, branded the United States with a moral stigma in the eyes of the world, and caused "the patriotic Negro population, ten per cent of the country, [to be] aroused to a high pitch of indignation by the treatment of its men in the armed forces." Browder also took exception to the concept that "we 'postpone' the fight against anti-Negroism and anti-Semitism until the war had been won, because, forsooth, this fight might 'interfere with the prosecution of the war!' " On the contrary, "Defeat and abolition of these doctrines of racial superiority, the complete removal of their influence from social and political relationships within the nation, are a necessary part of achieving victory in the war."

What actions, then, did Browder propose for confronting anti-Black racism? His concluding point was that "anti-Negroism in all its manifestations of Jim Crow segregation, poll-tax laws, and all their consequences, must be rooted out of American social and political practice by laws, by energetic administration, and by public education." Absent from his proposal were the usual endorsements of radical tactics of mass social action such as strikes, sit-ins, and any other activity that might be considered disruptive but could bring a more immediate redress. Moreover, Browder used the abstract but noble sentiments the Party shared with the Double V movement to provide cover for the unconscionable smear that the revolt in Harlem was created and manipulated by outside, Nazi agitators.[54]

In *The Street* there is not the least indication that fascist agents were manufacturing the potentially incendiary conditions so graphically depicted by Petry. The environment of domestic race and class oppression was an adequate justification for the eruptions. The triggering circumstances are foreshadowed. The only space relatively free of racism in the Harlem community is among gangsters, which insinuates that gangsters might have the capacity to gain yet more influence, even in the political sphere. Yet the main gangster in *The Street*, Junto, has fought his way up from the depths of the poverty-stricken sector of New York and is genuinely puzzled by Boots Smith's negative attitude toward the antifascist crusade. Although Petry obviously intends the Black-on-Black violence to be a misdirected expression of legitimate rage, there is no suggestion that appropriate targets of Black rage should be fifth columnists or American fascists such as the Ku Klux Klan. Petry's target is primarily the social, political, and economic system in the United States that fosters race, class, and gender oppression.

Even more compelling evidence of Petry's outlook on the homegrown nature of wartime rage in Harlem can be found in her 1947 short story, "In Darkness and Confusion." Her protagonist is named William Jones, who shares the same last name as the depraved and threatening building superintendent in *The Street*. But this Jones is the devoted husband of an enormously fat and very dark woman called Pink, and he is father to his son, Sam, and a niece, Annie May, who lives with them. Sam's plans for college were dashed when he was drafted into the army and sent to Georgia for training. Annie May is a defiant eighteen-year-old who stays out half the night and cannot hold a job. Much of Jones's reflections and conduct are devoted to protecting Pink. He is concerned about Sam, who has stopped sending the family letters; he worries about Annie May, who seems headed on an irresponsible and self-destructive course; and he is especially worried about Pink, whose obesity and hard life threaten to worsen her heart condition.

Jones is employed as a porter in a drugstore. After work he wanders over to a barbershop to get a haircut and participate in the latest discussion about the course of the war. Among the customers he spots a soldier on leave from Sam's base and quickly drags out of him the shocking news that Sam is in an army prison. Sam was shot in the stomach by a military policeman for refusing to obey the Jim Crow law requiring him to ride in the back of a bus. Sam, in turn, shot the MP in the shoulder. He was sentenced to twenty years at hard labor.

Jones returns home desperate to keep the upsetting news from Pink. But he has a run-in with Annie May, who is exceedingly rude to him and announces her intention of moving out. When Pink returns from work at midnight, she takes Annie May's side, and Jones is left to ruminate on the failures of his life. The next morning is Sunday, and Pink prepares to go to church all day by herself. After a few hours Jones goes to a bar to think more about Sam's situation. The bar opens into a hotel lobby, and at this point Jones witnesses events roughly identical to those that scholars now believe set off the Harlem Riot in August 1943.[55]

In the lobby a white police officer is involved in a conflict with an inebriated Black woman, and an African American soldier intervenes. The tall soldier resembles Sam, and Jones watches in horror as the soldier wrests away the policeman's nightstick and hits him on the chin. With a crowd gathering, the policeman reaches for his gun, and the soldier starts to run. A shot is heard, and the soldier drops to the ground; word starts to spread through the crowd that the soldier is dead. To Jones, "it was like having Sam killed before his eyes."[56]

An ambulance arrives to take the soldier to the hospital, and the crowd, now in the hundreds, starts to follow the vehicle. Mounted white police officers fruitlessly try to disperse the throng. Jones joins the mob as his rage against Sam's twenty-year sentence is transmuted into rage at the police. He also recalls that the hospital toward which he is marching was where he and Pink had been subjected to racist insults when their last child died there. He begins to take pleasure from the power of the throng and the fear visible on the faces of the white authorities: "He began to feel that this night was the first time he'd ever really been alive."[57]

He then runs into Pink, who is carrying a large bottle of cream soda, amidst a group of women emerging from late church services. Jones abruptly blurts out the news of Sam's twenty-year sentence and then tells her of the killing of the soldier in the bar—although he admits to himself that he does not definitely know if the soldier was killed. Jones's only explanation of the shift from his protective attitude toward Pink is "She had to know sometime and this was the right place to tell her. In this semidarkness, in this confusion of noises."[58] Pink emits a high-pitched wail and heaves her soda bottle through the plate glass window of a furniture store. She then grabs a footstool and uses it to break the window of a dress shop.

As Pink, whose name seems to have revolutionary political connotations, continues her destructive spree, the mob follows suit, and Jones feels a great pride in his wife. Jones also begins thinking about how old he will be when Sam is finally released from prison, and this spurs him to accompany Pink as she leads the mob in attacking one white-owned store after another. When Jones spots Annie May destroying a naked white clothes dummy, he suddenly feels compassion for her: "She never had anything but badly paying jobs—working for young white women who probably despised her. . . . She didn't want just the nigger end of things. . . . All along she'd been trying the only way she knew how to squeeze out of life a little something for herself."[59]

Before Jones can connect with Annie May, he is swept to another intersection where the police are clubbing and arresting looters, and cars with loudspeakers are calling on the "good people of Harlem" to desist. Jones is revolted by the loudspeakers, as he repeats the phrase "of Harlem": "We don't belong anywhere, he thought."[60] In response to the appeals, he grabs a summer suit from a clothing store, then finds himself in a music store smashing all the records. By the time he finds Pink again, her rage against "the world that had taken her son" has reached a zenith. She rips the iron gate off a liquor store and, with eyes "evil and triumphant," urges the mob "to drink up the white man's liquor."[61]

Yet Pink quickly finds that it is the iron gate (or the world) that had actually triumphed, for she starts to stumble as "the rage that had been in her was gone, leaving her completely exhausted."[62] Jones tries to lead her home; but she collapses along the way, and her heart gives out. In the final sorrowful paragraphs, Jones discovers that he has changed:

> All his life, moments of despair and frustration had left him speechless — strangled by the words that rose in his throat. This time the words poured out.
>
> He sent his voice raging into the darkness and the awful confusion of noises. "The sons of bitches," he shouted. "The sons of bitches."[63]

Petry's view of the crisis of the Harlem Riot is unambiguous: The riot in Harlem grew out of homegrown racism, as expressed in the terrible social and economic circumstances that were exacerbated by wartime conditions. In particular, drafting Black men from the North into a segregated army and sending them to the Jim Crow South for training for mainly menial service jobs added insult to injury.

The rage in Harlem grows in the absence of a radical social movement in which Harlemites could gain access to the ideas and ideology that might afford hope and a political strategy. It is not surprising that rage experienced "in darkness and confusion" might transmute into looting and violence. It is indicative of the failure of the Harlem Left that the unidentified community leaders who emerged in cars with loudspeakers to pacify the crowd are met with contempt by Petry's protagonist. To be sure, the perspective of the politically sophisticated Petry should not be confused with Jones's perspective. Nevertheless, in crafting this plot Petry was fully aware that the leaders of the Communist Party in Harlem and others grouped around the *People's Voice* (Adam Clayton Powell was out of town) had been central to the pacification efforts she depicts in the story.[64]

Petry's political and literary evolution after *The Street* is marked by several abrupt developments. These are likely connected to her increasing disillusionment with the organized Left and her understandable desire for some self-protective cover, given the onset of Cold War–McCarthyite political repression. As *The Street* was receiving national attention, Petry boldly announced a plan to write a series of novels addressing various facets of African American life. She was asked by *Ebony* in April 1946 if she might soon write about Euro-Americans. Her reply was reported as follows: "She admits to being primarily interested in writing about Negro life though she will not say she will never write a book with a non-Negro theme." She is then quoted: " 'For the moment . . . I am mainly concerned with Negro life.' "[65]

Yet only one year later she published her second novel, *Country Place* (1947), which focused on white characters in a rural setting with few African Americans. Taking into account the length of time it takes for editors to accept a novel, recommend revisions in the text, and move through the production process, it is hard to guess when this full-length work was written or how her decision to focus on white characters so quickly displaced her previously announced plans.

Country Place appears as if it were a partial retreat to Petry's earlier pulp-fiction literary strategies. Although she would always describe it as a novel about a storm in a rural area, *Country Place* is actually about the consequences of wartime adultery and features a womanizer who sleeps with both a mother and her daughter.[66] In 1971 Petry denied that she intentionally wrote the novel to extend her repertoire into new racial terrain. She explained that "I happened to have been in a small town in Connecticut during a hurricane—I decided to write about the violent, devastating storm and its effect on the town and the people who lived there." She subsequently identified the town as Old Saybrook and the year of the storm as 1938; her explanation for the predominantly white characters is that the novel reflects the actual racial composition of the town.[67] The text of the novel and her statements about it seem to contradict her statement a year earlier in the March 1946 *Daily Worker* that she regarded herself as an "emotional arouser" who aimed to write a series of books that will "move [the public] to action."

At the moment *Country Place* was published, Petry moved with her husband to her birthplace of Old Saybrook; this time there were no interviews in which she might be asked to explain her rapid change of circumstances. She was then thirty-nine, and she resided in Old Saybrook until her death fifty years later. Although Petry episodically reviewed novels for New York newspapers in the late 1940s and early 1950s, most of her literary efforts were devoted to writing fiction for children and young adults. These include *The Drugstore Cat* (1949), *Harriet Tubman, Conductor on the Underground Railroad* (1955), *Tituba of Salem Village* (1964), and *Legends of the Saints* (1970). In 1958 she wrote a screenplay for Columbia Pictures (intended to be "That Hill Girl," starring Kim Novak) and five short stories. Her political concerns are still evident in many of these stories. Moreover, her third and final novel, *The Narrows* (1953), which will be discussed in volume 3 of this series, would be a monumental work that reconfigured the issues of race, gender, and Cold War repression on a new and striking plane.

In later years, Petry claimed that she left the *People's Voice* in mid-1944 because it was closing. However, the newspaper lasted until 1948. Among Petry's personal papers is the notification of her dismissal in mid-1943 due to staff cutbacks made for financial reasons. After her departure, both her "Lighter Side" and "National Roundup" columns were briefly assumed by Marvel Cooke before they were dropped. Apparently Petry appealed her dismissal to the Newspaper Guild on the grounds that she had not been given proper advance notification. The dismissal did not alter her commitment to the People's Committee.

Petry would later assert that she left New York City because she could not cope with her fame there; in particular, she did not like to "answer questions."[68] Perhaps coincidentally, the timing of her move back to Connecticut was congruent with the launch of the Cold War and the purging of left-wing staff members from the *People's Voice*. By the mid-1940s, Adam Clayton Powell recognized how vulnerable he was to having the Communist label pinned on him. So in 1946 he fired Doxey Wilkinson and forced Max Yergan to resign from the *People's Voice*. Marvel Cooke left in protest, and the paper filed for bankruptcy in 1947 and ceased publication the next year. Petry never said a word about any aspect of this period in her autobiographical writings or in interviews. Indeed, the author of a 1996 dissertation subtitled "The Short Fiction of Ann Petry" observed with justification that Petry, all the way up until her death, "has not been particularly forthcoming or cooperative concerning her career."[69] This reticence is clearly corroborated by Petry's grumpy and brief responses to questions from various interviewers over the years.[70]

There is reason to distrust Petry's terse answers to some questions. In an exchange that might have cast light on her role with the *People's Voice* and the People's Committee, and their relationship to her writing, Petry was asked by an interviewer, "I know that you worked as a reporter in Harlem for six years. Did this experience affect your writing in any way, perhaps both your style and subject matter?" Petry's monosyllabic reply was "Doubtful." There is evidence that something other than "doubtful" could have been said in response to the question. A compelling example can be found in a March 1946 interview in the Left-liberal newspaper *PM*, to which Petry occasionally contributed and whose printing presses were used to print the *People's Voice*. Petry stated forthrightly that "the kinds of violence" she wrote about in *The Street* came directly from her work as a reporter. She specifically related how she covered the stabbing in the back of an African American youth by a white delicatessen owner. The same incident is introduced in *The Street*, but the delicatessen owner is a baker who stabbed a Black youth for taking a piece of bread, recalling the "crime" of Jean Valjean in Victor Hugo's *Les Miserables* (1862).

Petry's interviews in the 1970s and 1980s show that she was happy to provide the names of all her relatives, writing teachers, and authors whom she met, but long after the end of McCarthyism, not one of her fascinating *People's Voice* comrades is recalled. Marvel Cooke, the Communist and *People's Voice* managing editor subpoenaed by HUAC, nonetheless insisted that she and Petry were "very good friends" and that she had spent "many weekends" visiting with Petry. Cooke was also sure that Petry was well read in Marxism and that she considered herself to be "very friendly" to, although not a member of, the Communist Party.[71] As for providing a literary interpretation, Petry's interviews in 1946 reveal an eagerness to explain her fiction and its underlying purpose; after the 1950s, she resists interpretation of her work.

The degree to which her public persona was deliberately fashioned to obscure her connections to the Harlem crusade, and how much of it is the result of accident and personal eccentricity, is difficult to ascertain. Symptomatic of the enigma is Petry's collection *Miss Muriel and Other Stories*, published in 1971. Since no editor for the volume is listed, one must assume that the selection, design, and sequence of the stories are Petry's. Understandably, Petry's earlier fiction, "Marie of the Cabin Club" and "The Siren Sounds at Noon," are not included in the volume, no doubt due to their brevity and more limited scope.

Yet any reader attempting to gain a sense of Petry's literary roots and evolution as an artist will be thoroughly befuddled by the author's decision to arrange the stories to a large extent in the reverse order in which they came into print and not to clearly date when each was published.[72] For an author who formerly wrote so adamantly of the centrality of the historical matrix in the production of fiction, it is paradoxical that she would publish what appears to be a retrospective anthology in a manner that can easily foster fallacious interpretations. Is it possible that Petry, after 1950, applied to her own life the same method of subtraction that she employed in her Harlem-based literary work? Whatever the inducement, the effect has been to cause her work to be interpreted out of context of the precise political struggles in which her vision was molded. Moreover, her activist career is one of many severed from accounts of the tradition of the literary Left in the era of the antifascist crusade.

FIGHTING THE FIFTH COLUMN

In contrast to Petry's approach, the contention that fascists, racists, and pro-Hitler agents were deliberately promoting disorder in Harlem during World War II was the bugaboo of several fiction writers close to the Communist Party. The two most widely known efforts to dramatize this claim appeared in 1943, Carl Offord's *The White Face* and Benjamin Appel's *The Dark Stain*. Both novels were expansively reviewed in the mainstream as well as the Communist press within months of the Harlem rebellion. Both were also excerpted in the popular journal *Negro Digest*, an independent magazine that was edited by Jewish Communist Party member Ben Burns (who will be discussed in Chapter 6).

Carl Ruthven Offord (1910–90) came from a middle-class background in Trinidad.[73] When his mother died and his father migrated to the United States, he was unhappily placed with a grandmother. At age eleven he rebelled by resolving to become a writer and dropping out of school to read while working at odd jobs.

With assistance from other relatives, Offord left for New York at age nineteen. He spent much of the 1930s working as an actor and a journalist and devoting himself to the study of painting, drama, and writing at the New School for Social Research. While working for the *Crusader News*, a paper that presented a weekly digest of news pertinent to African Americans, Offord wrote *The White Face*.

The novel's narrative evokes other African American "escape" novels in which the protagonists flee the violence of the South only to find disillusionment in the North. What is appalling about *The White Face* is that the married couple at the novel's center, Chris and Nella Woods, take such extraordinarily different paths as they confront unanticipated forms of racism in the North. Chris is drawn to a militant Black nationalism and anti-Semitism that is the instrument of white fascist bosses, while Nella joins Jews in a Popular Front interracial committee for justice.

The *People's Voice* greeted *The White Face* in May 1943 with a glowing review, praising Offord for the book's "human element rather than any propaganda angle." [74] In contrast, a few weeks later the *Daily Worker* published a long analysis by the African American Communist Party leader Claudia Jones (1915–64) that treated the novel as if it were a political document. Offord is criticized for the "unclarity" of his solution to the issues of fascism and anti-Semitism in Harlem and because he "fails to give a clear-cut answer in his novel as to how these evils can be overcome." The novel was not "realistic" because it failed to demonstrate that Blacks and whites were in the process of coming together: "The initial talent of this new author could have been used to describe this period with all of its undercurrents as one of the richest in the great growth of Negro-white unity— a history which is today responsible for the growing understanding that integration of the Negro people into our national life and the war effort is a military necessity." [75] A month later, Samuel Putnam devoted his *Daily Worker* column to praising the power of the novel, although he endorsed Jones's criticisms, adding that the "dark, tragic side of the picture" was too heavily stressed in comparison with the "progressive forces." [76]

Shortly after the 1943 Detroit riot, the *New Masses* gave even more space to *The White Face* in an extensive review by editorial board member Barbara Giles (1906–86). Giles, a Communist from a well-to-do Euro-American Louisiana family, was publishing excerpts in the *New Masses* from her novel-in-progress, *The Gentle Bush* (1947), about racism at the turn of the century. She described Offord's book as mainly focusing on "a Negro 'nationalist' movement." She concentrated on the contrast between Chris, who is ensnared and destroyed by Black nationalism, and his wife, Nella, who escapes to the haven of "progressive Negro and white forces."

In Giles's interpretation, a succession of contingencies account for the Woods' divergent paths. Chris is wanted on fraudulent murder charges in Georgia and must remain in hiding and without employment, which is scarce in Harlem. He finds a receptive community among the nighttime rallies led by an anti-Semitic Black Nationalist named Reeves. Reeves's angry rhetoric against "the white face" and his clamor for equality for African Americans seize Chris's emotions, blinding him to puzzling aspects of the nationalist movement such as the appearance of a Japanese speaker at a rally and what seems to be the approval of the white police. Nella finds work with a Jewish family at the demeaning Bronx Slave Market and comes into contact with another friendly Jewish family whose members steer her toward an interracial "progressive" coalition.

Given Offord's counterposition of Nella's path to the disastrous course of Chris, one might imagine that the political content of this novel would have been positively hailed. It provides far more evidence of "the birth of the new within the old" than Chester Himes's *If He Hollers Let Him Go*, praised in 1945 as the Communist Party's wartime line on racism was being reappraised, or *The Street*, which appeared in the midst of the *New Masses* controversy over Albert Maltz. Yet Giles, who enthusiastically applauded Offord's craftsmanship and choice of subject, objected nonetheless to the novel's characterizations. She asserted that Chris, Reeves, and the Black Nationalist movement (which ultimately turns out to be manipulated by the Christian Front) are vivid and memorable, while Nella and the progressive characters are thin and less interesting.[77]

Unperturbed by the criticism, Offord debuted in the Communist press with a guest editorial in the 1943 issue of the *New Masses* that appeared immediately following the publication of Browder's "Hitler's Uprisings in America." Offord began with an analysis nearly identical to Browder's: In Detroit, Los Angeles, and elsewhere, "Hitler's Guerrilla Forces in America" had carried out actions to disrupt the production of war materials, create panic, and otherwise impede the war effort. The primary difference between Detroit and Harlem was that in Detroit "race hatred was the weapon used to prevent Negro Americans from contributing their all toward the war program," while the situation in Harlem turned out differently because the city administration was more democratic. Offord respectfully disagreed with Browder's view that the Harlem disturbance was not a "race riot"; in his view, "any rioting by Negroes is a 'race riot.'"

What occurred in Harlem, Offord argued, was a "revolt against the whole structure of ghetto life." Pursuing the same approach Ann Petry would take in "In Darkness and Confusion," Offord described the Harlem riot as "a revolt against all traces of Jim Crow and color discrimination. It was against lynching, against food and rent profiteering in the war crisis which is infinitely steeper in a ghetto." As such it constituted a "new determination of the Negro" that must be understood as "the war against fascism on the home front." Moreover, Offord contended that good leadership was required: "In the absence of organized help from his Negro and white leaders and allies there will inevitably be more blind and desperate Harlems." He raised the call to "abolish the ghetto" and insisted that the continuing existence of the ghetto was "to the benefit of Hitler's guerrillas in America."[78]

That autumn Offord joined the army and was assigned to the Negro Port Company. During the war Offord continued to write, and he contributed fiction to Edwin Seaver's Cross-Section (1944) and Story.[79] Discharged in late 1945 with the rank of first sergeant, Offord launched several unsuccessful businesses importing spices and coffee, and he episodically engaged in journalism. In early 1947 The White Face was surprisingly subjected to a harsh reexamination in the new Communist literary journal Mainstream. This reassessment occurred in a review essay by the playwright Theodore Ward that also critically reconsidered the work of Ann Petry, Chester Himes, and William Attaway and took swipes at Frank Yerby and Richard Wright.

Ward went far beyond the earlier fault-finding of Barbara Giles and Claudia Jones. He insisted that Offord, like the other authors whose work he reviewed in his essay, was bitten by the bug of "defeatism" and that his novel actually "represents what appears to be a distillation of the author's own bitter, nationalist feelings, which, by nature of the situation and the plot, comes near to being unbridled anti-Semtitism." Ward also offered a startling explication of Chris Woods's death in The White Face, after his freedom is won by the interracial committee. He maintained that the inclusion of Chris's death was Offord's proof that an African American "can not even afford to accept his freedom so long as the white man is instrumental in its procural."[80]

Ever thick-skinned, during the following two years Offord published two more stories in the Communist literary publication Masses & Mainstream, both of which treat relations between U.S. soldiers and Black inhabitants of an island in the Caribbean.[81] By 1954 he was no longer associated with Communist publications and wrote a paperback thriller, The Naked Fear, about a white couple who kidnap a baby. In 1961 he founded the Black American newspaper in New York, which later launched the United Black Appeal, aimed at providing relief to Africa. In 1977 he organized the first Black American Film Festival. At the time of his death in 1990 he was attempting to complete an autobiography.

Benjamin Appel (1907–77) was well known to the members of the Communist literary movement since 1935, when he joined the League of American Writers just before the launch of the Popular Front. He refused to join the Communist Party due to deep-rooted suspicions about potential informers, although his wife, Sophie Marshak, was a member in the 1930s.[82] Appel made political contributions through service on leading committees of the League of American Writers, including the National Council until its demise after Germany invaded the USSR in 1941.

Although Appel's parents came from wealthy Jewish families in Poland, he was raised in the gang-ridden Hell's Kitchen area on the midtown West Side of Manhattan. He graduated from Lafayette College in 1929, and his first literary efforts were metaphysical, including *Four Roads to Death* (written earlier but published in 1935), set in Asia. Soon he was writing poetry and fiction for the little magazines in the late 1920s and early 1930s, and he was increasingly drawn to the Left. Turning to experiences from his own life for subject matter, Appel was inspired by Upton Sinclair and Theodore Dreiser. The major achievement of his early years was the "Brain Guy" trilogy, comprised of *Brain Guy* (1934), *The Power House* (1939), and *The Dark Stain* (1943). This sustained narrative of almost 500,000 words traces the evolution of the college-educated Bill Trent as he emerges in the Depression as a gang leader, strikebreaker, and finally, a full-blown fascist who promotes white supremacy and seeks to foment a Harlem race riot.

Among Appel's twenty-five works of fiction are many others with explicit political themes. *Runaround* (1937) treats political corruption in New York, while *But Not Yet Slain* (1948) concerns the Washington, D.C., bureaucracy following President Franklin D. Roosevelt's death. *Fortress in the Rice* (1951) and *Plunder* (1952) are harsh critiques of the U.S. occupation of the Philippines, where Appel had worked for the U.S. high commissioner Paul V. McNutt in the mid-1940s. His labor novels include *The Raw Edge* (1958) and *A Big Man, a Fast Man* (1961), while his gangster novels include *Life and Death of a Tough Guy* (1973) and *Hell's Kitchen* (1977). The versatile Appel also published a classic documentary narrative, *The People Talk* (1940); a historical novel of two families before World War I, *A Time of Fortune* (1963); and numerous juveniles, travel books, and popular histories and biographies.

In 1941 Appel was severely burned in an accident and moved from New York City to Patchogue, Long Island, to recover. After that he was employed as an aviation mechanic on Long Island and then at the Office of Civilian Defense in Washington, D.C. Following his sojourn in the Philippines, Appel spent seven months at the Office of War Mobilization and Conversion and then moved to Roosevelt, New Jersey, where he resumed writing full time. For the rest of his life he remained a liberal, although he sometimes identified himself as a "utopian."[83]

Appel's novel of the home front, *The Dark Stain*, was prophetic in myriad ways. The events triggering the rage in Harlem depicted in the novel involve the same types of characters that would be on the scene during the August 1943 rebellion that occurred shortly after the book's publication. There are an African American woman, a Black man who behaves strangely, and a white police officer who becomes frustrated and shoots the Black man. However, in The Dark Stain the woman calls the police, the man is mentally ill, and the policeman is a "progressive" Jew.

In a description of the novel that Appel offered in The Writer magazine in 1944, he related the process by which he wrote The Dark Stain. He explained that in 1942 he read a news article about a white policeman who had been forced to kill a "deranged" African American after acting with restraint. Appel then began the process of imagining what it would be like for this policeman if he were "decent" and antiracist.[84]

Appel went on for several pages describing the imaginative process and grueling footwork involved in researching materials to create his story. But he never explained why the white policeman was portrayed in the novel as Jewish. Instead, he emphasized that an antifascist commitment was crucial to his motivation for selecting characters. Although Appel did not consciously credit his own Jewish American background, when he decided to make the policeman decent and antiracist, he also made him a Jew. Moreover, Appel's character is a secular Jew, not one who embraces religion or Old World culture. In contrast, the Jewish policeman's father, who embraces his Jewishness, is a racist and is at odds with the son. The decision to make the policeman a progressive Jew underscores the stressful dilemma the wartime Popular Front posed for radical Jews like Appel, who had previously been outsiders arrayed against the system. The politics of the Popular Front meant that they were now expected to maintain law and order in support of Roosevelt's antifascist crusade.

When the New Masses reviewed The Dark Stain, the reviewer, Alan Benoit, focused largely on the novel's political value as an exposé of domestic fascism. Benoit praised Appel's dramatization of "organized fascism as an active agent behind situations which a complacent man might dismiss as showing no trace of fascist inspiration." While Appel's earlier novels had depicted interlocking connections among criminals, big business, and the police, The Dark Stain revealed a fascist conspiracy coordinated at the highest levels by a well-heeled organization, the American Research Association, headquartered in a Manhattan skyscraper. When the policeman in Harlem is forced to shoot a deranged Black man, the fascists see an opportunity to incite a race riot, which would soil the wartime United States with the "dark stain" of racial conflict.

However, the policeman, Sam Miller, becomes aware of the fascist conspiracy after his fiancée, a progressive trade unionist, is kidnapped by the fascists. He begins to mobilize allies including trade unionists and Harlem residents. Miller's fascist counterpart is Bill Trent, a gangster from the pages of Appel's earlier novels who is now a key agent for the domestic fascists and assigned to Harlem. The novel thus foreshadows the fascist and antifascist forces that might one day come into decisive conflict in the United States.

Benoit was also critical of *The Dark Stain*, along the lines of other complaints that appeared in the *New Masses*. One grievance was that the novel was "defeatist," and the other had to do with Appel's failure to create a positive hero. Benoit noted that Appel's white fascists, such as Bill Trent, were seen to tower above the positive characters such as Sam Miller and the African American community leaders. More precisely, Benoit protested that Bill Trent's psychology as revealed by Appel is rich and compelling, while Sam Miller and his associates are "confused" and the Black community leader Clair is "ineffectual." Benoit asked, "Why do so few novelists put into their books some of the sanity, the great intellect and grandeur of character for which anti-fascist leaders throughout the world are known?"[85]

When Appel published a defense of his novel the following year in *The Writer*, he argued similarly to the way that Ann Petry would defend *The Street* in 1950. What Appel called the "message novel" linked contemporary writers such as Upton Sinclair and Theodore Dreiser with earlier exemplars Charles Dickens and Leo Tolstoy. The aim of such message literature is to "record the bitter meanings of twentieth century society." In writing *The Dark Stain*, Appel had moved from a general concern with fascism to the specific issue of "race hatred in America." After doing his research in Harlem in the summer of 1942, Appel decided that the mode of a detective novel was most appropriate to telling his tale, because the fascists operated as a conspiracy and therefore detective methods were required to expose them.[86] But he did not address the criticism that he needed to create more idealized antifascist characters.

In years prior to the 1943 Harlem Riot, the Communist Party and its allies in the Popular Front had an extensive history of widely distributing literature unmasking diverse forms of racist and fascist activities in the United States. Leading up to World War II, some of the most spectacular antifascist books were those of John L. Spivak (1897–1981) and Albert Kahn (1912–79). Both authors were Jewish and were close to the Communist Party; both had a flair for reaching a mass audience; and both displayed considerable personal courage by directly confronting violence-prone right-wing groups. Spivak, however, was the trailblazer of the exposé genre. He had been involved in the socialist movement during the World War I era and had acquired seasoning during his years as a reporter in Moscow and Berlin. While Spivak's focus was on uncovering subterranean Nazi groups and the Ku Klux Klan, he also wrote about prisons and fraudulent mental hospitals and corruption in the steel and coal industries.[87]

Spivak's bond with the Depression-era Left was sealed by the 1932 publication of his book *Georgia Nigger*, a novel blending techniques of pulp fiction and documentary journalism to depict peonage and chain-gang life among African Americans in the South.[88] The dangers of espionage by fascist and right-wing regimes was his theme in *Secret Armies: Exposing Hitler's Undeclared War on the Americas* (1939) and *Honorable Spy: Exposing Japanese Military Intrigue in the United States* (1939). Spivak's essays regularly appeared in the *New Masses*, but he also collaborated closely with *Ken* (1937–39), a glossy-photo Popular Front magazine published by the founders of *Esquire*.

In the post–World War II era Spivak's two pamphlets attacking the Cold War domestic Right were issued by the Communist publishing house New Century, *Pattern for Domestic Fascism* (1947) and *The "Save the Country" Racket* (1948). At the onset of the antiradical McCarthyite witch hunt, Spivak vanished for twenty years, living under the pseudonym Monroe Fry. As Monroe Fry he was a frequent contributor to *Esquire* and became the editor of *True Weird Magazine*, which he filled with many of his own writings. He also wrote for the broader world of pulp magazines as Howard Booth, Jack Marchant, Howard Blaise, and Al Lippencott. In 1967 he briefly surfaced as John Spivak when *A Man in His Time*, his autobiography up to 1939, was published to laudatory reviews.[89]

Albert Kahn, born in London in 1912, was a 1934 graduate of Dartmouth College. He remained a committed Marxist throughout his life. Believed by some scholars to have been a secret member of the Communist Party,[90] Kahn led a number of antifascist and peace organizations beginning with the American Council against Nazi Propaganda (1938–41). In 1939 Kahn collaborated with the former U.S. ambassador to Germany William E. Dodd in publishing *The Hour*, a confidential weekly newsletter devoted to exposing Axis intelligence operations in North and South America. Kahn's first three books were coauthored with journalist and short fiction writer Michael Sayers: *Sabotage! The Secret War against America* (1942), *The Plot against the Peace: A Warning to the Nation!* (1945), and *The Great Conspiracy: The Secret War against Soviet Russia* (1946).

During the Cold War Kahn was blacklisted by the publishing industry. In 1954 he founded his own publishing house, Cameron and Kahn Associates. His cofounder, Angus Cameron (1908–2002), had been forced for political reasons to resign as editor of Little, Brown and Company. The new publishing house immediately caused a sensation when it issued the confessions of informer Harvey Matusow, *False Witness* (1954).[91] While maintaining a political activism in the cause of world peace, Kahn in his final years became a successful biographer of performance artists, including the Soviet ballerina Galina Ulanova and the cellist Pablo Casals.[92]

Neither Appel nor Offord was a member of the Communist Party, and there is no evidence that they were encouraged in their efforts by the Party. Their novels nonetheless illustrate the widespread acceptance by pro-Communists during the Popular Front era of an improbable interpretation of the causes of the 1943 riots in the ghettos of urban America. As a cultural force in the 1940s, the pro-Communist leadership of the antifascist crusade achieved its authority through the day-to-day practical activity of its adherents and a misplaced faith in the Soviet Union as fundamentally a repository of humanity's best interests. Writers such as Appel and Offord voluntarily incorporated and idiosyncratically reworked themes that they felt demanded artistic depiction, whether inspired by Party publications, journalists such as Spivak and Kahn, or other experiences.

{ 5

Disappearing Acts

When recounting the fortunes of the Communist-led cultural movement during the antifascist crusade, one is tempted to explain the revolving door of personnel as a function of the Communist Party's political mutations. The apostatic drama is heightened when famous writers depart the Party at critical turning points, sometimes with public fanfare. One thinks of James T. Farrell (1904–79) and John Dos Passos (1896–1970) breaking ranks during the Moscow Trials and the Spanish Civil War, Granville Hicks and Malcolm Cowley resigning from the Party and the League of American Writers in response to the Hitler-Stalin Pact; Richard Wright withdrawing from Party activity in revulsion because of its World War II policy subordinating African American protests to national unity; Ruth McKenney enduring public expulsion from the Party (as an ultra-Leftist) in the wake of the removal of Party general secretary Earl Browder (as a right-wing revisionist); and veteran Communist Howard Fast venting his anguish in The Naked God (1957) at the time of Nikita Khrushchev's revelatory speech to the Twentieth Congress of the Communist Party of the Soviet Union.

Yet a focus on famous "breaks" with Communism tends to depreciate other salient factors in the forging of the Communist literary tradition. One factor is the ample number of writers whose departures from the tradition are not wholly explicable by political disillusionment at prominent conjunctures. Communist political beliefs do not always transcend other formidable facets of life. Overall, there is little evidence to substantiate the contentions of several pioneering books about the literary Left that writers were destroyed en masse by their Communist political commitments or that, after the early 1930s, only one-book authors and literary hacks were attracted to Communism. Such an assessment is essentially a reductionist conclusion to an abbreviated political critique.[1] To be sure, turnover was continuous, and oppositional cultural movements such as the one led by Communists tended to attract more neophytes than established writers. But departures and unfulfilled professional lives often had their own explanations. Among the leading causes among rank-and-file members of the literary Left are traumas carried over from youth, inherited mental illness, physical ailments, premature death, lack of time and energy due to work obligations, expatriation, accusations of espionage, and diversions of interest. Some of these instances will be discussed here; others, in volume 3 of this series.

A pattern of quiet departures from the movement and the cessation of writing by promising writers began with the creation of the movement itself. The year 1934, however, has a peculiar prominence due to the spectacular disappearing acts of two young writers, aged twenty-five and twenty-eight. One, Henry Roth, authored what is now judged to be perhaps the most highly regarded novel of the pre–World War II Left, *Call It Sleep*; the other, Lauren Gilfillan, wrote one of the most widely read books in the early 1930s, *I Went to Pit College*. In early 1935, both writers signed the call for the First American Writers Congress on the cusp of the turn toward the Popular Front. After that, one vanished for three decades and the other for life. The failure of these two neophyte writers to follow up their initial successes can be blamed on neither Communism nor political commitment, but instead on the social and biological tragedies of humanity.

Call It Sleep was unquestionably drafted during Henry Roth's accelerating political radicalization, although he drew on memories that had accrued during earlier decades. While attending City College of New York in 1924–28, Roth became sympathetic to the Left; his loyalties were not solely to the Communist Party, but he acutely judged the Soviet Union as "a new social order built on the proletariat."[2] He sensed such sentiments surfacing as a logical and organic outgrowth of the situation in which he and his contemporaries found themselves. One individual from City College he recalled was Morris U. Schappes. Like Schappes, many students were Jewish and the children of immigrants who worked in sweatshops. Characteristically, Roth's initial sympathies for the Left were based on an abstract attraction to Marxism rather than readings of Marx and Lenin, which would come later. Moreover, the poverty he had known in his youth was no longer a pressing factor. By 1927 Roth was living with New York University English professor Eda Lou Walton (1898–1961), ten years his senior. When the Depression began two years later, the suffering of ordinary working people seemed to him like a spectacle with himself as an observer.

Wearing an English jacket purchased for him by Walton, Roth walked the streets and watched men standing in soup-kitchen lines and living in Hoovervilles. As he hovered on the fringes of the discussions in Walton's literary salon, Roth observed the shift in the conversation of the salon's intellectuals from quasi-mystical ruminations about the poetry of William Blake to impassioned arguments about the relation of the artist to Marxism and "the Revolution." Be-

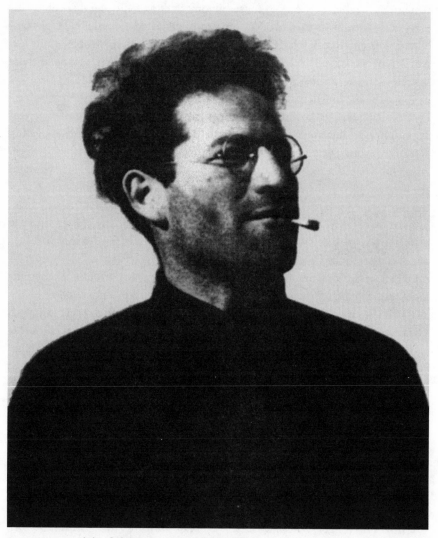

HENRY ROTH joined the Communist movement
in 1933 and remained sympathetic for the next three
decades. (Photograph by John Mills IV; courtesy of
John Mills V)

tween 1930 and 1932, Walton's soirees began to attract adherents of the Communist Party.

Hitherto the salon had been primarily attended by poets such as Leonie Adams (1899–1988) and Lynn Riggs (1899–1954); friends such as Ann Singleton and Hal White; the critic William Troy (1903–61); and the anthropologist Margaret Mead (1901–78). Among the new participants were the pro-Communist poets Horace Gregory (1898–1982) and Genevieve Taggard (1894–1948). Soon Richard and Louise Bransten, wealthy Jewish Communist activists from California, joined the salon. Richard Bransten, an aspiring but unsuccessful novelist, was for Roth an imposing figure; in contrast to the memory of Bransten held by others, Roth recalled him as handsomely built, articulate, and able to summarize the political situation in a personal and comprehensible way.[3] Roth's gravitation toward Communist Party commitment accelerated as *Call It Sleep* poured out onto paper.

In the summer of 1932, Hal White helped Walton locate a cottage in Maine where Roth was able to complete the major portion of the novel. When Roth returned to New York in the fall, he struck up an acquaintance with a carpenter who had been called to his building to do some work for Mary Fox, a Leftist neighbor affiliated with Theater Union. The carpenter's name was Frank Green, and Walton also subsequently employed him. Green was a Communist Party militant with a distinctive Irish accent who had traveled the world as a ship's carpenter. Roth was enchanted with Green, and soon they became intimate friends.

Unsuspecting of Roth's literary activities, Green brought him to a meeting of a waterfront unit of the Communist Party that had been organized to influence the International Longshoreman's Association. At the meeting, Communist Party leader Charles Krumbein gave a speech and asked all visitors to join the Party. Green had brought another guest who declined, but Roth agreed to join and was soon writing leaflets and attending classes on Marxism. Walton was horrified by the news of her protégé's Party membership; Roth recalled that she stayed up all night mourning what she feared would be the loss of his creativity. Walton's concerns were magnified when the 1934 West Coast longshoremen's strike broke out. The Party supported longshoremen's leader Harry Bridges and began to distribute literature on his behalf. Roth was caught passing out leaflets under a viaduct by goons working for Bridges's rival, and they beat him badly.

Roth's decision to join a proletarian unit of the Party, rather than a unit of other writers, was symptomatic of his tormented psychological makeup. While others saw brilliance in his novel and in his conversation, he mysteriously suffered from low self-esteem and a strong sense of guilt prior to making his Communist Party commitment. He knew he had an ability to produce narrative, which he had demonstrated in a student essay he had published at City College in 1925.[4]

EDA LOU WALTON was a New York University professor who
lived with and supported novelist Henry Roth during the 1930s.
She became pro-Communist in the latter part of the decade.
(From the Belitt Collection in the Howard Gotlieb Archival
Research Center at Boston University)

Yet he nonetheless felt incapable of grasping abstract theories and following through on their implications, whether Marxian or Freudian. He also felt incompetent to handle office work and was therefore drawn to manual jobs, although Walton supported him for most of the 1930s. For reasons he could not explain, Roth was dependent on older and stronger individuals to care for him; his mother had, in fact, accepted his relationship with Walton precisely because she knew that he was being well fed, clothed, and housed.

Roth remained an active Party member while he finished *Call It Sleep* in 1933. In 1934, with the help of David Mandel, a labor attorney and friend of Walton's who was part-owner of Ballou Publishers, the novel was published. Although the *New Masses* issued a short, unfavorable notice, the *Daily Worker* immediately hailed it as a masterpiece, and the *New Masses* judgment was buried under powerful letters to the editors hailing the novel.[5] Despite this reception, Roth minimized his contact with Party intellectuals, aside from an occasional discussion with Samuel Sillen. When Green went back to sea as a ship's carpenter, Roth transferred his need for a political mentor to a German American Communist who used the Party name Bill Clay.[6] Clay, who had worked baking cookies for the Nabisco Company, had lost a hand in an industrial accident and was also tormented by an unfaithful wife.

Roth's semiautobiographical *Call It Sleep* seemed to demand a sequel as the logical next step in the author's literary development. But Roth's fascination with Clay convinced him that he must instead write a novel based on Clay's life. Although scholars have speculated that pressure from the Communist Party caused Roth to change the subject of his projected novel, Roth contended that the primary influence of the Party on him was to broaden his horizons beyond New York City.[7] Roth's view of Clay as an exciting character on which to base a new novel was not the only reason why he could not plunge ahead with a sequel to *Call It Sleep*. More likely he was paralyzed because he found it impossible to move the autobiographical character David Schearl to the next level. To re-create his own experiences, he would have had to depict David in incestuous relations with his sister and cousin. Instead, in *Call It Sleep* Roth had not mentioned his sister and had shifted sexual tension to David's Oedipal complex in relation to an imaginary mother based on Eda Lou Walton.[8]

Sixty years later, when Roth finally wrote and published sequels to *Call It Sleep*, he revisited his early years. This time he included frequent episodes of incest between the autobiographical character, now named Ira, and his sister and his cousin. But Henry Roth in 1934 could not confront his youthful violation of sexual taboos, in fiction or personally. He created a persona free of the predispositions and temptations that would lead to sibling incest. His novel's title, *Call It*

Sleep, connotes the world of the unconscious to which he hoped to consign the guilt that haunted him, with unanticipated punishing consequences for his literary career.

During the mid-1930s, Roth was vexed by the double guilt over his sexual transgression and his situation of unearned privilege by virtue of Walton's financial support. Joining the Party, under the tutelage of older male mentors, Green and Clay, was a means not only of assuaging guilt but also of defying Walton, his mentor-protector, and making a belated transition from adolescence to manhood. His relationship with Walton was emotionally convoluted; she continued to have affairs with other men and to tell Roth about them. One of these was with David Mandel, whom she later married. Breaking with Walton seemed to be the logical next step, as a rupture with her held the promise of sexual well-being.

Throughout the time Roth labored over his unfinished manuscript about a German American worker, he was engulfed alternately by sexual reveries and self-loathing that he had hoped his Party commitment would purge from his consciousness. In his torment he felt that he alone suffered from such conflicts. The more he struggled to escape his distressed psyche by immersing himself in the "impersonal" class struggle, the more he began to feel that his mental state was afflicted by "aberrations in desire and sexuality and sexual fantasy." [9] To him, the effort to commit himself to an ideology functioned as a kind of corrective sexual puritanism; it was also a response to his mother, who held socialist ideas without having any concrete political perspective. But the contradiction was wrenching; he was emotionally caught up in sexual fantasy and uncontrollable desire while intellectually pledged to the revolutionary cause. For a while he succumbed to the former and dropped his Party membership, becoming a fellow traveler. It was in that capacity that he agreed to Richard Bransten's request to submit a statement of support for the Moscow Purge Trials—a thoroughly apolitical statement that appeared in the 2 March 1937 *New Masses*, in which his denunciation of Trotsky's "monstrous ego" was more likely a self-criticism. [10]

When Roth attended the Yaddo artists' colony in 1938, he met not only the writers James T. Farrell and Kenneth Fearing (1902–61) but also a radical composer, Muriel Parker. He then returned from Yaddo to find that Walton had become a Communist and that David Mandel, originally hostile to the Party, was a fellow traveler. At that point Roth informed Walton that he was involved with Parker and that their relationship was ended. Still under the influence of Clay, however, he decided that he might finalize his break from Walton by living on his own for a time. The plan was for the two men to travel to the West Coast for five or six months. En route they had a mission to carry out: Clay had been born in Ohio under such murky circumstances that he was unaware of his birth date.

In 1938 Roth accompanied Clay to city hall in Cincinnati to discover the truth. Clay was appalled to learn that he was fifty years old. The two friends continued their westward journey. Roth and Clay had conflicts while in California, but Roth returned to New York feeling stronger and more independent and finally free of his need for Walton.

At that time war was looming. Shortly after he married Muriel Parker, Roth rejoined the Communist Party, and his new wife joined as well. With millions of men being drafted, Henry trained as a tool-and-die maker and became active in the United Electrical and Machine Workers Union. Following the war he and Muriel decided that they did not want to raise their two children in New York City and moved to Boston, where Henry worked at making gauges and tools at the Keystone Company and attempted to carry out Party work. But they found a housing shortage in Boston and were unable to afford a comfortable apartment. They read about available cheap housing in Maine, and Henry moved his family into an old house on a 100-acre farm. Initially Henry remained in Boston alone, continuing his Party work, but he found himself unable to recruit a single worker. Muriel became the chief breadwinner, and Henry moved to Maine to raise geese and ducks while in 1949–50 also working at a mental institution.

Henry Roth continued to receive Party literature, and Party members visited his home to discuss the political situation. But he became increasingly suspicious that these visitors were really FBI agents. When he noticed that a car was following his, he canceled his subscription to the *Daily Worker*. In 1951 his confidence in the Soviet Union was badly shaken by the "Doctors' Plot" (Stalin's paranoid accusation that a group of Jewish doctors were engaged in an attempt to assassinate Soviet leaders). His sympathy for the Party was now accompanied by a degree of mistrust. His adherence was further eroded by the 1956 Khrushchev revelations, although his membership by then had lapsed, and he paid little attention to the resulting internal Party struggle. When the FBI came to his house to question him, partly out of a concern that the breed of ducks he raised was called "Muscovite," he told them, "If you want to know the closest thing for which I stand, I'm a Titoist." [11] With his literary aspirations long banished, he devoted himself to calculus problems for the next four or five years instead of reflecting on his personal and political past.

Until 1967 Roth still regarded himself as a Marxist and believed that the example of the Soviet Union as a model for socialism took precedence over all other concerns. Even when the USSR invaded Hungary in 1956, he thought that Soviet leaders were justified in halting what he perceived as a capitalist restoration there. When the Cuban Revolution occurred in 1959, he was wholly on the side of Fidel Castro. But at news of the 1967 war in the Middle East, he experienced a certain reversal. His training in the Party's version of Marxism told him that the Arab forces were the more "progressive," but he was terrified that several million Jews might be slaughtered. He had felt this way before, during World War II — as if his own life was at stake when the Red Army went into battle against Hitler — and again in 1962, as the Cuban revolutionaries faced down President John F. Kennedy.

This time, perhaps as a much-delayed aftershock of the Holocaust, the feelings of strength and power he derived from identifying with the victorious Israeli state were far more intense. Following the emergence of his new sense of ethnic belonging, Roth struggled to reestablish his identity as a writer, with occasional stories and interviews. After Muriel's death in 1990, what remained of his writer's block dissolved, and a new version of his childhood began to appear in a sequence of novels he wrote covering his adolescence and young manhood. Roth died just as the novels were coming off the press, but he had become something of a literary legend during the last three decades of his life. Although he was not exactly a literary phoenix rising from the ashes, his creative powers had been sufficiently restored to allow him to craft several new semiautobiographical novels. No such opportunity came to his female counterpart.

THE ORDEAL OF LAUREN GILFILLAN

Early in the summer of 1930, a twenty-one-year-old Smith College junior disrobed before an eminent physician in Kalamazoo, Michigan. The student's worried mother had brought her home from Northampton, Massachusetts, where she had been hospitalized in a "highly nervous state" following repeated episodes of unconventional behavior.[12] The student was Harriet Woodbridge Gilfillan (1909–78), and such episodes were not exceptional. Since age eight, when she had run away from home in quest of adventure, Harriet had exhibited high spirits and a rebellious temperament.

At age fourteen, Harriet displayed a precocious literary talent — producing diaries, poems, and letters — as well as an equally precocious preoccupation with sex. Harriet and her friends circulated "hot" books, one of which, *The Plastic Age* (1924), was about the dissipated life of a male college student; they disguised it inside the cover of Raphael Sabatini's swashbuckling adventure novel *The Sea Hawk* (London, 1915; New York, 1924). In her early teen years, Harriet continued to disappear from home and frequently kept the company of homeless people whom, like everyone else, she affectionately called "bums." She shocked her community by smoking in public, and she dreamed of having a Bohemian life. After graduating from Smith College, she planned to make a beeline for Green-

LAUREN GILFILLAN was a best-selling radical author of the early 1930s who disappeared from literary history. (Courtesy of Henry Gilfillan)

wich Village, where she would live in an artist's garret and forge a career as a successful writer.

At age twenty-one, Harriet's plans seemed threatened by incidents and episodes judged erratic by her family, friends, and teachers. The Kalamazoo doctor completed his examination, consulted with his colleagues, and presented Caroline Gilfillan, Harriet's mother, his diagnosis of a psychological complex based on biological abnormalities of a sexual nature. Caroline quickly conveyed the diagnosis in a letter to Harriet's Aunt Emily:

> Her genital organs are undeveloped.
>
> The uterus is infantile and she is so small that the doctors say she can never . . . deliver a child without a caesarian operation. . . . The doctors agreed that lack of development in the genital organs has its effects upon her mental make-up and that she will probably never be very stable. They say that her mentality is high and she may do splendidly in some congenial work—[but] she seems to live in a perpetual state of adolescence.[13]

Four years later, this perpetual adolescent who never grew taller than four feet, eight inches, was propelled to national fame when she published, under her new name, Lauren Gilfillan, the sensational best seller *I Went to Pit College* with the imprint of the Viking Press.

The book ostensibly was a nonfiction narrative in which a college graduate travels to the scene of the Great Coal Strike of 1931 in the coal town of Avella, Pennsylvania, thirty miles from Pittsburgh. "Pit College" is the ironic term that local miners use to refer to the mines, an allusion to the University of Pittsburgh, called Pitt for short, where the children of the wealthy went to college at that time. The protagonist, Laurie, disguises herself as a child, a boy, and a male coal miner, to gather information for a book during five weeks lived at a high-pitched intensity. The Pit College adventure includes hunger, violence, birth, death, romance, jealousy, and a sensational political trial—all the elements of a romantic or melodramatic novel. *I Went to Pit College*, however, was marketed as a mix of autobiography and reportage. Indeed, the very busy cover of the first edition features on the spine a photograph of the author in cap and gown at her graduation from Smith College; on the front jacket of the book are seven documentary pictures, one showing the author dressed in miner's overalls beside a real miner and the others depicting various scenes of demonstrations, military occupation, shacks, and so on.

Selected as the Literary Guild Book for March 1934, *I Went to Pit College* was guaranteed an initial sale of 50,000 copies. But that scarcely accounts for the national sensation it created. There were more than seventy-five reviews; most were wildly enthusiastic, and some appeared on the front page of book review sections. Across the country there were announcements of meetings at public libraries and of small-town literary clubs where discussions of *I Went to Pit College* were to be held, usually preceded by a presentation on the book by a local woman. Gilfillan was the subject of dozens of news articles in which a standard biography recounted her upbringing in a family of social workers who lived in the Washington, D.C., slums at the time of her birth; the family's subsequent move to the Midwest and Kalamazoo; Gilfillan's dismay at finding herself unemployable after graduation from Smith College in the depths of the Depression; and finally, her acceptance of the "dare" of a publisher, George Palmer Putnam (husband of the aviator Amelia Earhart), to relocate to a coal mining town in order to immerse herself in an "experience" that would become the basis for a successful first book.[14]

Invariably as well, the authors of these interviews—usually male—would dwell on Gilfillan's gender and physique to emphasize the contrast between her apparent female frailty and the horrors allegedly experienced by this "small Irish girl from Smith College" on her journey from middle-class security to the heart of darkness amidst western Pennsylvania's coalfields. Typical was the amazement expressed by the leading critic Burton Rascoe in the March 1934 issue of *Esquire*: "A very sprite of a girl, so tiny, so doll-like and so helpless-looking that the almost uncontrollable masculine impulse is to pick her up and stuff her into an overcoat pocket, has written a book displaying terrifying courage." The national acclaim accorded the book was well-summarized by the Raleigh, North Carolina, *News and Observer*. An article titled "Life in Mining Town Portrayed" referred to *I Went to Pit College* as the "book that has taken the country by storm" and went on to assert, "With one accord the book critics of the metropolis of New York have welcomed this volume as a harbinger of a new era in literature. A new star has swept into the literary firmament."[15]

This new star, however, was to some extent an invention of the media, an invention required by the national imagination. The personality depicted in the papers facilitated the mediation between the America of the urban and the small-town, book-reading public and the sudden, rather brutal emergence of an underclass that was forcing its way into the pages of literature and accordingly to the center of mass culture. The other America revealed in Gilfillan's book, among many additional books in the 1930s, was largely peopled by the horrifically impoverished and exploited, most of whom were of Southern and Eastern European and African American ethnicities.

OF GENDERS AND GENRES

The naive, Girl Scout–like "Smithie" of the newspapers bore little resemblance to the real Gilfillan, as her life can be reconstructed or even as she engagingly appears in her own narrative. *I Went to Pit College* is a book that the scholar Paula Rabinowitz so aptly characterized in 1991 as "probably the most thoroughly self-reflexive piece of proletarian writing to emerge from the 1930s."[16] The headlines of the reviews from across the nation invariably emphasize an encounter between innocent, middle-class female vulnerability and the brutal "raw life" of the proletariat. Gilfillan seems to stand for the known and familiar, an extension of the reader's sensibility, while the miners are both the other and the frightening reality. "College Girl in the Pennsylvania Mines" read the headline on the front page of the *New York Herald Tribune* books section, accompanied by a full-page color painting of a ramshackle Pittsburgh mine with two bent-backed workers walking in front of it. Other headlines include "College Girl among Striking Miners," "Girl Reporter in Coal Country," "Girl's Story of Mine Town Is Grim but Fascinating," "A Girl Writes of Miners," "Girl in Mining Town," "Smith Girl Observes Life among Poor Miners," and "A College Girl Paints Life of Coal Pit Folk."[17] The Communist *Daily Worker* headline was a bit less dramatic, but the contrast of gender and class was still evident: "A College Girl Writes about Western Pennsylvania Miners."[18] A typical variation of such headlines would be "Degree in Raw Life Was Hers." And to emphasize the corrosive effect of attending proletarian Pit College after the well-to-do and all-female Smith College, the issue of *Time* magazine for 5 March 1934 ran a photograph of Gilfillan looking quite prim and proper, while underneath the photograph a caption read, "Her make-up wore off."[19]

The problem of describing the narrative's relation to reality was as vexing for critics as articulating the exact genre of the narrative. Among the most tortured remarks were those of midwestern writer Zona Gale that appeared on the front page of the *Herald Tribune* books section: "In the accepted library classification of 'fiction' and 'non-fiction' . . . this book belongs to non-fiction, for it is a straight record of fact. But it is as absorbing as the best in fiction, and it is out of the stuff of which fiction is made." At the same time, however, Gale apparently saw *Pit College* as some kind of photographic fiction. She concludes, "There is no brief, no thesis, no accusation. It accuses no more than the picture of typhoid fever. . . . It is today's fiction—the new fiction that is about something vital concerning a group of today. Such fiction, being truth, is as strange and as terrible as truth always is. The book is fiction as *Les Miserables* is fiction—not because it tries to be, but because it cannot help it."[20]

Such riddles became commonplace as various reviewers tried to reconcile their belief that the events depicted must be true with their sense that they were reading a novel. William Soslon declared in the 2 March 1934 *New York American* that the book has "the feeling of true reporting." The *New York Sun* of the same date proclaimed it "good Reporting. . . . It is a superb piece of reporting." And yet, "It reads like a novel." *Time* magazine agreed that it "reads like a first-rate novel." Herschel Brickell, in his column "Our Table" in the *New York Post*, explained that "it becomes more of a novel than many books that are classified as novels" but it is also "a fine and valuable social document." "Social reporting after *Survey Graphic*'s heart," stated the *Survey Graphic* of Concord, New Hampshire. The *Nation* simply characterized it as "a document of the plight of one group of workers." "Essentially honest reporting" was the view of the "Books on Parade" section of the *New York East Side Home News*.[21]

Burton Rascoe went much further, proclaiming it "one of the great masterpieces of reporting." Yet, the *Yonkers New York Record* insisted that "what results is an almost unbelievable account of her experiences." Several other responses challenged the veracity of the text. Communists in the *Daily Worker* and the *New Masses*, although praising some aspects of the book, insisted that the portraits of Communist activists and the descriptions of YCL meetings were total fabrications. A minister who had worked in Avella insisted that the descriptions of the insensitivity of the church were slanderously false.[22]

Fifty years later an enterprising journalist for a western Pennsylvania newspaper went to Avella to interview participants in the Great Coal Strike. When the subject of Gilfillan's book came up, those interviewed universally condemned it as fiction. They claimed that Gilfillan had dramatically exaggerated the degree of poverty, hunger, and ignorance of the population — the very issues that had so captivated the reading public.[23]

As might be expected, the Communist press took the most searching approach. After all, the book was about "their class" — the industrial working class moved into action by Depression conditions. Moreover, the Gilfillan phenomenon — the middle-class artist seeking to represent the proletarian other — was then a central issue of debate within the Party-led John Reed Clubs. In the May 1934 *New Masses*, there was a review by Party member Helen Kay. This was a pseudonym for children's author Helen Goldfrank, who would later be revealed as a central character, Shirley, in Gilfillan's book. Kay stated, "Many of the chapters lose out by the author's efforts at fiction — which, if given in pure truth, would have added much to her work." Gilfillan's account of a Communist meeting, according to Kay, was typical of her fantastic fictionalizing. While acknowledging that other scenes, such as those of workers' daily lives, comprised "a fine piece of reporting," Kay nonetheless regarded *I Went to Pit College* as a "respectable college girl's adventure among the savages."[24]

Gilfillan posed an enigma for the Left. Clearly, she was sympathetic to the Communists' aims, but she was also satirically critical of the Party members she depicted. She was especially amused by what she saw as their inappropriate tactics and their illusions about workers being motivated by a higher class-consciousness rather than pragmatic economic self-interest. Thus, it was nothing less than sensational when Gilfillan herself appeared at the John Reed Club meeting on 16 April 1934 to speak on the topic "The Ideology, Political and Literary, behind My Book." What radicals called the bourgeois press, which covered the event, reported that Gilfillan admitted at the outset that she had had to look up the meaning of the word "ideology" in the dictionary before coming to the meeting. But all accounts—in the Communist as well as the mainstream press—agreed that she held her own in spite of a tumultuous situation that might have been any other author's worst nightmare.[25]

According to a long description of the event in the *Daily Worker* by Nathan Adler, later an eminent clinical psychologist in the Bay Area, the floor was immediately taken by the *New Masses* reviewer Helen Kay. Kay revealed that it was she who had been portrayed in *I Went to Pit College* as the exotically beautiful Jewish "villainess" Shirley. In the *Daily Worker*, the amazed Adler depicted Kay's intervention as that of "a character [who] was walking out of the pages of [Gilfillan's] book to challenge the author, her 'creator.'"[26] In the book Shirley, the Communist Party organizer who is to some extent motivated by her jealousy over the transfer of the affections of Johnny Cersil, a young worker aspiring to be a writer, from herself to Laurie, persecutes Laurie as a possible ruling-class spy. In a memorable scene, Shirley delivers a powerful tirade against "art for art's sake"—to which the awestruck and apparently worshipful Laurie can only reply, "Shirley, you're beautiful!"[27]

Next spoke Pat Touey, a leader of the National Miners Union, who said that he had come to the event with "blood in his eye," prepared to take revenge on the author—"but didn't have the heart, after he saw this honest and disarmingly charming slip of a girl."[28] The most extensive remarks appeared in *Partisan Review*, then an official organ of the John Reed Club. The reviewer was Ben Field, a pseudonym for Moe Bragin (1901–86), at that time a short-story writer and later a quite prolific novelist. Field complained that Gilfillan's work was corrupted by her insistence on remaining an outsider to the proletarian movement and that she could only shed her college miseducation and "imagery" of "middle class consciousness" by using Marxist analytical instruments and participating in the struggle.[29] The Daily Worker reporter lionized Field as an example of a writer from the middle class who had given himself totally to the workers' cause: "Field has come to us from her [i.e., Gilfillan's] world and he has come to us simply, giving all of himself. He is earnest and humble. He knows and spoke honestly of the middle class artist grappling to destroy his old self so that he may approach the revolution."[30]

Gilfillan defended her work, as reported in the Daily Worker, by saying that although she was struggling hard to make herself into a "revolutionary artist," she found that "Communists sometimes showed too much fervor and not enough tact or appreciation for the psychological problems the individual was faced with." She listened but did not capitulate to the onslaught of John Reed Club members, one of whom argued that "the writer with a middle class background dissects himself, all activity paralyzed; he retches painfully, tearing up clots of his innermost self; in the end he drowns in his own foul vomit." Gilfillan retorted that the Communist "technique was bad. She said we wanted to knock her down and drag her home. She would come in her own way."[31]

Gilfillan had been in dialogue with Communist Party members at least since the summer of 1931. In 1932 she cast her vote for Communist presidential candidate William Z. Foster. But she had consistently held her ground against the prevailing John Reed Club notion of writers transforming themselves into proletarian cultural soldiers in the Revolution. However, her insistence on retaining the "right" to her own personality was not so much due to her middle-class origins or Smith College education as the Communists and others thought it was. Despite her intense love for her family and a genuine adulation of her working professional mother, Gilfillan had long sought a release from middle-class conventionality. Her experiences at Smith College seem to have played a role only as a counterexample to a real education, which she identified with her work experience. It was Gilfillan's radical, proletarian, and Bohemian identity—one that she had worked so hard to construct—that she was unwilling to simply "destroy." It was by writing I Went to Pit College that she had finally and most fully given birth to her new identity, which was signaled by her abandoning the name Harriet, which she hated, for Lauren, which she thought was more colorful and less feminine.

THE WOUND AND THE BOW

The writer who went to Pit College was not at all a girl who clung to middle-class respectability or feared dirt, poverty, powerful emotions, and raw life. By and large, the middle-class values and ties demonstrated by the protagonist Laurie in the novel reflected Gilfillan's self-satirization as remnants of a Harriet who had not yet been fully purged. The author who wrote the book was neither Harriet nor Laurie but Lauren, which was the name she called herself and wanted others to call her. Lauren was the antibourgeois Bohemian who readily took to the road with bums without a penny in her pocket and who sought out the roughest and wildest neighborhoods in which to live, furnishing her room with odds and ends that she borrowed, picked up on the street, or stole. Lauren was scarcely a repressed, middle-class puritan. She led a fast-paced and varied sexual life, sometimes with three dates a day. From the time she was a teenager her engaging personality attracted so many ardent male admirers that she could not help but break hearts, including that of "Johnny" in Avella.

In such a context, Gilfillan's radicalism, although not essentially ideological, was strong and present as a natural expression of personal and cultural rebellion. After her stay in Avella, Gilfillan befriended the Left journalists Harvey O'Conner (1897–1987) and Jessie Lloyd (1904–88) in Pittsburgh. She was attracted to the idea of accompanying Lloyd to Kentucky to cover the murder trials that had grown out of the labor struggles there.[32] Later Gilfillan lived at the Michigan home of the Federated Press editor Carl Haessler (1888–1972). She was fascinated by this "millionaire Communist" whose troupe of visitors had freshly returned from the USSR.

In the year between her departure in the fall of 1931 from Avella and her writing of I Went to Pit College in the winter of 1933, Gilfillan lived in both the African American community and Bohemia of Chicago, where she knew Ben Ray Reitman (1897–1942), the famed whorehouse doctor and lover of Emma Goldman. In correspondence with friends, and with George Palmer Putnam, the editor who had dared her to write I Went to Pit College and who acted as her literary agent in selling several excerpts from it, she frequently told them that she might join the Communist Party. Yet she also reported hilarious episodes where both she and the Communists trying to recruit her looked downright silly. Then suddenly in the midst of the debate about Party commitment that had surrounded her appearance at the John Reed Club, Gilfillan announced (at the beginning of that meeting) that she had recently married a Communist—the Hungarian-born antifascist militant Andrés Kersetz. The two were already deep into studying Lenin and about to depart for the Soviet Union.[33]

A year later, however, they quietly divorced. Gilfillan's last publication, "Why Women Really Might as Well Be Communists as Not, or Machines in the Age of Love," an essay that appeared in the dissident Marxist journal Modern Monthly, had been published in February 1935. By midsummer Gilfillan had vanished completely from public view. I Went to Pit College continued to sell steadily through the 1930s, going into its sixth printing in 1938. It was one of 200 best sellers chosen for the library of the White House, and in 1936 it was declared one of 700 books necessary for a home library.[34]

Gilfillan's effort to tell what it was like to attend Pit College seems trapped between her need to respond to the Depression conditions by creating a character who behaved like many male role models in literature and the socially constructed female ideal that readers and reviewers attached to a female author and protagonist. The male role model character was, of course, the prevailing vehicle for a writer in quest of exciting material for a popular book; male experiences were normally acquired by fighting in a war, hitting the road, or seeking some other adventures. As the class struggle merged with antifascist sentiments after 1933, such a masculinist view of "real experience" was behind George Putnam's dare to Gilfillan to move to the strike venue to gain material for a book. Indeed, Putnam had dared his son, David, to go to Antarctica to acquire material for a book, which he had done.[35]

On the other hand, when she was among the working-class community in Avella, and again as she faced the critics who reviewed her book and publicized her story, Gilfillan was placed in the conventional idealized role of a middle-class young woman. Harriet's efforts to become Lauren were mostly misunderstood or not recognized. Nevertheless, the female protagonist of Pit College persists in trying to become Lauren. She smokes in public to the dismay of the Communists. She goes freely where she wants and speaks without restraint, to the astonishment of most of the men of the town who know only married or "bad" women. She cross-dresses without thinking twice. Then, after toying with her ardent lover Johnny, she goes absolutely gaga over the exotic Shirley. All of this is largely unremarked in reviews or in biographical sketches.

Like many women's autobiographies, I Went to Pit College aims to make the invisible visible. Yet the emotional terrain the heroine treads is subordinated to the disclosure of the portrait of the reality of class oppression of the "other America" comprised of Slovaks, Poles, Germans, Italians, Lithuanians, Greeks, Russians, Bulgarians, and African Americans. While there are other women in I Went to Pit College and there are a union, political parties, and families who want to take her in, Laurie remains isolated to the end.

Following Gilfillan's medical examination in Kalamazoo in 1930, her doctor prescribed a period of hospitalization for a nervous disorder; from this point, biological explanations continued to be sought to explain her unusual behavior. In 1931, following her stay in Avella and Pittsburgh, Gilfillan was again hospitalized, this time for malnutrition. Instead of returning to New York, she went home to Kalamazoo and unsuccessfully struggled to write her book, although she produced one chapter that Putnam sold for $300 to the magazine Forum. But her behavior became erratic once more; her symptoms included sudden rudeness, insomnia, impulsiveness, and a writing block that produced both a fear of failure and suicidal moods. She complained of a pain in her head that had lasted for more than a year, which she convinced herself was caused by vertebrae twisted out of shape at the base of her skull that pressed on a nerve center, the result of years of nervous tension. She called this affliction "sciatica neuritis" and thought that an operation to rectify the condition would make her more personally stable. In June 1931 she met a rambling poet at a Kalamazoo literary gathering, fell violently in love with him, and brought him home to live with her, thus precipitating a family crisis. Within days the man fell ill, was hospitalized, and then was forcibly taken back to Canada by his father, after which he apparently died.

In a distraught state, Gilfillan went to Chicago, where she believed the poet had left some manuscripts. A few months later she was again taken ill and returned home. This time she renewed an acquaintance with an old high school classmate, Clarence Young, an aspiring novelist who took a job as a handyman in the Gilfillan home. Young nursed and guided and harassed Gilfillan into writing I Went to Pit College during the winter of 1932–33. By the time the manuscript was completed, George Putnam had quit the publishing business, leaving Gilfillan herself to bring the work to New York City in the spring of 1933. Once there, she supported herself by taking jobs in department stores and kitchens while the manuscript was making the rounds to publishers. She sold another narrative, "Weary Feet," based on her new experiences.[36]

Her life becomes sketchier following her marriage in 1934, the publication of her book, and her appearance at the John Reed Club meeting. In the summer of 1934 she participated in a New Masses symposium on Marxist criticism,[37] and she won a fellowship to the Bread Loaf Writers Conference in Vermont. In February 1935 she published two more pieces, a portrait of her life residing near Union Square (in which she appears as a single woman) and the satirical essay on women and Communism in the Modern Monthly.[38] She signed the call for the Communist-led First American Writers Congress and joined the League of American Writers. To her friends and relatives, she announced her plans for a new book, based on the character of one Jimmy-the-Jockey, who had lived next door to her in Chicago.

On 18 August 1935, however, Gilfillan was taken by friends to a New York City hospital after she was discovered talking to imaginary characters from her new book. She was then brought back to Kalamazoo, and in October she was hospitalized at the University of Michigan in Ann Arbor. Over the next thirty-nine years, Gilfillan remained hospitalized primarily at the Kalamazoo State Hospital for the Insane, where she was treated with electric shock and insulin therapy and possibly underwent a lobotomy. In 1973 she showed small signs of improvement and was placed in a boardinghouse in Kalamazoo where five years later, at age sixty-nine, she died in obscurity.[39] Her only writings that survive from this entire period are some short notes to her aunts thanking them for gifts in the late 1930s; they were signed Harriet, rather than Lauren.

Gilfillan's diaries, which commence when she was fourteen, demonstrate that from an early age she used a highly dramatized imagination to take control of her life—to give it order—amidst a social and personal world of increasing confusion. The confusion was probably exacerbated by the social upheaval of the Depression, but there were more personal matters as well. Family correspondence indicates that in the 1920s, her older sister, Frederika, was removed from Smith College and hospitalized after suffering from delusions. In the mid-1930s her father, Edward, was advised by doctors to leave Kalamazoo and move to Chicago after he experienced violent obsessions regarding his wife as well as developing a compulsion to spank his children. Genealogical research on the Gilfillan family—which turns out to be Scottish, not Irish, as the newspapers had claimed—reveals a long history of "talented" members, sometimes poets, who are just as frequently described as "unbalanced."[40] Harriet's (or Lauren's) affliction seems to have been genetically inherited. Is the narrative of her remarkable journey in search of an "other America" and her rejection of middle-class values simply the work of a madwoman?

Edmund Wilson, in his writings collected as *The Wound and the Bow* (1941), uses the Greek mythological character Philoctetes—with his incurable wound and invisible bow—as a symbol of the creative artist. Wilson's image of torment producing art may have application to Gilfillan, but this is not to suggest that mental illness generates creative talent. Rather, a central feature of Gilfillan's writing is her remarkable recognition that her unconventionality, in part her mental instability but also her refusal either to be middle class or to give herself wholly to some fantastic and romanticized vision of the working class, was both her strength and her dilemma. *I Went to Pit College* mocks the less mature persona, Laurie; it courageously exposes Laurie much as it insists on her tenuous autonomy, harnessing her uncertain sense of self to prefigure the complex self-consciousness of James Agee and Walker Evans's far better known *Let Us Now Praise Famous Men* (1941).

Beyond that, however, *I Went to Pit College* is a text that redelineates the proletariat in a new borderland of the class struggle, one in which boundaries and norms are destabilized. Gilfillan, who came from the bottom rung of the middle class and a very dysfunctional family, sequentially assumed new identities ranging from an indigenous street urchin to an elite and pampered collegian to an irresponsible "art for art's sake" Bohemian to a suspected company spy. At the same time, her vision of America became transformed through her encounter with ethnicities and members of the working class that had not been part of her Smith College education. Her creative tropes—her bendings of borders, genders, and genres—were an expression not of madness but of the power of the creative imagination in the service of a humanizing art, to overcome the tragic consequences of biology. Both Gilfillan and Henry Roth left their mark on the 1930s. Roth's work will endure, but Gilfillan's has been lost to all but a handful of scholars.

AN ORDINARY LIFE

Not all disappearing acts were as spectacular as Roth's and Gilfillan's. Of the hundreds of young writers drawn to the pro-Communist movement, few had the talent that Roth displayed or the phenomenal instant success of Gilfillan. The career of Joseph Vogel (1904–90) is more representative of that of rank-and-file pro-Communist cultural workers. Like many others, Vogel was bonded to the Communist movement not as a Party activist but through his membership in Communist-led organizations, such as the John Reed Club in the early 1930s and the League of American Writers after the Popular Front, as well as his circle of friends on the Federal Writers Project. Their primary struggle was to find a way to keep writing and publishing with few financial resources and little or no institutional support, outside the occasional windfall from a patron. A profile of Vogel's career reflects the press of daily activities and work of writing, which became central in his drift away from the movement.[41]

Vogel was a warm and gentle man whose first novel, *At Madam Bonnard's* (1935), created the atmosphere of a Bohemian rooming house in the early Depression. His father, Morris Vogel, was a Jewish immigrant from Warsaw, Poland, who worked on the streets of New York pushing a scale on which people could weigh themselves for a penny. He then delivered milk for the Borden Milk Company using a horse and wagon. Finally he became a housepainter after the Vogels relocated to Utica. The family, while Jewish, was unconcerned with religion and attended services only two or three times a year.

Both of Vogel's siblings dropped out of school at an early age, but Vogel was remarkable in childhood for his extraordinary capacity for reading and writing. At four he was copying whole sentences from newspapers and was soon promoted a grade. He started taking several books a week out of the library, devouring them in the evenings. He also developed a knack for eavesdropping on

JOSEPH VOGEL in 1940. A promising novelist of the Great
Depression era, he drifted into obscurity in later decades.
(Courtesy of Joseph Vogel)

adult conversations while reading, which provided him with a store of material he would use when he began writing creatively.

Vogel graduated from the Utica Free Academy in 1922, specializing in drafting and printing as well as taking college preparatory classes. By chance he enrolled at nearby Hamilton College and worked his way through school as a waiter, librarian, tutor, and designer of wall charts for a geology professor. Prior to attending college Vogel had systematically read a large number of classic works of fiction, but he was particularly transfixed by Fyodor Dostoevsky, who inspired his first stories. Although Vogel's early efforts saw publication and even won prizes, his writing teacher at Hamilton declared that he must have gotten his material from "the sewers," a comment that in part prompted Vogel to switch to a major in philosophy.

Upon graduation from Hamilton, he turned his back on his earlier aspiration to study law and moved to New York City, where he held a long series of jobs for economic survival. He worked on a daily trade paper covering the men's clothing business; but his literary interests were too distracting, and he was fired. He then signed up as a crewman on an Italian ship taking a load of wild mules to Italy; this adventure became the subject of his first unpublished novel, of which some sections appeared as short stories. Next he edited his own publication in the clothing industry, meanwhile making a small name for himself with fiction he published in little magazines. In 1929, the year his magazine folded and he was married, the poet Louis Zukofsky (1904–78) approached him as an emissary from Ezra Pound, who was seeking promoters of his work in the United States. For a while Vogel corresponded with Pound, but he broke off the relationship when he became aware of the bizarre nature of Pound's economic theories.

For three years in the early 1930s, Vogel worked in a New York art gallery and bookstore hanging exhibitions, selling books, and writing pamphlets about artists. After that he worked as a shipping clerk, a researcher for a professor, and a part-time teacher of journalism in a private business school. Finally he had a breakthrough. Over the years he had kept up an acquaintance with a Hamilton College trustee, Charles A. Miller, who was a well-to-do banker and attorney. Miller had followed Vogel's literary career and occasionally took him to dinner when he came to New York. Suddenly, in 1934, he offered Vogel a $100-a-month stipend to write a novel. For his topic, Vogel chose life in a New York rooming house just before the onset of the Depression. At Madam Bonnard's was a literary success, although sales were modest and Vogel, now the father of a young daughter, was still plagued by lack of a steady income.

Vogel had considered himself a radical while at Hamilton, and among the places to which he successfully submitted his early work was the *New Masses*. This caused his classmate, the psychologist B. F. Skinner, to record in his autobiography that "Vogel was contributing to a communist magazine."[42] The magazines where Vogel published fiction—*Blues*, *Morada*, *Blast*, and *Anvil*—were generally associated with the Left, and many of his acquaintances were pro-Communist. Since writers in the Soviet Union were supported by the writers' union and could devote themselves full-time to their writing, Vogel fantasized that they lived in paradise. However, the struggle to earn a living and work hard at his writing was so time consuming that he did little more than discuss revolutionary politics. But politics did not determine his literary strategy; he always saw his artistic project as the creation of characters. In 1935 he wrote to Horace Gregory, who had reviewed *At Madam Bonnard's*, that "the test of good work is the creation of revealing characters; in a book like *Man's Fate* the incidents alone are sufficient to raise it above the level, but it is Malraux's creation of characters that raises the book to greatness."[43]

Vogel's next job was as a "relief investigator" for a public welfare office in Brooklyn, which paid about $100 a month. Vogel was assigned to what was dubbed the "silk-stocking district," where persons who had once earned a high income had been humbled by the Great Depression and were compelled to apply for welfare aid. Vogel interviewed applicants from this area and then wrote their case histories. Although *Man's Courage* (1938) was far from Vogel's thoughts at the time, the experiences he gained proved useful in writing the novel.

Once again, Vogel's benefactor, Charles A. Miller, came to his rescue when the Munson-Williams-Proctor Institute of Utica was organized with Miller as chairman of the board. Vogel was again offered $100 a month, this time as a creative writing fellowship. Vogel moved back to Utica, to an upstairs, back-door-entrance apartment, and planned his novel about a poverty-stricken Polish immigrant family. With his prior experiences in the welfare system and his choice of his hometown for a setting, Vogel literally wept as *Man's Courage* poured from him. The manuscript took little more than a year to complete and was published by Knopf to rave reviews. The *New York Times* carried one that began by calling the book "a novel of distinguished power" and concluded, "This novel takes first rank in this year's fiction."[44]

After the completion of *Man's Courage*, Vogel spent two weeks at the Yaddo artists' colony, where he began planning his next novel about a young man going away from home for the first time and encountering a world of violence unexpectedly connected with his own family. Upon returning to Utica, Vogel started writing the novel, which he set in an imaginary amusement park north of Utica,

near a village he dubbed Bridal Veil. *The Straw Hat*, which suggests a new, psychological direction in his art, was published by the left-wing house Modern Age
Books in 1940.

When Vogel returned to Brooklyn in 1938, he expected to resume his welfare
office job; but during his long absence the department had been taken over by
the civil service, and he was told to wait until the next series of exams was given.
He then turned to the Works Projects Administration (WPA),[45] hoping to find
an assignment that would allow him to write his own material. Instead he was
assigned to the folklore department, which required that he walk the streets of
Brooklyn to gather children's songs about jumping rope and bouncing balls. He
quickly accepted another offer from Charles A. Miller, but this time to assist in
the preparation of Miller's autobiography. Again the salary was $100 a month,
and Vogel's task was to type Miller's dictation.

Soon after he completed this job, in 1940 Vogel accepted employment as a
prison guard with the U.S. Bureau of Prisons. He hoped to gather enough material in a few months to produce future articles and books. Instead, a lack of
alternative prospects for economic subsistence led him to spend the next quarter
of a century working, mostly as a counselor, at the federal penitentiary at Lewis-
burg, Pennsylvania; the Federal Correctional Institution at Milan, Michigan; the
National Training School for Boys in Washington, D.C.; the Federal Prison Camp
at Maxwell Air Force Base in Montgomery, Alabama; Kilby State Prison in Montgomery, Alabama; West Virginia Penitentiary in Moundsville, West Virginia; and
the Ohio Penitentiary in Columbus, Ohio. During these years Vogel continued
to publish when and where he could, in periodicals such as *True Detective* and
publications related to his profession, such as the *Juvenile Offender*. As a result of
many years of chain-smoking, Vogel suffered a heart attack in 1964 and decided
to return to more sustained efforts at writing. He found work teaching English
composition at Ohio State University, and after a year he was given classes in advanced expository composition and narrative writing. Before he retired in 1970,
he had published a play and a piece called "Prison Notes" in the literary magazine of the English Department. After that, Vogel devoted himself to creating
handmade lettered books with the texts from Lewis Carroll and James Joyce. As
in the case of numerous other rank-and-file participants in the literary Left, few
knew that Vogel was still alive or that he had returned to his art.

FROM NEW MASSES TO MASS MARKET

Even a writer with a national reputation and who made a good living through
sales of his or her work could mysteriously disappear. Of all the pro-Communist
writers who made the transition to mass culture during the antifascist crusade,

Ruth McKenney (1911–72) is the one whose fame was greatest and the one who plummeted the farthest. She was born in Mishawaka, Indiana, and grew up in Cleveland, Ohio. Her mother, Marguerite Flynn, was a public school teacher and an Irish nationalist. She encouraged Ruth toward radical politics but died when her daughter was eight. John Sidney McKenney, her father, was employed as the manager of a factory. It was a sad childhood, and Ruth discovered how to disguise her unhappiness with humor.

Ruth McKenney attended but did not graduate from the Ohio State University in the late 1920s. Journalism was her passion. At age fourteen she began working on the *Columbus Dispatch*; she first learned the trade of printer and then, at seventeen, switched to reporting. In 1932 she started writing for the *Akron Beacon-Journal* and soon won awards for her feature reportage. Her radicalism became more pronounced as the Depression evolved. By 1933 she had a reputation as an independent Leftist and a good reporter who wrote funny stories, some of which exhibited the influence of humorist James Thurber, who had preceded her at Ohio State. Along with another Leftist, B. J. Widick, she organized the Columbus local of the Newspaper Guild, and Widick became its vice president. Widick remembered her as looking "Shanty Irish, vivacious with a mug face, heavy set and unhappy about it," and that she sometimes had the trace of a snarl on her face.[46] Widick also recalled that the men on the paper were quite jealous of her abilities, and that she was strongly supported by Jack Knight, owner of the paper.

By the mid-1930s McKenney was drawing close to the Communist Party and was much influenced by Heywood Broun, a Communist fellow traveler and a leader in the Newspaper Guild. With encouragement from the noted columnist Earl Wilson, McKenney moved to New York City and spent 1934 to 1936 employed as a feature writer on the *New York Post*. Subsequently she used her savings to launch herself as an author.

McKenney's first writings would be her best-known. These were short stories about her zany younger sister, Eileen, that initially appeared in the *New Yorker* starting in 1936. The wittiest were collected in her inaugural book, the best-selling *My Sister Eileen* (1938). In 1940 Eileen McKenney moved to Hollywood, where she married novelist Nathanael West, but the newlyweds were killed in a car accident in December of that year. The play version of *My Sister Eileen* opened only a few days later, in early 1941, and subsequently become a smash hit. Then a movie was made of it in 1942, a Broadway musical called *Wonderful Town* appeared in 1953, and a new film based on the musical came out in 1955. McKenney wrote many other madcap tales about her family that appeared in three subsequent collections: *The McKenneys Carry On* (1940); *The Loud Red Patrick* (1947), which also became a Broadway show; and *All about Eileen* (1952). Less successful were two autobiographical humor books about her later life, *Love Story* (1950) and *Far Far from Home* (1954).

Like Len Zinberg, McKenney learned very early to present a Marxist sensibility in forms accessible to a broad audience. *My Sister Eileen* provides many episodes in which the "truth" of experience is counterpoised to cultural myths that usually stem from institutionalized religion and the commodification of culture. Even though the work is a contribution to popular culture, McKenney repeatedly satirizes mass culture, such as the movies, which are said to attain value from a strictly consumerist point of view because they last longer than other forms of mass distraction. On the other hand, sometimes mass culture tells more about social reality than the versions offered by the cultures of family and church, as in the case of the "Chickie" cartoon featured in one episode. Rebellious behavior is the source of much of the humor of the tales, and such behavior is also valorized as superior to the foolishness that prevails among those who carry out their social roles unthinkingly. This unthinking quality is suggested by those whose lives are regimented in the summer camp that Ruth and Eileen attend. Implicit Communist attitudes are sometimes present in passing, as when Ruth acquires anticapitalist and atheist values from a robust unionist organizer. So are quasi-feminist opinions, as when Ruth's father, fascinated by capitalist gimmicks, is outsmarted by his clear-thinking daughter. In sum, the *My Sister Eileen* tales can be regarded as the story of the making of two inner-directed female rebels, during which the antinomies of mass culture are interrogated in a mass culture form.

In 1937 Ruth McKenney married a prominent Communist journalist, Richard Bransten, who used the pen name Bruce Minton. After Eileen McKenney's death, the couple adopted her son from an earlier marriage as well as Bransten's son from his first marriage; they also had a daughter of their own, named after Eileen. McKenney's political views were as ardently Communist as her husband's, and during the late 1930s and early 1940s she had her own weekly column, called "Strictly Personal," in the Party's *New Masses*.

McKenney considered her humor writing as merely a source of income, "to make a living while composing weightier *opera*."[47] The first of her "weightier" works was a nonfiction novel called *Industrial Valley* (1939), based on events in Akron from 1932 to 1936. The documentary form of the work, which uses experimental techniques to dramatize the Goodyear rubber strike and the beginnings of the CIO, led the *New Republic* critic Malcolm Cowley to declare it "one of our best collective novels."[48] *Jake Home* (1943), her second proletarian novel, was less enthusiastically received by the popular press and even caused a controversy in the pages of the *Daily Worker*.

Jake Home commences with the extraordinary, agonizing, three-day Cesarean birth of the twelve-pound Jake in 1901. It concludes with the third or fourth in a series of traumatic personal-political rebirths wherein Jake finally assumes his role as a working-class Communist leader. The overall style of *Jake Home* is much in the mode of John Dos Passos, a one-volume *U.S.A.* without the experimental interchapters. McKenney includes events in Pennsylvania, New York, Chicago, and the far West and dramatizes historical events such as the 1919 steel strike and the Sacco-Vanzetti defense campaign. There are suggestions that Jake is an embodiment of the leadership potential of the working class in the United States, perhaps an alternative to Dos Passos's character Mac in *U.S.A.* Her fast-paced, realist-naturalist prose technique catches the flavor of many decades, and her sketches include a range of familiar and symptomatic personality types. But her work is also similar to Dos Passos's in that she never quite achieves emotional depth in her main characters.

A primary source of contention among those who sent letters of complaint about the novel to the *Daily Worker* was McKenney's proletarian übermensch, Jake Home, who is tempted into co-optation by two women. One is Margaret, an upwardly mobile western Pennsylvanian; the other is Kate, a rich New York socialite who is slumming in the Communist movement. It was accepted by readers that effeminacy, literary interests, and sensuality were linked to middle- or upperclass corruption; the objections were to the lack of decent Communist women in the novel. The women in *Jake Home* never share Jake's fundamental loyalty to the working class. His first wife, Margaret, is simply unaware of his formative proletarian experiences; she marries him in ignorance of his underlying values. Treated with little sympathy by McKenney, Margaret is depicted as a corrupt hypocrite who has sex with Jake twice during her visit with him when she is supposed to be finalizing her divorce so she can marry a wealthy industrialist.[49]

Jake's second wife, Kate, is depicted as no less savory but is seen more as a victim of her class background. Kate enters the relationship with a full awareness of Jake's political convictions and, indeed, is drawn to him precisely for that reason. Moreover, Kate has outspoken feminist attitudes, declaring herself sexually a free agent and refusing the role of a "breeding machine."[50] However, Kate's umbilical cord to wealth and privilege prevents her from full integration into the Communist movement, despite her Party membership, as well as integration into her marriage to Jake. Kate's "infidelity" to the Communist cause is paralleled by her sexual infidelity to Jake, which usually occurs with wimpy, literary males.

Jake Home was intended to be a study dramatizing why a talented person who might rise to wealth as a boss or bourgeois politician would throw in his or her lot with the working class. It seemed, however, also to reflect McKenney's and Bransten's need to purge bourgeois ideas and temptations from their consciousness. The depiction of Jake as having a clear conscience and finding fulfillment only when he repudiates class corruption expresses the ideal that they sought but were incapable of sustaining.

From a regional perspective, western Pennsylvania functions primarily as a background in the novel. It is the proletarian cradle of Jake's Communism, distant from the fleshpots of New York, and the memory of his origins holds Jake steady.[51] The feminist politics of the book are hardly revolutionary; McKenney advances a progressive liberal view of gender relations in the home. The perspective is the same as that proposed in her autobiographical *Love Story*: A woman has a right to a career and a family; this can be hellishly stressful but is still a step forward from the traditional role of women in the nuclear family. However, the husband must share domestic duties, and it is strongly desirable to have modern appliances and maids, cooks, and nursemaids.[52]

The *Daily Worker* debate about *Jake Home* demonstrates the ongoing use by many Communist reviewers and activists of political criteria to judge fiction, and their obsession with the need to create admirable Communist leaders in fiction. At first the novel was overpraised, and then two Communist political militants — Peggy Dennis, the wife of leader Eugene Dennis, and Israel Amter, an admired leader in New York — attacked her portraits of Jake and Kate as miseducating the American public as to the real character of Communist leaders. There may be such individuals in the movement, the two insisted, but they would not be leaders. McKenney defended herself by stating that the depiction of Jake Home was the first part of a trilogy, and that his subsequent development would fulfill expectations for a man of his political stature — including the appearance of a loyal wife and family. As for Kate, she was not a wicked woman but one to be pitied because she lacked the strength to carry out the life required by Communist convictions.[53]

In her memoirs, McKenney reported that the criticisms were an all-out assault — Jake was "kicked black and blue" by the *Daily Worker*. In reality, most of the specific objections were couched in respectful praise showered on other aspects of the novel, and on her talents in general. McKenney's *Daily Worker* reply at the time expressed gratitude for the attention given to the novel and considerable humility, peppered with obsequious references to the Communist Party leadership and a quotation from Stalin. Yet in her memoirs she reported that she was "heart-broken." She had apparently regarded Jake as an "immortal" hero, and she had shown a draft to important Communist leaders in the labor movement as well as in the Party literary circles. Her explanation for the uproar was that "a famous personality in the left-wing movement" had let it be known that Jake was "a mean, nasty, overheated version of himself." Years later, McKenney concluded that she got what she deserved. She had attempted to fashion a novel to serve a cause and had been judged by the criterion of how "useful" the book might be to the cause.[54] A year after the debate, Ruth McKenney and her husband were living in Hollywood and collaborating on film scripts. Bransten planned to write a scholarly tome on economics; McKenney, a new novel about wartime Washington. Neither materialized.

During 1945 and 1946 the Communist Party was in turmoil as the Party's leader Earl Browder was accused of right-wing deviations, replaced, and cast out. Bransten and McKenney were publicly expelled a few months after Browder, although the accusation against them was "ultraleftism"; they were charged with being part of a faction that felt that the anti-Browder correction had not gone far enough. Subsequently McKenney and Bransten took their family to Western Europe to avoid the conservative atmosphere sweeping the United States with the onset of the Cold War. They eventually settled in England, and from there they coauthored a very successful travel book, *Here's England* (1950).

However, both were tormented by personal demons. Bransten committed suicide on McKenney's birthday in 1955, just before McKenney's last major work appeared. *Mirage* (1956) was a pedestrian historical novel about Napoleon in Egypt. A few years later McKenney returned to the United States, where she was periodically institutionalized for depression. Suffering from a heart ailment and diabetes, she died at Roosevelt hospital in New York at age sixty-one.

McKenney resembled Len Zinberg in holding a dual identity as a proletarian and a popular writer; yet their dispositions did not match. By all accounts, Zinberg declared that there were no contradictions between the two; as Ed Lacy he was pursuing Len Zinberg's life as a literary radical by other means. McKenney, in contrast, asserted that she was conflicted; her successful popular writing was merely a means of making easy money to sustain her serious, proletarian work. Other writers who found a home in mass and popular culture as the climate of the antifascist crusade mutated into that of the Cold War would offer a variety of other explanations for their choices. What is evident is that the conversion of proletarian writers from the *New Masses* to the new mass market did not require an abandonment of aims, only a new literary venue. A comparable conclusion might be drawn from a survey of the large number of Jewish Americans who converted to the internationalism of the antifascist crusade. For the most part, the conversion of the Jews neither obliterated nor fully obscured where they had come from.

The Conversion of the Jews

THE LOST WORLD

In a 1985 study in the *New Left Review*, "The Lost World of British Communism," the British Marxist Raphael Samuel recalled his upbringing in a Jewish Communist family in the 1930s and 1940s. Samuel wrote that to be a Communist was to have "a complete social identity." He recollected that, like practicing Catholics or Orthodox Jews, "we lived in a little private world of our own," which he described as "a tight . . . self-referential group." Samuel and his circle "maintained intense neighborhood networks and little workplace conventicles." They "patronized regular cafés, went out together on weekend and Sunday rambles," and took their holidays together at Socialist Youth Camps. They even had their own "particular speech. . . . Like freemasons we knew intuitively when someone was 'one of us,' and we were equally quick to spot that folk devil of the socialist imagination, a 'careerist,' a species being of whom I am, to this day, wary. Within the narrow confines of an organization under siege we maintained the simulacrum of a complete society, insulated from alien influences, belligerent toward outsiders, protective to those within."[1] Aaron Kramer (1921–97), a Jewish American Communist for two decades and a prolific poet who secured his reputation after the 1930s, conjured up a similar "lost world" when he reminisced about his own youth in the 1930s and 1940s.[2]

Kramer was born in 1921 to New York working-class Communist parents, Hyman, a bookbinder, and Mary, who, in the Great Depression, stamped laundry tickets. The Kramer family idolized Moissaye Olgin (1878–1939), for many years the Communist Party's leader in Jewish affairs and the most notable figure of that era in the Party's Yiddish-language daily newspaper, *Freiheit*. In 1931 Kramer was sent to an ultra-Bolshevik Yiddish School where his instructor had recently arrived from the USSR. In Kramer's public elementary school, teachers would ask the students for the "news of the day"; most read from the *New York Times*, but young Kramer leaped to his feet with the *Daily Worker* in hand. In 1990 Kramer recalled that his favorite "newsday" was always the day after 1 May, when he could announce to the class, "'A million people marched in this city, a million people marched in that city, fifty thousand here.' . . . That was my text, and it remained my text for a very long time."[3]

Kramer's impulse to write poetry emerged independently, but as he approached adolescence, it was harnessed to his revolutionary political spirit. Kramer's mother, who nearly outlived him and remained a Communist Party stalwart to the end, reported that at age two he was reciting rhymes, many inspired by the Yiddish, folk, and labor songs she sang. In first grade, at Public School No. 174 in the Bronx, Kramer wrote his first poem, a Mother Goose–inspired verse about a boy in a haystack. This came at the urging of Pearl Bynoe, the only African American teacher in the school in 1927 and probably the only Black person most of the all-Jewish class of students had ever seen. Kramer felt such gratitude toward Miss Bynoe, along with developing a mad crush on her, that forty-seven years later he established a poetry prize in her name for the student population of the school, now entirely African American and Latino/Latina.

Bynoe's encouragement launched him, at age six, into an outpouring of nature poems. Initially, Kramer did not realize that he was unique in the intensity of his reactions to nature, to the sound of a train, or to the sight of the bricks on a building in an old town in Connecticut that he passed by. "I thought all children reacted that way and had a sort of romantic haze around the things that they saw." The "nature phase" lasted through fourth grade. Then he experienced a clash in his emotions between the self-indulgence he associated with his immersion in nature and the seriousness he felt was demanded of him by his Marxist political environment. The resulting transformation was no doubt assisted by his first sighting of the poetry editor of the Communist children's magazine, *New Pioneer*—Martha Millet, about five years his senior and "an absolutely gorgeous creature."[4]

Overnight, Kramer tore up his notebook of nature poems and issued a ringing manifesto of socially conscious art:

Now is not the time for nature poems
When thousands upon thousands
Are losing their homes.
Not ballads of how princesses wed
When the problem is, "Where shall I find bread?"[5]

This annunciation of a new direction was promptly submitted to the *New Pioneer*, where Kramer became the principal poet for several years, until he graduated to the children's page of the *Sunday Daily Worker*.

Kramer was raised in *Yiddishkeit*, yet a chief theme of his poetry through the

AARON KRAMER and NORMAN ROSTEN were pro-
Communist poets in the 1940s and remained friends during
and after the Cold War. (Courtesy of Aaron Kramer)

1940s and early 1950s—and a strong presence even after that—was African American history and culture. Indeed, his poems in the *New Pioneer* included one on the Scottsboro case and another addressed to the imprisoned Black Communist Angelo Herndon. The latter begins

> You youthful proletarian,
> Of an oppressed and starving race;
> Your hardships are the hardships
> That all working youth must face.

It was signed "Aaron Kramer, 12½."[6] The choice of Black rather than Jewish identity, to the extent that Kramer would later insist that he "felt Black" and that he glowed with pride when a Black writer said, "Kramer, you have a Black soul,"[7] is partly explained by personal factors. These encompass his infatuation with Pearl Bynoe and the Communist political education he received through supporting the Party's defense of Angelo Herndon and the nine Scottsboro Boys. A facilitation of this cross-ethnic identification may also be associated with the decision of his parents to identify themselves as Yiddish but not Jewish.

Such a perspective was a point of principle in his family, as it was among many pro-Communist *Freiheit* readers, and also for the popular Proletpen writers —Jewish Communist working-class poets writing only in Yiddish, such as Yuri Suhl and Ber Green, who took the adolescent Kramer under their wing.[8] The Kramer parents spoke Yiddish, sang Yiddish, and ate Jewish foods (which they called Yiddish foods) but were not merely irreligious or nonreligious; they were actively antireligious. Living in a ground-floor apartment, they made a point of leaving their shades up so that the Orthodox Jews en route to the synagogue could see them eating on fast days. The Maccabees were worshiped as national liberation fighters, but Hanukkah, the Festival of Lights, was not celebrated. In fact, Kramer never missed a day of school during the Jewish holidays; in many classes he was the only child, staying all day and insisting on being taught, as an act of defiance.

Yet the Kramer family was not assimilationist. Like Proletpen and other *Freiheit* readers, the Kramers had no interest in taking on the dominant Christian bourgeois culture. Instead, they wanted to be internationalist and working class. The distinction to them was between dragging themselves back to their childhood memories and shtetl culture or looking forward to the future and fighting the oppression they faced today and would face tomorrow. From this perspective, the paramount issue in the United States became Jim Crow, anti-Black racism, and the struggle for liberation of Black Americans, who were indubitably working class, bearers of a rich and inspiring folk culture, and up against proponents of white supremacism that bore a striking resemblance to the ideology of those who carried out pogroms under the czar and fascist assaults under Hitler. "Yiddish but not Jewish" could mean, under these conditions, varieties of a Jewish identity integrated into an internationalist outlook, a standpoint scornful of Judeocentrism or Jewish chauvinism yet comfortable with Jewish secular traditions and history.

This brief profile dramatizes some of the salient features of the Jewish American experience with Communism, especially that of first- and second-generation Eastern European Jews. The inordinately large number of Jews in the intellectual apparatus of the Party as well as the panoply of cultural networks that appeared as part of the broader social movement was a pronounced feature that grew even more obvious during the antifascist crusade when Aaron Kramer found his poetic voice. How large was the Party's Jewish American constituency? Reliable statistics are difficult to obtain, but there was possibly a Jewish American presence of close to 50 percent of the total of those who published regularly in Party-affiliated venues and joined Party-led organizations such as the John Reed Club, the League of American Writers, and the National Council of the Arts, Sciences and Professions. This is a remarkable aggregate; only 2 or 3 percent of the population of the United States was Jewish in the mid-twentieth century. Some Jewish American writers, like Kramer, came from Communist families; many more came to Communism by choice, albeit in numbers disproportionate to those for the general population. The justification for such an inordinate Jewish presence may be ascribed to manifold circumstances. These provide an explanation for the flow of Jewish Americans as a group into the Communist movement; what triggered the individual choices of particular writers can only be understood through case studies.

The most compelling explanation for the high proportion of Jews is simply that the Communist movement in the United States had a solid foundation in Eastern European Jewish immigrant families; they brought to their new country not only an abhorrence of czarist autocracy but also working-class and socialist loyalties. Moreover, the Communist movement exhorted its members to adhere to a cultural pluralist and internationalist universalism, a stance that was attractive to young Jews emerging from families still shaped by the experience of shtetl and ghetto isolation. In contrast to the strict faith of their Orthodox elders, Marxist doctrine furnished the option of a moral life justified by supposedly scientific arguments and analysis. Jews nurtured by an atmosphere influenced by the study of holy books and ardent debates over segments of the Old Testament were well equipped for a political movement where hallowed writings by Marx, Engels, Lenin, and Stalin were fervently embraced as well as debated as guides to political practice. Such intellectually passionate individuals were excluded from many typical professions by anti-Semitism and the constricted economy of the Depression, while Communist institutions and organizations afforded a place to write, speak, teach, and interact on equal terms with non-Jews. In fact, a Jew entering the Communist movement had a range of choices through which to express his or her identity. On one hand, there were clubs and organizations immersed in *Yiddishkeit*; on the other, one could also assume a non-Jewish "party name" and a persona devoid of any ethnic attachment.

In the 1930s and 1940s, of course, the Communist movement was among the most aggressive forces in striving to prepare a response to the march of fascism across Europe. The effect on Jewish Americans can be seen in the large number of Jewish American youth who volunteered to battle the combined military might of Franco, Hitler, and Mussolini in Spain in 1936 by joining the Party-led Abraham Lincoln Brigade. Once overseas, they joined thousands of other Jewish internationalists from Europe and the Middle East to aid in the creation of a people's army that comprised the International Brigades under the leadership of the Communist International. The chief ethnic component of this initial campaign to halt fascism by military force of arms was most likely Jews from numerous countries. Yet most of the Jews in the Abraham Lincoln Brigade regarded themselves primarily as antifascists and partisans of democracy, which is also representative of the frame of mind of most Jewish American Communist cultural workers until the post–World War II years. Of course, when the non-aggression pact was suddenly signed between Hitler and Stalin in August 1939, the Party endured profound embarrassment. Then Germany invaded the USSR in June 1941, and antifascism was restored as a major Communist theme. As the Party leaped to the forefront of supporting the Allies in World War II, a younger generation of Jewish American cultural workers emerged.

Antifascism was vital, but left-wing Jewish cultural workers also adhered to other convictions that comprised an interlocking worldview. These include an exorbitantly romanticized assessment of the USSR, a zealous championing of the CIO, and a burning abhorrence of white supremacy. From 1936 to 1939, belief in the Soviet Union's steadfast antifascism certainly enabled many Jews to blind themselves to the criminal nature of the Moscow Trials; then, from September 1939 to June 1941, belief in the ultimate goodness of the Soviet Union was no doubt an important factor in the rationalization by many Jews of their acceptance of the eighteen months of the Hitler-Stalin Pact as a temporary tactical maneuver. What was perhaps singular in Jewish American left-wing antifascism was the political form it took: Jewish nationalism and any dependence on powerful Western protectors were eschewed; instead, Jewish Americans called for unified armed resistance among all the oppressed and expressed a sense of sympathy and solidarity with other non-Jewish groups suffering persecution, especially through colonialism and white supremacism. Their blind spot regarding anti-Semitism in the USSR flowed from the Soviet Union's status as a bulwark of social justice, not from insensitivity to Jewish suffering.

BETWEEN INSULARITY AND INTERNATIONALISM

Communism's appeal for Jewish American cultural workers profoundly affected intellectual life in the United States in the mid-twentieth century. Prior to the 1930s, the foremost authors in radical literary circles were the non-Jewish writers Jack London, Upton Sinclair, Floyd Dell, John Reed, and Max Eastman. During the Depression, when Communism displaced Socialism as the leading force on the Left, there was a sea change in the number of left-wing Jewish participants. A former playwright and journalist, Michael Gold, achieved international renown when his *Jews without Money* was published in 1930. Clifford Odets (1906–63) revolutionized the theater with *Waiting for Lefty* (1935), *Awake and Sing* (1935), and *Golden Boy* (1937). Lillian Hellman (1905–84) promoted anticapitalism with *The Little Foxes* (1939) and antifascism with *Watch on the Rhine* (1941). A legion of radical Jewish American poets emerged, such as Stanley Burnshaw (1906–2005), Joy Davidman (1915–60), Kenneth Fearing, Sol Funaroff (1911–43), Alfred Hayes (1911–85), Edwin Rolfe, Muriel Rukeyser (1913–80), and Louis Zukofsky.

Moreover, the post-Depression replenishment of the Communist literary tradition was already in progress, as the early writings of a younger group of Jewish American Left cultural workers developed from the Communist-led cultural milieu. In the 1940s, after the commercial failure of *Somebody in Boots* (1935), Nelson Algren, born Nelson Abraham (1909–81), won acclaim as the bard of the lumpenproletariat for *Never Come Morning* (1942) and *The Man with the Golden Arm* (1949), his novels about the Chicago urban underclass. Irwin Shaw published the best seller *The Young Lions*. Jo Sinclair, born Ruth Seid (1913–95), who likewise launched herself by writing radical fiction and drama (see the discussion in the Conclusion), brought out a prizewinning attack on homophobia and anti-Semitism, *Wasteland* (1946). Howard Fast, well regarded for his historical novels, publicly joined the Communist Party in 1943. Arthur Miller (1915–2005), a struggling Marxist playwright since the late 1930s, won the Pulitzer Prize for *Death of a Salesman* in 1949. Norman Mailer (b. 1923), a Communist fellow traveler, achieved both popular and critical success with his masterpiece of battle in the Pacific, *The Naked and the Dead* (1948). When HUAC hauled ten leading Communist screenwriters and directors before hearings in Washington, D.C., in 1947, which led to their imprisonment in 1950, six were Jews: Alvah Bessie; Herbert Biberman (1900–1971); Lester Cole, born Lester Cohn (1904–85); John Howard Lawson (1895–1977); Albert Maltz; and Samuel Ornitz (1891–1957).

Finally, the institutional presence of Jews in the cultural wing of the Communist movement was remarkable. The editor of the Party's publishing house, International Publishers, was Alexander Trachtenberg (1884–1966); the chair of the Party's cultural commission was V. J. Jerome, born Isaac Jerome Romaine (1896–1965); and the head of the Party's important Hollywood section was John Howard Lawson. There was a substantial Jewish presence on the editorial board of the Party's *New Masses* as well as its successors, *Mainstream* and *Masses & Mainstream*. The Party's theoretical organ, initially called the *Communist* and then *Political Affairs*, was edited in the late 1940s and early 1950s by Jerome.

Yet what did it mean to be a Jewish American Communist if so many declared themselves as internationalists first? The Aaron Kramer paradigm offers a perspective on how varied identities—a Jewish identity, an identity expressing solidarity with African Americans, a proletarian identity, or a Communist identity—can be the basis for political activity of various types. On one hand, the insularity of the Jewish Communist cultural milieu could facilitate its participants' adoption of a Communist outlook that was safeguarded from the effects of the dominant culture of the country or region. Thus many Jewish Marxists felt no temptation to adapt to middle-class Christian culture, detach themselves from Jewish folk culture, succumb to self-hatred, or embrace the various forms of ethnic prejudice widespread in the dominant culture of the United States. Many, although not all, especially if one's family was educated and secularized, retained an affection for Jewish songs, foods, earthy humor, and a tradition of heretical thought and resistance to oppression. On the other hand, the largely insulated Communist culture had a selective, outward-looking component that emphasized internationalism, antifascism, anticolonialism, and a strong sense of identification with other groups at the bottom of the social ladder. The resulting ethos, a product of both insularity and internationalism, was expressed by Kramer in his life and in his poetry, and especially in his combination of a non-chauvinist Jewish pride and a crossover identity with Black Americans. A similar ethos was diversely exemplified in Kramer's generation of Jewish Marxist activist cultural workers who were shaped by the specific problematic of the 1930s and who continued their work in the 1940s and 1950s.

In examining a range of writers and intellectuals, one finds that patterns of identity selection and construction could be constituted differently in different contexts. While the Jewish presence in the Communist cultural movement may lend itself to generalizations on a broad plane, these generalizations cannot in turn be imposed from the top on the complex individuals who comprised the movement.

Thus some Jews who took on the roles as spokespersons for the Party might ignore identity in all forms except that of a Communist. James Allen (1906–91), for instance, a University of Pennsylvania Ph.D. candidate, author of many of the Party's scholarly tomes on "the Negro Question," and eventually the president of the Party's International Publishers, left behind his posthumously published *A Communist's Memoir: Organizing in the Depression South*.[9] Although the memoir exemplifies the characteristic sense of solidarity with African Americans, in 130 pages there is not one word about any feeling of Jewish identity, even when Allen heard blatant anti-Semitic remarks during the Scottsboro trial. His changing his name from Sol Auerbach to Jim Allen is explained only as a desire for anonymity, since he saw Jim Allen as a common name. However, when writer Irwin Granich chose to mask his own identity, he became Mike Gold—another common name but one that affirmed his Jewish background.

Perhaps in the middle of the spectrum, between Kramer and Allen, is Ben Burns (1913–2000). In 1945 Burns was the founding editor of the famous African American magazine *Ebony*. A Jewish American Communist who had been born Benjamin Bernstein, Burns was a man whose political convictions alone led him to antiracist journalism, which in turn placed him in contact with many African Americans who worked for the Black publications the *Chicago Defender* and the *Negro Digest*. In his 1996 autobiography, *Nitty Gritty*, Burns recalled frequently being told that he was "not a real white man" by John Johnson, the Black owner of *Ebony*, and other staff members.[10] On occasion, curious visitors to *Ebony*'s offices would query, "Say, Burns, what are you anyway, Negro or white?" His response was "Neither—I'm Jewish."[11] This was not insignificant as an answer during the postwar era, when many Jews were identifying themselves as white.

Burns, Kramer, and hundreds of other journalists, editors, fiction writers, playwrights, scholars, film script authors, and poets belonged to this generation of midcentury left-wing Jewish American cultural workers whose sense of Jewish identity was largely informed by the belief that they shared with African Americans common goals and common enemies. Although they were antisegregationist on principle, their perspective for the most part cannot be understood as integrationist in the sense of "liberal integrationism," denoting equality in formal political rights within the existing social system. Whether they came from Left Jewish families, like Kramer's, or chose to link themselves to the antiracist tradition by identifying with the Communist Party was not decisive. The utopia of racial harmony to which they aspired would be forged in the process of common work not merely to "integrate" into a racist capitalist system but to overthrow the inegalitarian social system; it would be realized only in a world from which the underlying causes of racial oppression had been purged by collective action. The meeting ground for Blacks and Jews on the cultural terrain of the Communist-led social movement was envisioned mainly in the imagined narratives of left-wing plays, novels, and poetry. But in some cases it occurred in practice—on the battlefields of Spain, in clandestine meetings of self-organized and armed Black sharecroppers with Jewish union and Party organizers in the Deep South, and on the picket lines of industrial union struggles in the North.

The personal, political, and cultural commitments growing out of this movement were indissolubly linked to an ideology of antiracist radicalism as it evolved through two stages: first, in the context of the Depression and, second, during World War II and the Cold War. The view that anti-Black racism was the symptom of an inegalitarian capitalist economic order that was also dangerous for Jews and other oppressed groups was thus doubly reinforced. The rise of fascism illustrated that targeting of Jews in Europe was analogous to anti-Black racism in the United States; the era of the Cold War McCarthyite witch hunt revealed how racism, anti-Semitism, and anti-Communism were all linked as components of the assault on the Left.

Although Jewish American Left cultural workers and political activists of the generations of the antifascist crusade were passionate in their intellectualism, much of the foundation for such an ethos grew not from the study of particular party texts but from life itself, including the practice of the Party. According to Kim Chernin in her 1983 memoir, In My Mother's House, her mother, Rose Chernin, the California Jewish Communist imprisoned during the McCarthy era, joined the Communist Party after a demonstration by the unemployed. Rose Chernin recalled that she looked up and "I could see those horses coming. It was a nightmare. And we were paralyzed. They were riding straight toward us, riding us down." When she heard a scream, she imagined that she was "standing in a village and the cossacks were riding down." She then added, "You could go so far back in Jewish history and always you would find that cry. Always, in the history of every people. And then people were running all around me, racing for the subway, screaming, crowding together. And I ran with them, and I was thinking, this, this is the answer they give to the demands of the people." Chernin stood there, looking at the crowd: "My fear was gone. I felt angry, I felt exhilarated, and I felt purposeful. That was the day I joined the Communist Party."[12]

Like the Kramer family, Rose Chernin was as militantly opposed to Jewish theology as she was fervently in solidarity with the Jewish people. Of Freiheit she recalled that "it was against religion and never lost an opportunity to attack the tradition." Chernin noted further that in New York City in the 1930s there was an agreement that Yiddish papers would not come out during the Jewish holidays. Yet *Freiheit* appeared even on Yom Kippur, the holiest of holidays. She admired this policy and added, "To you this may not sound like anything very much, but to us it was the world turning upside down."[13]

Notwithstanding the antireligious stance of Chernin and other Jewish Communist militants, the alternative moral principles they constructed in the course of their political struggles resemble the collectivist ethics found in aspects of Judaism, Christianity, and many other religions. They rejected the Jewish religion's institutional forms but appropriated much of the moral content. Commenting on the efforts of the Party-led unemployed councils to get milk for children of Harlem and elsewhere in New York, Rose Chernin observed, "This struggle of people against their conditions, that is where you find the meaning in life. In the worst situations, you are together with people. If there were five apples, we cut them ten ways and everybody ate."[14]

Despite its claim to be based on scientific analysis, the predominant pro-Communist radicalism of this era was also marked by illusions, oversimplifications, and self-deceptions. Perry Anderson identified the problem as flowing from a new form of nationalism that had emerged following the victory of Stalin's faction in the Communist Party of the Soviet Union, based on the illusion that it would be possible to build socialism in a single, economically underdeveloped country. As a consequence, "the activities of the Third International were utterly subordinated to the interests of the Soviet state, as Stalin interpreted them." The result was "the arresting phenomenon, without equivalent before or since, of an internationalism equally deep and deformed, at once rejecting any loyalty to its own country and displaying a limitless loyalty to another state." The tragedy was played out "by the International Brigades of the Spanish Civil War, shadowed by Comintern emissaries—Codovilla, Togliatti, Gerö, Vidali and others—recruited from across all Europe and the Americas. With its mixture of heroism and cynicism, selfless solidarity and murderous terror, this was an internationalism perfected and perverted as never before."[15] Yet beneath this deformed internationalism, the antiracist radicalism to which Jewish Americans were attracted grew from heartfelt convictions and the situation in the United States; it was not imported from the USSR, and changes in Soviet policies did not decisively disrupt such commitments, even if tactics dramatically changed on various other fronts.

THE MIRROR OF RACE

As a chief theme in writing by Jewish American pro-Communists, the portrayal of racism against African Americans served a range of functions. Some

Jewish Americans had grown up in proximity to African Americans, but segregation reigned to the extent that actual contact was minimal. Most of their African American literary characters and experiences were therefore very much imaginary constructions; moreover, the literary texts can be regarded as mirrors, in which the Jewish American writers illuminated dark others but were also bringing to life aspects of their own psyches that they did not want to engage directly. Several varieties of this complex relationship of autobiography and antiracism can be especially observed in the work of three prolific Left writers: John Sanford, Vera Caspary, and Howard Fast.

John Sanford (1904–99) used African American characters to assert his anger and outrage about the U.S. social system and to unveil his utopian dreams of carrying out some action in opposition to the system. He was born Julian Shapiro in Harlem, the only son of Russian Jewish émigrés. He was devastated by the death of his mother when he was ten; it was she who had instilled in him a love of books and American history. Emulating his father, Sanford chose a career in law and was admitted to the bar after being awarded a law degree from Fordham University in 1929.

Instead of practicing law, he fell under the influence of his childhood friend Nathaniel Weinstein, who later called himself Nathanael West (1902–40), and started submitting stories to little magazines such as *Pagany* and *Contact*. In 1934 he published *The Water Wheel*, a stream-of-consciousness meditation on events in the life of a law clerk in the late 1920s. The book was praised for its graceful and clear prose and original language, but it seemed formless. Under West's influence, Sanford adopted his new name, only half-admitting to himself that it masked his Jewish identity. West had urged that "Shapiro" be changed to "Starbuck," a character in Herman Melville's *Moby Dick*, but "Sanford" seemed more suitable because it appeared to have no special significance.

In 1935, after some years living on a dole provided by his father, Sanford published *The Old Man's Place*, a horrific story of a group of World War I veterans who wreak havoc on a farm. The book was characterized by power and speed as if a bomb were about to explode, suggesting the influence of Erskine Caldwell, James M. Cain, and W. R. Burnett. Its success brought him an offer from Paramount pictures, and he moved to Hollywood. At Paramount he met his future wife, the screenwriter Marguerite Roberts (1905–89). Together they shifted from Paramount to MGM in 1938 and collaborated on a number of motion pictures. Following their success with *Honky Tonk*, starring Clark Gable, Sanford was offered a two-year contract. Instead of accepting it, he took up his wife's offer to stay home and write novels, living on her income.

By the late 1930s, Sanford had been drawn to the Communist Party. His first

JOHN SANFORD joined the Communist Party in the 1930s
while continuing to publish powerful and original novels. (From
the Sanford Collection in the Howard Gotlieb Archival Research
Center at Boston University)

step was to stop by Stanley Rose's Bookshop, next door to a restaurant where he ate, so that he could pick up the Communist publications *Labour Monthly* and *Imprecorr*. Party members noticed his interest and invited him to meetings. Meanwhile, he had met the novelist and screenwriter Guy Endore through an introduction from Alvah Bessie, one of the readers of the manuscript of *The Water Wheel* at Scribner's. They started playing golf together almost every morning, during which Endore discoursed on the situation in Spain. Although Endore was already in the Communist Party, he oddly discouraged Sanford from taking the same step. But they continued to be good friends and later taught a course together on the modern novel at the People's Educational Center, the Communist-led school in Los Angeles. Sanford eventually became a Party member and a very regular attendee at meetings; Roberts joined the Party to keep him company.

As a Marxist, Sanford was committed more emotionally than intellectually. He understood the Party's version of Marxist principles, but he never read much Marx. He did not consider himself theoretically astute, and the manifestation of Marxist ideas in his fiction and nonfiction was mainly in the form of broad principles. Even these had a Populist and Romantic aura, to wit that "the rich are thieves and the poor are decent people." [16] His first two novels, while not conceived with political aims, expressed some sympathy for the underdog, a sentiment that first emerged during his boyhood experience when he had to defend a cousin who was always being picked on. His politicization was more evident in his third book, *Seventy Times Seven* (1939). In this novel, he interspersed in the text chapters expressing his view of American history. The narrative involves a farmer accused of murdering a wanderer, who tells the story of his hard life to the district attorney. While his strategy bears some resemblance to the technique used by John Dos Passos in *U.S.A.* (1936), Sanford was more directly influenced by William Carlos Williams's *In the American Grain* (1925), which he had read nearly fifteen yeas earlier. To his surprise, when he found himself wanting to make historical judgments in the mid-Depression, he felt inspired by Williams's passion.

In his 1943 antiracist classic, *The People from Heaven* (reprinted in 1996), Sanford created a Black woman driven to shoot a local white bully who has raped her in an upstate New York town. There is no evidence that this tale came from material beyond Sanford's own imagination, how he believed oppressed people had the moral right to act, particularly when the rest of the community remains unmoved. The emotionalism of his narrative is underscored by his decision to publish the book despite the pleas of some of his Communist Party colleagues in Hollywood not to do so because they thought it would exacerbate racial tensions when wartime unity was required. [17]

Sanford's stubbornness in such matters made him feel that his work was produced entirely without the impact or influence of the Communist Party but came instead exclusively from his own beliefs and sympathy. When he ignored advice from the Communist Party committee in Hollywood that had been established to help writers with their work, he was not further pressured by his comrades. However, he was not promoted as a Communist Party writer. He only contributed a single poem to the *New Masses*, although he served as an editor of the *Clipper*, a publication affiliated with the League of American Writers, to which he submitted a half-dozen pieces.

Eight years later, in the middle of the witch hunt, Sanford self-published a 400-page modernist, proletarian novel, *A Man without Shoes* (1951). This novel depicts the developing political consciousness of a working-class youth, Dan Johnson, and the events that finally lead him to volunteer to fight with the International Brigades in Spain. To some extent, Dan Johnson is John Sanford as he might have been with a different class background that could have brought about an earlier political awakening. Dan reacts resolutely to events such as World War I and the execution of Sacco and Vanzetti and to race and class oppression — to which Sanford was oblivious in his youth. Dan is not Jewish, although he apparently has no particular religious or ethnic background. But the touchstone at every stage in Dan's political development is an awareness of anti-Black racism, and the main influences on Dan are two African American friends. One mirrors Sanford's background: His name is Julian, he aims to become a lawyer, but he ends up writing novels. The other, Tudor Powell, called "Tootsie," becomes Dan's partner in a shoeshine business that they call the Black and White Polishing Company. Tootsie's decision to go to Spain inspires Dan to follow him, thus recasting Sanford's decision to follow Nathanael West to Hollywood. There is but one Jew in the novel, Seymour Wolf, who appears in a paragraph. Wolf is subjected in school to anti-Semitic harassment, which Sanford depicts as being similar to but not as intense as anti-Black racism.

In 1951, Sanford and Roberts were named as Communists by the screenwriter Martin Berkely and subpoenaed by HUAC. Sanford, still a Communist, invoked the Fifth Amendment, and Roberts, her brief Communist involvement years behind her, invoked the First Amendment. Sanford the Communist had already abandoned his screenwriting career and could not be hurt by blacklisting. Ironically, the former Party member Roberts was terminated by MGM and blacklisted until 1960, when she wrote the film *True Grit*, starring John Wayne.

Following a trip to Europe financed with Marguerite's severance pay, the Sanfords had their passports confiscated and decided to reside in Montecito, near Santa Barbara, in 1955. Sanford had been attending Party meetings right up until the HUAC hearings. Then he stopped showing up at events and lost all contact with the organization when he traveled abroad and later moved to Montecito. Nevertheless, he considered it a matter of pride that he never actually resigned from the Party. His basic outlook was not particularly affected by the 1956 revelations of the Twentieth Congress of the Communist Party of the Soviet Union or the invasion of Hungary. For a few years he continued reading the *People's World*, but then he decided to read only materials that interested him or were relevant to his work.

Throughout much of the 1950s, Sanford struggled with a writer's block induced by a sense of guilt for being responsible for the destruction of Roberts's career. He simply could not get any words down on paper and was possessed by a sense that he was punishing himself. By 1947–48 he had already finished *The Land That Touches Mine*, about the disintegration of an army deserter; it was published first in England and then brought out by Doubleday in 1953. Another novel did not appear until *Every Island Fled Away* (1965), about a California minister who defends a draft resister.

In 1967 Sanford published his eighth and last work of fiction. *The $300 Man* treated the relationship between a man whose wealthy father had bought his way out of the military draft and the man who served in his place. Sanford then changed his literary interests and published four volumes of interpretative political commentary on U.S. history. The first, *A More Goodly Country*, was rejected by all of the eighty or so publishing houses that agreed to read it, but it was finally published to critical acclaim in 1975. It was followed by *View from the Wilderness* (1977), *To Feed Their Hopes* (1980), and *The Winters of That Country* (1984). Next he published a multivolume autobiography using an experimental, hybrid technique utilizing screenplays, prose poems, and a realist narrative. The overall rubric was called *Scenes from the Life of an American Jew*. The first volume appeared in 1985 as *The Color of the Air*. Four superb sequels were published over the next few years, along with four more that are semirelated spin-offs. His autobiographical strategy uses a blend of narrative and documentary forms. In a sequence of scenes, what Sanford and others said is recalled and dramatized, and letters and book reviews are reproduced verbatim. Many episodes were reconstructed with the assistance of Roberts's marvelous memory, and Sanford read the text to her as the work was in progress, believing that the quality of her listening drew from him a synthesis of perspectives that transformed his revisions.

Scenes from the Life of an American Jew covers many of the same years as *A Man without Shoes*; but in the latter most of the characters are Jewish, and there are hardly any African Americans. There is a dramatic polarity between Sanford's middle-class life experience and the imagined one of Dan Johnson. The central Black protagonists in Sanford's early novels were essentially idealizations and surrogates who were presented to the readers as teachers, guideposts, and role models.

Another Jewish American radical writer who used imaginary African American experiences to reflect on her own life was Vera Caspary (1899–1989).[18] Caspary was a notable popular writer of mysteries and romances whose political views were not known to her audience until she narrated a rather tame version of her 1930s Communist Party activities in her autobiography, The Secrets of Grown-Ups (1979). Earlier Caspary had fictionalized some of her experiences in a novel, The Rosecrest Cell (1967). Otherwise, her reputation was solely that of a skillful suspense writer who excelled at portraying characters under stress due to fear or as a consequence of a police investigation. The paradigmatic work of her career is Laura (1943), which features a police investigator who falls in love with a woman he believes to have been murdered. In Bedelia (1945), The Murder in the Stork Club (1946), Stranger Than Truth (1947), Thelma (1952), False Face (1954), Evvie (1954), The Husband (1957), and many other works, Caspary customarily employs multiple points of view and often presents a leading character dominated by a particular emotion.

In an earlier phase of her career, however, Caspary wrote novels with more visceral social themes. Her first novel, The White Girl (1929), is the story of a light-skinned southern African America woman who passes for white. Thicker Than Water (1932) is an "insider" narrative of the assimilation of a Jewish family as their Orthodoxy fades and materialism becomes dominant. The Dreamers (1975) traces the lives of three women from the late 1920s to the 1970s. Caspary also collaborated on writing plays with other Left writers, including Geraniums in My Window (1934) with Samuel Ornitz and an adaptation of Laura (1947) with George Sklar. Among her many screenplays, I Can Get It for You Wholesale (1951) was written in collaboration with Abraham Polonsky.

The use of race as a mirror is most apparent in The White Girl. The novel tells of a light-skinned African American who "passes" in Chicago and New York but commits suicide when the white man she loves rejects her after her dark-skinned brother accidentally shows up. In her 1979 autobiography, The Secrets of Grown-Ups, Caspary traced the origins of this novel to the day she read a newspaper article about a Black woman passing for white. Caspary was suddenly overcome with guilt and shame because she remembered a light-skinned African American girl in her high school class who apparently shunned both Blacks and whites. Although Caspary was fascinated by the woman's beauty, she could never bring herself to approach her and wondered why she shunned both races. Caspary explained: "So she became the heroine of my story. Our experiences and characters were woven together. I knew her loneliness, her fears, hopes and shame;

she shared my early jobs. I endured the snubs and insults of white people who believed themselves superior. When I walked on a crowded street or rode on the subway I was a black girl passing as white. She suffered and rejoiced as I had in love. I shed her childhood tears."[19] Caspary discussed how she acquired additional material from an African American male friend who had a cousin who passed for white.

Her memoir does not address the impossibility of her becoming the Black woman passing as white or that the blending of the two—herself, whom she knew very well, and the girl she hardly knew—created something quite different, a third person. This omission reinforces the impression that the story of the beautiful Black woman passing as white is also the story of Caspary's own experiences as a Sephardic Jew negotiating her own ethnicity.[20]

Another variant of the connection between Jewish identity and the mirror of race arises in the account that the Jewish historical novelist Howard Fast provides in his 1990 autobiography *Being Red*. It concerns his 1944 novel *Freedom Road*, the story of a Black southerner, Gideon Jackson, during Reconstruction. While Fast conducted extensive research on the post–Civil War era, he lived for a while in the southern mansion belonging to the old aristocratic family of the wife of his publisher. Concealing his Jewish identity from them, Fast listened to their stories and was amazed at the ease with which "cultured" people could hold such blatant prejudices. He studied their attitudes and examined the artifacts in their museumlike house.

What had originally prompted Fast to write this novel was the combination of four events that paired anti-Semitism and anti-Black racism. First, during his youth he had hoboed through the South and had been appalled by the racism he witnessed. Second, Fast and his wife had spent an afternoon with the novelist Sinclair Lewis and had been horrified to find him expressing "genteel anti-semitism." Third, while working at the Office of War Information during World War II, Fast had initiated a project to study the possibility of integrating Blacks into the segregated army. Finally, as Fast recalled, "Reports were beginning to filter out of Germany about the destruction of the Jews. . . . [Hence] all the notes and thinking that I had done for a novel about Reconstruction came together— and every moment I could steal from my work at the OWI was put to writing the new book."[21]

Thus Fast's correlation of anti-Semitism, in both genteel and vulgar forms, with anti-Black racism on the part of rich and poor compelled him to write his first novel with Black central characters. *Freedom Road* went on to become a literary sensation worldwide; there are claims that it was the most widely printed and read book of the twentieth century. W. E. B. Du Bois wrote a foreword praising its psychological insight into African Americans, and Paul Robeson offered to play Gideon Jackson in a Hollywood film version. However, the proposed film was never made as both Fast and Robeson were soon blacklisted in Hollywood.[22]

FASCINATING FASCISM

During World War II, the menace of German fascism was an obsessive theme of writers with pro-Communist backgrounds, many of whom were Jewish. Their novels began to emerge in 1946, and most authors were combat veterans or war correspondents. Few would endorse the point of view of *The Cross and the Arrow*. Albert Maltz's novel suggested that Germans were potentially normal citizens of the West, capable of decency but violently deformed by a monstrously indecent ideology and social system. Moreover, Maltz held that, while far more extensive, Nazism was nevertheless a continuation of other barbaric episodes in history.[23] To the contrary, Martin Abzug's *Spearhead* (1946), Stefan Heym's *The Crusaders* (1948), and Irwin Shaw's *The Young Lions* dramatized the argument that Nazi evil was sui generis. No Left novelist would admit to Vansittartism, but such a view is insinuated in these three novels principally by the displacement of a German penchant for militarism by an inordinate degree of anti-Semitism. This argument reached a climax in *The Wine of Astonishment* (1948), by Martha Gellhorn (1908–98), a Communist fellow traveler at the time of the Spanish Civil War. Her novel, which tracks the adventures of a Jewish GI in the last days of World War II, is close to a call for random retaliation against German civilians.

Spearhead was the first novel of Martin Abzug (1916–86). Abzug was born in New York City. He worked in his family's garment business from 1934 to 1960 before becoming a stockbroker. As a young writer in the late 1940s, he was associated with the Communist political and cultural movements. In 1944 he married a radical lawyer from the same milieu, Bella Savitzsky (later better known as the congresswoman Bella Abzug).[24] *Spearhead* reflected Abzug's military service and described the retreat of a U.S. Army artillery unit during the early days of the Battle of the Bulge. The plot centers on the tension between two of the unit's officers. Lieutenant Knupfer is a worldly German refugee who considers the peculiar German mentality as beyond redemption, while Captain Hollis believes that Germans are just ordinary people who had received a rotten deal. Antagonism initially erupts between the two over the taking of German prisoners. Knupfer insists, "You should have shot them instead. . . . They can't be changed—that much I know. A dead fanatic is better than a live one." Hollis replies, "They didn't act fanatic, Knupfer. They acted like you and I would have acted; they were scared and they gave up."[25]

Knupfer is convinced that the U.S. Army is incapable of fathoming the depth of German depravity; he fears that the United States will leave Europe too quickly after the war, and the task of cleansing will remain unfinished. The strain between the two men and their rival philosophies erupts again when a captured German prisoner, Wunderlich, cries out to alert his fellow soldiers that U.S. troops are nearby. Knupfer attempts to silence Wunderlich by strangling him, but he is stopped by Hollis, who insists that "we don't kill prisoners in cold blood." [26] As the novel moves toward its calamitous climax, Wunderlich manages to seize a pistol during the chaos of an attack and fatally shoots Knupfer. When Hollis finds out what has happened, he beats Wunderlich to death.

Stefan Heym's The Crusaders commences with a corresponding polarization of U.S. Army soldiers. Sergeant Bing, another German refugee, albeit Jewish, reacts to the taking of German prisoners of war in a manner similar to Lieutenant Knupfer's: "I hate 'em." Lieutenant Yates, formerly an assistant professor of German at a midwestern university, protests that "this is a scientific war" and offers a rationale for the humane treatment of German prisoners: "The man over there's been doing the same thing you've been forced to do: He's followed orders. . . . He's the victim of his politicians as we're the victim of ours." [27]

Other themes in The Crusaders are comparable to those encountered in Abzug's and Shaw's novels, notably the opinion that U.S. soldiers have never been educated about the democratic and antiracist goals of the war, and that the military defeat of Germany will not necessarily mean de-Nazification unless extreme measures are taken after the war's end. Moreover, Heym's treatment of the early postwar occupation period suggests that the United States is only interested in promoting an order where capitalism can flourish. General Farrish, whose behavior suggests General George S. Patton's, aims to create an efficient postwar administration by employing former Nazis.

Heym (1913–2001) was born Helmut Flieg into a Jewish family in Germany. Drawn to Marxism in his youth, he aspired to become a journalist and entered Humboldt University in Berlin in 1932.[28] In March 1933, following Hitler's ascendancy to power, Heym was forced to flee Germany at age nineteen; his father, after being held hostage, committed suicide. In Czechoslovakia Flieg adopted the name Stefan Heym, continuing as a journalist but also writing poetry, literary criticism, and drama. In 1935 Heym received a scholarship from the Jewish American academic fraternity Phi Sigma Delta, which was established to allow German Jewish students to continue their education.

Heym soon came to the University of Chicago to study German literature, but he also began publishing in German-language journals as well as in the Nation magazine in 1936. He received a B.A. and then an M.A. degree from the University of Chicago, with a thesis on the German poet Heinrich Heine. Sympathetic to Communism and fiercely anti-Nazi, Heym moved to New York to edit the pro-Communist German-language *Das deutsche Volksecho* until 1939. He later indicated that he had been a member of the Communist Party from 1936 onward. Subsequently he worked as a salesman for a printing company.

By 1942 Heym had published his first novel, *Hostages*, about life under the Nazis; it became an instant best seller. At that time he legally changed his name to Heym and fell in love with Gertrude Gelbin, a widow twelve years older than himself; they were married the following year. Likewise a member of the Communist Party, Gelbin was employed by MGM and, under the name Valerie Stone, published children's stories and articles on subjects of interest to women.

Heym joined the U.S. Army in 1943 and was trained in military intelligence. In 1944 he published *Of Smiling Peace*, a failure as a work of literature, although it portends the more ambitious *The Crusaders*. Based on research, the novel is set in North Africa (where Heym had never been) and uses the problems of an emancipated colonial state to consider the motivation for the war and the nature of the fascist cast of mind. In June 1944 Heym landed in Normandy just after D-day and spent the rest of the war close to the front lines. His work involved interrogating prisoners, writing leaflets, broadcasting using loudspeakers to enemy positions, and especially writing radio programs as part of a Mobile Radio Broadcasting unit. Since his unit was near to the front, there was often the danger of attack and capture, and Heym was awarded a Bronze Star for bravery. After the war Heym spent three years working on *The Crusaders*, which he cut down to 300,000 words from a much longer manuscript. The novel went through four printings in the first three weeks of publication, and eventually 2 million copies were sold in English and other languages.

The Crusaders differs from *Spearhead* and more closely resembles *The Young Lions* in that a Jewish soldier is killed and the naive liberal, Yates, eventually forms a mature understanding of the nature of the evil he must face. *The Crusaders* also resembles *The Young Lions* in that anti-Semitism in the U.S. Army is emphasized and Nazism is depicted as an all-encompassing corrupt force. The hard-bitten Sergeant Bing is taken aback and descends into a deep depression when he visits the German city where he had been born and raised, only to find its citizens thoroughly depraved by fascism. Where Heym differs from both Abzug and Shaw is in his placing a strong emphasis on the fascistlike behavior of U.S. officers, who make common cause with the Nazis to gain economic profit.[29] Like *Spearhead* and *The Young Lions*, however, *The Crusaders* admonishes the reader—to wake up, to develop a new consciousness, and to finish the sanguinary job of eradicating German fascism at its vile roots.

By the start of the next decade, the novels by Jewish pro-Communists had become less vituperative and waxed nostalgic for the fraternity of men who had worked together to save democracy. *The Sun Is Silent* (1951), by Saul Levitt (1911–77), traces the journey of a group of men from their army air force training through the completion of their bombing raids over Europe.[30] Levitt had served as a radioman-gunner on a B-17, and his novel was especially effective in dramatizing the elements of a bombing mission—the alert, the briefing, the takeoff, enemy fighter attempts at interceptions, the bomb run, and the return flight. Moreover, although his novel has a collective protagonist, Levitt managed to infuse members of the bomber crew with distinctive personalities.

Levitt was born in Hartford, Connecticut, and attended the City College of New York. A close friend of the Communist writer Arnold Manoff (1914–65), Levitt was a pro-Communist in the 1930s and published in the *Anvil*, the *New Masses*, and the International Publisher's collection *Get Organized!* (1939). During World War II he was a correspondent for *Yank* while serving in the air force, and he continued to write literary reviews and political commentary for the Communist press as Alfred Goldsmith. In the 1950s he was one of the writers for the television programs *Danger*, *You Are There*, *Wide Wide World*, *Climax*, and other shows while publishing short stories in *Harper's*, *Atlantic Monthly*, *American Mercury*, *Fortune*, and the *Nation*. In 1959 he produced a two-act play about an incident from the Civil War called *The Andersonville Trial*, which was rewritten and expanded to achieve acclaim as an Emmy Award winner in 1971. In 1971 he also produced *The Trial of the Catonsville Nine*, a play based on the trial of the pacifist Berrigan brothers.

Face of a Hero (1950) by Louis Falstein (1909–96) is noteworthy for its modest portrayal of an ordinary man who performs his duties as a committed antifascist. Falstein was born in the Ukraine and came to the United States at age sixteen.[31] His father had orchards in the Ukraine, but he became a businessman in the United States. The family had no interest in either radical politics or Zionism, and Falstein lacked direction as an adolescent. He was forced to go to Hebrew school but found it dull. He attended but did not graduate from high school in Chicago, although he later secured a diploma by taking a special course. During the early Depression he found work for a while as a shoe salesman, but he was mainly unemployed. In 1934 he came to Detroit to seek work in the auto plants. At this time he was drawn to the John Reed Club, where he became friends with the African American poet Robert Hayden and developed an admiration for the radical attorney Maurice Sugar. Occasionally he wrote skits for fund-raising events. His name appeared (as Lewis Fall) as one of the editors of the Detroit Left publication *New Voices*, but he published nothing. After changing his name for a while to Fallon, because of the Ford Motor Company's reputation as being anti-Semitic, he at

During the 1930s and 1940s, SAUL LEVITT published fiction
widely under his own name and wrote criticism for the *New
Masses* as Alfred Goldsmith. After World War II he published
a novel and achieved success as a playwright. (Courtesy of
Howard Gotlieb Archival Research Center at Boston University)

last found work. But when a union leaflet was discovered in his lunch bucket, he was fired and was forced to apply for "pick and shovel" work with the WPA. To his good fortune, he secured a job with the Federal Writers Project.

At the WPA Falstein found himself under attack by the Black Legion, a neofascist organization that denounced him and other radicals as Red spies and threatened their lives. Falstein recalled that he was referred to in the newspapers as an "agent of the Third International." Shortly afterward a coworker on the Federal Writers Project was murdered. In order to help save the WPA from elimination, Falstein joined the Save Our Jobs March in Washington, D.C., spending a week living in a tent in Potomac Park and lobbying congressmen. At this time, Falstein became obsessed with the Spanish Civil War. He generally felt like an unheroic, perhaps even cowardly person, but the logic of his political views made him susceptible to pressure to take action on behalf of the Spanish Republic.

When two of his friends joined the Abraham Lincoln Brigade and were killed in battle, Falstein volunteered. Before he could depart, however, he received a court order to appear as a witness at the impending trial of the members of the Black Legion. This was an event that attracted worldwide attention. Legion "executioners" paraded before a crowded courtroom and bragged about their exploits in killing scores of persons — sometimes by burying them alive in lime pits — because they were African American or "Red unionists." When the trial was over, Falstein found work at a General Motors plant, only a week before the famous sitdown strike began. He remained in his plant for six weeks. He was often frightened by the efforts of the police and vigilantes to evict the strikers, but he drew strength from his sense of solidarity with other men and women in the battle.

Just before the start of World War II he moved to New York. As a Communist he believed that he should participate in the war, even though he felt fearful and unsuited. To his amazement he was accepted for combat duty in the army air force and managed to fly fifty bombing missions from 1943 to 1945, receiving a Purple Heart and Air Medal with three clusters for his service. *Face of a Hero* was written to show that even a man with as little self-confidence as he had could survive and carry out his duties.

In the process of writing the novel, he discovered how easily he could put words together. The book's sudden best-seller status in the United States, along with its success in Britain, bolstered his ambitions. In the postwar period the *New Republic* published everything Falstein submitted. Politically, he remained outside the Party membership but was more loyal to the Party than ever. He faithfully read the *Daily Worker* and the *New Masses* and its successors. Through the dancer and poet Edith Siegal he met Michael Gold, and he knew Len Zinberg as well. He believed that Stalin could do no wrong and was unaffected by the revelations

LOUIS FALSTEIN, a pro-Communist from the 1930s until
the end of his life, wrote a popular novel about World War II.
(Courtesy of Louis Falstein)

at the Twentieth Congress in 1956, and he continued to read and study Marx in his spare time. His wife worked as a guidance counselor, and in 1946–48 he took courses at New York University, after which he taught writing there in 1949–50 and at City College in 1956.

Falstein's forte was writing popular literature. He greatly admired Harold Robbins's *A Stone for Danny Fisher* (1952), and in 1953 he published his own urban crime novel, *Slaughter Street*, billed on the cover as "a savage novel of crime and lust in the big city." In 1954 he published a thriller, *Sole Survivor*, about a concentration camp survivor who encounters his Nazi tormentor in New York. In 1965 he published a memoir of his family in Europe, *Laughter on a Weekday*, and in 1968 he wrote a biography of Sholem Aleichem. His last, unfinished work was an autobiographical novel based on his experiences with the WPA in Detroit.

FROM EMILY DICKINSON TO EMMA LAZARUS

If the Jewish cultural Left was literarily involved in a group of pro-Communist publications, it was the individuals who kept those publications afloat who gave the tradition its unique stamp. One of the most pivotal was Morris U. Schappes (1905–2004), who was born Morris Schappeslevetch in the Ukraine, although his family was already living in Brazil.[32] His father, an illiterate but skilled anarchist worker, had gone there in search of employment. Schappes came to New York in 1914 speaking Portuguese, Spanish, and Yiddish. A brilliant student at Public School No. 64, he skipped grades five times and was sent to a special high school on the City College campus where he completed a four-year curriculum in three years, during which time he developed a stuttering problem. After graduating from City College, he attended graduate school at Columbia University and received an M.A. in 1930. He commenced work on a dissertation on Emily Dickinson's poetry and joined a Marxist study circle whose participants analyzed the socialist classics "not just line by line, but comma by comma."[33] In 1932 his academic work encountered a crisis. Schappes had been the first to discover that Emily Dickinson's family had modified her unpublished poems. After he published his findings in *American Literature*, the Dickinson estate broke off all relations with him.[34] He concluded that to continue working on his doctorate would mean starting over with a new dissertation topic. Accordingly he turned his energies to teaching, writing, and left-wing activities. During the early 1930s, he published a great deal in the literary pages of the *New York Post*. He also wrote an essay for *Modern Monthly* in 1933 on T. S. Eliot's anti-Semitism, and he contributed to *Poetry* and the *Symposium*.

By 1932 academics were for the first time becoming attracted to the Communist Party, especially through the activities of the League of Professionals for Fos-

MORRIS U. SCHAPPES was a popular English teacher at
City College of New York who joined the Communist Party.
He was blacklisted after serving a prison sentence and became a
prominent editor and authority on Jewish American life. (Photo
by Nell Greenfield; courtesy of Morris U. Schappes)

ter and Ford and later the Pen and Hammer, a small group with a headquarters on Sixteenth Street that was similar to the John Reed Club but with a less visible Party presence. The Pen and Hammer was comprised primarily of scholars who were literary critics, historians, and social scientists, but it also included a few physical scientists. Schappes, who was already teaching at City College, joined the Pen and Hammer in 1931 and a year later became its national executive officer. For the Pen and Hammer magazine, he used the name Vetch, which was the last part of Schappeslevetch. The only active branch of the Pen and Hammer was in New York, although there were individual correspondents around the country. The Pen and Hammer fell apart in the period leading up to the Popular Front.

In 1934 V. J. Jerome signed Schappes's application to the Communist Party, wherein he enrolled under the name Alan Horton. What convinced Shappes to join was an incident in which the Communist Party members active in the Pen and Hammer took what he believed to be the wrong side in a dispute. He met with Party leader Earl Browder to complain. Browder agreed with Schappes, who concluded that the best way to influence Party policy was from the inside. Since there did not yet exist any units for Party academics, Schappes joined a branch of industrial workers and became its educational director.

By 1936 Schappes had taught at City College for eight years without gaining tenure, which was at the time a prerogative of full professors and a status conveyed by the president. In April 1937 the English Department chairman happened to walk into his class and heard Schappes reading from the work of Percy Bysshe Shelley, which he mistook for a writing by Marx. Soon thereafter, Schappes received a notice that he would not be reappointed in the fall. Within a short time protests came from unions all around the country, and hundreds of students staged a sit-in.[35] When Schappes was reappointed, further left-wing activity was galvanized on the campus.

The first Communist Party unit at City College had been connected with the Harlem section of the Party because of the college's location. The three founding members began recruiting around issues of tenure, working conditions, and the need to combat fascism, for which they set up the Anti-Fascist Association of Staff of City College. In 1934 separate units had been established at the Brooklyn branch of City College, Hunter, and Queens College. The Communist publication *Teacher-Worker* was an eight-page printed bulletin issued anonymously, and Schappes was among the editors. The publication was distributed through the college's mailroom. The Communist Party's influence was so great in the Instructional Staff Association that the Party members had a policy of deliberately maintaining a majority of non-Communists on the association's executive committee; the Party members thought that it was better to lead, and sometimes be outvoted, than to merely dominate the organization. Through the efforts of Party members, a more democratic tenure system was proposed, and strong ties with the labor movement were created.

As a result of his encounters with anti-Semitism at City College, Schappes experienced his first sense of his connections to Jewishness. There were anti-Semites on the college faculty, and a German professor was accused of anti-Semitic behavior. After a brief period of doing research on the English poet Christina Rossetti (1830–94), Schappes found himself captivated by the Jewish New York poet Emma Lazarus (1849–87). His fascination with women poets seemed to be connected with the education on "the Woman Question" that he had received in Communist circles. The Communist orientation did not address sexual issues; it was primarily aimed at securing the rights of women in trade unions. It also had a goal of electing women to leadership positions in local Party units and state committees. Schappes discovered that nothing of significance had been published about Lazarus since the early 1900s; scarcely more than one of her sonnets was known to the public. Since he had become active in the Communist-led Jewish People's Fraternal Order, Schappes applied for and received $100 to subsidize his research on Lazarus.

Schappes's scholarship and political activism went hand in hand. In 1938 the Anti-Fascist Association of City College persuaded the administration to call a collegewide antifascist meeting. Schappes was chosen to speak for the faculty, and 3,000 students attended the assembly. This was a time of great influence by and prestige for the Party, but much of it evaporated at news of the Hitler-Stalin Pact. Then, while the Party was at its weakest and most isolated, the Rapp-Coudert investigation of subversives in the New York state school system began.[36]

Schappes had used a Party name and published anonymously to protect his job, but he nonetheless sold the Daily Worker on campus. Faculty, students, and staff knew that he was a Party member. He was investigated and faced the dilemma of lying about his Party membership or admitting it at the cost of his job. Schappes lied, claiming that he had left the Party a year earlier and that all the members he had known had vanished from the scene. He was then tried for perjury. While he was out on bail, he completed his project on Lazarus. At the New York Public Library he was befriended by Joshua Bloch, who had been chief of Jewish acquisitions for thirty years. Bloch made available to Schappes unpublished writings of Lazarus and introduced him to the New York Public Library Bulletin, in which Schappes published a group of Lazarus letters.[37] The library's board of trustees was upset by this, but Bloch vouched for Schappes, telling them that he was a first-rate scholar.

While serving his prison sentence for perjury in the Tombs, Schappes began research on the history of Jews in the United States. Bloch arranged for publishers to send him books, which is the only way that prison authorities would allow him to receive them. In prison Schappes completed the major portion of his background reading on the topic and decided what he wanted to do. In 1944 he was paroled on condition of obtaining employment. A friend procured for him a job producing electronics in a war production plant. After he finished his parole, he began his history of the Jews in the United States in earnest. He also lectured on the topic for small fees. His lectures were from time to time sponsored by the International Workers Order, an organization that not only sold insurance but promoted a rich cultural life. His wife, Sonya, was a teacher but found that she had been blacklisted because she had refused to shed the Schappes name. She then began working for booksellers and reprint houses and for the Communist Party bookstore at the Party-led Jefferson School of Social Science. The two lived frugally and decided not to have children so that they could devote themselves fully to the revolutionary cause.

While in prison, Schappes had been offered a contract by the Alfred Knopf publishing house to write a history of Jewish Americans, but Schappes was hesitant to make a commitment at that time. His main interest was to do literary and scholarly work, and so far as he knew, no history of Jews in a particular country had been published by a Marxist anywhere in the world, not even in the USSR. But Schappes was concerned that it would seem like a retreat to emerge from prison and bury himself in writing a book, as if he had gotten scared and was dropping out of political activity. So he went to Earl Browder to ask for a political assignment from the Party to prepare the history. Browder, who was always sympathetic to scholarly and cultural work, gave him a written statement declaring that he was to be assigned to the Jewish history project full time. William Z. Foster, too, had a close relationship to Jewish workers, especially garment workers, and looked favorably on the effort. Schappes was forced to carry out most of his research by correspondence, but he found archivists quite willing to help him.

In 1938 the New York State Committee of the Communist Party had sponsored a publication called *Jewish Life*, which was an official Party organ. Schappes had been a member of the editorial board, along with Rabbi Moses Miller and Party leader Alexander Bittleman. The Communist Party financially supported and sponsored the magazine but did not promote it. *Jewish Life* lasted only sixteen months, collapsing after the Hitler-Stalin Pact. The Party then published *Jewish Survey*, which lasted a year and a half, followed by *Currents*, which appeared during World War II.

In October 1946 a new version of *Jewish Life* appeared, again led by Communists but without a specific Party connection. Unfortunately, at the same time an Orthodox Jewish magazine with the identical name appeared. In the early 1950s, when the Communist editors of *Jewish Life* were called before investigating committees, the editors of the Orthodox magazine became fearful of being identified with alleged subversives. Consequently its publisher approached the district attorney and charged the pro-Communist *Jewish Life* with a copyright violation. In 1958 Schappes and the other editors were forced to put several notices in the magazine explaining that the two publications were unrelated. The name of the Communist periodical was changed to *Jewish Currents* at the beginning of the next year.

In the late 1940s Schappes began to realize that his thinking about Jews had evolved dramatically. At first he held views akin to an assimilationist indifference about Jewish culture. Then, provoked by Hitler, he became concerned with anti-Semitism. He now realized that he had developed a genuine fascination with Jewish affairs. Previously his main association with Jewish culture had been through his parents. He had eaten with them once a week until he was married. However, instead of using the visits to improve his Yiddish, he had tried to get his mother to upgrade her English. But after the battles against anti-Semitism on the City College campus, Schappes began to frequently interrogate his parents about their own experiences. Schappes's father died while Morris was in prison, but after his release he visited his mother and sister regularly to ask them about their Jewish experiences.

Throughout the Cold War Schappes rendered his services to *Jewish Life* and to *Jewish Currents* on a voluntary basis. His wife continued to support him, although he had a small income from lectures and some of his publications. The magazine was published in the offices of the Party's Yiddish-language paper, *Freiheit*, so there was no phone bill, rent, or printing costs. In the early 1950s, when the Party began sending a section of its leadership underground, the magazine moved to Union Square due to fear that there might be a police raid on the old building and the subscriber list would be confiscated. The new space had been previously occupied by the Jewish Labor Committee, which had been created by Communist Party member and union leader Ben Gold during World War II. Although the committee had folded, its furniture remained, and *Jewish Life* took possession of it.

Working on his book on Jewish American history and putting out the magazine were Schappes's major political responsibilities, but he also taught at the Communist Party's training school. Originally, he had taught the theory of "the Negro Question" until the Black Party leader Doxey Wilkerson produced a study arguing that the Black Belt region in the South had shrunk to a point where

Marxists could no longer refer to it as a nation. The Black Belt nation had been the basis of the Party's theory and program relating to African Americans. Schappes supported Wilkerson, and they became a minority opposed to the Party's traditional view. Accordingly, they were both switched to teaching other topics. Schappes began to specialize in propaganda techniques and "the Jewish Question." For him, like other Jewish Communist cultural workers, the topic of anti-Black racism was a major issue of concern. But his politics had formed first through developing an internationalist identity and then by turning to Jewish history and culture within an internationalist framework.

From the time that *Jewish Life* began, it had followed Party orthodoxy, such as supporting the expulsion of Earl Browder and ignoring the implications of the infamous Doctors' Plot in the Soviet Union in 1952. The magazine's policy, being so adamantly pro-USSR, had the effect of allowing Schappes greater flexibility in his other relations with the Party. When the Party leader Bob Thompson lambasted Schappes's old friend Bill Lawrence (a pseudonym for William Lazar) at a Party convention, Schappes felt he could protest the attack with impunity. Likewise, Schappes violated the Party injunction not to recognize expelled members by continuing to talk to Bella Dodd, the onetime leader of the Communist teachers. But the connection between orthodoxy and privilege was not discerned. The editor Louis Harap defended the 1952 Prague trials in Eastern Europe not because he believed that this would give him wider latitude in other arenas but because he sincerely believed the charges. Later, Schappes and Harap came to see themselves as having been like horses wearing self-imposed blinders; they could not see the crimes of Stalin and the other Soviet leaders, and they confidently dismissed criticisms of Stalin and the others because they believed that the sources of such criticism were contaminated. Within such a framework, they imagined themselves to be absolutely honest and consistent. The premise that the Soviet leadership was benign had to be accepted if one were to be part of a wonderful movement for a better world.

However, there were certainly moments of intellectual grappling and questioning. When friends of Schappes returned from World War II and told stories about Russian soldiers misbehaving and expressing anti-Semitic views, the *Jewish Currents* editors could neither believe nor entirely disbelieve the stories. Consequently, they attributed the stories to the fact that U.S. troops had entered the war late and that the Soviet troops were the recently drafted, backward peasant elements.

Such illusions necessarily meant that the reaction to the Khrushchev revelations was particularly extreme, perhaps even more so among the *Freiheit* editors. Many of the Jewish editors would have left the Communist Party after the 1957 convention, but they had control of two institutions that published organs, in contrast to Communist Party members around John Gates at the *Daily Worker*, who rebelled in the pages of the newspaper but eventually quit the Party. Since 4,000 to 5,000 Communists still identified with *Jewish Life*, the editors decided to make their own policy decisions and no longer heed orders from Party officials. They did not bother to consult the Party's National Committee or Central Committee. *Freiheit* editor Paul Novick, however, remained on the National Committee of the Party, and Schappes continued to hold a seat on the Party's National Jewish Commission.

While Schappes served on the commission, its meetings were occasionally contentious. Schappes recalled that at one point the question of anti-Semitism within the Party was raised, and the Party leadership's representative, William Weinstone, said that this was impossible. However, after the African American attorney William Patterson, also a member of the committee, said that he witnessed anti-Semitism in the Party all of the time, Weinstone backed down. Differences on the National Jewish Commission were exacerbated over the Soviet interventions in Hungary and Czechoslovakia in 1956 and 1968. At the time of the 1967 Six Day War in the Middle East, *Jewish Currents* and *Freiheit* took a pro-Israel position and were at odds with the Party's support for the Arab nations. The Party leadership, however, was hesitant to punish the dissenters; it was reluctant to force the Jewish membership to choose between the positions of the Party leadership and those of the Jewish publications. Criticisms, according to Schappes, began of himself and the others privately but nonetheless through Party channels.

In late 1968 Schappes got a phone call from a *New York Times* reporter asking his response to a memorandum that had been sent to Party branches that claimed that Schappes could not be trusted because he had deviated from the Party's positions on Hungary and Czechoslovakia and was guilty of "White chauvinism." Schappes replied that *Jewish Currents* was and would continue to be a publication independent of the Party. Soon, the Party launched a rival publication, *Jewish Affairs*, which devoted major attention to criticizing *Jewish Currents* and *Freiheit*. Eventually Schappes, whose other activities had interfered with his attendance at Party unit meetings for some time, received a letter from the membership committee of the Party's state committee informing him that he was no longer connected with the Party. The other *Jewish Currents* editors drifted away from the Party. Paul Novick was denounced in Communist parties abroad as an expelled renegade, although nothing was said about him to the Party membership in the United States so as not to alienate the milieu around *Freiheit*.

Jewish Currents, however, survived and actually thrived during the 1970s and

1980s. Prior to the 1967 war in the Middle East, the editors were kept outside the Jewish community. But their new espousal of the need for Jewish culture and for Jews as a people to survive gave them new entry. In 1970 the American Jewish Committee published a series of pamphlets on uniting the Jewish community, and Schappes was stunned to learn that he had been invited to a meeting to present his views along with his longtime antagonist Irving Howe.[38]

The conversion of Jewish Americans to a pro-Communist perspective was thus a journey with myriad ends, usually involving a reclamation of Jewish identity in some form. While many might have changed their names and aspired to write about Jewish life with dispassion, the intensity of anti-Semitism during the antifascist crusade compelled all but a handful to address some aspect of their Jewish upbringing and background. For many, their focus on the plight of African Americans was a surrogate for their own anxieties. For one famous Jewish American playwright, antifascist sentiments were so overwhelming that he constructed a bifurcated persona in the 1940s that eventually allowed his rage and art to find a middle ground in Broadway theater.

{7

Arthur Miller's Missing Chapter

MILLER THE MARXIST

On 3 July 1945 the *New Masses*, a weekly magazine of culture and politics published in Manhattan and principally staffed by members of the Communist Party, printed a curiously disarming essay about the New York stage. Double-edged in its admixture of bluntness, anguish, and eloquence, "Sincerity in the Theater" scolded Broadway dramatists of the 1940s as well as creative writers loyal to left-wing politics. The author of the essay reprimanded all of them for shared complicity in failing to grasp the proper link between theme and character. In the contemporary plays written by members of both groups, the dramatis personae tended to be "fabricated in the mills of theme's demand." The *New Masses* critic allied himself with "Progressive" writing but warned Leftist playwrights about the dangers of devising characters who promoted "a call to action"; one's characters should be "in themselves a condemnation of society as it is constructed." Further, "the drama of our time lies in the man next door."

"Sincerity in the Theater" reads today as if it were an outpouring of personal grievances against the treatment of a rejected play, or a brief for some work-in-progress blocked from completion due to the prevailing rules of the game. The wounded author is disdainful of the Broadway critics' "exercises in award-making" that overlook "the basic ingredient of good theater," which is "sincerity." He alleges that no other art form "produces as much that is not heartfelt as does the theater," a result of the metastasis of Broadway drama into a "technical exercise in which creativity is deemed to be present if a new twist is given an old plot, if laughter rings out no matter how simulated." He retorts that "sincerity" is nothing less than the "path that leads from the heart" and is to be found in "honest characterizations."

As an antidote to the fashionable tenor on Broadway, "Sincerity in the Theater" champions only two plays, notwithstanding their artistic weaknesses and the absence of political characters. One is the recent production of Tennessee Williams's *The Glass Menagerie* (1944), which by surprise controverted the expectations of the critics because "the play seems true, and today on Broadway this astonishes." Earlier, Sean O'Casey's *Juno and the Paycock* (1924) ignited in Ireland an even more spectacular reaction because "the truth of the picture drawn upon the stage was so convincing, so close to life, that those responsible for that life were pierced to the heart." In a conceivable self-reference, the *New Masses* critic declared that authentic theater will arise again when "a playwright comes along who will face the dirtiest corners of our world and set about cleaning them out with real characters." Nothing must endanger the artist's "search for the truth," for "the truth itself is political."[1]

The author of "Sincerity in the Theater" was Matt Wayne, identified only as the current drama editor of the *New Masses*. His name first appeared in print in the 6 March issue and would vanish forever one year later. The brief tenure, about two dozen columns, prompts the conjecture that drama criticism was perhaps not Wayne's intended vocation. Upon further inspection, one can not help but notice that the central themes of "Sincerity in the Theater" and additional writings in the *New Masses* by Matt Wayne between March 1945 and March 1946 dovetail with the prevailing opinions of playwright Arthur Miller (1915–2005).

In the summer of 1945 Miller was still nursing his wounds from the calamitous critical response to his first Broadway play. *The Man Who Had All the Luck* had closed after four performances in November 1944, following a barrage of notices dismissing it as "confused" and "addled."[2] He recollected afterward that his bitterness culminated in a pledge: "I would never write another play, that was for sure."[3] Something changed in 1945, however; by 1946 he had found his way back with an older manuscript, "The Sign of the Archer," which under the fresh title *All My Sons* won the New York Drama Critics Circle Award in 1947 and secured the career he had thought was lost.

In his autobiography, *Timebends* (1987), Miller appraised "Broadway in the forties" in a manner identical to that of "Sincerity in the Theater": "There were absolutely definite rules of playwriting" wherein "the author could only be a sort of conductor who kept order rather than a sneaky deviser of some meaning at which the play would finally arrive."[4] Throughout his career, Miller emphasized the primacy of emotional truth in the creation of character in relation to dramatic action.[5] Forty years later he was still asserting that the success of *The Glass Menagerie* took the critics by surprise because "it aimed for the heart."[6] *Juno and the Paycock* would steadfastly be estimated as "a great piece of work,"[7] and in *Timebends* he recalled a performance in which the actors "humbled the heart as though before the unalterable truth."[8] In 1949 in the *New York Times*, Miller wrote his now famous line, "I believe that the common man is as apt a subject for tragedy in its highest sense as kings were."[9]

"Sincerity in the Theater" also encapsulates the core argument of a "lost" Marxist essay that Miller would synopsize in 1956, at the time he testified before HUAC in respect to the federal government's withholding of his passport. Referring back to 1947, Miller volunteered that he prepared a manuscript following a series of meetings with Communist Party writers, "in which, for the first time in my life, I would set forth my views on art, on the relationship of the artist to politics." Miller further told the committee, "I think it is the best essay that I ever wrote, and I have never been able to find it in the last 2 or 3 years. I wish I could. I would publish it, as I recall it, because it meant so much to me." His oral summary was no less a cri de coeur than the words of Matt Wayne ten years earlier:

> That great art like science attempts to see the present remorselessly and truthfully; that, if Marxism is what it claims to be, a science of society, that it must be devoted to the objective facts more than all the philosophies that it attacks as being untruthful; therefore, the first job of a Marxist writer is to tell the truth, and, if the truth is opposed to what he thinks it ought to be, he must still tell it because that is the stretching and the straining that every science and every art that is worth its salt must go through.[10]

In *Timebends*, Miller appended the information that he read this essay to a large meeting of left-wing writers in the midtown theater area, and that they were confused by its theme that "a writer cannot make truth but only discover it."[11]

Circumstantial evidence is overwhelming that Matt Wayne was, indeed, Arthur Miller. Following a request that I turn off my tape recorder and not take notes, I was advised of this identity by two former Communists, A. B. Magil (1905–2003) and Lloyd Brown (1913–2003), editors of the *New Masses* during the 1940s. Magil served as acting editor of the magazine during Wayne's tenure, and Brown, an African American air force veteran, joined the staff during a March 1946 reorganization when Wayne departed without public explanation. Brown also believed that Miller had belonged to a writers' unit of the Communist Party around 1946 under the same pseudonym.[12] Although Miller never confirmed the pseudonym or the *New Masses* column, he did not dispute the association either; he simply was not directly asked. Having risked a prison sentence for his refusal to identify Communist writers before HUAC, Miller sensibly cultivated a silence about select portions of his youth and personal life; this broadened into a prickly defensiveness regarding his later marriage to actress Marilyn Monroe. He went to his grave carrying many secrets, and portions of his personal papers remain closed to the public.[13] Miller's biographer, Martin Gottfried, observes of *Timebends*, "It is abridged and calculated autobiography, selective and sometimes misleading about his personal life and unilluminating about his work."[14]

A more recent work by a scholar, Enoch Brater's *Arthur Miller: A Playwright's life and Works*, speculates that *Timebends* was a "preemptive strike" against would-be biographers, "omitting many details while dramatizing others at the expense of 'mere fact.'" Brater observes a disappointing response to the autobiography in the United States, and he quotes Miller's opinion that the factual revelations found wanting were mainly in regard to his relationship with Marilyn Monroe.[15]

No doubt a hunger for more details about Monroe, whom Miller met in 1951, has detracted from more prosaic questions, especially about radical politics in a decade less associated with Left commitment than the 1930s. Almost no direct information about 1945–46 is provided in *Timebends*. The strategy of the book is true to its title in that it violates strict chronology, substituting instead the plea-sures of associative colloquies across the decades. Miller scholars have not yet filled in the details of those two years; the most complete calendar of Miller's life notes only that his novel *Focus* was published on 30 October 1945. There are no references to 1946.[16] However, at least six radio plays survive from that period; two are adaptations, and three were never published.[17] Only a few other publications in 1945–46 appear on Miller bibliographies. These include a brief excerpt from his 1944 volume of reportage about soldiers on military bases, *Situation Normal*, in the April 1945 issue of *Science Digest*; a contribution to the sym-posium "Should Ezra Pound Be Shot?" in the 25 December 1945 *New Masses*; and an April 1946 short story that appeared in *Encore*, which draws on the experiences of *Situation Normal* and which was never reprinted.[18] Even the most comprehen-sive bibliographies of Miller's work do not cite reviews of his plays published in the Communist press in the 1940s or 1950s or, for that matter, most of the con-tributions under his own name to Communist-led publications such as *Currents* and *Jewish Life*. To be sure, Miller's broad alignment with pro-Soviet Commu-nism is affirmed by the first-rank scholars of Miller's life and writing, such as Martin Gottfried and Christopher Bigsby.[19] Most information about his connec-tion to the Communist movement is derived chiefly from the vague allegations with which he was confronted by congressional investigators during his HUAC testimony and the discursive ruminations in his memoirs.

Notwithstanding, the confusing metamorphosis of political culture in the United States over the past fifty years could be observed in the journalistic spin on the news of Miller's death. The impulse of well-meaning obituarists and eulo-gists was to elide mention of Miller's artistic and intellectual journey through Communism. The *New York Times* obituary, as colossal as it was laudatory, ignored Miller's profound encounter with Marxism, reporting only that he "was cited for contempt of Congress, although he said that he had never joined the Commu-nist Party."[20] This is a misreading of the HUAC contempt citation, which was the result of his refusal to identify other people rather than his political philosophy. The obituary furnishes a highly abbreviated rendition of Miller's tortured response to the question of whether he ever held Communist Party membership.[21]

Of Miller's political awakening during the Depression, playwright Tony Kushner eulogized in the *Nation* that Miller was "one of those political people who refused an identification with a specific race or nation or movement or party. He certainly wasn't a communist, and he wasn't a socialist."[22] To demonstrate a primal source for Miller's consistent devotion only to "democracy and self-reliance," Kushner quotes an anecdote told by Miller about his Republican grandfather. In the 1930s the old man urged the unemployed Miller to travel to the USSR to take advantage of business opportunities in a "new country." When informed by his grandson of the government ownership of business in the Soviet Union, the old man made a face that "would have put fears into Karl Marx himself" and muttered, "them bastards." Kushner does not provide a citation, but Miller's reminiscence appeared in his essay "A Boy Grew in Brooklyn," published in 2000 in *Arthur Miller: Echoes down the Corridor, 1944–2000.* The essay was first published in a 1955 issue of *Holiday* magazine.[23]

The same anecdote is recounted at greater length in a short story by Miller, "Grandfather and Emperor Franz Joseph," that appeared in the June 1943 issue of *New Currents* published under the auspices of the Jewish Survey Corporation.[24] This magazine was close to the Communist Party. The short story was never mentioned by Miller and has been omitted from all biographies, bibliographies, and other Miller scholarship.[25] What is most consequential in a comparison of the two accounts, beyond an illustration of Miller's facile fusing of fiction and autobiography, is that the 1943 version of the story presents a political view quite contrary to the message extracted from it by Kushner. In the 1943 story Miller's grandfather is not portrayed as a political inspiration but someone who is tragically deluded and driven by a fantastic longing for a return to a feudal past that Miller attributes to his refusal to acknowledge his deteriorating health and imminent death. After the onset of his fatal illness, Miller's confused grandfather spends his small savings on a closet full of fancy new suits that he will never wear.

The story that appeared in *Holiday* might be seen as a synecdoche for the "missing chapter" of Arthur Miller's life of the mid-1940s. Miller's 1943 fictionalized anecdote is recast as autobiography in 1955 but is stripped of the grandfather's primordial identification with Emperor Franz Joseph and many other details that render the grandfather an unsuitable role model. There is a political opacity in the 1955 version, one that Kushner finesses in depicting Miller as a consistent liberal icon rather than the complex human that he was.

What is lamentable is that the pains of liberal commentators to protect Miller from being stereotyped as a onetime Communist fellow traveler achieve results parallel to the efforts of those who might depict Miller as an apologist for totalitarianism. Both interpretations deny the acquisition of the wisdom Miller gained as he abandoned a pro-Soviet orientation and embraced the independent radicalism with which he infused culture in the United States during the second half of his life. Ultimately, the excising from Miller's biography of this transformative experience, which coincided with momentous steps forward in his career as a dramatist as well as the excruciating unraveling of his first marriage, obscures a discernment of the maturation of his artistic as well as political legacy.

SOCIALISM WAS REASON

Could Miller have avoided confusion had he offered a plainspoken version of the customary Cold War confession, "I believed in Communism for most of two decades, until I discovered that I had been duped"? The anti-Communist culture of the Cold War and its aftermath combined with the paradoxical nature of Miller's own relationship with the Left made it virtually impossible for him to offer such a statement. In a more painstaking manner, however, Miller does furnish evidence for a similar judgment in his autobiography. His method is to re-create the worldview and emotional state in which his convictions about the need for political virtue in the face of economic exploitation and racist hatred were forged under the bewitchment of the Soviet version of Communism that endured for most of the 1930s and 1940s.

According to *Timebends*, Miller was captivated by Marxism in 1932 because of the remarks of a college student he encountered, after which he promptly set about lecturing his father that "profit is evil, profit is wrong." [26] He depicted his youthful radicalization as coming like a thunderbolt, then quickly normalizing itself as an ingredient of faith. He suggestively acknowledged that the transformation was abetted by an unconscious parricidal proclivity and was less intellectually based than morally inspired — "a violent revelation of the hypocrisies behind the facade of American society." To the young Miller, the appeal of Marxism's grounding in reason afforded "the same privileges of joining the elect that enthrall religious communities." He noted that his brother, Kermit, agreed with his politics "in principle" and that in the circumstances of the Depression "the prospect of deep social change became less and less the subject of intellectual conversation and more the common property of everyone." [27]

Miller arrived at the University of Michigan in 1934. His new political philosophy was shared by his future wife, Mary Slattery. The two dreaded the irrationality that they saw embodied in the growth of fascism, and "we enjoyed a certain unity within ourselves by virtue of a higher consciousness bestowed by our expectation of a socialist evolution of the planet." To them, "socialism was reason," and "it was the Soviet Union that upheld reason's light by doing what was best for the majority." Doubts about the democratic character of the "one-party Soviet system" were deflected by the "illusions" created by the need for "hope." Roosevelt's New Deal was but a temporary respite: "All that could save us was harsh reason and socialism, production not for profit but for use." [28]

Miller remembered that from 1932 to 1939 he had "literally been having night-mares about the Nazis," yet he found himself accepting the Hitler-Stalin Pact with the belief that the victory of fascism in Europe would produce an empire "no worse than that of the British and French." Miller later observed that am-bivalence about supporting capitalist democracies "was very much part of the radical mind-set of the thirties." Part of the confusion in response to the early days of World War II stemmed from a post-1929 cynicism about the capitalist social order coupled with the horror of World War I, which was perceived as a sacrifice of working people to make the rich richer.

In 1939 it seemed transparent to Miller that the Western democracies, by handing Spain and then Czechoslovakia to fascism, were actually rooting for a "German victory in Russia," which would mean "a long future without any Com-munists at all in a world comfortably divided into spheres, none of them social-ist." [29] Miller's rationale here was identical to the official Communist position, as it appeared in *Jewish Voice*, the monthly publication of the National Council of Jewish Communists: "Hitlerism was nourished and kept alive by the financiers of England, France and the United States. Hitlerism grew and expanded because the imperialists of other countries wanted to build a strong Nazi Germany as a weapon against the Soviet Union." [30]

Miller wrote with a similar degree of haunting obliqueness about the psycho-logical dimensions of his ensuing disillusion with pro-Soviet Communism. He alluded to the 1939 Hitler-Stalin Pact seeming to be justified "if that is what you wished to see"; spoke of the need to understand "human illusion" by discovering what it is based on, notably the "logic of the illogical"; and attributed his politi-cal obtuseness to a substitution of "moral considerations" for an understanding of the workings of power. With the sagacity of the chastened he concluded, "It was our desire for a moral world, the deep wish to assert the existence of good-ness, that generated, as it continues to do, political fantasy." [31]

Since the political narrative of *Timebends* is episodic, not chronological, and dispersed among personal and literary digressions, some translation of his com-ments in more direct language may be needed for their full impact to be regis-tered. Readers in the twenty-first century may also be encumbered by a relative scholarly inattention to the literary politics of World War II. The 1940s was a decade dwarfed by events before and after—a transitional decade sandwiched between the trauma of the Depression, which created a magnetic pull toward the Left, and the conservative counterassault of the 1950s, with its resultant orgy of apology and obfuscation. Although an eminently commendable cause, the "antifascist crusade" that preceded the Cold War had a jumbled consistency. Political identities were obscured behind terms such as "Progressive," which might refer to a Communist or a pro-Soviet liberal. The light that the antifascist Left focused so brightly on German totalitarianism could also be blinding as to the Soviet counterpart.

As for political matters, the meditations of *Timebends* provide a credible recounting of why, during the 1930s and 1940s, Miller was incapable of discerning what he later realized were "the clear parallels between the social institutions of the fascist and Nazi regimes and those of the Soviet Union."[32] It is the 1945–46 engagement of Miller with the more narrowly cultural Communist movement that comprises the "missing chapter" of his life, thus precluding a rounded appreciation of his artistic development. A cautious retracing of his life during these years will render more intelligible the means by which Miller hammered out his ingenious strategy of reaching Broadway audiences with somber political themes.

Such a reconstruction will also make evident the mechanism through which Miller came to terms with his Jewish identity in the formative years of his writing career. Throughout his professional life he was hounded by the accusation that his plays of the 1940s and early 1950s manifest what the novelist Mary McCarthy called an "impatience with the particular" in favor of "a hollow, reverberant universality."[33] The inference that Miller might have been suppressing his Jewishness for invidious reasons has caused his defenders to enumerate Jewish aspects of *All My Sons* and *Death of a Salesman*. Some of the assessments of Miller's Jewishness rely on doubtful claims about his familiarity with the Yiddish language as well as assertions about Jews as uniquely "rooted in the strong sense of mutual responsibility in the family."[34] An examination of different and previously unnoticed opinions of Arthur Miller in the mid-1940s may facilitate a more accurate appreciation of Miller's ethnicity in relation to his artistic and moral stature. A rounded understanding of the significance of Miller's evolution in the 1940s cannot be extracted from the paradoxical particularities of the pro-Communist literary Left in the closing days of World War II.

The thirteen months of Matt Wayne's association with the *New Masses* were marked by incessant turmoil in the Communist Party. Miller was attracted to Communism in the early 1930s. He then found his calling as a young playwright in the post-1935 period of the antifascist unity of the Popular Front, only to be challenged by a new Communist policy turn in the wake of the 1939 Hitler-Stalin Pact. With the German attack on the Soviet Union in June 1941, a new policy that became known as Browderism (after Communist Party general secretary Earl Browder) was forged. This was a more intemperate version of the Popular Front in which the Party membership was whipped into a patriotic fervor that was actually to the right of many liberals.

Most alarming during Browderism was the Communist Party's rigid policy of subordinating the demands of labor and of protests against racism to the requirements of national unity believed necessary to defeat fascism. The Party also carried on a relentless campaign in support of government suppression of "fifth columnists," a rubric under which it amalgamated alleged supporters of the Axis, racists and anti-Semites, and left-wing critics of U.S. war policy and Communist policy such as the Socialist followers of Norman Thomas and Trotskyists. On 20 May 1944, as Miller was finishing *The Man Who Had All the Luck* and awaiting the appearance of *Situation Normal*, the subsuming of Browder's Communist Party into the U.S. war machine came to a logical conclusion when the Party was dissolved and reformed (on a much looser basis) as the Communist Political Association.

The situation remained unchanged until April 1945, when Matt Wayne was in the second month of his *New Masses* post. Then a thunderbolt struck: Without warning, the French Communist leader Jacques Duclos denounced Browder's recent pronouncements about the Teheran conference in Iran as a revision of Marxism. No one doubted that Duclos spoke as a proxy for Moscow, and the U.S. Communists began to turn against their helmsman when news of Duclos's criticism reached the Party membership in May. Tensions were already heightened because of Franklin D. Roosevelt's death in April and the imminent surrender of Germany. By June the once-lionized Browder had been stripped of power by his comrades and condemned as a pro-imperialist "enemy of the working class"[35] and as a traitor who had sought to dissolve the Communist Party into an educational club. In July, shortly after Wayne published "Sincerity in the Theater," the Communist Party reemerged with Eugene Dennis as national secretary and William Z. Foster as chairman. The following month atomic bombs were dropped on Hiroshima and Nagasaki, and Japan surrendered.

As Matt Wayne produced a steady stream of theater reviews and commentary during the fall of 1945 and winter of 1946, the Communist Party was consumed by lacerating self-criticism. Pro-Communist writers and intellectuals were caught up in the cross-currents of a complicated reevaluation of past practice. The dethroning of Browder provided an opening to cast off some of the embarrassing political baggage that had collected during the National Unity Front. Yet it was unclear as to whether this meant a return to the more latitudinal Popular Front of 1935–39 or to the extreme leftism of the early 1930s or was a step toward something new. The notion of creating a fresh, new militant cultural leadership was attractive to diverse constituents of the Left. It would provide a larger role for seasoned veterans, Communist Party professionals who had felt sidelined by the wartime focus on antifascist liberals, as well as for a generation of angry young writers eager to challenge the literary establishment and make their own mark.

But what were the boundaries of the changes under way? A left turn was required, but how far left? How many of the past problems were due solely to Browder, rather than to an organizational culture that was ultimately in thrall, albeit voluntarily, to a horribly corrupt caricature of socialism? Had Browder not been untouchable until orders came from Moscow to depose him? The campaign against revisionism plunged ahead while masking the ambiguities entailed in the liberation from above and a scapegoating of Browder. Writers, in particular, found themselves in an unexpected and unwanted predicament; the efforts of some to discuss what they saw as literary matters would necessarily have to engage issues relating to the eradication of Browderism. Concurrently, artistic life in the Soviet Union was further deteriorating under the rigid political control of Stalin's disciple Andrei Zhdanov (1896–1948). Ironically, when Browder was officially expelled in February 1946, the Communist Party was convulsed not by political dispute but by a literary debate over competing interpretations of the concept of "art as a weapon." With the close of the debate, Matt Wayne and Arthur Miller vanished as contributors to the *New Masses*.

What role did Matt Wayne play in this political drama and restoration of a Left orthodoxy in the Party, and what were its repercussions for Arthur Miller's return to Broadway? Part of the answer may be illuminated by the melancholy career of a Bohemian intellectual on the Left, Isidor Schneider (1896–1977), remembered today, if at all, chiefly as a confidant of the poet Hart Crane. On 19 December 1944 the *New Masses* announced with considerable fanfare that the forty-eight-year-old Schneider was joining the staff as literary editor at the start of the new year.

Schneider was an able critic who published widely in the prewar years and who was employed by various publishers to do editorial and publicity work. His professional life had spanned the modernist 1920s and the proletarian 1930s. In each decade he published a novel (*Dr. Transit* in 1926 and *From the Kingdom of Necessity* in 1935) as well as a volume of poetry (*The Temptation of Saint Anthony and Other Poems* in 1927 and *Comrade, Mister* in 1936) that vocalized the moods of the two eras.

"Izzy" was remembered by the *New Republic* literary editor Malcolm Cowley in his autobiographical *The Dream of the Golden Mountains* as "an amiable furry creature, easily wounded." He had a "mop of black-brown hair" and "an untrimmed mustache," under which a pipe was usually inserted. As "an idealist and a believer," Schneider inspired a "protective" attitude in Cowley, "surmising as I did that his transparent goodness would get him into trouble."[36] The New Masses described Schneider only as "lovable and learned" and pointed out that he had served as its literary editor eight years earlier, prior to his winning a Guggenheim Fellowship that enabled him to reside in the Soviet Union. Most importantly, the New Masses announced that Schneider was making plans for an expanded editorial board with new editors for both political and cultural matters.

The political atmosphere at the New Masses at this point can most accurately be described as High Browderism. The Marxist editors were busy admonishing the liberal newspaper PM, a publication uncommonly friendly to the USSR, for criticizing the U.S. Congress as a millionaires' club, arguing that unity of all classes against fascism was all that mattered. The editors also lambasted the left wing of the labor movement, declaring that anyone striking while the war was in progress should be regarded as a fifth columnist; they even criticized United Autoworkers leader Walter Reuther, who, although personally opposed to strikes, was willing to allow a referendum on the issue.[37] Thus the late 1944 reorganization at the New Masses was originally projected as a deepening of Browder's political strategy and had as its goal reaching out to a new generation of left-wing writers.

The older generation was represented by the writings of Harry Taylor, Matt Wayne's predecessor as the New Masses theater critic. Taylor was an activist with the Stage for Action, a Communist-led theater group that had performed Miller's That They May Win a year earlier.[38] The one-act audience-participation playlet about women on the home front came to be regarded as the major success of Stage for Action.[39] In his review column, Taylor habitually offered political advice, connected plays to current events, referred to his long personal history of involvement in New York radical theater, and displayed a special knowledge of the Yiddish theater.[40]

In early January 1945 the New Masses "Between Ourselves" column described a large gathering that the magazine had hosted to welcome back Isidor Schneider, who would oversee the nourishing of a wide spectrum of literature for a unified antifascist movement. The report mentioned that several playwrights had been in attendance.[41] A few weeks later photographs were carried of a number of continuing as well as newly appointed New Masses editors, with an announcement that more were to come.[42] A photograph of Matt Wayne did not appear, but on 6 March he was first listed as the drama editor. The official announcement was coupled with the news that Harry Taylor, after a year and a half in the post, had been compelled to resign due to the pressure of other work: "We are fortunate in obtaining as his successor Matt Wayne, who has considerable experience in the theater. His first review appears in this issue."[43] Unlike the situation with many other staff members, the "Between Ourselves" page of the *New Masses* never published any biographical information about Wayne or any tidbits about his adventures as a reviewer or reports on his other literary activities. Wayne was never among the staff members listed as speaking at one of the regular *New Masses* symposia, nor did he appear in group photographs taken at receptions aimed at increasing circulation.

BECOMING MATT WAYNE

Arthur Miller was a plausible if green successor to Harry Taylor at the *New Masses*, inasmuch as he passionately admired the Group Theater and especially the early left-wing plays of Clifford Odets. Miller had also reviewed plays and fiction as a student for the *Michigan Daily*, then worked for the Federal Theater Project in 1939–40. In 1942 he was frequently writing radio scripts for NBC's *Cavalcade of America* series.[44] Compared to Taylor's, the writings by Matt Wayne plainly revealed a newcomer to the Broadway scene. Wayne's columns often dwelled on themes that one easily associates with Miller's later essays on the theater, especially the need for poetry in the creation of character. Even when reviewing James Gow and Arnaud D'Usseau's *Deep Are the Roots* (1945), an acclaimed work whose authors were pro-Communist, Wayne modified his approval with a demur about the authors' lack of poetry.[45] While Wayne, like Taylor, attended the Yiddish theater, he protested that comprehension was difficult "for those like me who have no Yiddish."[46] The point is also made in *Timebends*, where Miller describes listening to his grandfather's stories even though "I understood no Yiddish."[47] Only on occasion did Wayne assert Marxist bromides such as "Race problems are, after all, economic problems first."[48]

By and large Matt Wayne's *New Masses* critical commentaries are estimates of the quality of writing, production, and acting, unencumbered with mechanical political content. Other than "Sincerity in the Theater," Wayne's most sustained discourse on theater technique was his July 1945 commentary on Bertolt Brecht's *Private Life of the Master Race*. Wayne presented a vivid synopsis of the play and described Brecht's epic method as focusing on creating characters to occasion not sympathy but understanding. Yet Wayne also asserted that dramatic theories, while absorbing, can never be executed in their pure form. He noted that Brecht's *Private Life of the Master Race* has conventionally realistic aspects that are effectively realized. As a consequence of stylistic blending, Brecht's play is in danger of being overwhelmed by an episodic character but is ultimately rescued because "it is forged in a spirit so honest as to command attention for the sake of its point of view alone, which is that of a man who has suffered from the German calamity and will not relent in his driving pursuit of the evil that destroyed his country and very nearly the whole world. There is not a trick in the play. It is as direct as a revolver and very nearly as compelling."[49] In later years Miller had little to say about Brecht's technique, although he repeated the point that Brecht himself was inconsistent in applying his own theory. Yet Wayne's frank admiration for Brecht's skill in dramatizing the relentless pursuit of evil seems to reverberate in the tension producing the climax of several of Miller's own productions.[50]

A. B. Magil, the acting editor of the *New Masses*, recalled that it was *Daily Worker* columnist Samuel Sillen who brought Miller to the magazine's office, where Miller agreed to become the staff writer known as Matt Wayne.[51] In the *Daily Worker* Sillen had published one of the few favorable reviews of *The Man Who Had All the Luck*, concluding that "it is gratifying to find a young playwright breaking intelligently with current theater stereotypes."[52] But Miller had a greater intellectual rapport with Isidor Schneider, and Miller and his college friend, the left-wing poet Norman Rosten (1914–95), would habitually lunch with him.[53] Who influenced whom may never be known, but the impact of the relationship was revealed in Schneider's critical writings during the year of Wayne's *New Masses* affiliation and in Schneider's subsequent role as the most reflective and ardent defender of Miller's plays in the Communist press.

Matt Wayne's columns, frequently under the rubrics "On Broadway" or "On and Off Broadway," garnered only modest attention in the letters section of the *New Masses*. No one was perturbed that the reviews centered on more technical aspects of theater, and at least one reader was certain that Wayne's "Sincerity in the Theater" was intended as a repudiation of Browder's revisionism.[54] But the direction of the *New Masses* cultural pages under Schneider and Wayne was made plain when Schneider published an essay that autumn called "Probing Writers' Problems." Schneider reported on a series of meetings held by the *New Masses* staff members and associates, three of which were devoted to culture. In his summary, Schneider dispensed a number of startling assertions.

One was minimalization of the existence of any Marxist canon of critical principles. Even the contributions of the Soviet critics were put aside by Schneider as unsuited to the situation in the United States. Schneider also argued that the momentary imprint of the Left on literary criticism in the 1930s was detached from any noteworthy attainments in aesthetics: "What gave the work of the Left critics of the thirties its impact was their enthusiasm, tenacity and their boldness in applying social criticism to current work."[55] While Schneider touted the victory of the Left in establishing the necessity of placing "a work within its social frame," he also noted that the Marxists of the 1930s promoted "a number of incidental concepts which have lost their value." These were the categories of "escapism,"

Photograph taken in the City Room of the Communist Party's
Daily Worker in 1941. Visible from the top down are George
Morris, David Platt, Dorothy Low, Louise Mitchell, Bill Mardo,
Nat Low, Joseph Starobin, and Arnold Sroog. (Courtesy of Bill
Mardo)

"ivory tower," and "decadence," which addressed moral, not aesthetic values. The application of such classifications had led to a misevaluation of novelist Henry James and had resulted in a disparagement of "experiment in form and exploration into states of consciousness" that resulted in the underappreciation of the achievements of the critic Kenneth Burke and the modernist James Joyce.

Such faultfinding with the Communist cultural tradition had occurred before. Criticisms of this type had been advanced by writers who forsook the movement in the 1930s and were privately nursed by veterans such as Schneider who nonetheless persisted as loyal Communists due to larger considerations. More heretical was Schneider's view that judgments as to whether a writer had fulfilled his or her social responsibilities should not be made at the discretion of the Communist Party. He rejected the notion that the *New Masses* should perform such a guiding role and called attention to the manner in which the Association of Revolutionary Writers in the USSR had abused such power in the early 1930s.

Instead, the *New Masses* staff meetings had concluded that "the safest authority, as yet, is the writer's own experience. Through the reactions of labor audiences and the organizational or agitational work that he does, the writer gradually defines his responsibility to the labor movement." Such a stance would free writers on the Left from a feeling of entrapment by immediate political crises and pressures, which had induced a "sense of emergency." Such an atmosphere of impending political crisis occasioned writers to subordinate artistic values and even to show their work to people they perceived as "labor leaders" for their opinions, and to regard adverse reviews of their work in the Left press as official repudiations.

According to Schneider, the *New Masses* board believed that the journalism and reportage produced from such concerns were "honorable," but there was "equal value in producing lasting works." With feeling and eloquence, Schneider restated the proposition of Matt Wayne's "Sincerity in the Theater," and he used language almost identical to that in the "lost" essay that Arthur Miller summarized before HUAC in 1956:

> No writer need worry about being politically correct if his work is faithful to reality. One important aspect of Marxism is its facing up to reality in everything. And the classics are eternally "correct" because they are representations of reality. And that is why the socialist Soviet Union is preeminently the country in which the classics live. The Marxist writer adds this to his advantages: his Marxist understanding enlarges his capacity to understand reality. Let him use it![56]

The aftereffects of Schneider's essay are well known to historians of the literary Left as well as of the role of Communism in the film industry. The novelist and screenwriter Albert Maltz, a member of the Communist Party since 1935, responded with an article essentially sympathetic to Schneider called "What Shall We Ask of Writers?" When Maltz's contribution was received at the *New Masses* in New York City, the hunt for vestiges of Browderism was at fever pitch, and Maltz's essay was seized upon by Party writers and political leaders as an opportunity to prove the sincerity of their anti-Browder credentials.

Maltz's primary contention was that the traditional slogan of the Communist Party's cultural movement, "Art as a Weapon," was accurate as a proposition but should be abandoned inasmuch as it had lent itself to simpleminded disparagement of art for its alleged political failures. This judgment probably had widespread support, but Maltz stepped over a critical boundary when he further insisted that writers who had broken with the Communist Party, such as James T. Farrell and Richard Wright, should be judged primarily by their books and not their current political views.[57] While it might be tolerable to forgive Henry James or James Joyce their political indiscretions, the mention of Farrell and Wright hit too close to home. As radicals who broke with the Party while still holding socialist and even Marxist principles, both were regarded as "Trotskyites" — that is, the worst form of renegades. The capacity to excommunicate someone as a renegade was, for Communists as for adherents of every orthodoxy, a means of discouraging dissent and disaffection when the Party's political policies or practices seemed to contradict the ideals that had drawn one to the Party.

Accepting responsibility for the controversy he had unwittingly unleashed, Schneider agreed to publish a vague disassociation, "Background to Error," in the same issue of the *New Masses* in which Maltz's essay appeared. Since Schneider had not recommended the embracing of writing by any "renegades," his transgression was less harshly viewed than Maltz's; he was able to criticize Maltz merely for inadequately analyzing the social background to the errors he had noted.[58] The *Daily Worker*, however, ran two vehement denunciations of Maltz on the same date as the issue of the *New Masses*. One was a personal attack by longtime Communist writer Mike Gold, "The Road to Retreat," labeling Maltz a sellout; the other was the first of a series of six columns titled "Art and Politics," by Samuel Sillen, imputing Browderism to Maltz and quoting Zhdanov. Dozens of other indictments of Maltz were published in both the *New Masses* and the *Daily Worker*, alongside a few cautious defenses. In the end, Maltz published "Moving Forward" on 9 April in the *New Masses* (it also appeared on 7 and 8 April in the *Daily Worker*), agreeing that his notions, "if pursued to their conclusion, would result in the disillusion of the left-wing cultural movement." A series of public meetings was held in New York and Los Angeles where Maltz was welcomed back into the fold.[59]

Matt Wayne's columns continued to appear through the publication of Maltz's essay, which coincided with Browder's official expulsion from the Communist Party. Yet within weeks of Maltz's recantation, Wayne's departure was in the works. The *New Masses* of 26 March reported that a lunch had been held the previous Friday at a Fourth Avenue restaurant where plans for expansion of the board were addressed. The gathering ostensibly developed proposals to counteract what was declared to be British prime minister Winston Churchill's plan for a new world war. The historian Herbert Aptheker (1915–2003) and Lloyd Brown were added to the board. A meeting of the "new" *New Masses* was scheduled for 13 April at the Paramount Restaurant. In that issue, the "On Broadway" column was written by Schneider, not Wayne, and the substitution was repeated on 2 April.[60]

When Maltz published "Moving Forward" on 9 April, no editorial board members were listed. There was an announcement that changes in the *New Masses* board were under way, and once more a notice was run of a meeting for new editors and contributors, this time described as a delegated conference, scheduled for 13 April. On 16 April the *New Masses* published a special issue called "Winning the Peace," and Matt Wayne and Isidor Schneider were still listed as members of the board. The announcement of the 13 April Paramount Restaurant conference was repeated, along with a new one for the 18 April Manhattan Center symposium "Art as a Weapon."[61]

However, on 23 April, in the "Between Ourselves" column, there was a letter from Schneider announcing his resignation as literary editor, and Matt Wayne was mysteriously absent from the staff roster.[62] Schneider's letter stated that he had resigned in March to devote time to finishing a novel, but he would continue to participate in broader cultural tasks as a member of the *New Masses* board. In a box called "Just a Minute," there is a list of nine new additions to the editorial board.[63] In the 30 April issue, Schneider was switched to the board, and Matt Wayne's name was nowhere to be found. A report claimed that thousands of people had attended the delegated *New Masses* conference and that 3,500 had come to the "Art as a Weapon" symposium.[64]

Wayne's departure from the *New Masses* coincided with Arthur Miller's return to writing *All My Sons*, which would be produced on Broadway less than a year later. Despite being sympathetic to Schneider and Maltz, Miller did nothing publicly that would estrange him from the *New Masses* editors. For their part, with the recantation of Maltz under their belt, the editors wished to reestablish orthodoxy without ruffling too many feathers. On 25 June the playwright Arnaud D'Usseau (1916–90) published a moderate essay on the topic of "Theater as a Weapon." He insisted that the slogan need not be abandoned but required a more imaginative approach.[65] On 17 December 1946 Harry Taylor returned to write theater criticism. On 7 January 1947 there was a brief skirmish between Schneider and A. B. Magil over the plays of Lillian Hellman that had emerged as a side issue in the Maltz dispute, suggesting tensions between Schneider and others remained.[66]

Shortly afterward, on 18 February 1947, Miller's *All My Sons* was favorably reviewed by Schneider, who added retrospective praise for *The Man Who Had All the Luck*. He called Miller a "natural playwright" who had achieved a strategy of presenting his ideas through "whole action" and "emotions." The main political idea of the play was that "self-fulfillment is possible only within a social frame."[67] On 14 October 1947 Miller was listed as the first speaker for a public meeting cosponsored by the *New Masses* and the new Communist journal *Mainstream* to defend the novelist Howard Fast, an early target of HUAC. On 13 January 1948 the *New Masses* announced that financial limitations were forcing the publication to combine with *Mainstream*. The journal offered a parting survey of "books written and plays produced" in 1947 that "come within the orbit of our thinking and our values"; *All My Sons* was among the eight plays that were named.[68]

What do we know of Miller's politics at that time? As a writer with views similar to those of Isidor Schneider, Miller was no doubt dismayed by the treatment of Maltz and Schneider. To some extent, Miller withdrew to the sidelines. Yet his personal confidence was sufficiently restored so that he was able to resume his career as a playwright with a strategy very different from that of the person who had written *The Man Who Had All the Luck*—a new strategy based on the principles championed by Matt Wayne. Following the success of *All My Sons*, Miller remained at arm's length from the Party's institutions, becoming increasingly dubious of the Party and the Soviet Union. Yet he loaned his name to select campaigns against political repression of pro-Communists and was to some extent propelled back into militancy by the HUAC investigations.[69] His work was discussed at length in Communist publications, and there is evidence that he followed some of the discussions.[70]

In the 1950s, whatever his misgivings about the Communist Party and the USSR, Miller resisted what he saw as a dangerous domestic repression in which anti-Communism was the wedge issue of right-wing demagogues. Just as pro-Soviet Communism had emerged in the Depression as a sign of hope for Miller in its intrinsic alliance with sentiments that were pro-union and antiracist, the offensive against Communism in the Cold War seemed to Miller to be part and parcel of an onslaught against the labor movement and civil rights. The Cold

Warriors were so strong that it was nearly impossible for a public figure of Miller's stature and his background of pro-Communist activities to publicly break with Communism without joining the conservative crusade, and without becoming an informer to prove that his anti-Communism was bona fide. But he did neither.

INNOCENCE WAS SHATTERED

It is a curious coincidence that during Matt Wayne's tenure at the *New Masses*, Arthur Miller's name began to appear in the magazine, and he began to write for it using his own name. In the issue where Matt Wayne's column initially appeared, a full-page advertisement for Miller's *Situation Normal* was published. This was rare in the *New Masses*, as if it were spotlighting Miller's new relationship with the publication.[71] A copy of *Situation Normal* next became part of a special offer accompanying a subscription to the *New Masses*. The same arrangement was made for *Focus* in the fall of 1945 and for the published edition of *All My Sons* when it appeared in 1947.[72] Usually the books offered with *New Masses* subscriptions were by well-known Communists; it was uncommon to see three by one author.

Unlike the reviews by Matt Wayne, the writings that appeared under the name Arthur Miller in the *New Masses* and several other publications of the Communist movement are strictly political, militantly angry, and focused on one issue: anti-Semitism. The time was ripe for Miller to feel close to the magazine about this topic. During Miller's association with the magazine, many pages of the *New Masses* were devoted to the situation of Jews in America and to the anti-Semitic dangers of Father Coughlin's Christian Front. This issue was also a central concern in Miller's novel-in-progress, *Focus*, which appeared about six months after the first of Matt Wayne's columns. Upon publication, *Focus* was celebrated almost uncritically in the *New Masses* as a dramatization of a political priority of the Left on the home front. The review was titled "On the 'Christian Front.'"[73]

Shortly afterward Miller contributed to the *New Masses* symposium "Should Ezra Pound Be Shot?"[74] In contrast to the paucity of political commentary in Matt Wayne's theater reviews, Miller's political line was unwavering and occasionally sectarian. Whether Pound deserved a traitor's fate was not a serious question for anyone who had heard Pound's speeches.[75] Indeed, Miller launched an attack against the literary establishment, the "leaders in the field," specifically meaning e. e. cummings, William Carlos Williams, Conrad Aiken, Karl Shapiro, and F. O. Matthiessen. They had claimed in the liberal *PM* that Pound's status as a poet exempted him from being taken seriously as a political activist. To Miller, this was proof of the literary establishment's lack of seriousness: "In asking us to laugh away Ezra Pound they have demonstrated that they regard themselves as poseurs and harmless clowns, facile entertainers who do not really mean what they say but simply speak and write in a modishly elevated sphere of life." [76]

It is apparent that Miller felt politically at home with the left turn of the post-Browder Communist Party and its growing differentiation from its onetime liberal allies. Four months later, the *Daily Worker* featured Miller in an interview, complete with a photograph. In the interview he continued to polemicize against the lack of serious commitment on the part of other writers: "I sincerely hate this false separation of the writer from people." He pointed out that he episodically took work "as a regular guy at a regular job" in order to "keep on learning about people and from them." What was required to solve the political problems of the postwar era, including anti-Semitism, was an understanding that "the main fight is the fight to raise the living standards of people all over the world and the enemy is imperialism." [77]

Around the same time that Miller was appearing in the *New Masses*, his wife, Mary, was employed by Philip Jaffe, a longtime intimate friend of Earl Browder. This was another significant link to the Communist Left. Jaffe was a public fellow traveler who in 1937 launched the publication *Amerasia*.[78] In June 1945 Jaffe and his closest associates were arrested by the FBI on charges of trying to pass government secrets to a foreign power. The case was weak in that it was based on break-ins and wiretapping. Eventually a deal requiring Jaffe to pay a fine was struck in February 1946. The magazine closed in 1947.[79] *Timebends* states that Mary was employed by Jaffe before the case, but her work as Jaffe's editorial secretary actually occurred several years later.[80]

Miller gave the USSR the benefit of the doubt in the 1930s and 1940s, but he tended to follow his own political drummer when it came to the domestic situation in the United States. A zealous antifascist, he was not blinded to the negative aspects of the Communist wartime Popular Front. Two things troubled him in particular: One was the prevalence of greedy wartime profiteering, which crystallized the idea for *All My Sons*. The other was the lack of consciousness among U.S. servicemen about the similarities between fascism and white supremacism, which he addressed in *Situation Normal* and again in *Focus*. During his HUAC testimony and in *Timebends*, Miller vehemently insisted that had *All My Sons* been completed and released before the end of Browderism, the play would have been roundly denounced by the Communist movement as disruptive of wartime unity, and perhaps as even profascist.[81] *Focus*, too, grew out of Miller's distress about racial prejudice, including anti-Semitism, that he witnessed while working at the Brooklyn naval yard. But it appeared during the Party's postwar turn in orientation.[82]

In assessing the missing chapter of 1945–46 in Miller's life, one can visualize more definitely the thirty-one-year-old writer en route to his artistic self-definition. The Matt Wayne columns sift through dozens of performances to gradually hammer out a strategy to sustain artistic seriousness while reaching a mass audience. A concurrent enchantment by and revulsion against Broadway is ubiquitous. Moreover, it is clear that Miller was coming to terms with his sense of Jewish identity. His means of doing so was to separate his rage at anti-Semitism, which was authentic and required expression, from the artistic conundrum of creating a politically serious theater for a mass audience. Until he created his alter ego, Matt Wayne, Miller was unable to reconcile the relationship between the urgency with which he wanted to speak out as a Jew and an artistic strategy that could reach a Broadway audience.

As noted above, the writings of Matt Wayne scarcely address Jewish matters in direct terms; yet the concurrent writings published under the name Arthur Miller are obsessed with the topic. Writers customarily construct masks and assume pseudonyms, and these often flow from entangled motivations. If, in becoming Matt Wayne, Miller merely wanted to protect himself from pigeonholing by critics or from political harassment by prospective employers who might notice a regular column, he would have had adequate justification. But the effect of his dual identity was liberating: The persona of Matt Wayne, searching for the poetry of emotion in the broad-minded atmosphere fostered by Isidor Schneider, seemed to speak independently of Arthur Miller, the admirably earnest antifascist polemicist. One voice balanced the other. Wayne sprang forth as a part of Miller's personality that drew upon his emotional life in some respects without being impeded by the ardently felt Jewish-specific opinions that were voiced under his birth name. The persona Matt Wayne thus prefigured the nonethnic Jews of Miller's *All My Sons* and *Death of a Salesman*.[83]

The content of *Focus* has some relevance to this transitional moment for Miller. The original title for the novel was "Some Shall Not Sleep," and the events depicted occur in 1944, a year before the novel's publication. Although *Focus* was praised by reviewers and sold well, it was not particularly promoted by Miller and was out of print for many years. The literary strategy of *Focus* falls between the old and new Miller and is a link to his pre-1947 writing, which Miller generally did not allow to be republished. *Focus* discloses a powerful truth; however, contrary to Matt Wayne's aesthetic, the character development is thin and the plot is carefully controlled by the theme.

The central character in *Focus* is Lawrence Newman, who waivers between intense social pressure to join an anti-Semitic gang modeled on Father Coughlin's Christian Front and a sense that this would be too extreme. In his lack of understanding about the relationship of racism in the United States to fascist enemies, Newman resembles the GI's Miller had interviewed for *Situation Normal*. And Newman was a veteran of World War I. Newman also anticipates Joe Keller of *All My Sons* and Willie Loman of *Death of a Salesman* as a non-Jewish protagonist and head of a family who undergoes a moral crisis. All three share a spiritual and cultural emptiness, which enables their giving in to foolish temptations.

In Newman's case, the emptiness is due less to economic insecurity and failed dreams than to a longing for a more vivid and sensual existence, represented for him by the reappearing image of a woman's body. He is transformed into a "Jewish" victim of bigotry because his diminishing vision causes him to wear glasses that endow him with an allegedly Semitic appearance. This occurs just as he meets a woman, Gert, who responds to him passionately. To sustain the sexual fulfillment with Gert, who has links to the anti-Semitic gang, he prostrates himself before the anti-Semites in order to gain acceptance. But he discovers that his lack of wholehearted commitment to the gang's values remains an obstacle.

Crucial differences set *Focus* apart from Miller's plays of 1947 and 1949. Unlike Keller and Loman, Newman is regenerated, not destroyed. Moreover, since Newman is treated as if he were a Jew when he dons his new glasses, he has a simulacrum of Jewish experiences with prejudice unlike Keller and Loman. Newman also develops an arm's-length relationship with a Jew, Finkelstein, who becomes something of a double. Most consequential is a scene that would be difficult to perform on a stage but that communicates Miller's belief that the dramatization of a powerful truth in a form accessible to a mass audience can transform humanity. Toward the climax of *Focus*, Newman and Gert accidentally walk into a film about the holocaust in which a priest sides with the Jewish targets of Nazi violence. They view the film all the way through to the climax, when the priest dies as a Jew.

After leaving the theater, Newman narrowly escapes an assault by the band of anti-Semitic thugs. He does so by directing them toward Finkelstein, the Jewish storekeeper and interloper in the neighborhood. But as he sees the Jew fighting back with a baseball bat, Newman undergoes a transformation. Like the priest in the film, Newman follows the Jew's example; he picks up a bat and fights the thugs. Later he tells the police that he, too, is Jewish. Thus Newman, under the influence of the humanizing film and the example of Finkelstein, finds his manhood by choosing an identity as an ally of the Jew. Newman becomes a new man, his own man, by defining himself as a Jew, and he is no longer in thrall to Gert or psychologically subordinate to the gang of anti-Semites.

There are close parallels between Miller and Finkelstein. Miller appears in the pages of the *New Masses* and the *Daily Worker* as a fighting Jew; like Finkelstein, he is not a Jewish nationalist but is forced to strike out in defense of his people by the threat of anti-Semitism abroad and at home. Just as Finkelstein's courageous act enabled the non-Jewish Newman to render his life more vivid and expansive by embracing a Jewish identity, Miller's polemics allow Matt Wayne to become a voice of a universalism not grounded on the evasion of a Jewish identity but empowered by its concurrent expression.

This analysis of Miller's artistic block regarding the utilization of Jewish subject matter in his writing in the 1940s is not speculative. In a little-noticed article, Miller explicitly stated that in the 1940s he felt he could not create Jewish dramatis personae without transforming his art into propaganda—which would muffle the complexities and ambiguities with which he wished to infuse his characters. In 1948, in remarks published by the pro-Communist magazine *Jewish Life*, Miller recalled the innocence of his 1936 University of Michigan play about a Jewish family, *No Villain* (revised under the title *They Too Arise*): "There was good and evil in the most delightfully true proportions, with never a qualm about 're-vealing' anything about Jews."[84] In a section of the piece called "Innocence Is Shattered," Miller explained that the shock of learning what Hitler was "saying about Jews and doing to Jews" sent him into a rage that was intensified by what he perceived to be the complacency of those around him.

Moreover, his political rage was felt personally. Miller's closest friend, a wealthy student he had met in an English class, refused to recognize Miller after Miller's *No Villain* was produced; the play had identified him to the broader public as a Jew who did not deny his Jewish identity. When the play was optioned by three Broadway producers, all declared that the presence of a Jewish villain (albeit a likable one) rendered it unproducible because it would inflame anti-Semitism. Miller's reaction was extreme: "I gave up on the Jews as literary material because I was afraid that even an innocent allusion to the individual wrong-doing of an individual Jew would be inflamed by the atmosphere, ignited by the hatred I suddenly was aware of, and my love would be twisted into a weapon of persecution against Jews. No good writer can approach material in that atmosphere. I cannot censor myself without thwarting my passion for writing itself."[85] Miller next compared Jewish writers of the postwar era with radical writers of the 1930s. Echoing concerns expressed by Isidor Schneider, he observed that writers who wanted to be socially significant in the 1930s felt a political obligation to include a strike in their text. In contrast, Jewish writers who want to use their art to protect Jews "must do a very difficult thing with our minds. We must lift ourselves out of the present. We must move into the area of Jewish life with a new vision, a vision that excludes defensiveness."

Miller concluded by invoking Sholem Aleichem's literary philosophy, which "excluded no part of Jewish life or psychology, which made excuses for noth-

232

ing but never hesitated to arraign society where society was at fault." Miller's remarks echo sentiments from Matt Wayne's "Sincerity in the Theater": "It is the attitude of total truth. . . . We ought to be able to create a gallery of Jewish characters so powerful in their reality, so hearty in their depictions, so deeply felt in their emotional lives, that the audience or the reader, by the pure force of the characters themselves will be brought to that state of love and innocence in which I once so briefly lived." Jewish characters will once again be "people trying to make some sense out of life, people out of a common pool of humanity, people lazy, people ambitious, people in love, people in jail, people running away, and people dying bravely on some military mountain."

Miller was calling for action by Jewish American writers, but how was such action to be taken in his forthcoming play, *Death of a Salesman?* Jews, he insisted, have a special knowledge of Jewish life that the world needs to know. Therefore,

> to face away from Jewish life when one has a story to tell is not more universal and less parochial; it is to refuse to do best what no one else can do at all; and equally important, to draw upon Jews for our works is to bring into the family of people—our people, our beloved and creative people, who have been edged away from the table to wait in the shadows like ghosts or pariahs. . . . We wrong ourselves and our own art, by drawing a curtain upon them.[86]

In *Death of a Salesman*, Miller resolved this contradiction as he had in *All My Sons*. The emotional foundations of both plays stem from Miller's own Jewish American life; but the issues are presented on the terrain of universalist, somewhat Marxist categories, and the characters are dressed in nonethnic garb. The characters in *All My Sons* and *Death of a Salesman* are indeed Matt Wayne's relatives.

The invention of Matt Wayne probably allowed Miller to maintain a critical distance from other psychological pressures impeding his artistic consciousness. He seemed to have had a need to step back from a family drama that had obsessed him throughout his life. The origins of an apparent trauma in Miller's family relationships have not come to light in biographical research to date, but a substantial portion of his major works, *All My Sons, Death of a Salesman*, and *The Price*, is haunted by complex feelings of guilt that must have been rooted in his dealings with his father and brother. In a 1955 autobiographical entry for *Twentieth Century Authors*, Miller stated emphatically that he knew his destiny was that of a writer from the moment he read Dostoevsky's *The Brothers Karamazov* (1880), a novel about rivalry between brothers, the hereditary sin of sensuality, a guilt complex, and an impulse toward parricide against a businessman father.[87] Strangely, no mention of this transformative moment occurs in *Timebends*.

Inasmuch as many of the prototypes of Miller's characters were derived from his own Jewish family members, they had an inherently Jewish dimension. Yet for reasons that he explains in "Concerning Jews Who Write," Miller could not portray the fictionalized brothers and fathers in his plays as Jews. In *The Man Who Had All the Luck* and stories such as "The Plaster Masks" and "It Takes a Thief," he used the strategy of retaining the guilt but excising the theme from its family source. The artistic results were diminished, and only the first was ever reissued (in a revised version in England in 1989).[88]

Another source of Miller's guilt stemmed from his awareness of his limitations as a political activist. He had become a revolutionary with minimal revolutionary practice. At first he seemed embarrassed about his somewhat privileged class origins. In his 1944 autobiographical statement for *Cross-Section: A Collection of New American Writing*, he did not mention that he was the son of a businessman. He wrote as if he had no family, accentuating his experiences with poverty and his few proletarian work adventures, imputing to himself an anti-intellectual background.[89] Miller was haunted by his decision not to go to Spain and especially by the death there of his friend Ralph Neaphus from the University of Michigan. His guilt is dramatized in *Timebends*, where he reported that a feeling of personal debt to the memory of Neaphus, who was captured and executed by fascists in Spain, impelled him to cross a picket line of nuns when he attended the Waldorf Peace Conference in 1949.[90] In World War II, it was his brother, Kermit, who went to fight (and returned shell-shocked), while Miller was not drafted because of a football injury. Yet he wanted to do his share to stop fascism, and this emotional need was partly met through a gut-level loyalty to Soviet Communism and the Communist Party. Consequently, becoming Matt Wayne enabled Miller to engage more fully in the Communist movement that seemed to embody his revolutionary aspirations, while still shielding that part of him necessary for artistic creativity.

How do the disclosure of Matt Wayne's identity and the reinsertion of nearly thirty unacknowledged prose texts (a few written under the playwright's own name) into the career of Arthur Miller modify his reputation? This documentation of his substantially more extensive engagement in Communist cultural activities than hitherto recognized reveals an unexpected dimension: Miller's creation of a "secret self" in the pages of the Communist *New Masses*, who wrote sound articles on drama that were absent of political hectoring or rewarding political "correctness," and that were dedicated to the integration of Marxist convictions with a vision of successful popular theater. Although one might expect a pseudonymous column in a Communist publication to serve as an instrument for venting political dogma, Matt Wayne's column was primarily a vehicle for fending off the pressure of Communist politics on Miller's creative artistic process.

In his *New Masses* columns, Wayne revealed virtually no autobiographical detail, beyond noting the plays that he attended. He rarely spoke as an ideologue— and never directly as a Jew. Wayne was the terrain on which Miller wrestled weekly with the crisis in his art that followed his 1944 abdication of a career in theater. But Miller's construction of the Matt Wayne persona, sans a biography and ethnicity, also seems to have emancipated Miller to write under his own name in a much more political register than Wayne. His writings appearing under the byline "Arthur Miller" in the mid-1940s are almost exclusively focused on anti-Semitism and the responsibility of Jewish intellectuals.

The missing chapter of Arthur Miller's biography is marked by a double life: Miller the crusader against the oppression of Jews, and Wayne the artist seeking a strategy to reconcile politics and art on a conceptual level. In the end, Matt Wayne freed Miller to come to grips with his feelings of guilt, rooted in family tribulations, as creatively reworked in his drama. It was a crucial transitional moment in Miller's life that allowed him to create the non-Jewish Jews of *All My Sons* and *Death of a Salesman*.

In 1992 Miller published a novella covering the late 1930s through the postwar era, *Homely Girl, a Life*. As an allegory of Miller's political evolution, the work makes perfect sense if Miller himself is understood to be the homely girl. Janice Sessions, the daughter of well-to-do Jewish immigrants, lacks self-confidence and allows herself to become married to Sam Fink, a more ethnically identified Jew and a Communist "man of action." Initially disturbed by Sam's fanatic behavior during the Hitler-Stalin Pact, Janice becomes unfaithful to him while he is away during World War II. Following the war, she makes a brief attempt to recommit to Sam, only to seize on the knowledge of a sexual indiscretion of his own as an excuse for finally parting company.

In the late 1940s Janice by accident encounters David, a blind, non-Jewish man who is employed as an expert on music for a record company. David finds her beautiful body a compensation for her (unseen) homely face and provides Janice with years of happiness throughout the postwar era. The narrative, told retrospectively from Janice's point of view, commenced long after David's death. But the fulfilled homely girl has no regrets about the past and confidently faces the future. As was the case with Miller, the 1940s for the homely girl was a transitional decade that, with the pain of loss, would ultimately generate a more complete sense of self.

CONCLUSION

The Fates of Antifascism

THREE LIVES

In the frigid winter months of early 1939, a small group of antifascist writers, artists, and intellectuals in Cleveland, Ohio, conceived a new literary quarterly they named *Crossroad*. The inaugural issue, published in April, showcased three Cleveland authors: Chester Himes, Jo Sinclair (born Ruth Seid), and Dan Levin (b. 1914). All were in the formative stages of their writing careers, and each dreamed of becoming a professional author. Within a decade, each published a first novel to conspicuous acclaim.

Himes's *If He Hollers Let Him Go* is a classic of African American protest fiction. Sinclair's *Wasteland* is a pivotal work in the postwar Jewish American reclamation of identity and a breakthrough in lesbian fiction. Levin's *Mask of Glory* (1949) is a compelling account of combat in the Pacific. Throughout the mid- to late twentieth century, these three novels were periodically reissued. Himes would publish twenty volumes; Sinclair, five; and Levin, six. None is cited in literary histories or reference works as principally a writer who had been associated with the Communist movement, which is fitting and yet deficient. The literary origins of these writers are intimately coupled with their early experiences with Communism, especially the policies promoted by the Party in the antifascist era.

Crossroad had an attractive format, a copious supply of young modern artists, and a mandate to publish all writing that qualified as "an efficient and distinguished expression of significant thought or feeling."[1] Such a nonpolitical recipe stood in stark contrast to the effort of Cleveland radical writers six years earlier to launch *The Red Spark: Bulletin of the John Reed Club of Cleveland*. The initial editorial of the *Red Spark* merely reiterated the injunction of the national John Reed Club, the Communist-led cultural organization founded in New York City in 1929, "to create and publish art and literature of a proletarian character. . . . To make familiar in this country the art and literature of the world proletariat, and particularly that of the Soviet Union."[2] The original editors of and contributors to the *Red Spark* were all members and supporters of the Communist Party; the bulletin's artwork primarily offered cartoonlike fat capitalists, gaunt workers, and brutal-looking policemen, and the literary component was dwarfed by Communist political reportage and analysis.

Nevertheless, there was a slender strand of ideological continuity between the Red Spark and Crossroad. The catalyst for Crossroad was Dan Levin, a twenty-five-year-old Russian-born secularized Jew and a secret member of the Cleveland branch of the Communist Party. Others inaugurating the new journal comprised a cross section of the segment of the Cleveland intellectual community attracted to the ethos of the Popular Front promoted by the Communist Party: sympathy for the Spanish Republic, support of the CIO, warm feelings toward the Soviet Union, and a passionate hatred of the racial injustice perpetrated against African Americans. Much of the cultural material accepted by the editors addressed working-class life, such as unemployment and labor conditions on the New Deal's WPA; themes of social justice, such as international war and segregation; and politically committed writing, such as the fiction of John Steinbeck.

When the first issue of Crossroad appeared in April, the editorial board included Cleveland College English professor Winfield Rogers, a specialist on the writing of liberal Ohio farm novelist and Popular Front supporter Louis Bromfield (1896–1956); journalist Spencer D. Irwin, associate editor of the Cleveland Press and a Communist fellow traveler; Rowena Woodham Jeliffe, cofounder of Cleveland's interracial community center, Karamu House, and a lifelong civil rights activist; and Manuel G. Silberger, a lithographer and printmaker who had previously passed through the Communist Party and now worked for the Cleveland WPA. Levin was, in effect, the editor of Crossroad, although for reasons of modesty he was not so listed until the fourth issue. By that time, January 1940, his associate editor was a young Zionist, Sidney Z. Vincent, the future executive director of the Jewish Community Federation of Cleveland.

Just as the novelist Len Zinberg was summoned forth at the outset of Trinity of Passion, so Himes, Sinclair, and Levin are evoked at the conclusion. These three midwesterners are not the most notable writers who might be identified with the Left during the years of the Spanish Civil War and World War II; their distinction cannot compare with that of Arthur Miller, Lillian Hellman, Richard Wright, Howard Fast, Nelson Algren, and others mentioned. Yet, due to the vital association of each with the genesis of critical strands within post-Depression writing, they suitably bring to a close this investigation of the literary aspect of the antifascist crusade. Literary significance is based not solely on the authority of a few highest-ranking authors; it can also be found in the substructure, at the very foundation of modern literature, where half-forgotten writers who variously passed through the Communist experience left ineradicable marks.

As members of a new generation of Left writers, none of the three young nov-

DAN LEVIN was attracted to the Communist movement in
Cleveland, where he edited *Crossroad*. After service in World
War II in the Pacific, he skillfully explored the contradictions of
ideological commitment in a series of novels. (Courtesy of Dan
Levin)

ices featured in the first issue of *Crossroad* was a veteran of the first Communist literary organization of the Depression era, the John Reed Club, which inspired numerous publications, including the *Red Spark*. Moreover, none had published sufficiently to become a member of the League of American Writers, initiated by pro-Communists in 1935 and subsequently transformed into a Popular Front organization. All were recent employees of the Cleveland Library Project of the federal government's WPA, where attraction to Communism was prevalent if diffuse.

The senior member of the trio at the time of the founding of *Crossroad* was Chester Himes, a thirty-year-old African American born in Missouri and who had fleetingly attended the Ohio State University. In 1928 Himes had been sentenced to twenty years' hard labor in the Ohio State Penitentiary for armed robbery. In 1932 he began publishing short stories in African American publications, and by 1934 he was appearing in *Esquire*. Paroled in 1936, Himes was married in Cleveland the following year. He then commenced writing a novel about his prison experiences variously called "Yesterday Will Make You Cry" and "Black Sheep" that would eventually be published in two versions, *Cast the First Stone* (1952) and *Yesterday Will Make You Cry* (1998). Himes helped to launch *Crossroad* with an accomplished story about the emasculating repercussions of poverty.[3]

Four years younger than Himes was the twenty-six-year-old Jewish working-class woman Ruth Seid, who had been submitting fiction to the Communist Party's *New Masses* as Jo Sinclair for the preceding five years. She had chosen the second part of her pen name out of admiration for the socialist novelist and activist Upton Sinclair. Throughout the Depression she carefully worked her way through the many drafts of a novel about her adolescence. Provisionally titled "Now Comes the Black," the manuscript featured African American and Jewish American proto-lesbian protagonists from segregated neighborhoods in Cleveland who combine in a battle against patriarchy and white chauvinism. "Now Comes the Black" would eventually appear as *The Changelings* in 1955. A novel reassessing her experiences with Communism, *Anna Teller*, in which she moved her cast of characters from Cleveland to Detroit to disguise her models, was published in 1960. For the inaugural issue of *Crossroad*, Sinclair provided "Dead Man," a short, well-crafted antiwar poem.[4]

Dan Levin was the only one of the three who was Cleveland-born and had a college degree. After he graduated from Adams High School, he took a B.A. degree in classics from Western Reserve College (later Case Western Reserve University) and spent a year at the Columbia School of Journalism, where he became radicalized. He joined the Communist movement after he returned to Cleveland

RUTH SEID was a left-wing writer in Cleveland in the 1930s.
As Jo Sinclair she became famous in the 1940s and 1950s for her
novels portraying a Jewish American lesbian rebelling against
racism. (From the Seid Collection in the Howard Gotlieb
Archival Research Center at Boston University)

and worked there for a while as a journalist. From 1943 to 1945 he served with the U.S. Marines in the Pacific theater. Subsequently Levin published two additional novels as well as scholarly studies of Maxim Gorky and Baruch Spinoza.[5] To the inaugural issue of Crossroad, Levin contributed a poem commemorating the burial service of a Cleveland worker killed in a strike.[6]

The history of the journal Crossroad embodies the tensions that would plague the literary component of the antifascist crusade. The magazine was founded in the months following the withdrawal of the International Brigades from Spain in the autumn of 1938; Madrid fell one month before the first issue of Crossroad went on sale. Through a strategy developed by Levin, the magazine attempted to deepen, continue, and expand the Popular Front in culture. Critical to Levin was the conviction that the politics of the journal be broadly antifascist, and that Communists and non-Communists agree with that principle in their quest to publish writing of artistic merit.

At the outset, such a goal seemed logical and noncontroversial, with Communist Party members participating as individuals in the planning meetings. The announcement of the Hitler-Stalin Pact on 23 August 1939 dramatically changed the situation. In an instant the Communist Party members stopped pressing for the United States to join with the USSR in stopping Hitler; instead, the Party began to demand peace. In mass organizations Communist supporters put forward motions opposing U.S. aid to England and France; when the Communists were successful in winning the vote, the independent-minded members of the organizations would walk out. Thus a number of Popular Front alliances became hollow fronts during the Hitler-Stalin Pact; seeds of suspicion were sown that would bear bitter fruit in the years to come.

Crossroad had published two issues and the third was under way by the time of the pact. When Communist Party members on the editorial board began pressing Levin to introduce the new political line into the journal, Levin regarded their efforts as an inappropriate attempt at a takeover. As pressure on him mounted to betray the very individuals whom he had recruited to the magazine, he took the matter personally; some of these writers and artists were unaware of his own Party membership and that of other board members. Levin brought his complaint to the Central Committee of the Cleveland branch of the Communist Party, where his passionate defense of the value of the present course of Crossroad resulted in a temporary vote of confidence. The fourth issue appeared shortly after the start of the new year. By that time Levin realized that it was not solely the literary tactics of his comrades to which he was opposed; he also objected to the political policy behind the tactics. In 1940 Levin quietly resigned from the Communist Party, and Crossroad folded.

Himes and Sinclair, less entangled in the Communist Party than Levin, were more at ease with Communist policy during the pact. Sinclair continued her regular submissions to the *New Masses* and her friendly correspondence with the editors. She was evidently unruffled by the rapid changes during the pact, the switch in political line when the USSR was invaded in 1941, and the advent of Browderism. Her efforts to publish in the Communist press ceased in 1944, when she was on the precipice of her entrance into the mainstream literary world through publication of her award-winning novel, *Wasteland*. Himes moved to California shortly after *Crossroad* folded. During the pact he became more intimate with the Party and was probably a member for a brief time.[7] But his mellow attitude mutated into loathing when the Popular Front was reinstated, after which Himes concluded that the Party's commitment to antiracist activity was compromised. His fury was manifest in his 1947 novel, *The Lonely Crusade*.[8]

The three writers were also friends, even though their friendships did not survive the passage of time and migrations from Cleveland. Levin met periodically with Sinclair, who talked earnestly of her uncertainty about her sexual orientation. Levin also conferred many times with Himes, and the two became sufficiently close to form a plan to live together in Paris in the postwar years. On the other hand, Himes and Sinclair were confidants at the Cleveland Public Library WPA project. In the 1940s, Himes and Sinclair exchanged a few letters, and Himes induced Richard Wright to review *Wasteland* for *PM*.[9]

As might be predicted of young writers, each left a literary record of his or her association with some of the others in published and unpublished writing. In Levin's autobiographical manuscript of 1940, "The Education of a True Believer," Himes appears as a minor character: Hank Crawford, a gifted Black writer who is in a rage about racism but who is desperate to be regarded as a writer first. Seid's unpublished book manuscript of the same year, "They Gave Us a Job," uses Himes as a model for a major character: Aaron Wright, a proud and angry Black writer. Himes, in his autobiographical *The Quality of Hurt*, relates his friendship with Levin in Cleveland.[10] He also appropriated aspects of Levin's moral earnestness and Sinclair's ethnic self-consciousness to fashion his memorable portrait of a Jewish Communist intellectual, Abe "Rosie" Rosenberg, in *The Lonely Crusade*.

THE WOUNDED HEART

The outcome of the Spanish Civil War is customarily referred to as "The Wound in the Heart," a defeat of the forces of good by those of evil. There were other wounds to hearts during that era as well, including a wrenching of the emotions of novelists whose utopian visions were beguiled by an identification of socialist ideals with Communist Party policy. A few writers from the antifascist crusade would persevere as Communists into the 1950s, during which they and talented newcomers waged a feisty battle against McCarthyism. But most departed the Communist movement with considerable dismay in the first five or six years after World War II. Their frustration was sometimes searing and was sporadically expressed in public denunciations of the Party in their fiction, such as Chester Himes's mesmerizing *The Lonely Crusade*.

Mainly, their disaffection was expressed in subtler ways; the wound could be deep and recovery from disillusionment slow. For the young writers whose careers partly began in the pages of *Crossroad*, the attractions of Communism had been transformative, and their letdown was painful. Not only in the novels of Himes but also in those of Dan Levin and Jo Sinclair were imaginative battlegrounds where these writers in the antifascist crusade negotiated and resolved their crises of belief.

In his 1940 unpublished novel, "The Education of a True Believer," Levin was the first of the three to record the stages by which he became enchanted with and ultimately disappointed by the Communists' worldview. Echoing the religious title, Levin gave his autobiographical protagonist, an aspiring young writer in a midwestern city, the name David Zaddick. (*Zaddick*, or *tzaddik*, is Yiddish for "a righteous man.") David Zaddick is initially enamored of the Marxist notion that the "system" more than the individual bears responsibility for the problems faced by young people in the Depression. Zaddick is further delighted that this analysis had appeared in a Communist Party publication in an article written by a noted literary critic.

In the novel, Levin insinuates that Zaddick's embracing Communism is as much psychological as it is political. Zaddick is portrayed as a young man frightened by the degree of his own self-absorption; he feels that a commitment to an ostensibly unselfish cause will foster a much-needed equilibrium in his personal life. Moreover, he believes that his making a commitment to the Communist Party will buttress the commitment he had difficulty in making to his lover, Carla.

Jewish characters and allusions are attendant in "The Education of a True Believer," but the self-portrait does not emphasize Levin's later judgment that the basis of his attraction to Communism lay in his family's Russian Jewish origins. His parents were prosperous intellectuals in czarist Russia. His mother, Dr. Charissa G. Levin, was a surgeon, and his father, Joseph D. Levin, became a high official in the Alexander Kerensky government. The Levins remained in Russia throughout World War I. Joseph Levin felt in some danger from the Bolshevik regime, so the family left Russia when Dan was seven. After they arrived in the United States, the Levins went directly to Cleveland, where Charissa obtained a medical license and Joseph scrambled to launch an insurance agency.

Dan Levin's memories of his privileged childhood in Russia were idealized, happy ones, and it seemed as if only in the United States did he encounter anti-Semitism. Thus he grew up with a very positive feeling about Russia as a motherland that was abandoned by his parents in the wake of the revolution, but which over the next decades came to portend the future of humanity. His connections with his Jewish background, however, were limited; he grew up speaking Russian but not Yiddish. His father had had a religious childhood but had become thoroughly secularized during his professional career in Russia. In Cleveland, however, Joseph Levin gravitated back toward a Jewish religious community, although his wife continued to profess a nonreligious Enlightenment orientation. The Levins lived in a lower-middle-class neighborhood comprised of Jewish Americans, Italian Americans, and Polish Americans; by and large the community was devoid of African Americans, there being only one in Dan's school.

Levin's literary interests began at an early age, when he started writing for his high school paper. At first he fancied himself a poet and was attracted to Walt Whitman, Robert Frost, and E. A. Robinson, but eventually journalism became his main interest. After high school he went to Western Reserve College, where he majored in Greek and Latin. He graduated in 1935. At Western Reserve he met his wife, the painter Kathleen Miller. For a while Levin was employed in social work, providing welfare relief, and while doing so he experienced his first stirrings of interest in Communism. He then took a brief trip to Greece on a freighter. Upon his return he enrolled in the Columbia University School of Journalism, from which he received an M.A. Returning to Cleveland more radicalized, he was not able to find a job. Reading the *New Masses* helped prepare him for membership in the Communist Party.

Like David Zaddick in his novel, Levin became a leading activist in Cleveland's Communist-led Popular Front organization, the American League for Peace and Democracy.[11] Then he began producing publications for the Cleveland CIO and subsequently found work on the WPA. The fictional Zaddick replicates Levin's progress as he becomes involved in a writers' group that founds a literary journal, the *Midwesterner*.[12]

"The Education of a True Believer" has a breezy style; the narrative moves quickly as its characters, background, and positions are sketched rather than fully crafted. Yet it is an eerily troubled novel in several critical respects. Although the political implications of the novel are mostly latent and are dramatized rather than explained, ideological and psychological tensions are present throughout. Spain is the one issue about which David Zaddick feels a "purity of passion."[13] This allows his haunting doubts about the nature of the Soviet Union to be counterpoised to his certainty about the justness of the cause in Spain.

Simultaneously, Zaddick is bedeviled throughout the novel by an imaginary alter ego, Irving. This chimerical friend first appears during Zaddick's young manhood and tantalizes Zaddick by his Bohemian life and womanizing. Then, when Zaddick joins the Communist Party, Irving mysteriously disappears. Later, when Zaddick resigns from the Party, disgusted by its Machiavellianism, he has a vision of Irving marching in his place in a May Day parade. Irving had become an example of Communist rectitude. Alternately taking on characteristics of the id and the superego, Irving at first embodies the fantasy of the Jew as a Bohemian libertine and later appears as a disciplined revolutionary. Zaddick is incapable of accommodating his conflicted self to either of these imaginary Jews.

In 1940 Levin quietly dropped his Party membership. Then came a long withdrawal. At first he poured his passion into writing "The Education of a True Believer." He later recalled that he had submitted it to Modern Age, a left-wing publishing house, which accepted the novel and considered nominating it for a prize. Then the publishing house shut down, and Levin was unable to locate another publisher. Meanwhile, he found himself continuing to think like a Communist Party member. The complete break that he had fantasized in his unpublished novel was harder to carry out in his own life. He had been consumed by the idea of a just society, and the Communist Party seemed the only available vehicle for realizing such a goal.

As the end of the WPA neared, Levin at first planned to work in a defense plant, and he enrolled in night courses to learn how to run a lathe. Then he took a half-dozen civil service exams and, test scores in hand, went to live with relatives in Washington, D.C., where he hoped a job would materialize. After Pearl Harbor he found a government job working for the Office of War Information and the Department of Agriculture. Although no longer a Communist Party member, he participated in a group comprised of Party sympathizers. He knew that the Communists and fellow travelers felt that he was one of them in spirit; despite his traumatic experiences in Cleveland, he realized that he was still, like his comrades in the group, a Communist by inclination.

One difference, however, was that his Communist ideology was becoming displaced by the Popular Front view that World War II was a "righteous war unlike any other," a glorious campaign to destroy Nazism and fascism. The bitter price of international war, which he had opposed during the 1930s, receded into the background. As when he joined the Communist Party, Levin realized that he would accrue psychological benefits if he enlisted: "In my green uniform I could leave behind my disappointments over career, quandaries over marriage, and struggles over identity. War could even give me my theme, for I needed a theme in order to become a writer. I seized the chance as if I had been lying in

245

wait for it."[14] In March 1943 Levin enlisted in the U.S. Marines as a combat correspondent and traveled to Parris Island, South Carolina, to be trained. Levin was thirty, and the typical recruits were between eighteen and twenty. As a combat correspondent with the rank of sergeant, Levin participated with these young marines in the battles of Saipan, Tinian, and Iowa Jima in the Pacific.

Returning home in 1945, Levin was employed as an editor at the State Department and then as a reports officer on the staff of the U.S. mission to the United Nations. It was in Washington that he wrote *Mask of Glory*. From the outset he aspired to write a momentous poem and a great novel out of his war experiences. He had read Tolstoy's *War and Peace* three times; he also knew Stefan Heym's work and had read *The Crusaders*.

Mask of Glory was a war novel in the tradition of the proletarian novel of the 1930s. Nineteen-year-old Glenn Manson, a Polish American from Cleveland, is both a working-class hero and a projection of Levin's own personality. In contrast to the tough guys of Norman Mailer's *The Naked and the Dead*, Levin chose to render his characters as essentially good American kids. His continuing loyalty to the antifascist crusade prompted him to include a character with Communist views as one of the marines. Moreover, the question is raised in the novel as to whether the fight against fascism should have commenced in Spain. Levin also went out of his way to incorporate Jewish characters, hoping to break stereotypes about Jews and to dramatize friendship between Jews and non-Jews. However, he made the Jewish characters neither realistic nor important.

The Communist Party no longer held an attraction for him, but his "true believer" mentality remained. Through two later novels, *The Dream and the Flesh* and *Son of Judah*, Levin slowly worked his way out of this state of mind. In the former, which he published after his 1950–53 sojourn in Paris, he focused on liberals and their disillusionment with New Deal liberalism. The subtext, however, was his own commitment to the Communist Party and his personal struggle to preserve his marriage. The novel recounts the life of David Hyatt from 1938 to 1948 as he leaves Cleveland and moves with his wife to the nation's capital. Hyatt is a true-believing liberal in much the same way that Levin subscribed to Communism, but in wartime government service he finds his liberal ideals have become tarnished by greed and personal cowardice. Like Levin, Hyatt escapes both the disillusionment of his Washington experience and its corresponding effects on his marriage by joining the marines.

After returning from Paris, Levin moved back to Cleveland. His father had died, and prospects for employment seemed bleak during the Cold War. With the help of his mother, he decided to carry on his father's insurance agency, which he did for the remainder of the decade. In his spare time he continued writing fiction, and in 1961 he published *Son of Judah*, which was set in the first century A.D. As in his previous novels, Levin continued to wrestle with his revolutionary and utopian dreams, but he was now in the final stage of the struggle. Jesus is depicted in the novel as a raving young radical, obsessed with the fantasy of revolution. The protagonist, Ben Yehudah, is taken from his homeland and pressed into a Roman legion. Sent back to Judea to subdue an uprising led by the Jewish "Messiah," Yehudah is won over to the rebels' cause. After a terrible defeat, he wanders the Roman Empire torn between his love for a courtesan and for the mother of his two children. The narrative is substantially an allegory of Levin's own journey through the Left, but he was no longer as close to the Communist dream as he had been in Washington or Paris.

At age fifty Levin decided to sell the family insurance company and seek a Ph.D. in Russian literature at the University of Chicago. After he received his degree, he began a teaching career at Wayne State University and later taught at Kent State University, Western Reserve University, and eventually Long Island University. Although he continued to write fiction, drama, and poetry, his last published books were all nonfiction: *Stormy Petrel* (1965), a study of Maxim Gorky; *Spinoza: The Young Thinker Who Destroyed the Past* (1970); and *From the Battlefield: Dispatches of a World War II Marine* (1995).

When Levin and Himes began to see each other regularly in 1939, Levin was immediately struck by how bitter and caustic Himes's opinions were about African American leadership. This shocked Levin, who had a tendency to romanticize everything about Black America, although his personal experiences with Black Americans were limited.[15] He imagined that Himes's relation to Communist politics as a Black man was similar to that of his as a Jew; moreover, they had a further bond in that they both desperately wanted to become writers. Despite the sentiments he had expressed, Himes began submitting manuscripts that did not mention race. Jo Sinclair and other *Crossroad* contributors addressed racism in their stories and poems, but Himes's three short stories submitted in 1939–40 ("With Malice toward None," "A Modern Fable," and "Looking Down the Street") were class-based and Marxist. When Himes contributed "The Shipyards Get a Welder" that same year to a projected WPA collection (that never appeared), the issue of race was not mentioned. Himes had published stories about African Americans before and would again soon; but *Crossroad* appeared at a moment when his views were undergoing a political metamorphosis that would mark his first two novels.

Interviewed by the *Chicago Defender* in 1945, Himes asserted that the origins of his "race consciousness" came in the middle of the Depression, simultaneous with his attraction to the trade union movement. It was through the union movement that Himes and other African Americans gained an education about the world—"made contacts with new outlooks, came to understand things about segments of society from which they had been excluded, and with whom they had no means of contact." Himes developed "a hatred of the ruling class of whites" but not of white workers: "I identified myself with labor" and "worked for the CIO in Cleveland."[16]

As Himes remembered it, what had propelled him toward the political writing that emerged in If He Hollers Let Him Go was the shocking racist prejudice that he encountered when he moved to Los Angeles in 1940. The city seemed in thrall to white racist prejudice, fueled by the prewar migrations of southern whites to California. Although his literary aspirations drew him toward the Los Angeles chapter of the League of American Writers, he primarily worked for American Federation of Labor unions and collaborated in Communist Party activities with several African American veterans of the Abraham Lincoln Brigade. When the Communist Party turned pro-war, he at first tried to raise his concerns about its abandonment of antiracist struggle and its anticolonial policies in a friendly manner. To the Communist Party's West Coast paper, the People's World, he wrote a long letter explaining why the struggle for national independence in India should not be subordinated to building a national unity against the fascist war. His essays supported the Double V campaign but did not attack the Communist Party by name.[17] As late as 1946, he submitted a book review (unpublished) of Ann Petry's The Street to the New Masses that laid bare a Marxist orthodoxy.[18]

As the war drew to a close, Himes concluded that the Communist Party's wartime political evolution had been a betrayal; instead of fighting fascism both at home and abroad, the Party had downgraded the struggle against racism on the domestic front. For Himes, however, it was not an issue of the subordination of the Communist Party to needs of the Soviet Union; as late as his 1945 Chicago Defender interview he called himself a "great admirer of the Soviet Union," and indeed the Soviet Union is of no consequence in The Lonely Crusade. Rather, for him the failure of the Communist movement lay in its arrogance—in its members' zealotry for pleasing its leadership and in the culture of blind loyalty that it created. Even African American Communists, who understood the Party's capacity for racial chauvinism, are portrayed as doing whatever is necessary to retain their privileges of being part of the movement. The Lonely Crusade was not written as an anti-Communist polemic but sprang from passionate belief in communist principles above and beyond Communist organizations. The title refers to the unhappy demise of the antifascist crusade; when the principles of antifascist forces were not marshaled against domestic racism, the true communist was abandoned by the Party and left to fight alone.

Of the novel's sensational narrative, Himes would later insist, "There wasn't a single event in the story that hadn't actually happened. My characters were real people, living in familiar situations."[19] This is likely an exaggeration, although prototypes for various characters can be identified. The extraordinary Black Communist from Mississippi, Luther McGregor, is somewhat modeled on Spanish Civil War veteran Eluard Luchell McDaniel.[20] The Black Communist Party leader Bart is inspired by Los Angeles Communist official Pettis Perry. The industrialist Lewis Foster resembles Louis Bromfield, the novelist who had employed Himes on his Ohio farm (although his last name links him to Communist Party leader William Z. Foster). Abe "Rosie" Rosenberg has the moral earnestness of Dan Levin. Lee Gordon has aspects of Himes, and Gordon's wife, Ruth, resembles Himes's first wife, Jean Lucinda Johnson.

Luther McGregor, however, is the most unforgettable character in the novel. Attractive and repulsive, civilized and savage, he is a man beyond good and evil who lives without illusions. Two other Black characters, Lee Gordon and Lester McKinley, together with Luther McGregor, may be fictional facets of Himes's own fractured persona. Although his novel has been called anti-Semitic, the only character with a firm moral center is the Jew, Rosie Rosenberg. At first, Rosie's aggressive, ethnic self-identity is grating, especially since he seems oblivious to its ill effect on Lee Gordon, but eventually Lee realizes that Rosie's acceptance of his own ethnicity is the reason that Rosie can feel such a genuine connection with all humanity.

In his conversations in Cleveland in 1939 with Chester Himes, Levin did not dwell on his Jewishness. Moreover, Levin was never taken with the Marxist dialectical materialist philosophy that Rosie frequently expounds. While there were many Jewish Communists from whom Himes might have recycled those particular attributes in depicting Rosie, Lee Gordon's reaction to Rosie's personality in *The Lonely Crusade* recalls a letter that Himes sent to his old friend Jo Sinclair in 1945. Upon receiving her congratulations on the publication of *If He Hollers Let Him Go*, Himes responded to her concern about the novel's explosiveness: "Even you, with your goddamn insidious Jewish chauvinism, used to pump frustration through me. . . . But even so, I always liked you for all your very human qualities."[21] Himes as a writer and a person thought on many levels simultaneously and responded to criticism accordingly. His explosive rage at what he perceived as "Jewish chauvinism" might have been inextricably tied to his genuine affection for Sinclair, much as his brutal assault on the Communist Party in his fiction complemented his devotion to the essence of the Party's antifascist crusade.

CHANGELING

Jo Sinclair had been born to Nathan and Ida Kravetsky Seid, Jewish Russian immigrants, in Brooklyn, New York, in 1913. Three years later they moved to Cleveland. Her neighborhood was originally Jewish and Italian but became transformed into a Black district in the late 1940s and 1950s. Sinclair fictionalized her teenage self as Judith Vincent (called Vincent) in The Changelings and herself as a woman in her late twenties as Deborah Brown in Wasteland.[22]

The adventures of the fictional Vincent are rooted in Sinclair's years at Kennard Junior High School, where she led a gang of boys who lived on her street. From the outset Sinclair's family life was complicated by continual difficulties with her father and brothers.[23] From 1926 to 1930 Sinclair attended John Hay, a vocational high school, excelling at athletics, academics, and dramatics; she was also a popular president of the student council. Although class valedictorian, she could not afford to attend college. Consequently, Sinclair worked as an apprentice in the advertising office of a department store and then at a knitting mill. Subsequently she made boxes and was a cashier. She had begun writing poetry at fourteen, and she educated herself at the Cleveland public library.

Sinclair first submitted her work to the New Masses in December 1934, but nothing was accepted for two years. When a story of hers was finally published, it turned out to be a brilliant exploration of racial dynamics that prefigured many of her later crucial themes about the corruption of the young by their elders and by individuals in authority. "Noon Lynching," which was her first publication, is set in an elementary school. Throughout the first two-thirds of the narrative the reader is not provided with an explanation for the teacher's rudeness toward one of the students, Herman Jackson. The grounds for her accusation that he stole money from her also remain puzzling. Only when Herman is sent to the basement at noon, where the janitor is supposed to transfer him to police custody, does the reader learn that Herman is Black and that the teacher is white. This is revealed in the epithets used when the janitor and the police officer stage a mock lynching, terrorizing Herman into a false confession. Earlier in the story, Herman had playfully displayed a tough-guy persona, fantasizing for himself a romantic life of crime as a route to self-empowerment. At the story's conclusion, as the police officer drags Herman away and places him in the Hudson Farm reformatory, Herman feels the cold stone floor beneath his feet and is filled with a new and vicious hatred for society, upon which he will act when released: "Just you wait, he said, his feet rapping the words out of the stone; just wait. Just wait!"[24]

Other of Sinclair's writings would be accepted by the New Masses, but at least twenty-seven more submissions were rejected, the last in March 1944. In spite of that, her connections with Communist publishing ventures remained unchanged. In January 1943 she submitted a novelette about U.S. veterans of the Spanish Civil War to the Communist Party's International Publishers. She also sent material to publications close to the Party, such as *Ken*, *The Fight against War and Fascism*, and the organs of the New Theater League. In March 1943 her story "The Blood of an American" was accepted by the *Negro Quarterly*, a journal edited by the pro-Communists Angelo Herndon and Ralph Ellison, but the issue in which it was to appear was never published. Sinclair's literary contributions brought her into communication with a range of Communist writers of the antifascist era, including Joe Pass, Isidor Schneider, Samuel Sillen, Barbara Giles, Willard Maas, Richard Rovere, Theodore Ward, and John Stuart.

In August 1939 Sinclair attempted to persuade Maxim Lieber, a Communist Party member who specialized in representing writers in or close to the Party, to become her literary agent; but Lieber declined on the grounds that he found her writing too political for popular magazines and too satirical for working-class publications. Barbara Giles of the *New Masses* considered Sinclair's antiwar contributions during the Hitler-Stalin Pact to lack clarity about the relationship of the upper classes to warmongering. Generally the Communists encouraged Sinclair's writing even when particular submissions were not accepted. Samuel Sillen was adamant that the *New Masses* wanted more contributions from her and that the editors preferred to wait for her best work. When *Wasteland* appeared, it became a selection of the Book Find Club, which had left-wing connections.

The *Daily Worker*, however, cast a cold eye on the novel. The reviewer Albert Stevens complained that the potential power of the theme of family relationships worked only on a "descriptive psychological level." Stevens contended that the self-hatred of the Jewish male protagonist, who had changed his name from Jacob Braunowitz to John Brown, was insufficiently explained by anti-Semitism. What was lacking was an "emphasis on the social and ideological forces that make this family such an extreme example of Marxist teaching as to the corruption of the family under capitalism." Stevens observed that Brown's sister, Debby, played a positive role in teaching him self-love, and that there were strong indications that she is linked to left-wing causes. Then he demurred that this was "at the cost of her having to assume the masculine paternal role in which her father and brother have failed, sacrificing her femininity and becoming a Lesbian." [25] The *Daily Worker*'s review of *Wasteland* was so dogmatic that it likely discouraged any remaining sympathies Sinclair might have had for the paper, if not the Party as well. Saul Levitt's review in the *New Masses* (under the pen name Alfred Goldsmith), although more sympathetic to the potential of psychoanalysis, contrasted Sinclair's work unfavorably with Mike Gold's *Jews without Money*.[26]

In 1940, when Sinclair assembled materials for her (unpublished) volume "They Gave Us a Job," her sentiments were much the opposite. Sinclair had brought her project to completion simultaneously with Dan Levin's "The Education of a True Believer," but unlike Levin's, Sinclair's manuscript was a testament of faith in the Left. The central character, modeled on Chester Himes, is Aaron Wright, a twenty-eight-year-old writer married to an attractive woman named Virginia. Wright has previously worked for newspapers, as a busboy, and as a bellhop. Like Himes, Wright has a fine face with light brown skin, but a "too sensitive mouth" and long eyelashes "gave almost an effeminate, lovely look to the Negro's face." He had a trembling mouth and was always on the alert for possible insults or snubs from whites. Wright had also spent five years in the state penitentiary. While incarcerated, he had gradually learned to control his voice and face, and he emerged from prison with impeccable manners of speech and habits of dress.

For the most part Wright was painstakingly courteous and grammatical. But after a few drinks and a marijuana cigarette he became transformed, acting egotistical as if he were a master of men, recklessly spending money. Sinclair also portrays Wright having difficulty with other men in prison because his "girl's lashes" had aroused them. At first Wright took gifts in return for bestowing sexual favors, but then he pulled back from such behavior. Wright witnessed a prison fire, which he recounted in a story called "Prisoners of Mankind" and sold to Esquire, thus initiating a career as a writer. This success brought him an early release from prison and the confidence to marry Virginia. But being unemployed soon reduced Wright to securing a manual labor job with the WPA. Unsatisfied, he campaigned to obtain a WPA writing job, emphasizing that he had faced discrimination because he was Black.

Sinclair's Aaron Wright is paired with Ben Levine, a Jewish veteran of the Spanish Civil War. Levine is now a WPA worker in the history division of the public library. Two years in Spain left him with spells of dizziness and headaches, but he is still dabbling with Communism. Levine hopes to write for a Yiddish newspaper. When the two men discuss politics, Wright tells Levine that he has a cousin who has been trying to recruit him to Communism for the past five years: "He says it's the only place for our people."

The most political character in the novel is Molnar, who secretly reads the New Masses and the Daily Worker at work. He is a translator of Hungarian literature and talks incessantly about the importance of unions and unionizing the WPA. Eventually Levine and Wright join a union, and Wright starts to become decidedly more political. Both become enthusiastic after a large union meeting is held, but then layoffs begin. The situation at the WPA is uncertain at the novel's conclusion, but there is little doubt that the seeds of future political developments have been planted.

Sinclair was already highly politicized when she first encountered Helen Buchman, who became the most significant woman in her life. According to Dan Levin, Sinclair previously had been living with Helen Miskell, a WPA official who was a regional representative of the League of American Writers. Sinclair met Buchman in May 1938 through the left-wing Contemporary Theater in Cleveland, which Buchman had founded. Helen was married to Morton Buchman, who came from a family of many diverse radicals.

Morton's brother, Alex, was initially a Communist. He traveled to China, where he worked with pro-Communist foreign correspondent Agnes Smedley (1892–1950); then he returned to the United States and become involved in the Trotskyist movement for many years, helping among other assignments to arrange security for Trotsky at his compound in Mexico. The poet Helen Sharnoff was Morton's and Alex's sister. She was married to Philip Sharnoff, a leading intellectual in the Communist Party in Cleveland and a teacher at the Party's Workers School. Helen Sharnoff shared her husband's politics, and they traveled several times to the Soviet Union. Helen Buchman, however, seemed primarily interested in the theater, antiracist activities, literature, and psychoanalysis. Jo Sinclair moved in with the Buchman family, and she and Helen became companions for the next twenty-three years. During that time she honed to perfection her masterwork about Blacks and Jews in Cleveland.

Like Ann Petry's The Street, which appeared nine years earlier, The Changelings centers around the theme of African Americans searching for suitable housing. The focus is on a particular block of East 120th Street in Cleveland. Petry had set The Street in November 1944, while World War II was in progress. The setting of The Changelings is not as precise; the book gives the time as 1945 but sometimes suggests several years after the end of the war. Yet a war at home is still in progress—a struggle for survival, a war of class conflict and of racial and ethnic hatred. Early in the novel, Sophie Golden, the mother of the radical poet Jules Golden, stresses the urgency of keeping African Americans (Schwartze) from moving into empty flats in the neighborhood: "If 120th falls—if one Schwartze is permitted to move in and we fall—the other streets go, too. Then the whole neighborhood goes. It is a war. And we, we on 120th are the ones who will win it or lose it for a whole neighborhood."[27]

The Street, however, contrasts dramatically with The Changelings, with the latter's setting in the Midwest. The African Americans search for decent housing outside the ghetto in a neighborhood of Jews and Italians. The Golden and Valenti houses have empty apartments upstairs, and the Zigmans' upstairs apartment soon becomes vacant. Moreover, 120th Street is adjacent to the "Gully," a venue dominated by young people.

The Gully functions as a fantasyland, where choices must be made whether to continue or to challenge the racist and sexist order imposed by the adults on the street. At first, the children's gang in the Gully seems to compare with a primitive society of cave dwellers; they sit around a fire roasting potatoes, erupt in adolescent sexuality, and battle each other for control of the gang. As in William Golding's *The Lord of the Flies* (1954), the children's gang is a commentary on the larger society of adults who, behind masks of religious piety and devotion to family, are consumed by greed and a jealousy of those who have moved out to the wealthier "Heights" section of the city. The adults use self-righteousness and ethnic chauvinism to cover their criminal activities, infidelity, lust, and hypocrisy.

Even the family of the protagonist, Judy Vincent, is corrupt; her father becomes involved in an illegal plot to burn down their house for the insurance money and then betray his neighbors by running off to the Heights and selling the vacant lot to a Black family. Yet it is not foreordained that the children of the Gully must follow their parents' paths. After all, it is in the Gully that two of the novel's "changelings," the African American Clara Jackson and the Jewish American Judy Vincent, can meet on common ground and cast off the social roles foisted on them by the parents of 120th Street, the schools, and other societal institutions.

The Changelings addresses the very issue for which the Communist press incessantly criticized *The Street*: the possibility of building an interracial alliance for change. What is extraordinary about the racism depicted by Sinclair in distinction to racism portrayed by Petry is that Sinclair's anti-Black racism is ethnically generated; it is not produced simply by "whites," but by Jewish Americans and Italian Americans. In the case of Jewish Americans, a specific Yiddish term is used to illustrate their racist fears: *Schwartze* (the Black ones), which plays a role similar to the epithet "niggers." But the ethnic character of bigotry complicates the issue of racism in *The Changelings* because the Jewish perpetrators were themselves only recently the victims of a racist holocaust. Moreover, the Italian Americans and Jewish Americans are often at odds with each other but become bonded as whites in their opposition to the African Americans. They might not like each other, but their common disparagement of Blacks allows them to assume a superiority even if their economic status is equal to or lower than that of the Blacks. Clara Jackson's father and mother, for example, work, respectively, in a post office and a beauty salon. Jules Golden accuses his mother, in her refusal to concede Blacks the same property rights as others, of acting like a "White Russian landowner." [28]

The Changelings recalls traditional left-wing literature not only in its argument for the need to put together an interracial alliance but also in the revolutionary role envisioned for political art. Jules Golden keeps a "red notebook" in which he writes poems that can be used to convey the problems of young people and provide political guidance to them. Jules suffers from a heart condition and could die at any time; but his legacy of literary radicalism must be passed on to a new generation of changelings who can carry forward the radical tradition. Like many Left writers, Jules has two voices. Privately he composes love poems to his neighbor, Ruth. But he never writes these down, so that the truth of Jules's inner life, like Sinclair's, is never fully revealed.

What the poems in the red notebook teach is an understanding of the relationship between racism and self-hatred, which Judy Vincent and another changeling, David Zigman, will later apply to male chauvinism. In several verses of a poem called "Die *Schwartze*," Jules describes how Jewish immigrants have transformed themselves into imaginary "owners" of American cities and then, out of their self-hate, create an imaginary Black devil to objectify their guilt and fear:

> Now comes the Black
> From out the secret dark cell of my heart
> Now comes the Black Enemy, unnamed, unseen,
> For I fear his name, his face,
> For I will not admit his name is mine,
> His face is mine!
> Now comes The Black to overwhelm me,
> From out the sky, from out the street,
> From out the heart of me![29]

Judy Vincent, however, is not merely a passive recipient of knowledge. She understands immediately that race hatred is a product of self-hatred, that the image of the Black is a projection of one's own insecurities and guilt. But she goes a step further and wonders whether her new friend Clara, who had rescued her when her own gang had turned on her, was an avatar of some new and different self-identity. "From out of the heart of me," she ponders, "From out of the heart of me!"[30]

Sinclair applies Jules's analysis to the sexist behavior of Dave Zigman, a sexism that he manifests in relation to Judy Vincent even as it fills him with self-loathing. From the novel's outset, Dave is depicted as if the culture of East 120th Street is destined to transform him into something unnatural. He resents being asked about his imprisoned gangster brother, Ziggy, who is much admired by the Gully gang. Their fascination with Ziggy makes Dave feel as if there is an expectation that he should act in a like manner. As the oldest son still at home, Dave

255

is also outraged at having to enforce the racist housing policy. The neighbors expect him to carry out his duty. He irrationally blames Phil Rosen, the son in the family who had occupied the upstairs rooms, for the Rosen family decision to move out. At the root of these feelings of uncertainty about his tough-guy role is Dave's love and respect for his mother; he feels that she was exploited by his father, and he does not want to carry on such a tradition. Throughout the novel Dave dreams of replacing a valued bracelet that had once belonged to his mother but which his father had stolen when he left her for a prostitute.

These inner doubts are what will lead Dave toward becoming one of the changelings. As Judy Vincent puts it to Clara, "It means somebody who's left in a place secretly, instead of the person who's supposed to be there." Describing Jules's poem "The Changelings," Vincent uses the example of a child who has been replaced without the knowledge of the parents: "There's this new kid—this changeling—in a house, and his parents think he's theirs. But he isn't—not in his heart. They think one way and talk one way, and the kid who's a changeling thinks entirely different."[31]

Sinclair's understanding of the changeling mentality is in many ways a compelling interpretation of Marxist praxis, with a primacy placed on the creative imagination. As in Ann Petry's novel, the social forces in the world are reified in "the street," which stands as a symbol of social institutions and systems. The street in both novels reproduces the larger society by eliding historical consciousness and maintaining separations of ethnic groups and genders. There is a strained and artificial feeling about the street, but it is clear that one method of assuaging insecurities is to project an object to hate and dominate, as in race hatred and sexual chauvinism. Changelings in Sinclair's novel refuse to participate in the generational reproduction of false consciousness, but such resistance is only possible through bonding in a new form of community.

Why do Vincent and Clara bond? They share outrage as women threatened by men, they feel separated from their parents, and they seek an intimacy that they cannot find within prescribed heterosexual culture. Clara's decision to come to the aid of Vincent when Vincent is attacked by her gang is shown not so much as an act of compassion as one of self-interest. They face a common enemy in fighting male control of their bodies and behavior, as adolescents. Moreover, both young women sense that standing up for gender rights is of a piece with standing up against racism and ethnocentrism. Racial hatred and gender oppression are interconnected in that all are derived from a socialization process that fosters self-hatred, fear, and projection. When Jules learns that Clara and Vincent have become friends, he declares that they have beat "the street."[32]

Ann Petry's The Street climaxes in the defeat of the isolated individual in a reified world; *The Changelings* concludes with intimations of a group-based model of social change. Jules dies, but Vincent inherits his red notebook and she, Clara, and Dave form of a new kind of community as the changelings. Moreover, Sinclair does not limit her new revolutionary vanguard to young people. The combination of art, exemplary action, and passion can influence others, even members of the older generation, if the younger one can be affected. In his final dialogue with his mother, Jules gives her a graphic description of a war different from the one described by Sophie at the outset of the novel:

> The *Schwartze*—what are they? Just a name you gave a lot of stuff you're afraid of. You gave it a name and then you were able to curse it. . . . Here's another way to look at it. The *Schwartze*—they're a wall that you made yourself. . . . It stands between you—and the right kind of world. . . . A wall . . . higher than any kind there is. Higher than the no money wall, the sickness wall. . . . Like you made it yourself, brick by brick. A mistake! People make mistakes. But now you've got to climb over it, Ma. You first, then the whole family—after you show them how.[33]

Jules's final act is to read his last poem, a paean to the socialist dream that concludes,

> I will no longer be afraid of death
> When life has opened for all to see
> My mother's heart—the beautiful flower,
> The song, the dream that never dies.[34]

Jules's speech to his mother is linked to his passing on the red notebook to Vincent. The vision of the poem's dream must be shared, but Jules's final gesture suggests not only that it requires forgiveness of those who tried to mislead, but that the leadership must evolve into the hands of women. Jules, with his red notebook of radical poems, is Jo Sinclair's tribute to the Left of the antifascist crusade that had initially helped her to form a humanizing artistic vision. Jules is an avatar of those long-held hopes and dreams, but now he is dying of a weakened heart; his wound in the heart, both physical and emotional, is also imprisoning his family, insofar as his mother and siblings are prevented from going forward with their lives as long as he requires constant care. In the novel's closing scene, two weeks after the death of Jules, Vincent sets out to emulate his role as teacher by conducting with Dave and Clara a discussion of poems from the red notebook.

Through the writings of Jo Sinclair and others, what the poet Edwin Rolfe called the "trinity of passion" lived on in manifold forms. It would not be a simple legacy. Chester Himes had foregrounded the anguish of his disillusionment in

The Lonely Crusade, then switched to more directly autobiographical themes before remaking his life abroad during the Cold War. For Dan Levin, the emotional struggle to come to terms with his political crisis took decades. Levin's experience was like that of the former Communist leader George Charney, who wrote in his 1968 memoir *A Long Journey* of his resignation from the Communist Party: "I was now free of the past. But in truth, neither was I free nor could I shake off the past."[35] This was because the shaping of one's consciousness during the antifascist crusade went far beyond organizations and formal political positions: "To discard doctrine was one thing; but to discard ideology involved mind and heart, the total commitment, the mystique of the revolution itself."[36]

The *Changelings* received only scant attention when it was published, and Sinclair drifted through decades of obscurity. She was devastated by the death of Helen Buchman and became increasingly withdrawn. Yet three of her novels—*Wasteland*, *The Changelings*, and *Anna Teller*—combine to represent a literary version of a continuous attempt to recapture the idealistic spirit of the antifascist crusade and recast it in a form that could outlast the desecration of the original dream. Edwin Rolfe's poem "Elegia" initially invoked the trinity of passion for "Madrid" as an emotion of purity, one identified with a lifelong fidelity to the antifascist cause in phrases more elegant than those of the youthful Jules Golden:

> I love you, therefore I am faithful to you
> And because to forget you would be to forget
> Everything I love and value in the world.
> Who is not true to you is false to every man
> And he to whom your name means nothing never loved.

Yet on closer inspection one can see that beneath the passionate language of Rolfe's poem there resides a knot of impure, clashing, and perhaps menacing emotions. In particular, Rolfe's poem conceals logical contradictions behind its profession of an idealized, fused love that a male might feel toward a lover, wife, and mother, all called Madrid. These masculine forms of love come in every variety and are often at war with one another. Beyond this, to swear devotion and fidelity to a cause is an abstraction; in the mix of life the meaning of fidelity and the nature of causes become variously defined and often hindered by the delusions and blindness that so frequently accompany passion.

Just as Rolfe fails to unravel the contrarieties of passion, so the antifascist crusade encompassed its own shrouded secrets, many of which were barely fathomed by its passionate partisans. Some of the veiled mysteries were grounded in the common tragedy of life: humanity's uphill battle to metamorphose dreams into actuality while faced with overwhelming obstacles, both biological and historical. Others are more uniquely coupled with the perilous political situation of the antifascist militant. Rolfe and his comrades confronted ferocious adversaries while ensnared between the realpolitik of the Western "democracies," such as the United States and England, rooted in class, racial, and colonial oppression, and a professed "socialist" ideology, promoted by the USSR, that screened a barbarous despotism.

In retrospect, the literature of the antifascist crusade, intermittent in its quality, recounts many stories pivotal to apprehending the lives of idealistic yet diversely flawed men and women committed to the revolutionary fashioning of a better world in the mid-twentieth century. George Charney made another observation about the post-Communist experience of those who retained an idealistic vision that has importance for the literary imagination: "We could express . . . the disillusionment and the yearning, the moral and intellectual effort to understand our past and bridge the gap to the present."[37] Such a legacy of hard-won wisdom, in which socialist convictions were recast in new forms, is movingly expressed in many novels that variously reclaim versions of the antifascist legacy. It is poignantly evident in Jules Golden's paraphrasing of Marx, when he exclaims to Vincent upon learning of her new bond with Clara, "A changeling can change the world!"[38]

NOTES

PREFACE

1 See the discussion of Josephine Herbst's statement that the 1930s was "a humanscape
   —the setting of my loves and discoveries" in Alan M. Wald, *Exiles from a Future Time: The
   Forging of the Mid-Twentieth-Century Literary Left* (Chapel Hill: University of North Carolina Press, 2002), 6–7.

2 See Kai Bird and Martin J. Sherwin, *American Prometheus: The Triumph and Tragedy of J. Robert Oppenheimer* (New York: Knopf, 2005), 112.

3 Ernest Hemingway, *For Whom the Bell Tolls* (New York: Scribner's, 1940), 381.

4 See Albert Fried, ed., *Communism in America: A History in Documents* (New York: Columbia
   University Press, 1997), 226–47; Geoff Eley, *Forging Democracy: The History of the Left in
   Europe, 1850–2000* (New York: Oxford University Press, 2002), 282–87; Ernst Fischer,
   "The People's Front of Yesterday—The National Freedom Front of Today and Tomor-
   row," *Communist*, October 1942, 841–48.

5 See the fascinating analysis in Frank A. Warren, *Noble Abstractions: American Liberal Intellectuals and World War II* (Columbus: Ohio State University, 1999).

6 This view is expressed, for example, in the essay entry "Stalinism" by Ralph Miliband
   in the Harvard University Press *Dictionary of Marxist Thought*, which is also a source
   for definitions of further political terms used in this book, such as fascism and colonialism. See Ralph Miliband, "Stalinism," in *A Dictionary of Marxist Thought*, ed. Tom
   Bottomore, Laurence Harris, V. G. Kiernan, and Ralph Miliband (Cambridge: Harvard
   University Press, 1983), 461–64.

7 Michael Harrington, "Liberalism and the Left," in *Taking Sides: The Education of a Militant Mind* (New York: Holt, Rinehart and Winston, 1985), 8.

INTRODUCTION

1 Ed Lacy, *In Black and Whitey* (New York: Lancer Books, 1967), 9.

2 Ibid., 142.

3 Ibid., 29.

4 Ibid., 99.

5 Ibid., 97.

6 Ibid., 28.

7 Ibid., 100.

8 Ibid., 127.

9 See the biography by Doris Willens, *Lonesome Traveler: The Life of Lee Hayes* (New York:
   Norton, 1988).

10 Lacy, *In Black and Whitey*, 238.

11 Ibid., 224.

12 Zinberg's story "The Right Thing" was included in Nick Aaron Ford and H. L. Faggett, *Best Short Stories by Afro-American Writers, 1925–1950* (Boston: Meador, 1950), 184–88.

13 Lacy, *In Black and Whitey*, 239.

14 Ibid., 249, 253.

15 "Leonard Zinberg, Wrote as Ed Lacy," *New York Times*, 8 January 1968, 85.

16 Biographical information about Zinberg is based on Papers of Leonard S. Zinberg, Mugar Memorial Library, Boston University, Boston, Mass.; Alan M. Wald interview with Annette T. Rubinstein, September 1990, New York, N.Y.; Alan M. Wald interview with Harold Cruse, November 1991, Ann Arbor, Mich.; Alan M. Wald, "The 1930s Left in US Literature Reconsidered," in *Writing from the Left* (London: Verso, 1994), 100–113; Alan M. Wald, "Popular Fiction," in *Encyclopedia of the American Left*, 2nd ed., ed. Mary Jo Buhle, Paul Buhle, and Dan Georgakas (New York: Oxford University Press, 1998), 620–27; Alan M. Wald, "The Urban Landscape of Marxist Noir: An Interview with Alan Wald," *Crime Time: The Journal of Crime Fiction*, no. 27 (2002): 81–89; Robert Niemi, "Ed Lacy, 1911–1968" (draft manuscript, 2005); Ed Lynskey, "Ed Lacy: New York City Crime Author," from <http://www.mysteryfile.com/Lacy/Profile.html> (March 2006).

17 Ralph Ellison, "Negro Prize Fighter," *New Masses*, 17 December 1940, 26–27.

18 George Schuyler, *Pittsburgh Courier*, 28 December 1940, 11, and 18 January 1941, 6.

19 For a summary of the debate, see Gavin Cologne-Brookes, *The Novels of William Styron: From Harmony to History* (Baton Rouge: Louisiana State University Press, 1995).

20 "Hargrove's Post Spurned by Legion," *New York Times*, 13 September 1946, 4.

21 Ed Lacy, *Sin in Their Blood* (New York: Mcfadden-Barell Books, 1966), 18. The original edition was by Eton Books, 1952.

22 Ibid., 7.

23 Ed Lacy, *Moment of Untruth* (New York: Lodestone Books, 1964), 14.

24 See n. 19 in Chapter 1.

25 See my review essay about Lipsitz, "Learning from Labor," *Monthly Review*, February 1996, 53–62.

26 I first discussed these debates in book form in *James T. Farrell: The Revolutionary Socialist Years* (New York: New York University Press, 1978), esp. chap. 2.

CHAPTER 1

1 Wolff was officially the last commander. After the return of the volunteers, the term "Abraham Lincoln Brigade" was used to refer to the preponderance of U.S. participants, although some had participated in the George Washington Battalion, the Canadian MacKenzie-Papineau Battalion, the John Brown Artillery Battalion, or other units.

2 Milton Wolff, *Another Hill* (Urbana: University of Illinois Press, 1994), 353.

3 Ibid.

4 See the lengthy discussion in the chapter "Art Is a Class Weapon" in Walter Rideout, *The Radical Novel in the United States: Some Interrelations of Literature and Society, 1900–1954* (Cambridge: Harvard University Press, 1956), 165–224.

5 In *Crusade on the Left: The Lincoln Battalion in the Spanish Civil War* (New York: Pegasus, 1969), Robert Rosenstone estimates that 30 percent of the Lincolns were Jewish, although the number could be as high as 40 percent, and believes that only 5.73 percent of the volunteers held positions as teachers of any kind. Communist Party members may have comprised as much as 80 percent of the volunteers. See pp. 97–121, 367–72.

6 The episode seems roughly based on the climax of Sherwood Anderson's *Beyond Desire* (New York: Liveright, 1932).

7 Peter N. Carroll, *The Odyssey of the Abraham Lincoln Brigade: Americans in the Spanish Civil War* (Stanford, Calif.: Stanford University Press, 1994), 205.

8 Hemingway facilitated publication of Bessie's manuscript as well as lauding it in print and in private correspondence; see Carroll, *Odyssey of the Abraham Lincoln Brigade*, 236. Sheean's lengthy endorsement appears on the back jacket of the first edition of *Men in Battle*.

9 According to Bernard Dick, Sheean had been attracted to Marxism and fell in love with a Spanish Communist in Spain. Dick also links Lang to the playwrights Emmet Lavery and Maxwell Anderson. See *Radical Innocence: A Critical Study of the Hollywood Ten* (Lexington: University Press of Kentucky, 1989), 115–16. The character may additionally have some reference to scenarist and novelist Michael Blankfort, who had written a novel and play about Spain and was regarded by his onetime Communist friends to have behaved poorly during the HUAC hearings.

10 Alvah Bessie, *The Un-Americans* (New York: Cameron and Associates, 1957), 257.

11 Bessie was the principal author of the open letter, but Wolff assisted; see Carroll, *Odyssey of the Abraham Lincoln Brigade*, 237, 238.

12 Bessie, *Un-Americans*, 258–59.

13 For the assault on Thompson, see Sylvia Thompson, "The Arlington Case," in *Red Scare: Memories of the American Inquisition*, by Griffin Fariello (New York: Norton, 1995), 544–48; for the murder of Bodenheim, see Jack B. Moore, *Maxwell Bodenheim* (New York: Twayne, 1970), 172–73.

14 Bessie, *Un-Americans*, 370, 371.

15 Ibid., 371.

16 See the insightful discussion in Dick, *Radical Innocence*, 106.

17 Bessie, *Un-Americans*, 383.

18 See, for example, the statements by Paul Berman and Martin Peretz on the back jacket of Herrick's autobiography, *Jumping the Line: The Adventures and Misadventures of an Ameri-*

can Radical (Madison: University of Wisconsin Press, 1998), and by Thomas Berger on the back jacket of Herrick's novel *Hermanos!* (New York: Simon and Schuster, 1969).

19 There is a vast body of high-quality scholarship on U.S. literature about the Spanish Civil War, often combining genres and political perspectives and sometimes providing an international context. The only study to include a substantial discussion of both Bessie and Herrick is the unpublished dissertation by José Morales-Serrano, "Spanish Civil War Fiction" (University of New Mexico, 1979). Other volumes on this topic include Frederick R. Benson, *Writers in Arms: The Literary Impact of the Spanish Civil War* (New York: New York University Press, 1967); Allen Guttmann, *The Wound in the Heart: America and the Spanish Civil War* (New York: Free Press, 1962); Peter Monteath, *Writing the Good Fight: Political Commitment in International Literature of the Spanish Civil War* (Westport, Conn.: Greenwood Press, 1994); John M. Muste, *Say That We Saw Spain Die: Literary Consequence of the Spanish Civil War* (Seattle: University of Washington Press, 1966); and Stanley Weintraub, *The Last Great Cause: The Intellectuals and the Spanish Civil War* (New York: Weybright and Taley, 1968).

20 Biographical information on Wolff is based on Carroll, *Odyssey of the Abraham Lincoln Brigade*; "Milton Wolff's Homepage" on the Internet, which includes a summary and excerpt of "A Member of the Working Class"; and the private papers of Milton Wolff in the Abraham Lincoln Brigade Archives, Tamiment Library, New York University, New York, N.Y.

21 Letter from Milton Wolff to Anne, 3 April 1943, Wolff Papers, Lincoln Brigade Archives.

22 Dan Bessie, *Rare Birds: An American Family* (Lexington: University of Kentucky Press, 2001), 235.

23 Ibid., 87.

24 Sources for this biographical sketch include Bessie, *Rare Birds*; Carroll, *Odyssey of the Abraham Lincoln Brigade*; correspondence between Alvah Bessie and Guy Endore, Guy Endore Papers, University of California, Los Angeles; the Alvah Bessie Papers, Wisconsin Historical Society, Madison (including the text of a 1978 M.A. thesis at California State University, Northridge, "Alvah Bessie: A Study of One of the Hollywood Ten," by Jerrold Zinnamon, and correspondence with Zinnamon); the Bessie Papers, Lincoln Brigade Archives; Dick, *Radical Innocence*; Gabriel Miller, "Alvah Bessie," in *Dictionary of Literary Biography*, 26:30–33; and personal correspondence with Dan Bessie, 19 October 1988 and 1 September 1995.

25 Alvah Bessie to Guy Endore, 22 January 1934, Endore Papers.

26 Ibid., 4 February 1934.

27 Ibid., 18 March 1934.

28 This biographical portrait of Herrick is based on personal correspondence between Alan M. Wald and William Herrick between 1995 and 1998; Herrick, *Jumping the Line*;

Carroll, *Odyssey of the Abraham Lincoln Brigade*; Cecil Eby, *Between the Bullet and the Lie: American Volunteers in the Spanish Civil War* (New York: Holt, Rinehart, and Winston, 1969); and materials from the Herrick Papers, Boston University, Boston, Mass.

29 Herrick, *Jumping the Line*, 3.

30 The organization was internationally associated with the Bolshevik Bukharin, and in the United States it was led by Jay Lovestone.

31 See letter from Bernard Wolfe to William Herrick, 16 December 1952, Herrick Papers. In this letter Wolfe indicates his intention of using some of Herrick's anecdotes in his own fiction.

32 Cary Nelson and Jefferson Hendricks, eds., *Edwin Rolfe: Collected Poems* (Urbana: University of Illinois Press, 1993), 13–15, 294. The poem "For Arnold Reid" was published in *New Masses*, 25 July 1939, 11.

33 Al Richmond, *A Long View from the Left: Memoirs of an American Revolutionary* (New York: Delta, 1972), 202.

34 Letter from Joseph Freeman to Daniel Aaron, 7 July 1958, Daniel Aaron Papers, Cambridge, Mass.

35 Information on Reid is based on material found in the microfilm of the Comintern Archives section on the International Brigades, Fond 545, Opis 3, Delo 453, in the Lincoln Brigade Archives at Tamiment Library. The information on Reid is found variously under the names Reid, Reed, and Reisky. Some of this material is summarized as well in Herbert Romerstein, *Heroic Victims: Stalin's Foreign Legion in the Spanish Civil War* (Washington, D.C.: Council for the Defense of Freedom, 1994). Romerstein provides the identification of Bittleman, who is referred to in the archives as "B." However, Romerstein seems unaware of the crucial correspondence of Earl Browder and Robert Minor in regard to Reid's fate, suggesting that not all files were available to him when he carried out his research in Moscow in 1993.

36 Herrick, *Hermanos!*, 50.

37 Carroll, *Odyssey of the Abraham Lincoln Brigade*, 204.

38 Of course, this assessment of the Popular Front was defended in recent years by a number of anticommunist and conservative historians. See Ronald Radosh, Mary R. Habeck, and Grigory Sevostianov, eds., *Spain Betrayed: The Soviet Union in the Spanish Civil War* (New Haven: Yale University Press, 2001). At the time of the fiftieth anniversary of the Spanish Civil War, Radosh was particularly prominent in assailing the notion of any positive contributions from the Lincolns. See Ronald Radosh, "My Uncle Died in Vain Fighting the Good Fight," *Washington Post*, 6 April 1986, and the reply by Christopher Hitchens, "Re-bunking," *Grand Street*, Summer 1986, 228–31. See also the following exchange in the *Nation*: Brian Morton, "Pathetic Fallacies," 29 November 1986, 614–17, and letters from Ronald Radosh and Brian Morton, 27 December 1986–January 1987, 722, 748. One of the more ambitious attempts of recent scholar-

ship to treat the International Brigades veterans and their cause with respect, while simultaneously holding no illusions about the aims of the Stalin regime, is James K. Hopkins, *Into the Heart of the Fire: The British in the Spanish Civil War* (Stanford, Calif.: Stanford University Press, 1998). The quantity and quality of Hopkins's research, as well as its polished prose, sets a high standard for future scholarship.

39 Law is discussed throughout the indispensable volume edited by Danny Duncan Collum, *African Americans in the Spanish Civil War: "This Ain't Ethiopia, but It'll Do"* (New York: G. K. Hall, 1992).

40 To my knowledge, there is only one other published novel focusing directly on the war in Spain by a U.S. citizen who was a combat veteran. James Norman Schmidt (1912–83) served in a French antiaircraft battery during 1937–38. Subsequently he broadcast English-language news programs from Madrid. He then returned to Chicago, the city of his birth, and passed briefly through the Communist Party. His 1960 *The Fell of Dark: A Novel of War in Spain*, published under the name James Norman, is about the evacuation of antifascist leaders from Madrid and Valencia as Franco's forces move toward final victory, and it might be read as an allegorical meditation on several of the different factions in the war.

Other radical novels about Spain were produced by authors who visited Spain briefly or sympathized from afar. John Dos Passos, who was in Spain in 1937 to help Ernest Hemingway with the film *The Spanish Earth* (1937; directed by Joris Ivens), was already disaffected from the Communist Party; his experiences there prodded him to write a two-dimensional polemic against Stalinism, *The Adventures of a Young Man* (1939). Charles Yale Harrison, also a former pro-Communist, wrote an attack on Communist policy in a more satirical vein in *Meet Me on the Barricades* (1938). Two other novels about Spain in the 1930s, William Rollins's *The Wall of Men* (1938) and Upton Sinclair's *No Passaran* (1938), are romances intentionally written in the style of pulp fiction, with no pretense of verisimilitude, although they generally share the Communist outlook on the war. Michael Blankfort, a fellow traveler, published a pro-Republican novel about the siege of Alcázar, *The Brave and the Blind* (1940), preceded by a play in 1937 of the same title, and two years later Dorothy B. Hughes published a mystery novel featuring a Spanish Civil War veteran, *The Fallen Sparrow* (1942). The Spanish Civil War continued to be a literary theme of interest into the late twentieth century, spawning novels appearing around the time of the fiftieth anniversary of the war, such as Pael Leaf's *Comrades* (1985) and Clive Irving's *Comrades* (1986), as well as short fiction such as David Evanier's "How Sammy Klarfield Became a Vacillating Element in Spain," *Journal of Contemporary Studies*, Summer/Fall 1985, 89–106.

Short fiction about the Spanish Civil War includes three stories by veteran Alvah Bessie: "In the Line of Fire," *New Masses*, 25 July 1939, 11–12; "Soldier! Soldier!," *New Masses*, 2 October 1939, 15–16; and "My Brother, My Son," *Story*, January–February

1940, 48–55. Prudencio de Pereda, who was born in the United States of Spanish parents, traveled to Spain with Hemingway to assist with *The Spanish Earth* and published a number of short pieces related to Spain: "The Runners," *Partisan Review and Anvil* 3, no. 2 (March 1936): 21–24; "In Asturias," *Partisan Review and Anvil* 3, no. 4 (May 1936): 12–14; "The Bullfighter," *New Masses*, 16 March 1937, 15–16; "The Spaniard," *Story*, May 1938, 9–18; "My Brother Goes Back," *New Masses*, 16 July 1938, 20; and "Fascist Lament," *New Masses*, 28 February 1939, 11. Other fiction by Leftists about Spain includes Howard Fast, "Departure," *Mainstream*, Summer 1947, 338–34; Marjorie Fischer, "Angela," *Direction*, January–February 1939, 16–17; Martha Gellhorn, "Visit to the Wounded," *Story*, October 1937, 58–61; Lillian Hellman, "A Bleached Lady," *New Masses*, 11 October 1938, 20–21; Dorothy Parker, "Soldiers of the Republic," *New Yorker*, 3 February 1938, 13–14; Hyde Partnow, "Madrid to Manhattan," *New Masses*, 7 December 1937, 17–23; and Tennessee Williams, "In Spain There Was a Revolution" (previously unpublished), *Hudson Review*, Spring 2003, 50–56.

In cooperation with International Publishers, associated with the Communist Party, Alan Calmer edited *Salud: Poems, Stories, and Sketches of Spain by American Writers* (1938). The volume was intended to be a contribution from the perspective of proletarian literature and features short work by veterans as well as visitors to the front and other sympathizers of the Popular Front cause, the majority of whom were close to the Communist movement: James Neugass, Edwin Rolfe, David Wolff (a pseudonym for Ben Maddow), Sol Funaroff, Prudencio de Pereda, Kenneth Rexroth, Norman Rosten, Edward Newhouse, Kenneth Fearing, Erskine Caldwell, John Malcolm Brinnin, Vincent Sheean, and Joseph North. Another collective effort was . . . *and Spain Sings* (1937), edited by M. J. Bernadette and Rolfe Humphries, featuring fifty pro-Republican poems by Spanish authors translated into English by writers such as William Carlos Williams, Stanley Kunitz, Millen Brand, Muriel Rukeyser, Willard Maas, Edna St. Vincent Millay, and Ruth Lechlitner. A recent poetry collection that expands the literary terrain of Spanish Civil War verse is Cary Nelson, ed., *The Wound and the Dream: Sixty Years of American Poems about the Spanish Civil War* (Urbana: University of Illinois Press, 2002). A decade after the war ended, Alvah Bessie edited *The Heart of Spain: Anthology of Fiction, Non-Fiction, and Poetry* (New York: Veterans of the Abraham Lincoln Brigade, 1952), and at the time of his death he was collaborating with Albert Prago on *Our Fight: Writings by Veterans of the Abraham Lincoln Brigade* (New York: Monthly Review, 1987). The participation of veterans in the writing of science fiction, detection fiction, and other popular genres will be discussed in volume 3 of this series.

41 This was particularly the case in 1986, the fiftieth anniversary of the start of the war. In his *Village Voice* article, "Spanish Betrayals," 22 July 1986, 22–23, 25, Paul Berman mistakenly equates the reasoned and documented *Homage to Catalonia* with the exagger-

ated and highly speculative *Hermanos!* In an essay for the *New Criterion*, Ronald Radosh declares that "Herrick has given us what is perhaps the first honest portrayal of the war from within the Brigades in Spain"; see "'But Today the Struggle': Spain and the Intellectuals," *New Criterion*, October 1986, 13. However, the use of Herrick's fiction and memoirs to attack the brigade has provoked sometimes erroneous counter-charges. The following letters of exchange in the *Village Voice* debate the issue: "To Lie in Madrid," with contributions by Harry Fisher, Bob Gladnick, and Paul Berman, 19 August 1986, 4, 6; "The Spanish Civil War, Cont.," with contributions by Rose Smorodin and Paul Berman, 2 September 1986, 4; and "The Guns of August," by William Herrick, 16 September 1986, 6.

42 Bailey's version, along with copies of newspaper articles as documentation, appears in Bill Bailey, *The Kid from Hoboken* (San Francisco: Citrus Lithograph Prepress, 1993), 257–67.

43 Herrick, *Hermanos!*, 26–27.

44 Herrick to Wald, 24 February 1997.

45 See Berman, "Spanish Betrayals."

46 See the references in n. 38 above and letter from Herrick to Wald, May 1996.

47 I tried to address a number of issues involving understandable human failings of brigade members in relation to some of the political contradictions in Spain in my review of Harry Fisher's *Comrades: Tales of a Brigadista in the Spanish Civil War* (1997), in "Humanizing the Lincolns," *The Volunteer* 21 (Winter 1998–99): 5–7.

48 Rosenstone, *Crusade on the Left*, 114.

49 See Berman, "Spanish Betrayals." Carroll, in *Odyssey of the Abraham Lincoln Brigade*, investigates the death of Oliver Law and finds Herrick's version untenable; see pp. 135–39. See also the materials on Law sent by Herrick to Victor Berch in the Lincoln Brigade Archives.

50 Herrick to Wald, 24 February 1997.

51 Ibid.

52 These letters are available on microfilm in the Comintern Archives material on the International Brigades, Lincoln Brigade Archives. I am also grateful to Lincoln veterans Abe Smorodin and Bill Susman, as well as Cary Nelson, for sharing with me their own information regarding Reid in Spain. However, they are not responsible for my conclusions about Reid's fate.

53 Herrick also diminished his credibility by giving anti-Communist testimony under pressure during the McCarthyite witch-hunt era, although he says it was to preserve his union and that he later regretted doing so. See Herrick, *Jumping the Line*, 260–61.

54 William Herrick, "Contemporary American Fiction," *Michigan Quarterly Review* 26, no. 4 (Fall 1987): 745.

55 A subsequent essay by Nelson raises further questions about who pulled the trig-

ger during the execution of Lincoln volunteer Bernard Abramofsky, and whether the issue is important. See "Milton Wolff, Ernest Hemingway, and Historical Memory: The Spanish Civil War Sixty Years Later," *North Dakota Quarterly* 63, no. 3 (Summer 1996): 81–89.

56 The assertion that an individual might be faking injuries out of cowardice was apparently not unusual in Spain. In Harry Haywood's *Black Bolshevik: An Autobiography of an Afrio-American Communist* (Chicago: Liberator Press, 1978), the author describes on p. 471 an incident when he was accused of faking an asthma attack and might have been shot had a doctor not been present to confirm his condition.

57 Carroll, *Odyssey of the Abraham Lincoln Brigade*, 186–87. This description contradicts the version related by Romerstein in *Heroic Victims*, 37–38, where he expresses the belief that Abramofsky was shot in a café by a Lincoln Battalion officer named Tony DeMaio. His evidence is that a witness had identified DeMaio's victim as "Aronofski."

58 Wolff, *Another Hill*, 195.

59 Ibid., 117.

60 Ibid., 378.

61 Characteristic of such views is Isidor Schneider's "P.S. on Hemingway," *New Masses*, 14 January 1941, 12–14.

62 Alvah Bessie, review of *For Whom the Bell Tolls*, *New Masses*, 15 November 1940, 27–28.

63 *Salmagundi*, no. 76–77 (Fall 1987–Winter 1988): 128. Nelson's memory is confirmed by the series of articles covering the dispute over Hemingway's novel in the *People's World* between 30 October 1940 and 12 February 1941.

64 Dwight Macdonald, "Reading from Left to Right," *Partisan Review* 8, no. 1 (January–February 1941): 407.

65 Lionel Trilling, "An American in Spain," review of *For Whom the Bell Tolls*, ibid., 63.

66 A fuller statement of this political perspective on the nature of the war appears in Franklin Rosemont, "Spanish Revolution of 1936," in *Encyclopedia of the American Left*, 2nd ed., ed. Mary Jo Buhle, Paul Buhle, and Dan Georgakas (New York: Oxford University Press, 1998), 792–93. The fullest documentation appears in Burnett Bolloten, *The Spanish Civil War: Revolution and Counterrevolution* (Chapel Hill: University of North Carolina Press, 1991). Paul Buhle provides a useful perspective on the contradictions of the Spanish Civil War in "Still a Good Fight," *In These Times*, 14 November 1994, 30–31. "The Spanish Civil War: The View from the Left," a special issue of *Revolutionary History* (4, no. 1–2 [Winter 1991–92]) presents material expressing the orthodox Trotskyist view.

67 Paul Preston, *Revolution and War in Spain, 1931–1939* (London: Methuen, 1984). See the informative discussion of this volume by Helen Graham, "The Recuperation of Historical Complexity: The Spanish Experience of Republic and Civil War," *European Historical Quarterly* 16 (1986): 491–96.

68 *Salmagundi*, no. 76–77 (Fall 1987–Winter 1988): 126–27; Sam Tanenhaus, "Innocents Abroad," *Vanity Fair*, September 2001, 302.

69 Alan M. Wald interview with Saul Wellman, October 1995, Ann Arbor, Mich.; Tanenhaus, "Innocents Abroad."

70 See the excellent discussion in Warren Rosenberg, *Legacy of Rage: Jewish Masculinity, Violence, and Culture* (Amherst: University of Massachusetts Press, 2001), 1–2.

71 Perhaps the most familiar version of the symbiosis is the mild Clark Kent transforming himself into the iron-fisted Superman, in the cartoon originally created by two Jewish artists, Jerry Siegel and Joe Schuster. See Rosenberg, *Legacy of Rage*, 4, and Paul Breines, *Tough Jews* (New York: Basic Books, 1990), x.

CHAPTER 2

1 John Oliver Killens, *And Then We Heard the Thunder* (New York: Knopf, 1963), 6. The 1963 Knopf volume states that it is the first edition, although the copyright is 1962. About half the scholarly sources give the date of publication as 1962 and half as 1963.

2 Ibid., 438.

3 Ibid., 79.

4 Sometimes the slogan was expressed as "double victory for democracy at home and abroad." See Albert Parker [George Breitman], "Why Communist Party Attacks 'Double V,'" in *Fighting Racism in World War II*, ed. Fred Stanton (New York: Monad, 1980), 157–58. A history of the evolution of the slogan in the *Pittsburgh Courier* can be found in Lee Finkle, *Forum for Protest: The Black Press during World War II* (Cranbury, N.J.: Associated University Presses, 1975), 112–13.

5 Killens, *And Then We Heard the Thunder*, 79.

6 Ibid., 79–80.

7 According to Alan M. Wald interview with Grace Killens, 20 February 2002, Brooklyn, N.Y., the location of the events was Brisbane. Information on race conflicts in the U.S. military remains sketchy to this day. A useful and well-footnoted survey appears in the chapter "Good War, Race War, 1941–1945," in Gary Gerstle, *American Crucible: Race and Nation in the Twentieth Century* (Princeton, N.J.: Princeton University Press, 2001), 186–237. Rumors of a 1943 massacre of rebelling Black soldiers at a military base in Mississippi are reported in "Missing in Action," *In These Times*, 11 July 2001, 16, 21.

8 Killens includes the full quotation as the novel's frontispiece: "And then we saw the lightning, and that was the guns. And then we heard the thunder and that was the big guns. And then we heard the rain falling and that was the drops of blood falling. And when we came to get in the crops, it was dead men that we reaped." The novel's four section titles are also drawn from the quotation: The Planting, Cultivation, Lightning-Thunder-Rainfall, and The Crop.

9 For a useful review of the segregationist practices in the U.S. military during the war, see W. Y. Bell Jr., "The Negro Warrior's Home Front," *Phylon* 5, no. 3 (third quarter, 1944): 271–78.

10 Killens, *And Then We Heard the Thunder*, 450. In particular, Killens's character Scotty exhibits many characteristics of demoralized Black soldiers in World War II, deserting and rebelling as a form of refusing to accept racist treatment. See Bell, "Negro Warrior's Home Front," 276–77.

11 Killens, *And Then We Heard the Thunder*, 436.

12 Ibid., 465.

13 Ibid., 476. According to Grace Killens, Robert Samuels and many of the soldiers in the novel are based on individuals Killens knew and encountered during his wartime experiences; see Wald interview with Grace Killens.

14 See the following studies and collections of writings: Stanton, *Fighting Racism in World War II*; Irving Howe and Lewis Coser, *The American Communist Party: A Critical History* (Boston: Beacon, 1957); Ernest Mandel, *The Meaning of the Second World War* (London: Verso, 1986); and Wilson Record, *The Negro and the Communist Party* (Chapel Hill: University of North Carolina Press, 1951). Maurice Isserman's *"Which Side Were You On?" The American Communist Party during the Second World War* (Middletown, Conn.: Wesleyan University Press, 1982) offers a fresh and far more sympathetic interpretation of the Communists' policy. Although the book is convincing in arguing that the Party did not entirely "abandon the struggle for black rights during the war" (141), its treatment of the Party leadership's hostility to the Double V campaign is far too cursory.

15 Earl Browder, "Partisanship—A Luxury America Cannot Afford," *Communist*, March 1944, 200. Earlier, Browder had been explicit in stating that the Party was making itself available to defeat all those who might raise "socialistic proposals" that might "disturb" national unity:

> The Communist Party of the United States has completely subordinated its own ideas as to the best possible social and economic system for our country, which are the ideas of scientific socialism, to the necessity of uniting the entire nation, including the biggest capitalists, for a complete and all-out drive for victory. We give the formal assurance, which is backed up by our deeds, that we will not raise any socialistic proposals for the United States, in any form that can disturb this national unity. To all those still haunted by "the specter of communism," we offer the services of the Communist Party itself to lay this ghost. [Earl Browder, "The Communist Party and National Unity," *Communist*, September 1942, 691]

16 Quoted in James Gilbert, *Writers and Partisans: A History of Literary Radicalism in America* (New York: John Wiley and Sons, 1968), 54.

17 Killens, *And Then We Heard the Thunder*, 438, 439.

18 According to Killens's widow, he returned from World War II with several volumes of notebooks but only began to work on the novel in the mid-1950s; see Wald interview with Grace Killens.

19 According to Grace Killens, her husband remained a Marxist and socialist all his life; see ibid.

20 Biographical information on Killens is based on the following: Alan M. Wald interview with Grace Killens and Barbara Killens, 20 February 2002, Brooklyn, N.Y.; FBI file of John Oliver Killens, courtesy of Keith Gilyard; William H. Wiggins Jr., "John Oliver Killens," *Dictionary of Literary Biography*, 33:144–52; John Oliver Killens, "Rappin' with Myself," in *Amistad* 2, ed. John A. Williams and Charles F. Harris (New York: Vintage, 1971), 97–136; John Oliver Killens, "The Half Ain't Never Been Told," *Contemporary Authors Autobiography Series* (Detroit: Gale Group, 1985), 2:279–306; Papers of John Oliver Killens, Boston University, Boston, Mass.; Alan M. Wald interview with Howard "Stretch" Johnson, March 1995, by telephone from the Virgin Islands; Alan M. Wald interview with Lloyd Brown, October 1990, New York, N.Y.; and Alan M. Wald correspondence with Phillip Bonosky, 21 May 1997.

21 Killens, "Half Ain't Never Been Told," 284.

22 I am grateful for a 16 August 2004 letter from Keith Gilyard, which corrects many biographical details about Killens's youth, some of which Killens seems to have embellished in memoirs and interviews.

23 Letter from Keith Gilyard to Alan M. Wald, 17 August 2004.

24 Wald interview with Grace Killens.

25 Ibid.

26 Useful information about the radical culture at Howard University in the 1930s can be found in Jonathan Scott Holloway, *Confronting the Veil: Abraham Harris Jr., E. Franklin Frazier, and Ralph Bunch, 1919–1941* (Chapel Hill: University of North Carolina Press, 2002).

27 See Robert Cohen, *When the Old Left Was Young: Student Radicals and America's First Mass Student Movement, 1929–1941* (New York: Oxford University Press, 1993), 23–37. Cohen gives evidence that most of the organization's leaders had been quietly recruited to the YCL.

28 See Paul Buhle, "National Negro Congress," in *Encyclopedia of the American Left*, 2nd ed., ed. Mary Jo Buhle, Paul Buhle, and Dan Georgakas (New York: Oxford University Press, 1998), 535–36.

29 Killens, "Half Ain't Never been Told," 286.

30 There was little public acknowledgment of the race conflict. See Kay Saunders, "In a Cloud of Dust: Black GI's and Sex in World War II," in *Gender and War: Australia at War in the Twentieth Century*, ed. Joy Damousu and Marilyn Lake (Cambridge: Cambridge University Press, 1995), 178–90. I am grateful to Keith Gilyard, Killens's biographer, for

calling my attention to this essay. Grace Killens is certain that at some point Killens visited Australia, probably for "rest and recreation" from his duty in combat areas.

31 Wald interview with Grace Killens.

32 Killens, "Rappin' with Myself," 98.

33 In 1950 the union was expelled from the CIO for its alleged Communist influence, and it was put out of business in 1952. See Buhle et al., *Encyclopedia of the American Left*, 650.

34 See Penny Von Eschen, *Race against Empire: Black Americans and Anti-Colonialism, 1937–1957* (Ithaca: Cornell University Press, 1997).

35 The YCL had dissolved itself into American Youth for Democracy in 1943, when the Communist Party dissolved into the Communist Political Association to reaffirm the sincerity of its Popular Front pledge to raise no socialist agitation. See Buhle et al., *Encyclopedia of the American Left*, 922. The statement of purpose of *New Foundations* appears on the inside of the issue of vol. 2, no. 4 (Summer 1949). A useful commentary on the history of *New Foundations* by Alan Trachtenberg appears as the introduction to the 1968 Greenwood Reprint Corporation edition.

36 See Harvey Klehr, "Harry Haywood," in *Biographical Dictionary of the American Left*, ed. Bernard K. Johnpoll and Harvey Klehr (Westport, Conn.: Greenwood Press, 19), 189–91, and William Eric Perkins, "Harry Haywood," in Buhle et al., *Encyclopedia of the American Left*, 297–98.

37 Joseph Walker, "An American Author's Views on Freedom," *Muhammad Speaks*, 4 March 1963, 19.

38 John O. Killens, "For National Freedom," *New Foundations* 2, no. 4 (Summer 1949): 245.

39 Ibid., 245, 248.

40 Ibid., 254: "Indeed, as a result of the special character of oppression under which they have lived, the Negro people in the South have developed all the attributes of nationhood; they constitute an historically evolved, stable community of economic life, language, territory, and psychological makeup, manifested in a community of culture. Within the borders of the United States, under the jurisdiction of a single central government, there are today two nations: a dominant white nation, with its Anglo-Saxon hierarchy, and a subject black one."

41 Ibid., 258.

42 Ibid., 249.

43 Wald interview with Johnson, March 1995.

44 There is some uncertainty about Ralph Ellison's date of birth, as it was not recorded. In *Ralph Ellison: Emergence of Genius* (New York: John Wiley, 2002), Lawrence Jackson points out that although the date is traditionally recorded as 1914, he believes it was 1913; see n. 3 on p. 447.

45 Wright came in contact with the Communist Party in 1932 and apparently joined in 1933; his disaffection was pronounced after 1942, and he resigned in 1944. See the

discussion of Wright in Alan M. Wald, *Exiles from a Future Time: The Forging of the Mid-Twentieth-Century Literary Left* (Chapel Hill: University of North Carolina Press, 2002), 90–93.

46 Ralph Ellison, *Invisible Man* (New York: Random House, 1952), 558.

47 Ibid., 563.

48 See the extraordinary history of the editorial changes made in the original version of *Invisible Man* in Jackson, *Ralph Ellison*, 420–31. Barbara Foley discusses the earlier evolution of the manuscript in "From Communism to Brotherhood: The Drafts of Invisible Man," in *Left of the Color Line: Race, Radicalism, and Twentieth-Century Literature of the United States*, ed. Bill Mullen and James Smethurst (Chapel Hill: University of North Carolina Press, 2003), 163–82.

49 See my discussion in "The New York Intellectuals in Fiction," in *The New York Intellectuals: The Rise and Decline of the Anti-Stalinist Left from the 1930s to the 1980s* (Chapel Hill: University of North Carolina Press, 1987), 226–63.

50 See *Freedom*, June 1952, 7.

51 For a discussion of that schema, see Wald, *Exiles from a Future Time*, 294–97.

52 See ibid., 281–94.

53 In *The Black Atlantic: Modernity and Double Consciousness* (Cambridge: Harvard University Press, 1993), Paul Gilroy insists (pp. 134–35) that Du Bois's writings are selectively rooted in Hegel, which suggests that Killens might have indirectly imbibed the approach. Yet Adolph Reed Jr. disputes this interpretation of Du Bois in *W. E. B. Du Bois and American Political Thought: Fabian and the Color Line* (New York: Oxford University Press, 1987), 229–30.

54 "Cracker" is a derogatory term for a poor southern white, usually in Georgia; the other expression frequently used in the same manner is "peckerwood," which is believed to be an inversion of "woodpecker."

55 John Oliver Killens, *Youngblood* (New York: Knopf, 1963), 232.

56 See Jerry Gafio Watts, *Heroism and the Black Intellectual: Ralph Ellison, Politics, and the Afro-American Intellectual Life* (Chapel Hill: University of North Carolina Press, 1994), 48–49.

57 Inasmuch as the Harlem Writers Guild played an important role in gestating African American writers during the Cold War, it will be discussed in volume 3, along with predecessors such as the Harlem Writers Club and the Committee for the Negro in the Arts.

58 See my study of the significance of this volume, "Narrating Nationalism: Black Marxism and Jewish Communists through the Eyes of Harold Cruse," in Mullen and Smethurst, *Left of the Color Line*, 141–61.

59 According to Keith Gilyard, Killens made a central contribution to a founding document of the organization. See *Liberation Memories: The Rhetoric and Poetics of John Oliver Killens* (Detroit: Wayne State University Press, 2003), 59–62.

60 Killens, "Half Ain't Never Been Told," 296.

61 See John Oliver Killens, *Great Gittin' Up Morning: A Biography of Denmark Vesey* (Garden City, N.Y.: Doubleday, 1972) and *A Man Ain't Nothin' but a Man: The Adventures of John Henry* (Boston: Little, Brown, 1975). Unpublished plays include "Lower Than Angels" (1965), "Cotillion" (1975), and "Ballad of the Winter Soldier" (1964), with Loften Mitchell.

62 According to Grace Killens, John Killens's contribution was small but significant; see Wald interview with Grace Killens. A lesser-known film partly written by Killens is *Slaves* (1969), which also appeared as a mass-market paperback called *Slaves* (New York: Pyramid, 1969).

63 Wald interview with Grace Killens.

64 Quoted in *New York Times* obituary, 30 October 1987, D22.

65 According to a 21 May 1997 letter from novelist Phillip Bonosky to Alan Wald, there was a discrepancy between Killens in his polemical writing, where he put things "extravagantly," and in his private self. Grace Killens also described her husband in person as soft-spoken and quiet; Wald interview with Grace Killens.

66 According to Finkle, *Forum for Protest*, 211, the term "People's War" was widely used by left-wing African Americans.

67 Bernard C. Natty and Morrio J. MacGregor give the figure of 700,000 for African Americans in the U.S. Army alone, at the time Japan surrendered, in *Blacks in the Army: Essential Documents* (Wilmington, Del.: Scholarly Resources, 1981), 103. Chap. 20, pp. 592–638, "Service Units around the World," gives information about the various roles played by such troops.

68 Indeed, the letters supporting Attaway's application for a Rosenwald Fellowship to finish up the manuscript are all dated during the spring of 1940. See letters in File for William Attaway, Julius Rosenwald Foundation Papers, Fisk University, Nashville, Tenn.

69 See William Attaway, "Plan of Work," 1, File for William Attaway.

70 See Ralph Ellison, "Transition," *Negro Quarterly*, Spring 1942, 87–92, and Ralph Warner, "Blood on the Forge Is Story of Negro Brothers," *Daily Worker*, 8 November 1941, 7.

71 See the discussion of Attaway and the story in Wald, *Exiles from a Future Time*, 282–83.

72 See John Oliver Killens, foreword to *Blood on the Forge* (New York: Monthly Review, 1987), 7. Killens dates the meeting around 1946–48 and describes it as "a left wing session to hammer out a liberation ideology for black writers." Attaway was perceived as one of the "big time theorists."

73 All of these writers will be discussed in volume 3.

74 Some of the policies had been put in place while Browder was in prison on old charges of a passport violation, 25 March 1941 to 16 May 1942, and many other leaders had enthusiastically championed them. Despite new books about the Communist Party, the most substantial sources for the issue of the Party's approach to antiracism dur-

ing the war remain earlier studies such as Howe and Coser, *American Communist Party*, 441–49, and Record, *Negro and the Communist Party*, 227–35.

75 The most informative discussion of *Negro Story* to date appears in Bill Mullen, *Popular Fronts: Chicago and African-American Cultural Politics, 1935–46* (Urbana: University of Illinois Press, 1999), 106–47.

76 Such incidents were common and the subject of protest in the African American press. See Sgt. Aubrey E. Robinson, "Correspondence," *Opportunity*, Winter 1945, 48.

77 Margaret T. Goss, "Private Jeff Johnson," *Negro Story*, July–August 1944, 28–31. This statement is similar to the quotation attributed to the African American Communist journalist Eugene Gordon in a 4 April 1942 article in the *Militant*, newspaper of the Socialist Workers Party, "Why Communist Party Attacks 'Double V,'" by Albert Parker [George Breitman]: "Hitler is the main enemy. . . . The foes of Negro rights in this country should be considered secondary." The article is printed in Stanton, *Fighting Racism in World War II*, 157–58. Other World War II writings in *Negro Story* that are not informed by a Double V perspective include Lieutenant Robert A. Davis, "Sketches from the Army," July–August 1944, 55–56; Corporal Theodore Black, "Fighter's Fury," December 1944–January 1945, 31–34; Herman A. Mitchell, "At Taps," December 1944– January 1945, 53; and John Woodford, "Prisoner of War," December 1944–January 1945, 40.

78 Chester Himes, "Looking Down the Street: A Story of Import and Bitterness," *Crossroad*, Spring 1940, five unnumbered pages.

79 See the discussion of Ellison and *Negro Quarterly* in Wald, *Exiles from a Future Time*, 283–85.

80 "Now Is the Time! Here Is the Place!," *Opportunity*, September 1942, 271–73, 284.

81 "Zoot Suit Riots Are Race Riots!," *Crisis*, July 1943, 200–201, 222.

82 Chester Himes, "Negro Martyrs Are Needed," *Crisis*, May 1944, 159, 174.

83 Earl Conrad, "Blues School of Literature," *Chicago Defender*, 22 December 1945, 11.

84 This is the theme of Earl Browder's collection of writings, *What Is Communism* (New York: International Publishers, 1936), echoes of which can be found in Himes's World War II statements.

85 Chester Himes, "Lunching at the Ritzmore," *Crisis*, October 1942, 314–15, 333.

86 Chester Himes, "Two Soldiers," *Crisis*, January 1943, 13, 29.

87 Chester Himes, "So Softly Smiling," *Crisis*, October 1943, 314–16, 318.

88 Chester Himes, "Heaven Has Changed," *Crisis*, March 1943, 78, 83.

89 Chester Himes, "All He Needs Is Feet," *Crisis*, November 1943, 332.

90 Chester Himes, "Let Me at the Enemy—an' George Brown," *Negro Story*, December 1944–January 1945, 9–18.

91 Chester Himes, "A Penny for Your Thoughts," *Negro Story*, March–April 1945, 14–17.

92 Chester Himes, "He Seen It in the Stars," *Negro Story*, July–August 1944, 5–9.

93 Chester Himes, "All God's Chillun Got Pride," *Crisis*, June 1944, 188–89, 204. When the story was reprinted in *The Collected Stories of Chester Himes* (New York: Thunder's Mouth Press, 1991), the prologue indicating that the main character is already in the guardhouse was omitted.

94 Chester Himes, "Make with the Shape," *Negro Story*, August–September 1945, 36.

95 Chester Himes, *If He Hollers Let Him Go* (1945; reprint, New York: Thunder's Mouth Press, 1986), 4.

96 Ibid., 60–61.

97 Ibid., 89.

98 Ibid., 78.

99 Ibid., 112–15.

100 Ibid., 117, 158.

101 See the biographical sketch of Gordon in Wald, *Exiles from a Future Time*, 83–85.

102 Eugene Gordon, "Powerful Novel of Negro Life," *Daily Worker*, 30 December 1945, 9. See the quotations from letters to the *Daily Worker* in Record, *Negro and the Communist Party*, 228–34. For example, there is this passage from a letter by Thelma Dale: "In the win-the-war camp, a false illusion existed that Negroes would automatically win their rights through all-out support of the war effort. Even the Communists, as part of the revisionist policies, to an extent were affected by this illusion which resulted at times in soft-pedaling of the fight against the inferior status of Negroes in the armed forces."

103 Herbert Aptheker, "Together for Freedom," *New Masses*, 25 December 1945, 24.

CHAPTER 3

1 *New York Times*, 22 September 1944, 17.

2 See the discussion of Vansittartism and quotations from Maltz's correspondence on the subject in Jack Salzman, *Albert Maltz* (Boston: Twayne, 1978), 74–75. Maltz also refers to his preoccupation with the issue in his oral history, "The Citizen Writer in Retrospect" (1983), tape 14, side 1, University of California, Los Angeles.

3 Lola Paine, "The Degeneration of the German Woman," *Daily Worker*, 26 November 1944, 11.

4 See Mike Gold, "Not Until the Germans Repent," *Daily Worker*, 4 October 1944, 7.

5 This appeared in *Krasnaya Zvezda*, 24 July 1942, and is cited in Joshua Rubenstein, *Tangled Loyalties: The Life and Times of Ilya Ehrenburg* (New York: Basic Books, 1996), 192.

6 For a comprehensive collection of essays on Goldhagen's book, which includes references to earlier studies, see Robert R. Shandley, *Unwilling Germans? The Goldhagen Debate* (Minneapolis: University of Minnesota Press, 1998).

7 Michael Gold, "Germany Today: Suddenly All Good Little Anti-Nazis," *Worker*, 20 May 1945, sec. 1, p. 9.

8 Larry Ceplair and Steven Englund, *The Inquisition in Hollywood: Politics in the Film Community, 1930–1960* (Berkeley: University of California Press, 1979), 171.

9 Maltz, "Citizen Writer in Retrospect," 523.

10 Biographical information on Albert Maltz and Margaret Larkin Maltz is based on the following: Bernard Dick, *Radical Innocence: A Critical Study of the Hollywood Ten* (Lexington: University Press of Kentucky, 1989), 104–20; Salzman, *Albert Maltz*; Maltz, "Citizen Writer in Retrospect"; Alan M. Wald interview with Tiba Wilner, July 1990, Ojai, Calif.; Papers of Albert Maltz, Mugar Memorial Library, Boston University, Boston, Mass.; Papers of Margaret Maltz, Mugar Memorial Library; Papers of Albert Maltz, Wisconsin Historical Society, Madison; three reels of taped interviews with Albert Maltz by Victor Navasky, Library of Social History, Los Angeles.

11 Maltz, "Citizen Writer in Retrospect," 98.

12 Ibid., 14.

13 Ibid., 11–16.

14 Errol Segal, "George Sklar: Playwright for a Socially Committed Theater" (Ph.D. diss., University of Michigan, 1986), 90–95.

15 See the biographical sketch of Walker in Alan M. Wald, *The New York Intellectuals: The Rise and Decline of the Anti-Stalinist Left from the 1930s to the 1980s* (Chapel Hill: University of North Carolina Press, 1987), 55–56, 151–52.

16 Carl Reeve, "Despicable Role of Scab Portrayed in *Black Pit*," *Daily Worker*, 23 March 1935, 7.

17 Joseph North, "The Theatre: Theatre Union's *Black Pit*," *New Masses*, 2 April 1945, 42–43.

18 Jack Stachel, "On the Theater Union's Play *Black Pit*," *Daily Worker*, 29 April 1935, 5.

19 See Margaret Larkin, *Nation*, 9 October 1929, 382–83; "The Story of Ella May," *New Masses*, November 1929, 3–4.

20 Albert Maltz, *The Underground Stream* (Boston: Little, Brown, 1940), 341.

21 Michael Gold, introduction to Albert Maltz, *The Way Things Are* (New York: International Publishers, 1938), 14, and Michael Gold, "Review," *Daily Worker*, 16 July 1940, 7.

22 For Kazin, see Alfred Kazin, "Youth at the End of the Parade?," *New York Herald Tribune Books*, 24 July 1938, 2, and "Here Is a Left-Wing Writer Who Can Write," *New York Herald Tribune Books*, 30 June 1940, 5.

23 Samuel Sillen, "Profile of a German Worker," *New Masses*, 3 October 1944, 23–24.

24 Howard Fast, "Howard Fast Reviews Albert Maltz's New Book," *Worker Magazine*, Sunday *Worker*, 8 October 1944, 10.

25 Harry Martel, "The Problem of German Evil in *The Cross and the Arrow*," *Worker*, 18 March 1945, sec. 2, p. 8.

26 Robert Raven, "Book Strengthens People's Hatreds," *Worker Magazine, Sunday Worker,* 1 April 1945, sec. 2, p. 3.

27 Howard Silverberg, "Gives Exact Nature of German Guilt," ibid.

28 Undated manuscript by Howard Selsam, "On Martel's Criticism of *The Cross and the Arrow,*" Papers of Albert Maltz, Wisconsin Historical Society.

29 Further complicating the situation, the Trotskyist movement tended to present an idealized picture of the German working class and to place much of the blame for the triumph of fascism on policies of the Communists in the 1920s and 1930s. Trotskyists also held that the demand for "unconditional surrender" would only strengthen the resolve of the German population to fight longer and harder, for fear of being subjected to a new version of the hated Versailles Treaty. See Felix Morrow, "Stalin Blames the German Proletariat," *Fourth International,* June 1942, 186–91.

30 Biographical information on Irwin Shaw is based on the Irwin Shaw Papers, Mugar Memorial Library, Boston University, Boston, Mass.; Michael Shnayerson, *Irwin Shaw: A Biography* (New York: Putnam, 1989); and James Giles, *Irwin Shaw* (Boston: G. K. Hall, 1983).

31 Irwin Shaw, "Residents of Other Cities," in *Sailor off the Bremen and Other Stories* (New York: Random House, 1939), 267, 262.

32 Irwin Shaw, "Sailor off the Bremen," in *Sailor off the Bremen,* 8.

33 Shaw's play *Sons and Soldiers* (New York: Random House, 1944), originally called "Labor for the Wind" in 1940, is dedicated "To David Shaw, artist, brother, soldier."

34 Shaw, "Sailor off the Bremen," 10, 9.

35 Ibid., 19.

36 Shnayerson, *Irwin Shaw,* 33.

37 Ibid., 27.

38 Ibid., 55.

39 Ibid., 45.

40 Shaw wrote all or part of the following film scripts, in the United States and abroad: *The Big Game* (1936), *The Hard Way* (1942), *The Talk of the Town* (1942), *Commandos Strike at Dawn* (1942), *Take One False Step* (1949), *Easy Living* (1949), *I Want You* (1951), *Act of Love* (1954), *Ulysses* (1955), *Fire Down Below* (1957), *This Angry Age* (1958), *Desire under the Elms* (1958), *The Big Gamble* (1961), *In the French Style* (1963), and *Survival* (1963).

41 See the analysis in Morgan Y. Himelstein, *Drama Was a Weapon: The Left-Wing Theater in New York, 1929–1941* (New Brunswick, N.J.: Rutgers University Press, 1963), 45–46; see also Si Gerson, "Great Anti-War Play," *Daily Worker,* 21 April 1936, 7.

42 See John Cambridge, "Gentle People," *Daily Worker,* 7 January 1939, 7, and H. M., "Gentle People in Trouble," *New Masses,* 17 January 1939, 29–30.

43 Giles, *Irwin Shaw,* 172.

44 Most of the names appearing in the 28 April 1938 issue of the *Daily Worker,* includ-

ing Shaw's, are reproduced in Eugene Lyons, *The Red Decade: The Stalinist Penetration of America* (New York: Bobbs-Merrill, 1941), 248.

45 See Wald, *New York Intellectuals*, 128–39.

46 See Nancy Lynn Schwartz, *The Hollywood Writers' Wars* (New York: Knopf, 1982), 63.

47 Maltz, "Citizen Writer in Retrospect," 486.

48 Shnayerson, *Irwin Shaw*, 105.

49 Stanley J. Kunitz and Howard Haycraft, eds., *Twentieth Century Authors: A Biographical Dictionary* (New York: H. W. Wilson, 1942), 271.

50 Shnayerson, *Irwin Shaw*, 71.

51 Lionel Trilling, "Some Are Gentle, Some Are Not," *Saturday Review*, 9 June 1951, 8.

52 Shnayerson, *Irwin Shaw*, 161.

53 Ibid., 182.

54 Shaw, *Sons and Soldiers*, 99.

55 Leslie Fiedler, "Irwin Shaw: Adultery, the Last Politics," *Commentary*, July 1956, 73.

56 Collins was called to Washington, D.C., along with the Hollywood Ten in 1947 but was not asked to testify at that time.

57 In her 1956 testimony, Jigee Viertel minimized her Communist activities, stating that she joined mainly for educational reasons and that after 1940 her association was very loose. See *Investigation of Communist Activities in the Los Angeles, Calif., Area*, pt. 2 (Washington, D.C.: U.S. Government Printing Office, 1956), 5789–5804. Budd Schulberg's version is that he only joined a Marxist study group in 1936, which changed itself into a chapter of the YCL and Communist Party without notifying him. See *Investigation of Communist Activities in the Los Angeles, Calif., Area*, pt. 3 (Washington, D.C.: U.S. Government Printing Office, 1956), 581–624.

58 Salka and Berthold Viertel had come from Germany in the 1920s. She was an actress turned screenwriter (intimately associated with Greta Garbo), and he was a director and poet. Their legendary Hollywood salon was home to many famous writers from Europe. Salka Viertel published a successful memoir, *The Kindness of Strangers* (New York: Holt, Rinehart and Winston, 1969).

59 See Shnayerson, *Irwin Shaw*, 70–71, 111–12, and Schwartz, *Hollywood Writers' Wars*, 297–99. Another source for details about Jigee Viertel and others in her circle is Peter Viertel, *Dangerous Friends: At Large with Huston and Hemingway in the Fifties* (New York: Doubleday, 1992).

60 Irwin Shaw, *The Troubled Air* (New York: Random House, 1951), 116–17.

61 Ibid., 367.

62 Ibid., 293.

63 See the discussion of the novel in Wald, *New York Intellectuals*, 243–46.

64 See Howard Blue, *Words at War: World War II Era Radio Drama and the Postwar Broadcasting Industry Blacklist* (Lanham, Md.: Scarecrow Press, 2002), 128–31, 351. Blue's book pro-

vides original information on the background to the blacklisting in radio, although *Troubled Air* is not cited.

65 In *Memoirs of a Bastard Angel: A Fifty Year Literary and Erotic Odyssey* (New York: William Morrow, 1989), 45, Harold Norse recalls White, for whom he uses the pseudonym David Blake, as follows: "At thirty-four he was stony bald with sunken cheeks."

66 Actually, Shaw's memory was wrong about this. The Rapp-Coudert hearings began in 1940, and White had resigned from Brooklyn College to serve in the Spanish Civil War, which was over by 1939. However, White's name may well have been mentioned during the hearings, since the chief informant was a former Communist Party member, Bernard Grebanier, from White's own English department. See Ellen W. Schrecker, *No Ivory Tower: McCarthyism and the Universities* (New York: Oxford University Press, 1986), 75–83.

67 Shaw, *Troubled Air*, 330–31.

68 Norse, *Memoirs of a Bastard Angel*, 48.

69 Irwin Shaw, *The Young Lions* (New York: Random House, 1948), 70.

70 Irwin Shaw, *Welcome to the City and Other Stories* (New York: Random House, 1946), 106.

71 Ibid., 107.

72 See Giles, *Irwin Shaw* (1991), 62–65, and Chester E. Eisinger, *Fiction of the Forties* (Chicago: University of Chicago Press, 1963), 110.

73 Shaw, *Troubled Air*, 339.

74 Ibid., 380–81.

75 Ibid., 403–4.

76 Shaw, *Young Lions*, 19.

77 Herbert Mitgang, *Dangerous Dossiers: Exposing the Secret War against America's Greatest Authors* (New York: Ballantine, 1989), 92.

78 Eisinger, *Fiction of the Forties*, 109.

79 Shaw, *Young Lions*, 689.

80 Irwin Shaw, *Act of Faith and Other Stories* (New York: Random House, 1946), 109.

81 In his crudely polemical review of *Young Lions* in the *Daily Worker*, 15 October 1948, 12, Robert Friedman mistakenly points to the episodes involving Ackerman and Green as evidence that Shaw believes that anti-Semitism can only be fought as "the individual acts of men of good will."

CHAPTER 4

1 See Will Haygood, *King of the Cats: The Life and Times of Adam Clayton Powell, Jr.* (Boston: Houghton Mifflin, 1993), 88–91.

2 "Editorial Policy of the *Voice*," *People's Voice*, 14 February 1934, 34.

3 Ibid., 20, 34.

4 Although Robeson was certainly a supporter of the Communist Party at this point,

his main biographer believes that he kept his distance on the tendency to subordinate antiracist militancy to wartime exigencies. See Martin Duberman, *Paul Robeson: A Biography* (New York: Ballantine, 1989), 255.

5 Benjamin A. Davis Jr., contribution to "Round Table: Have Communists Quit Fighting for Negro Rights?," *Negro Digest*, December 1944, 64–65. Taking a position critical of the Party, sociologist Horace R. Cayton argued, "It is my feeling that the Communists misjudged the situation; that more aggressive action for Negro rights would indeed have aided the war effort"; see 66–68.

6 Haygood, *King of the Cats*, 88–90. See also Rob Teel, "The Color of Music in American History," *Oklahoma Daily*, 2 February 2001, 2.

7 See Paul Milkman, *PM: A New Deal for Journalism* (New Brunswick, N.J.: Rutgers University Press, 1997).

8 Haygood, *King of the Cats*, 44–45.

9 Kenneth O'Reilly and David Gallen, *Black Americans: The FBI Files* (New York: Carroll and Graff, 1994), 268–69.

10 For the most detailed study of Davis's career, see Gerald Horne, *Black Liberation/Red Scare: Ben Davis and the Communist Party* (Newark, Del.: Associated University Press, 1994). Davis's autobiography is available as *Communist Councilman from Harlem: Autobiographical Notes Written in a Federal Penitentiary* (New York: International, 1969).

11 See Maceo Crenshaw Dailey Jr. and Ernest D. Washington, "The Evolution of Doxey A. Wilkerson," *Freedomways*, Summer 1985, 101–15. Also see Brace Lamert, "Doxey Wilkerson Is Dead at 88," *New York Times*, 18 June 1993, D16.

12 See David H. Anthony, "Yergan, Max," in *Encyclopedia of the American Left*, 2nd ed., ed. Mary Jo Buhle, Paul Buhle, and Dan Georgakas (New York: Oxford University Press, 1998), 912.

13 See Rodger Streitmatter, *Raising Her Voice: African-American Women Journalists Who Changed History* (Lexington: University Press of Kentucky, 1994), 84–94.

14 Ibid., 93–94. Alan M. Wald telephone interview with Marvel Cooke, February 1998.

15 Nat Brandt, *Harlem at War: The Black Experience in World War II* (New York: Syracuse University Press, 1996), 97–98.

16 "Ann Petry," *Contemporary Authors Autobiography Series* (Detroit: Gale Research Corporation, 1988), 6:254, 259.

17 Ann Petry, "Marie of the Cabin Club," *Afro-American* (Baltimore), 19 August 1939, 14.

18 Ann Petry, "On Saturday the Siren Sounds at Noon," *Crisis*, December 1943, 368–69.

19 James W. Ivy, "Ann Petry Talks about First Novel," *Crisis*, February 1946, 48–49.

20 Examples of her articles about protests are "An Open Letter to Mayor LaGuardia," *People's Voice*, 22 May 1943, 4, and "Doomed Boys May Live Due to Layman's Plea," *People's Voice*, 26 June 1943, 13.

21 Ann Petry, "Harlem Urged to Attend First Meeting of 'Women, Inc.,'" *People's Voice*, 2 May 1942, 17.

22 Robert A. Hill, ed., *The FBI's RACON: Racial Conditions in the United States during World War II* (Boston: Northeastern University Press, 1995), 180.

23 Hazel Arnett Ervin, *Ann Petry: A Bio-Bibliography* (New York: G. K. Hall, 1993), 99.

24 Ibid., xiv.

25 Earl Conrad, "A Woman's Place in Harlem," *Chicago Defender*, 2 February 1946, 13.

26 "First Novel," *Ebony*, April 1946, 35–39.

27 Norman Markowitz, "Progressive Party, 1948," in Buhle et al., *Encyclopedia of the American Left*, 636–37.

28 "Winners of Houghton Mifflin's Literary Fellowship Awards," *Daily Worker*, 3 March 1945, 11.

29 John Meldon, "The *Street*—A Powerful Novel of Harlem Tragedy," *Daily Worker*, 20 March 1946, 11.

30 Milton Puretz, "Disagrees with Meldon's Review of *The Street*," *Daily Worker*, 30 March 1946, 8.

31 Albert Maltz, "What Shall We Ask of Writers?," *New Masses*, 12 February 1946, 19–22.

32 Samuel Sillen, "Better Politics and Better Art," *Daily Worker*, 14 April 1946, *Worker Magazine* section, 8.

33 Beth McHenry, "Says *The Street* Is First of Series on Negro Life," *Daily Worker*, 29 March 1946, 13.

34 Alfred Goldsmith [Saul Levitt], "Struggle for Survival," *New Masses*, 21 May 1946, 25–26.

35 Theodore Ward, "Five Negro Novelists: Revolt and Retreat," *Mainstream*, Winter 1947, 110.

36 Ibid., 107–8.

37 Ann Petry, "Harlem," *Holiday*, April 1949, 110–16.

38 Albert Maltz, "Moving Forward," *New Masses*, 9 April 1946, 21–22.

39 Certainly the novels written by African American Leftists prior to *The Street* did not offer trade union salvation or feature the CIO riding to the rescue. Richard Wright wrote only one short story, "Fire and Cloud," in *Uncle Tom's Children* (1938), that showcases mass interracial action at its climax. But the story was preceded by three disaster tales, and in its 1940 edition it was followed by "Bright and Morning Star," in which the proletarian interracial alliance is betrayed by a white comrade and the African American heroine goes down in a hail of bullets.

40 Ann Petry, "The Novel as Social Criticism," in *The Writer's Book*, ed. Helen Hull (New York: Harper and Brothers, 1950), 32–39.

41 Ann Petry, "Doby's Gone," *Phylon* 5, no. 4 (fourth quarter 1944): 361–66.

42 "Ann Petry," 256.

43 Petry's consciousness of triple oppression is strongly evidenced in nonfiction in her essay "What's Wrong with Negro Men?," *Negro Digest*, March 1947, 4–7.

44 Ann Petry, *The Street* (Boston: Houghton Mifflin, 1944), 258–60.

45 Ibid., 200.

46 Ibid., 323–24.

47 Ibid., 8.

48 Ibid., 15.

49 Ervin, *Ann Petry*, xiv.

50 See Rich Cohen, *Tough Jews: Fathers, Sons, and Gangster Dreams* (New York: Simon and Schuster, 1998), 161.

51 Harvard-educated Edwin Seaver (1900–1987) was a close fellow traveler of the Communist movement in the 1930s and author of two left-wing novels, *The Company* (1930) and *Between the Hammer and the Anvil* (1937). In 1938 he began to work for the Book-of-the-Month Club, and during the 1940s he edited four volumes of new fiction that included work by a large number of Communist and pro-Communist writers.

52 See Eduardo Obregón Pagán, *Murder at the Sleepy Lagoon: Zoot Suits, Race, and Riot in Wartime L.A.* (Chapel Hill: University of North Carolina Press, 2003); Dominic J. Capeci Jr., *The Harlem Riot of 1943* (Philadelphia: Temple University Press, 1977); Hill, *FBI's RACON*; Brandt, *Harlem at War*.

53 Max Weiss, "Fifth Column Diversion in Detroit," *Communist*, August 1943, 698–710.

54 Earl Browder, "Hitler's Uprisings in America," *New Masses*, 14 September 1943, 3–5.

55 See Brandt, *Harlem at War*, 185–206. The precipitating event occurred on a Sunday at 7:30 P.M. in the lobby of the Braddock Hotel at 126th Street and Eighth Avenue. An altercation began between a rookie patrolman and a woman who had apparently left a drinking party in one of the rooms. Pvt. Robert Bandy then hit the patrolman with his own nightstick and was shot while fleeing. The wound was slight, but word soon spread among a growing crowd that Bandy was dead.

56 Ann Petry, "In Darkness and Confusion," in *Miss Muriel and Other Stories* (Boston: Beacon, 1989), 281.

57 Ibid., 284.

58 Ibid., 286.

59 Ibid., 290.

60 Ibid., 291.

61 Ibid., 294.

62 Ibid.

63 Ibid., 295.

64 According to Brandt, *Harlem at War*, 194, among those exhorting Harlemites from

sound trucks to return to their homes peacefully were Walter White, Roy Wilkins, Max Yergan, Ferdinand Smith, Hope Stevens, and the Reverend John H. Johnson.

65 *Ebony*, April 1946, 39.

66 Paula Rabinowitz of the University of Minnesota has also observed that there are strong links between *Country Place* and the early section of *The Street* in which Lutie is employed as a domestic for a decadent family in upstate New York; see private conversation, February 2004. One might also speculate that "In Darkness and Confusion," which among Petry's short stories is unusually long, may have been part of a larger literary project about other aspects of Harlem life that she did not develop.

67 Ervin, *Ann Petry*, 75, 99.

68 Hill, *FBI's RACON*, 180.

69 Muriel Wright Brailey, "Necessary Knocking: The Short Fiction of Ann Petry" (Ph.D. diss., Miami University, 1996), 3–4.

70 Characteristic is the following excerpt from a 1971 interview with John O'Brien: "IN-TERVIEWER: Do you like talking about your writing? PETRY: No. I find it painful."

Other classic Petry responses include "Once I've written something I don't have anything more to say about it. That's it. . . . If a critic wants to analyze it, let him. Fine. But I don't want to" and "I think it is an imposition to ask me to 'explain' a story or novel." One interviewer, Mark Wilson, in 1987 maintained that the tape recorder could not communicate the warmth of the responses he got, often punctuated with laughter. But Wilson never asked her about her politics or the *People's Voice*. What Petry does talk extensively about are her ancestors and her family's drugstores and her Columbia University writing teacher. She also lists names of actors and writers she had occasion to meet. See Ervin, *Ann Petry*, 69–103.

71 Wald telephone interview with Marvel Cooke, December 1996. Queries about Petry's politics in published interviews are sometimes confusing because some interviewers fail to distinguish between what she thought during the late 1930s and 1940s and what she felt after the Cold War began and later.

72 It is customary for stories in an author's single-volume collection spanning several decades to appear in the order of publication or, if not, for there to be some means for the reader to ascertain the date and place of original publication. In this volume, the publisher gives only seven copyright dates without connecting them to particular stories. The book has no preface, introduction, or acknowledgments. The stories appear absent of bibliographical matter.

73 The main source of biographical information about Offord is Thelma Barnaby Thompson, "Carl Ruthven Offord," *Dictionary of Literary Biography*, 76:130–33.

74 Nell Dodson, "Carl Offord's First Novel, *White Face*, Is Startling," *People's Voice*, 15 May 1943, 10.

75 Claudia Jones, "Maiden Book of New Author Deals with Negro Problems," *Daily Worker*, 13 June 1943, 4. On 29 June 1943, p. 7, letters pro and con the Jones review were published in the *Daily Worker*.

76 Samuel Putnam, "Calls Offord Novel 'Thrilling Experience,'" *Daily Worker*, 16 July 1943, 7.

77 Barbara Giles, "The White Face," *New Masses*, 3 August 1943, 24–26.

78 Carl Ruthven Offord, "America's Ghettos," *New Masses*, 21 September 1943, 11–12.

79 See Offord, "Low Sky," in *Cross-Section: A Collection of New American Writing*, ed. Edwin Seaver (New York: Fischer, 1944), 304–13, and "So Peaceful in the Country," *Story*, May–June 1945, 81–86.

80 Ward, "Five Negro Novelists," 100–110.

81 See Carl Offord, "Gentle Native," *Masses & Mainstream*, September 1948, 8–16, and "The Green, Green Grass and a Gun," *Masses & Mainstream*, February 1949, 39–43.

82 Alan M. Wald interview with Franklin Folsom, May 1989, Boulder, Colo.; see Christina Baker, *In a Generous Spirit* (Urbana: University of Illinois Press, 1996), 100, 145.

83 Alan M. Wald interview with Willa Appel, December 1992, New York, N.Y.

84 Ben Appel, "The Message Novel," *The Writer*, February 1944, 36.

85 Alan Benoit, "Home Front Enemies," *New Masses*, 21 December 1943, 24–26.

86 Benjamin Appel, "The 'Message' Novel," *The Writer*, February 1934, 35–38.

87 One of the few scholars attentive to Spivak's methods and impact is William Stott, in *Documentary Expression and Thirties America* (New York: Oxford University Press, 1973).

88 See the valuable essay by Alex Lichtenstein, "Georgia History in Fiction," *Georgia Historical Quarterly* 79, no. 3 (Fall 1995): 633–58.

89 Spivak's papers are at Syracuse University, Syracuse, N.Y. The most extensive study of Spivak is a senior honors thesis done at the University of Michigan by Martin Wayne Friedman, "Towards an Effective Committed Reportage: A Study of John L. Spivak" (Program in American Culture, 1982).

90 See John Earl Haynes and Harvey Klehr, *Venona: Decoding Espionage in America* (New Haven: Yale University Press, 1999), 375–76. These authors also believe that Kahn assisted with pro-Soviet espionage.

91 See Robert M. Lichtman and Ronald D. Cohen, *Deadly Farce: Harvey Matusow and the Informer System in the McCarthy Era* (Urbana: University of Illinois Press, 2004).

92 Kahn's *Matusow Affair* (Mount Kisco, N.Y.: Moyer Bell, 1987) was posthumously published.

CHAPTER 5

1 The tendency to blame the Communist Party for literary failures was most powerfully expressed by Irving Howe and Lewis Coser in *The American Communist Party: A Critical History* (Boston: Beacon, 1957), 306: "In the long run, the damage wrought by the party

in its passion to conquer or destroy what it could not conquer was the same in literature as in the trade unions, the same in cultural matters as in politics. In the long run, that is, our story is the story of human waste." The theme that the Communist Left destroyed writers is also prevalent throughout Murray Kempton's *Part of Our Time: Some Monuments and Ruins of the Thirties* (New York: Dell, 1955).

2 Alan M. Wald interview with Henry Roth, 21 December 1988, Albuquerque, N.M. Biographical information on Roth is primarily based on this interview, along with correspondence from Roth on 30 November 1988 and 5 May 1989. Scholarship on Roth is quite substantial, including numerous essays, interviews, and lengthy book reviews. Most important are Bonnie Lyons, *Henry Roth: The Man and His Work* (New York: Cooper Square, 1976); Mario Materassi, ed., *Shifting Landscape: A Composite, 1925–1987* (Philadelphia: Jewish Publication Society, 1987); and Hanna Wirth-Nesher, ed., *New Essays on Call It Sleep* (New York: Cambridge University Press, 1996). Additional sources include a letter from Roth to Horace Gregory, 25 July 1933, in the Horace Gregory Papers, Syracuse University, Syracuse, N.Y. Steven G. Kellman's *Redemption: The Life of Henry Roth* (New York: Norton, 2005) contains new details about Roth's family and confirms the incidents of incest; his decades-long Communist activity, however, remains opaque.

3 This is how Stanley Burnshaw recalled Bransten, as reported in Hazel Rowley's *Christina Stead: A Biography* (New York: Henry Holt, 1993), 277: " 'spectacularly thin' and 'unathletic-looking, with a tension in his expression that could be gloriously dissolved when he laughed.' He suffered deeply from lack of self-esteem."

4 See Materassi, *Shifting Landscape*, 3–10.

5 See the following in *New Masses*: "Brief Review," 12 February 1935, 27; David Greenhood, "Another View," 19 February 1935, 21; Kenneth Burke, "More about Roth's *Call It Sleep*," 26 February 1935, 21; Alvah C. Brothers, "Bourgeois-Critical Exploitation," 26 February 1935, 21; Edwin Seaver, "Caesar or Nothing," 5 March 1935, 20.

6 Roth believed that Green died when his ship was torpedoed during World War II.

7 See Mark Shechner, "The Unquiet Past of Henry Roth," *Chicago Tribune*, 2 February 1995, book section, 1, 14: "Like many Depression-era writers, Roth fell under the spell of the Communist Party, which employed him as a literary foot soldier to write a 'proletarian novel' about a worker who had been injured in an industrial accident. Roth abandoned the project early on. . . . A stubborn man, Roth wouldn't be harnessed to literary number painting."

8 Genya Schearl is close in appearance to Eda Lou Walton, to whom *Call It Sleep* is dedicated; his own mother more likely resembled the repulsive Aunt Bertha of the novel. This point is made in Werner Sollers's essay "A World Somewhere, Somewhere Else," which also provides an explanation of the source for Roth's use of the Oedipal complex. See Wirth-Nesher, *New Essays on Call It Sleep*, 127–88. The evidence is lacking that

Roth had ever read Freud as a young man; like Marxism, talk of Freud was in the air at Walton's salon, which is where Roth might have absorbed the fundamental ideas of both.

9 Wald interview with Roth.

10 The statement is reprinted in Materassi, *Shifting Landscape*, 48–51.

11 Wald interview with Roth.

12 Biographical information about Gilfillan is based on the collection of Lauren Gilfillan papers (hereafter LGP) assembled over a ten-year period by the author, with the assistance of Henry Gilfillan. These papers consist of photocopies of more than fifty letters exchanged between relatives of Gilfillan (especially her mother and aunts) and letters from Gilfillan to various friends and relatives; photocopies of diaries, journals, and unpublished writings by Gilfillan from World War I through the early 1930s; letters and e-mails from Henry Gilfillan to Alan M. Wald from 1988 through 1999; photocopies of a large collection of book reviews, interviews, and other newspaper and journal articles about Gilfillan in connection with *I Went to Pit College*; copies of memoirs, genealogies, and family histories by Henry Gilfillan and other relatives; copies of letters from the Johns Hopkins University Hospital regarding Gilfillan's father; and Alan M. Wald's correspondence with the Kalamazoo Psychiatric Hospital about Gilfillan. Since many of the letters, newspaper articles, and other items are not dated very well, a general chronology of events has been reconstructed by cross-checking and cross-referencing. For background information on psychiatric treatments and analyses in the 1920s–40s, I consulted Charles Gibbs, "Sex Development and Behavior in Female Patients with Dementia Praecox," *Archives of Neurology and Psychology* 11 (1924): 179–94, and L. Kerschbaumer, "Endocrine Maldevelopment in Schizophrenia," *Journal of Nervous and Mental Diseases* 98 (November 1943): 521–25. I acknowledge and appreciate additional guidance from Dr. Gina Morantz-Sanchez and Dr. Isabel Bradburn. I also appreciate background information on the 1931 coal strike provided by Dr. James Barrett. Most citations will be from LGP, although I have attempted to provide more specific information about Gilfillan's writings in the Communist press and other places where her own writings appeared.

13 LGP.

14 LGP.

15 LGP.

16 Paula Rabinowitz, *Labor and Desire: Women's Revolutionary Fiction in Depression America* (Chapel Hill: University of North Carolina Press, 1991), 150. It was Rabinowitz's work that first drew my attention to the importance of Gilfillan's book. Her interpretation of *I Went to Pit College* remains unsurpassed.

17 LGP.

18 Edwin Rolfe, "A College Girl Writes about Western Pennsylvania Miners," *Daily Worker*,

3 March 1934, 7. Of course, most of the book is not just about the miners, who were all men, but equally about the women and children of the community.

19 LGP. Of course, as a Bohemian rebel of the 1930s, Gilfillan preferred not to wear makeup before, during, or after her Pit College sojourn.

20 LGP.

21 LGP.

22 LGP.

23 See the three-part series by Linda Morton in section C of the Washington, Pa., *Observer-Reporter*, 19, 20, 23 October 1981.

24 LGP.

25 LGP.

26 Adler's report was incorporated into the "Change the World!" column of the *Daily Worker*, 17 April 1934, 7.

27 Lauren Gilfillan, *I Went to Pit College* (New York: Literary Guild, 1934), 289.

28 "Change the World!," *Daily Worker*, 17 April 1934, 7.

29 Ben Field, "From Smith College to Pit College," *Partisan Review* 1, no. 1 (February–March 1934): 54–56.

30 "Change the World!," *Daily Worker*, 17 April 1934, 7.

31 Ibid.

32 LGP.

33 LGP.

34 LGP.

35 LGP.

36 Lauren Gilfillan, "Weary Feet," *Forum*, October 1933, 201–8.

37 "Authors' Field Day: A Symposium on Marxist Criticism," *New Masses*, 3 July 1934, 29–30.

38 Lauren Gilfillan, "Why Women Really Might as Well Be Communists as Not, or Machines in the Age of Love," *Modern Monthly*, February 1935, 747, 753.

39 LGP.

40 LGP.

41 The biographical sketch of Vogel is based on personal correspondence with the author.

42 B. F. Skinner, *Particulars of My Life* (New York: Knopf, 1976), 241.

43 Vogel to Gregory, 13 October 1935, Gregory Papers.

44 "Man's Courage," *New York Times Book Review*, 23 March 1938, 2.

45 The agency was established in 1935 by executive order of President Roosevelt as the Works Progress Administration, but the name was changed in 1939. Its aim was to assist individuals on relief by employing them in useful projects.

46 Alan M. Wald interview with B. J. Widick, 27 June 1990, Ann Arbor, Mich.

47 "Ruth McKenney," in *Twentieth Century Authors: A Biographical Dictionary*, ed. Stanley Kunitz and Howard Haycraft (New York: H. H. Wilson, 1942), 883.

48 Malcolm Cowley, "Collective Novel," *New Republic*, 22 February 1939, 77; Ruth McKenney, *Love Story* (New York: Harcourt, Brace, 1950), 122.

49 Jake, in contrast, is portrayed as celibate during the long separation preceding this encounter and is unstigmatized for his participation in the sexual encounter.

50 Ruth McKenney, *Jake Home* (New York: Harcourt, Brace, 1943), 390, 371.

51 His last name, Home, probably refers to the critical roots of his experiences in his Pennsylvania community.

52 See McKenney, *Love Story*, 120–21.

53 See articles discussing *Jake Home* in *Daily Worker*: 16 March 1943, 7; 3 May 1943, 7; 1 June 1943, 7; 2 June 1943, 7; 2 July 1943, 7; 25 June 1943, 7.

54 McKenney, *Love Story*, 231.

CHAPTER 6

1 *New Left Review*, November–December 1985, 11–12.

2 See summary of Kramer's career by Alan M. Wald in *Encyclopedia of the American Left*, 2nd ed., ed. Mary Jo Buhle, Paul Buhle, and Dan Georgakas (New York: Oxford University Press, 1998), 677–78. See also Aaron Kramer, *Wicked Times: Selected Poems*, edited and with a biographical essay by Cary Nelson and Donald Gilzinger Jr. (Urbana: University of Illinois Press, 2004).

3 Alan M. Wald interview with Aaron Kramer, 15 September 1990, New York, N.Y.

4 Ibid.

5 Quoted from memory in ibid.

6 Aaron Kramer, "To Angelo Herndon," *New Pioneer*, September 1934, 6.

7 Wald interview with Kramer.

8 See Aaron Kramer's entry on Proletpen in Buhle et al., *Encyclopedia of the American Left*, · 643–44.

9 This appeared as a special issue of *Nature, Society, and Thought* 13, no. 1 (2000).

10 Ben Burns, *Nitty Gritty: A White Editor in Black Journalism* (Jackson: University of Mississippi Press, 1966), 113; Alan M. Wald interview with Ben Burns, October 1995, Chicago, Ill.

11 Burns, *Nitty Gritty*, 136.

12 Kim Chernin, *In My Mother's House: A Daughter's Story* (New York: Harper and Row, 1983), 91.

13 Ibid., 60–61.

14 Ibid., 95.

15 Perry Anderson, "Internationalism: A Breviary," *New Left Review*, March–April 2002, 15.

16 Biographical information is based on Alan M. Wald interview with John Sanford,

March 1989, Montecito, Calif.; the John Sanford Papers at Boston University, Boston, Mass.; and Alan M. Wald correspondence with Sanford, 1988–99.

17 Wald interview with Sanford and correspondence with Sanford.

18 Biographical information about Vera Caspary is based on the Vera Caspary Papers, Wisconsin Historical Society, Madison, and Alan M. Wald interview with Ben and Norma Barzman, October 1992, Los Angeles, Calif.

19 Vera Caspary, *The Secrets of Grown-Ups* (New York: McGraw Hill, 1979), 36.

20 Two other Jewish American pro-Communist women who wrote of their personal experiences with anti-Black racism in the 1930s were Tess Slesinger in "White on Black" and Dorothy Parker in "Arrangement in Black and White." Both stories were anthologized in an influential collection on racism published in 1945, *Primer for White Folks* (Garden City, N.Y.: Doubleday, Doran, 1945). Moreover, all three of these radical women writers were associated in 1939–40 with the journal *Equality*, which was launched under Communist Party direction "to defend democratic rights and combat anti-Semitism and racism." Caspary served on the editorial council of *Equality*, along with another Jewish American pro-Communist woman, Lillian Hellman, and both Slesinger and Parker were contributors. The managing editor of *Equality* was Abraham Chapman, a Jewish Communist who fled to Eastern Europe during the Cold War but eventually returned to the United States. Chapman resurfaced as an English professor in the 1960s, publishing excellent and influential collections of African American, Native American Indian, and Jewish American literature.

21 See Howard Fast, *Being Red: A Memoir* (Boston: Houghton Mifflin, 1990), 75–77.

22 A film version did not appear until NBC produced a poorly done miniseries in the late 1970s starring the boxer Muhammad Ali as Gideon Jackson and costarring the singer Kris Kristofferson.

23 In this sense, Maltz prefigures Enzo Traverso's *The Origins of Nazi Violence* (New York: New Press, 2003). Traverso argues that the gas chambers of Auschwitz, rather than constituting a "break in civilization," confirm extermination "to be one of the faces of civilization itself" (2).

24 Abzug published one other novel, *Seventh Avenue Story* (1947), dealing with the garment industry. See also Abzug's correspondence with Charles Humboldt of *Masses & Mainstream* at Yale University. My interviews with Helen Yglesias and Barbara Zeluck in February 2004 in New York City indicated that both Abzugs may have been Communist Party members in the postwar years, but such affiliations were never publicly acknowledged and have not been documented. The *Daily Worker*, 11 January 1947, 11, singled out Abzug's novel for praise in "First Novel Illuminates G.I. Side of War," reviewed by John Hudson Jones.

25 Martin Abzug, *Spearhead* (New York: Dial, 1946), 74–75.

26 Ibid., 211.

27 Stefan Heym, *The Crusaders: A Novel of Only Yesterday* (Boston: Little, Brown, 1948), 9.

28 Sources for Stefan Heym include Peter Hutchinson, *Stefan Heym: The Perpetual Dissident* (Cambridge: Cambridge University Press, 1992); Inge Dube, "Stefan Heym," *Dictionary of Literary Biography*, 69:135–42; Reinhard Konrad Zachau, "Stefan Heym in Amerika" (Ph.D. diss., University of Pittsburgh, 1978); David Binder, "Stefan Heym, Marxist-Leninist Novelist, Dies at 88 on Lecture Tour in Israel," *New York Times*, 18 December 2001, A21. The *Daily Worker* ran a laudatory review by Robert Friedman, "Stefan Heym's *Crusaders* Outstanding War Novel," 5 September 1948, sec. 2, p. 11.

29 Heym's novel has been the subject of a thoroughgoing commentary in Joseph J. Waldmeir, *American Novels of the Second World War* (The Hague: Mouton, 1969), 56–76.

30 Biographical information about Saul Levitt is based on the Saul Levitt Papers at Boston University, Boston, Mass., and Alan M. Wald interview with his widow, Deena Levitt, September 1991, New York, N.Y.

31 Sources for biographical information on Louis Falstein: Alan M. Wald interview with Falstein, September 1991, New York, N.Y.; Falstein Papers, Wayne State University, Detroit, Mich.

32 Biographical information on Schappes is based on Alan M. Wald interviews with Morris Schappes, 14 November 1989 and 4 June 1990, New York, N.Y.

33 Wald interview with Schappes, 14 November 1989.

34 See Morris U. Schappes, "Errors in Mrs. Bianchi's Edition of Emily Dickinson's Letters," *American Literature* 4, no. 2 (January 1933): 369–84. See also his review of Emily Dickinson: "Unpublished Letters with Notes and Reminiscences," *American Literature* 5, no. 1 (March 1933): 82–85.

35 See the discussion in Ellen W. Schrecker, *No Ivory Tower: McCarthyism and the Universities* (New York: Oxford University Press, 1986), 66–67.

36 See the discussion in ibid., 75–83.

37 See Morris U. Schappes, "The Letters of Emma Lazarus, 1868–1885," *New York Public Library Bulletin*, no. 53 (1949): 315–34.

38 Wald interview with Schappes, 14 November 1989.

CHAPTER 7

1 Matt Wayne, "Sincerity in the Theater," *New Masses*, 3 July 1945, 29–30.

2 Benjamin Nelson, *Arthur Miller: Portrait of a Playwright* (New York: David McKay, 1970), 45.

3 Arthur Miller, *Timebends: A Life* (New York: Grove Press, 1987), 105.

4 Ibid., 103.

5 In his April 1956 *Atlantic Monthly* essay, "The Family in Modern Drama," he affirmed that "there lies within the dramatic form the ultimate possibility of raising the truth-

consciousness of mankind to such a level of intensity as to transform those who observe it." See Robert A. Martin and Steven A. Centola, eds., *The Theater Essays of Arthur Miller*, rev. and expanded ed. (New York: Da Capo Press, 1996), 84.

6 Arthur Miller, "The American Writer: The American Theater," in Martin and Centola, *Theater Essays of Arthur Miller*, 376 (originally in *Michigan Quarterly Review*, Winter 1982).

7 Matthew C. Roudané, ed., *Conversations with Arthur Miller* (Jackson: University Press of Mississippi, 1987), 274.

8 Miller, *Timebends*, 230.

9 Arthur Miller, "Tragedy and the Common Man," in Martin and Centola, *Theater Essays of Arthur Miller*, 7.

10 "The Testimony of Arthur Miller, Accompanied by Counsel Joseph L. Rauh, Jr.," in U.S. House of Representatives, Committee on Un-American Activities, *Investigation of the Unauthorized Use of United States Passports*, 84th Cong., Congressional Record, pt. 4, 21 June 1956 (Washington, D.C.: U.S. Government Printing Office, November 1956), 4687.

11 Miller, *Timebends*, 237.

12 Alan M. Wald interview with A. B. Magil, August 1990, New York, N.Y.; Alan M. Wald interview with Lloyd Brown, 2 September 1991, and telephone conversation, 13 December 1995. I do not regard Brown's recollection as definitive proof of Miller's Communist Party membership, but it sounds plausible in the context of the other circumstances.

13 The primary repository of Miller's papers is the Harry Ransom Humanities Research Center at the University of Texas, Austin. The materials are still not fully processed. Just before Miller's death an additional collection of Miller's papers and correspondence arrived, "but for legal reasons, those are not presently available either for processing or research. . . . It will be quite a while before they [any letters contained in the material] are available to scholars" (letter from Richard Workman to Wald, 24 May 2005).

14 Martin Gottfried, *Arthur Miller: His Life and Work* (New York: Da Capo Press, 2003), x.

15 Enoch Brater, *Arthur Miller: A Playwright's Life and Works* (London: Thames and Hudson, 2005), 130.

16 Martin and Centola, *Theater Essays of Arthur Miller*, xiii.

17 *Bernadine, I Love You* (unpublished, 1945); *Grandpa and the Statue*, in *Radio Drama in Action*, ed. Erik Barnouw (New York: Farrar and Rinehart, 1945); *The Philippines Never Surrendered* (unpublished, 1945); *The Guardsman* (adaptation, 1945), in *Theater Guild on the Air*, ed. H. William Fitelson (New York: Rinehart, 1947); *Pride and Prejudice* (unpublished adaptation, 1945); and *Three Men on a Horse* (adaptation, 1946), in Fitelson, *Theater Guild on the Air*. There are a number of references to Miller in Howard Blue, *Words at War:*

World War II Era Radio Drama and the Postwar Broadcasting Industry Blacklist (Lanham, Md.: Scarecrow Press, 2002). The most detailed study of Miller's radio plays is by Gerald Weales, "Arthur Miller Takes the Air," *American Drama* 5 (Fall 1995): 1–15.

18 Martin and Centola, *Theater Essays of Arthur Miller*, 591–92.

19 Christopher Bigsby, *Arthur Miller: A Critical Study* (Cambridge: Cambridge University Press, 2005).

20 Marilyn Berger, "Arthur Miller, Moral Voice of American Stage, Dies at 89," *New York Times*, 12 February 2005, A1, A14–15. Other obituaries in the major papers were shorter but similar. See Bart Barnes and Patricia Sullivan, "Playwright of Broken American Dreams," *Washington Post*, 12 February 2005, A1, and Ed Siehel, "Playwright Arthur Miller Dies," *Boston Globe*, 12 February 2005, 1.

21 The contempt citation was due to Miller's honorable refusal to answer questions about the identity of other individuals at a meeting of Communist writers—in particular, whether the playwright Arnaud D'Usseau chaired one such meeting. Of himself, Miller stated that he signed a form in 1939 that might have been used as an application for Communist Party membership but could not remember its exact nature, and that he did not know if a woman named Sue Warren had proposed him for membership in 1943 or 1947 (the question was unclear in regard to the date). His answer was less a forthright denial than an assertion of not having "memory" or "knowledge." He was unequivocal that he was never under Communist "discipline," which was a view that might be conceivable for a maverick writer in a Party Cultural Unit who saw his or her work as artistic and choices of activity as voluntary. See "Testimony of Arthur Miller," 4685, 4688–89. Moreover, in *Timebends*, 407, Miller seems to leave open the possibility that HUAC interrogator Richard Arens might have come up with some evidence of Communist Party membership, and that Miller would have had to concede the point: "How to explain that even if he had produced a Party card with my signature on it, I could only have said yes, I had probably felt that way then."

22 Tony Kushner, "Kushner on Miller," *Nation*, 13 June 2005, 6.

23 Steven R. Centola, ed., *Arthur Miller: Echoes down the Corridor, 1944–2000* (New York: Viking, 2000), 1–13. The full citation for the original appearance is "A Boy Grew in Brooklyn," *Holiday*, March 1955, 54–55, 117–24.

24 The original story was in *New Currents*, June 1943, 9–10. Miller is identified as "a young short story and radio script writer."

25 *New Currents* was inaugurated in March 1943, as a result of the reorganization of *Jewish Survey*. Miller had appeared in the first issue of *Jewish Survey*, May 1941, with an essay called "Hitler's Quarry," about the U.S. State Department's failure to help European Jews trying to escape the Nazis. The piece was published beneath one by the Communist writer Albert Maltz, "War Boom in Jew-Baiting," and Miller was identified as "a promising New York writer." *Jewish Survey* was marketed as a non-Party publication that

focused on anti-Semitism in all countries but did not advocate U.S. military intervention against Germany. Following the German invasion of the USSR in June 1941, the publication dramatically changed its policy and published an editorial headlined "Aid the Soviet Union against Hitler" (July 1941, p. 3). The managing editor of *Jewish Survey* was Louis Harap, a member of the Communist Party, and the editorial board included such well-known pro-Communists as Marc Blitztein, Rockwell Kent, Dashiell Hammett, Albert Maltz, and the painter Max Weber. The change of the magazine name from *Jewish Survey* to *New Currents* after several issues of the former failed to appear was an attempt to broaden the publication by giving overwhelming focus to the Nazi threat. The new "Statement of Policy" placed exclusive emphasis on "the total defeat of Hitlerism" as the precondition of Jewish survival. See *New Currents*, March 1943, 3. *New Currents* retained a strong component of pro-Communists on its editorial board, with some changes occurring as members entered military service. Miller's appearance in *Jewish Survey* as well as *New Currents* confirms how strongly he identified his opposition to anti-Semitism with his support for Soviet foreign policy in its various incarnations.

26 Miller, *Timebends*, 105, 114.

27 Ibid., 116.

28 Ibid., 71.

29 Ibid., 85, 86.

30 Editorial, "From Month to Month," *Jewish Voice*, March–April 1941, 2.

31 Miller, *Timebends*, 85, 86.

32 Ibid., 86.

33 Mary McCarthy, "The American Realist Playwrights," in *On the Contrary* (New York: Noonday, 1962), 309.

34 Some of these claims are summarized in Louis Harap, *Dramatic Encounters: The Jewish Presence in Twentieth Century Drama, Poetry, and Humor and the Black Jewish Literary Relationship* (Westport, Conn.: Greenwood Press, 1987), 122–28.

35 "CP Raps Press Hubbub on Browder," *Daily Worker* 30 April 1942, 2.

36 Malcolm Cowley, *The Dream of the Golden Mountains* (New York: Viking, 1980), 298.

37 The political views of the *New Masses* editors can be seen in the issues of late 1944 and early 1945; see esp. the issue of 19 December 1944, 22.

38 Stage for Action was a resuscitated version of the celebrated Theater of Action of the 1930s. Circumstantial evidence suggests that "Harry Taylor" might have been a pseudonym for Harry Lessin, a longtime member of the inner circle of both groups. The original Theater of Action was founded in 1929 as the Workers Laboratory Theater. The troupe was in the orbit of the Communist Party, concentrating on works of agitation and propaganda aimed at bringing political education to workers. After a period of friendly association with Group Theater, Theater of Action folded into the Federal Theater Project as the One Act Experimental Theater. When the Federal The-

ater Project closed in 1940, groups such as Current Theater and New Theater emerged to carry on the tradition. See "Workers Laboratory Theater/Theater of Action," in *Encyclopedia of the American Left*, 2nd ed., ed. Mary Jo Buhle, Paul Buhle, and Dan Georgakas (New York: Oxford University Press, 1998), 899–900. For a more substantial study, see Dorothy Jeanne Friedman, "From the Workers' Laboratory Theatre to the Theatre of Action: The History of an Agitprop Theatre," M.A. thesis, Theater Arts, University of California, Los Angeles (1968).

When Stage for Action was organized toward the end of 1943, a young Gene Frankel, later recognized as a pioneer of off-Broadway theater, took over the directorship. What differentiated Stage for Action from its predecessors was its highly professional staff and a greater degree of focus on theater entertainment values. Like Miller at the time, its writers, actors, composers, lyricists, and directors earned their living by working in the commercial theater of stage, screen, and radio. Stage for Action was supported by yearly subsidies from left-wing unions, such as the National Maritime Union and United Electrical Workers Union. See Harry Taylor, "Stage for Action," *New Masses*, 2 January 1945, 29–30.

39 The performance date was December 1943. *That They May Win* appears in Margaret Mayorga, ed. *The Best One-Act Plays of 1944* (New York: Dodd, Mead, 1945), 45–59. In a subsequent *New Masses* account of Stage for Action, Taylor judged Miller's work to be "sturdiest production so far" and announced a schedule of future performances, mostly reflecting Communist Party concerns about fifth columnists, support for the no-strike pledge, and the significance of the Teheran conference. See Taylor, "Stage for Action."

40 For example, see Taylor's review in the issue of *New Masses*, 26 December 1944, 27–28, where Taylor correlated the stage version of John Hersey's *A Bell for Adano* to the current moment in World War II.

41 "Between Ourselves," *New Masses*, 9 January 1945, 2.

42 Ibid., 23 January 1945, 2.

43 Ibid., 6 March 1945, 2.

44 The most detailed study of Miller's radio plays is Weales, "Arthur Miller Takes the Air."

45 Matt Wayne, "Deep Are the Roots," *New Masses*, 23 October 1945, 27.

46 Matt Wayne, "On and Off Broadway," *New Masses*, 27 March 1945, 27.

47 Miller, *Timebends*, 39.

48 "On Broadway," *New Masses*, 12 March 1946, 30.

49 Ibid., 10 July 1945, 27–28.

50 This prefigures his comments on Brecht in his essay "About Theater Language." See Martin and Centola, *Theater Essays of Arthur Miller*, 542; see also the remarks on Brecht on pp. 159–60.

51 Wald interview with Magil. On 13 February 1945, p. 2, there was a notice in the *New*

Masses that editor Joseph North was departing for England; A. B. Magil took charge in North's absence.

52 Sillen made the astute point that there is an imbalance between the play's philosophical content and dramatic action, a flaw that Miller was able to address in his later plays. See Samuel Sillen, "Three New Broadway Plays Add Little to Season's Total," *Daily Worker*, 2 December 1944, 11.

53 Alan M. Wald interview with Norman Rosten, September 1992, New York, N.Y.

54 J. B. M., "The Truth Is Political," *New Masses*, 11 September 1945, 21.

55 Isidor Schneider, "Probing Writers' Problems," *New Masses*, 23 October 1945, 22.

56 Ibid., 22–25.

57 Albert Maltz, "What Shall We Ask of Writers?," *New Masses*, 12 February 1946, 19–22.

58 Isidor Schneider, "Background to Error," *New Masses*, 12 February 1946, 23–25.

59 The events are summarized most sympathetically in Jack Salzman, *Albert Maltz* (Boston: Twayne, 1978), 85–95. A listing of most of the contributions to the debate can be found in Lee Baxandall, ed., *Marxism and Aesthetics: An Annotated Bibliography* (New York: Humanities Press, 1968), 174–76.

60 "Between Ourselves," *New Masses*, 26 March 1946, 2; ibid., 2 April 1946, 2.

61 Ibid., 9 April 1946, 2; ibid., 16 April 1946, 2.

62 Ibid., 23 April 1946, 2.

63 These included James Allen, Herbert Aptheker, Richard O. Boyer, Lloyd Brown, Howard Fast, Charles Humboldt, V. J. Jerome, Albert Kahn, and Charles Keller. See "Just a Minute," *New Masses*, 26 March 1946, 2.

64 "Between Ourselves," *New Masses*, 30 April 1946, 2.

65 Arnaud D'Usseau, "The Theater as a Weapon," *New Masses*, 25 June 1946, 15–18.

66 "Theater" and "*The Forrest*: Another Comment," *New Masses*, 7 January 1947, 26–27.

67 Isidor Schneider, "All My Sons," *New Masses*, 18 February 1947, 28–29.

68 Charles Humboldt, "Taking Stock," *New Masses*, 13 January 1948, 18.

69 In the early 1950s Miller defended the Reverend William Howard Melish, rector of the Episcopal Holy Trinity Church, who was ousted from his position because he was an official of the National Council of Soviet-American Friendship. Melish was a neighbor of Miller's in Brooklyn and had started a *New Masses* column at the same time that Matt Wayne's was launched. See Gottfried, *Arthur Miller*, 160–61.

70 Two of the most important exchanges were Isidor Schneider, "*Death of a Salesman*," and Samuel Sillen, "Another Viewpoint," *Masses & Mainstream*, April 1949, 88–96, and Edwin Berry Burgum, "Playwriting and Arthur Miller," *Contemporary Reader*, August 1953, 24–32, and Ira Wallach, "Playwright and Audience," *Contemporary Reader*, February 1954, 61–64. In addition to the 1944 review by Sillen of *The Man Who Had All the Luck*, other *Daily Worker* reviews include Mike Phillips, "Letter on Arthur Miller," *Daily Worker*, 1 March 1949, 12; Lee Newton, "Arthur Miller's Hit Play," *Daily Worker*, 14 February

1949, 11; Harry Miller, "*The Crucible*: Arthur Miller's Best Play," *Daily Worker*, 8 January 1953, 7; David Platt, "Letters to *Times* Assail Unfair Criticism of Miller's *Crucible*," *Daily Worker*, 18 February 1953, 7. In his testimony before HUAC, Miller referred on a number of occasions to commentary on his work in the Communist press.

71 *New Masses*, 6 March 1945, 27.

72 *New Masses*, 23 September 1947, 26.

73 Allan Crawford, "On the 'Christian Front,'" *New Masses*, 20 November 1945, 23.

74 Arthur Miller, "Should Ezra Pound Be Shot?," *New Masses*, 25 December 1945, 4.

75 The same point was made by contributors Albert Maltz and Norman Rosten. In contrast, Eda Lou Walton raised the matter of Pound's sanity.

76 Miller, "Should Ezra Pound Be Shot?," 4–6.

77 Beth McHenry, "*Focus* Author Hopes to Make Anti-Semitism Understood," *Daily Worker*, 17 April 1946, 13.

78 A successor to *China Today*, *Amerasia* was a monthly magazine that treated U.S. involvement in the Far East.

79 Frederick Vanderbilt Field, "Amerasia," in Buhle et al., *Encyclopedia of the American Left*, 22. See also Harvey Klehr and Ronald Radosh, *The Amerasia Spy Case: Prelude to McCarthyism* (Chapel Hill: University of North Carolina Press, 1996).

80 On p. 183 of *Timebends*, Miller states that he purchased a country house in Connecticut from Jaffe in the spring of 1947, having received early news of the sale because Mary was then Jaffe's employee. He states, "In a year or two he would be on trial for publishing without authorization." That would place the trial in 1948 or 1949, instead of 1946. Gottfried's *Arthur Miller* states on p. 113 that Mary's employment started after Jaffe's arrest (June 1945) and that she departed with the birth of her second child (31 May 1947).

81 See "Testimony of Arthur Miller," 4687–88. Of *All My Sons*, Miller explained that "I started that play when the war was on. The Communist line during the war was that capitalists were the salt of the earth just like workers, that there would never be a strike again, that we were going to go hand in hand down the road in the future." However, by the time the play was finally produced, "the Communist line changed back to an attack on capitalists." Miller speculates that, had the play been produced earlier, it would "have been attacked as an anti-Communist play" by the Communist Party. Also see Miller, *Timebends*, 238:

> The play could not have been written at all had I chosen to abide by the party line at the time, for during the war the Communists pounced on anything that would disturb national unity; strikes were out of the question, and the whole social process was to be set in amber for the duration. . . . I knew this was nonsense and that profiteering on a vast scale, for one thing, was rampant and that the high moral aims of the anti-fascist alliance, if they were to be given any reality at all, had to be contrasted to what was actually going on in society.

Miller speculates that had *All My Sons* appeared when the war was still going on, it would have exploded in the face of both the business community and Communists.

82 Miller also went out of his way to challenge the perception that *The Man Who Had All the Luck,* "seemingly a genre piece mid-America," was unconnected to the political questions of the 1940s: "The fear of drift, more exactly a drift into some kind of fascism, lay hidden somewhere in the origins of *The Man Who Had All the Luck*" (Miller, *Timebends,* 86).

83 The name "Wayne" had primarily mass culture associations, decidedly masculine. The actor Marion Morrison had taken the pseudonym John Wayne in the 1930s because a director thought his birth name was too sissified for the future star of westerns and World War II movies. Bruce Wayne was also the alter ego of the comic book hero Batman, introduced in 1939. Possibly Miller was thinking of the Wayne County CIO Council in Michigan, which had spearheaded the militant organizing of autoworkers that had so entranced him during his University of Michigan days. Moreover, Miller customarily borrowed names of relatives, sometimes employing them ironically. Matthew was the name of his Catholic father-in-law, a man not especially sympathetic to Jews or the Left.

84 Arthur Miller, "Concerning Jews Who Write," *Jewish Life,* March 1948, 9. Harold U. Ribalow refers to Miller's remarks as a "speech," without giving any publication sources in his introduction to an anthology of Jewish American writing, *This Land, These People* (New York: Beechurst Press, 1950), 4.

85 Miller, "Concerning Jews Who Write," 9.

86 Ibid., 10.

87 Stanley J. Kunitz, *Twentieth Century Authors: A Biographical Dictionary of Modern Literature,* 1st supplement (New York: H. H. Wilson, 1955), 609.

88 Arthur Miller, *The Golden Years and The Man Who Had All the Luck* (London: Methuen, 1989).

89 Edwin Seaver, ed., *Cross-Section: A Collection of New American Writing* (New York: Fischer, 1944), 556.

90 Miller, *Timebends,* 298.

CONCLUSION

1 Frederick J. Hoffman, Charles Allen, and Carolyn F. Ulrich, *The Little Magazine: A History and Bibliography* (Princeton, N.J.: Princeton University Press, 1947), 345.

2 "To All Intellectuals, Artists and Writers!," *The Red Spark: Bulletin of the John Reed Club of Cleveland,* October 1932, 2.

3 Chester Himes, "Looking Down the Street," *Crossroad,* April 1939, pages unnumbered.

4 Jo Sinclair, "Dead Man," *Crossroad,* April 1939, pages unnumbered.

5 Dan Levin, *Stormy Petrel: The Life and Work of Maxim Gorky* (New York: Appleton-Century, 1965), and *Spinoza: The Young Thinker Who Destroyed the Past* (New York: Weybright and Tally, 1970).

6 Dan Levin, "The Burial," *Crossroad*, April 1939, pages unnumbered.

7 Alan M. Wald interview with Lloyd Brown, October 1995, New York, N.Y. Brown remembered that African American Communist leader Pettis Perry had told him that Himes was a member of the Los Angeles branch of the Party but had been expelled by Perry on the charge of sexual harassment. Brown speculated that Himes had his revenge on Perry through the creation of the Black Communist leader Bart in the novel.

8 I have discussed *The Lonely Crusade* and other works of Himes in two essays: "Chester Himes (1909–1984)," in *African American Writers*, 2nd ed., ed. Valerie Smith (New York: Scribner's, 2001), 1:333–47, and "Narrating Nationalisms: Black Marxists and Jewish Communists through the Eyes of Harold Cruse," in *Left of the Color Line: Race, Radicalism, and Twentieth-Century Literature of the United States*, ed. Bill Mullen and James Smethurst (Chapel Hill: University of North Carolina Press, 2003), 141–61.

9 Richard Wright, "Wasteland Uses Psychoanalysis Deftly," *PM Magazine*, 17 February 1948, 8.

10 Himes wrote the following of Levin in *The Quality of Hurt* (New York: Paragon House, 1990), 141:

> I had known Dan back in Cleveland during my WPA days, when he had been editing one of those little literary magazines to be found all over the country; and I had seen him again in New York after the war when he had been working as an instantaneous translator for the United Nations. Dan had served in the Pacific and had written one of the first war novels, which in a way was a forerunner of the Jewish writers' treatment of the war theme which had its culmination in Norman Mailer's *The Naked and the Dead*. Jewish writers never glorified war like the Hemingway school. Thinking of it, I remember that Dan fought in the Spanish Civil War before that and had written a short story from that experience which I will never forget. It was about a young poet in the line of prisoners to be shot by the soldiers of Franco. He wanted to write a poem to tell his story to the world.

This passage gives an indication of Himes's faulty memory as an autobiographer: Levin was never in Spain, and Mailer's novel preceded *Mask of Glory*.

11 This organization was founded in 1933 as the American League against War and Fascism.

12 Levin's fictional re-creation of the *Crossroad* experience is consistent with his memory sixty years later. Certain characters bear a close resemblance to real prototypes. Milt and Agnes Bruster, for example, are based on Philip and Helen Sharnoff, relatives of Helen Buchman, who would soon become Jo Sinclair's mentor and companion. Philip was an instructor at the Party's Workers School, specializing in dialectical materialism, while Helen was a promising poet. During the crisis surrounding *Crossroad*, Philip supported Party control of the magazine and pressured Helen to do likewise. Joe Rieber was based on a Communist artist, severely crippled and deformed,

who lived in the poorest African American community. The *Midwesterner* mirrors *Crossroad*. It was not intended to be a Party organ but antifascist and liberal, yet not a front. However, in Levin's recollection, certain Communists around the magazine exhorted that it be subordinated to Party guidance. Zaddick's insistence that the focus of the magazine be "anti-Nazis" is shattered by news of the Hitler-Stalin Pact, which places even greater pressure on the Communists to shape the magazine to reflect the new Party orientation. Zaddick desperately performs intellectual somersaults to please the Party, in order to avoid becoming a "renegade," while at the same time maintaining the publication's autonomy and not violating the trust of its non-Party supporters.

13 Dan Levin, "The Education of a True Believer" (unpublished manuscript, 1940), 22.

14 Dan Levin, *From the Battlefield: Dispatches of a World War II Marine* (Annapolis, Md.: Naval Institute Press, 1995), 3.

15 Primarily Levin had worked with Karamu House, the African American cultural center in Cleveland, and had acted in plays performed there that had antiracist themes. One such play was *Stevedore*; another involved a stupid white detective and a brilliant black detective of which Levin later thought he heard echoes when he read Chester Himes's Harlem detective thrillers. See Alan M. Wald interview with Dan Levin, February 2005, New York, N.Y.

16 Earl Conrad, "Blues School of Literature," *Chicago Defender*, 22 December 1945, 11.

17 *People's World*, 14 August 1942, 4.

18 The review was made available to me by one of Himes's biographers, Michel Fabre. It is noteworthy that Himes complains about Petry's treatment of African American men.

19 Michel Fabre and Robert E. Skinner, eds., *Conversations with Chester Himes* (Jackson: University Press of Mississippi, 1995), 126.

20 See the biographical summary in Alan M. Wald, *Exiles from a Future Time: The Forging of the Mid-Twentieth-Century Literary Left* (Chapel Hill: University of North Carolina Press, 2002), 285.

21 Letter from Chester Himes to Ruth Seid, 21 December 1945, Jo Sinclair Papers, Boston University, Boston, Mass.

22 In the first version of *Wasteland*, she used the name Ruth instead of Judy; the novel was written in 1943 and was published almost unrevised.

23 She apparently softened her view of her father over time; the portrait of the father underwent five rewritings in *Changelings* and became increasingly sympathetic.

24 Jo Sinclair, "Noon Lynching," *New Masses*, 22 September 1936, 16–18.

25 Albert Stevens, "A Wasteland of Distorted Humans," *Daily Worker*, 28 April 1946, 9.

26 Alfred Goldsmith, "Troubled Journey," *New Masses*, 2 April 1946, 25–26.

27 Jo Sinclair, *The Changelings* (New York: McGraw-Hill, 1955), 34.

28 Ibid.

29 Ibid., 33.

30 Ibid., 34.

31 Ibid., 135.

32 Ibid., 197.

33 Ibid., 280.

34 Ibid.

35 George Charney, *A Long Journey* (Chicago: Quadrangle, 1968), 308.

36 Ibid., 317.

37 Ibid., 316.,

38 Sinclair, *The Changelings*, 199.

ACKNOWLEDGMENTS & SOURCES

As the second volume of a trilogy, *Trinity of Passion* overlaps considerably with the first volume with respect to foundational source materials and classroom experiences as well as consultation with friends, students, and scholars. The "Acknowledgments and Sources" page of *Exiles from a Future Time* should therefore be consulted by anyone wishing to gain a comprehensive grasp of the influences on my work and the debts that I have incurred. Moreover, the first volume's "A Note on Terminology and Illustrations" still applies, especially in regard to the capitalization of "Communist," "Black," "Party," and "Left" and to citation of periodicals. Here I will primarily offer augmentation concerning specific information in *Trinity of Passion*.

From the very outset of this volume, I have received emotional support and rigorous intellectual exchange from my partner, Angela Dillard. For nearly five years she has tolerated a house overflowing with old books and journals, file boxes of correspondence and photocopies, scattered tapes, and all-night work marathons, not to mention endless monologues and even rants about the contradictions of the Popular Front, the tragic nobility of the socialist dream, and the fascinating (for me, at least) features of the lives and writing of many neglected and forgotten authors. All the while, Angela has worked away diligently on her own pathbreaking scholarship about conservatism, religion, and the history of Detroit.

A second special debt is owed to my friend and comrade of more than three decades, Patrick Quinn of the Northwestern University Archives. At a crucial moment, when I first assembled my argument and evidence into a sprawling narrative, Patrick went through my rough-draft chapters line by line. Using his extraordinary knowledge of the politics, culture, and history of the twentieth century, Patrick not only pointed out all my missteps in writing and documentation but in almost every such instance he preternaturally proposed a more effective way for me to express my own intention. Only after Patrick's intervention did I feel confident in sharing the manuscript with three other scholars who provided much-appreciated additional feedback—Howard Brick, Laurence Goldstein, and Angela Dillard.

As always, financial support has been crucial. In this instance, I am grateful to the University of Michigan for a semester leave and research funds in connection with my directorship of the Program in American Culture (2000–2003) and a sabbatical in the fall of 2003. I am also grateful for receiving the Resident Fellowship for Manuscript Research, Longfellow House, Cambridge, Massachusetts, April 2004. In the spring of 2005 I received a research partnership grant from the Rackham Graduate School; my research partner, Rachel Peterson, was a fabulous colleague who went above and beyond the call of duty locating materials that no one else could find, and often in providing insightful observations. Portions of *Trinity of Passion* were presented as lectures delivered at or sponsored by the following venues: American Literature Seminar, Harvard University; American Civilization Program, Brown University; English Department, University of Massachusetts, Boston; English Department, Tufts University; English Department, University of California, Berkeley; the conference "The Legacy of the British Marxist Historians" at Edgehill College, Ormskirk, England; the conference "Capitalism and Its Culture," Santa Barbara, California; the conference "Outside American Studies," Dartmouth Summer Institute, Hanover, New Hampshire; the conference "The Noise of History," Dylan Thomas Center, Wales, November 2003; Tamiment Library, New York University; several events sponsored by the Future of Minority Studies at the University of Michigan, the University of Wisconsin, and Cornell University; and the English Department, the Program in Modern Thought, African American Studies, and Jewish American Studies, Stanford University. Portions of the manuscript were also presented at national conventions of the Modern Languages Association, the American Studies Association, and the Organization of American Historians. I appreciate the critical comments and suggestions from fellow panelists and audience participants on those occasions.

In *Trinity of Passion*, I cite materials from the following libraries and institutional collections, and I am grateful for assistance and in some instances for permission to quote from letters and manuscripts: FBI Reading Room (for the FBI files of Chester Himes, John Oliver Killens, and Irwin Shaw); Fisk University; Labadie Collection, University of Michigan; George Arents Research Library, Syracuse University; Library of Social History, Los Angeles; Mugar Memorial Library, Boston University; Harry Ransom Research Center, University of Texas; Walter Reuther Archives, Wayne State University; Schomburg Center for the Study of Black Culture; State Historical Society of Wisconsin; Tamiment Library, New York University; University of California at Los Angeles Oral History Collection (for the history of Albert Maltz); and University of California at Los Angeles Research Library. The following individuals gave me access to material from their private collections: Daniel Aaron, Cambridge, Massachusetts; Michel Fabre, Paris, France; Henry Gilfillan, Occidental, California; Robert Hethmon, Los Angeles; Aaron Kramer, Long Island, New York; Dan Levin, Long Island, New York; and Bill Mardo, New York City.

I cannot possibly list all the individuals who afforded me stimulating conversation and information that have variously worked their way into the making of this volume. Daniel Aaron has remained my foremost mentor in the field, and the time I spent with him in Ann Arbor, Michigan, in the fall of 2002 and in Cambridge, Massachusetts, in the spring of 2004 will always be remembered. Fredric Jameson has long been an inspirational figure, and his visit to the University of Michigan in the fall of 2004 came at a critical time in my thinking. Paula Rabinowitz is usually two steps ahead of me in contemplating new connections between gender and culture, and I am especially indebted to her for drawing my attention to the writings of Lauren Gilfillan. Likewise, it was Gay Wilentz who first pointed out to me Jo Sinclair's association with the Left; her unexpected death in February 2006 was a stunning loss to scholars working in the borderlands of African and Jewish diaspora cultures. Keith Gilyard has been extraordinarily generous in sharing his work on John Oliver Killens and in commenting on my own. Dick Meisler (who read a draft of my chapter on Arthur Miller) and Miriam Meisler have been the most faithful of friends, without whom I simply could not have survived the hard times in order to appreciate the good ones. Michael Löwy and Eleni Varikas, whose wide reading and imaginative perspectives are a reliable source of intellectual invigoration, accompanied me to the Greek Islands and housed me in Athens and Paris during a crucial period of reading for the project. Lewis Pepper and Moira Cunningham housed and fed me during a research period in the Boston area. My colleagues at the University of Michigan have always been available to provide insight and information helpful to my work, most recently Paul Anderson, Enoch Brater, Kevin Gaines, Sandra Gunning, James McIntosh, Gina Morantz-Sanchez, Tobin Siebers, Penny Von Eschen, and John Woodford, as well as members of the American Culture Faculty Reading Group, who have tolerated my ornery responses to many of our monthly readings over the years. Scholars in the field of the U.S. cultural Left comprise a generous community, always available to share ideas and information: Stanley Aronowitz, Graham Barnfield, Paul Buhle, Michael Denning, Brian Dollinar, Peter Drucker, Al Filreis, Barbara Foley, Jim Hall, Robert Hethmon, Rob Kauffman, Robbie Lieberman, William Maxwell, James Miller, Bill Mullen, Cary Nelson, Aldon Nielsen, Christopher Phelps, Mark Pittenger, Arnold Rampersad, David Roessell, Rachel Rubin, E. San Juan Jr., James Smethurst, Jon Christian Suggs, Michael Szalay, Harvey Teres, Alan Trachtenberg, Zaragosa Vargas, Doug Wixon, and Richard Yarborough. Associates on the editorial boards of *Against the Current* and *Science & Society* have also left their imprint on my thinking. It was an extraordinary honor to be able to meet and talk with a number of writers featured in this volume, especially Louis Falstein, Howard Fast, Aaron Kramer, Dan Levin, Henry Roth, John Sanford, and Morris Schappes. Correspondence with William Herrick, Joseph Vogel, and Milton Wolff was also prized. Family members of Benjamin Appel, Alvah Bessie, Lauren Gilfillan, John Oliver Killens, and Ann Petry were enormously obliging. My daughters, Sarah and Hannah, are the loves of my life. Angela is my angel.

For material used in this volume, the following people participated in personal interviews of varying degrees of formality, some of which were tape-recorded: Irving Adler, Ruth Adler, Willa Appel, Phillip Bonosky, Lloyd Brown, Alex Buchman, Victor Burch, Ben Burns, Marvel Cooke, Harold Cruse, Peter Filrado, Hy Fireman, Franklin Folsom, Sender Garlin, Henry Gilfillan, Erika Gottfried, Louis Harap, Esther Jackson, James Jackson, Paul Jarrico, Howard Johnson, Barbara Killens, Grace Killens, Aaron Kramer, Dan Levin, Deena Levitt, A. B. Magil, Bill Mardo, Elizabeth Petry, Norman Rosten, Henry Roth, Muriel Roth,

Acknowledgments and Sources

Annette T. Rubinstein, John Sanford, Alexander Saxton, Morris U. Schappes, Janet Sillen, Barbara Snoek, Saul Wellman, B. J. Widick, Tiba Wilner, Helen Yglesias, and Barbara Zeluck.

The following people shared information with me, usually through discussions, correspondence (including e-mail), and phone conversations: Bill Bailey, Dan Bessie, Martin Buchman, Paul Buhle, Jeff Cabusao, Michel Fabre, Milt Felsen, Dan Georgakas, Marvin Gettleman, Margaret Goostray, Julie Herrada, Mary Janzen, Alan Johnson, Andrew Lee, Maria Morelli, Steve Nelson, Sean Noel, Donald Pease, Christopher Phelps, Philip Sharnoff, Mark Solomon, Maynard Solomon, Joseph Vogel, Seama Weatherwax, Tom Weatherwax, and Eben Wood.

Once again I am grateful to the entire staff of the University of North Carolina Press, but especially Sian Hunter, Stephanie Wenzel, and the two readers of the manuscript.

This book is dedicated to my older sister and younger brother, Sharon and Michael, who have always supported me and my work over the years. They and their partners, children, and pets have often opened their doors and shared their hospitality during my research trips. None of these individuals or anyone else who was interviewed or who rendered assistance is in any way liable for the opinions or judgments expressed in this book.

INDEX